Fodor's 12th

Sweden

The Guide for All Budgets, Completely Updated, with Many Maps and Travel Tips

Where to Stay, Eat,
and Explore

On and Off
the Beaten Path

When to Go,
What to Pack

Post-it® Flags,
Web Sites, and More

Excerpted from *Fodor's Scandinavia*

Fodor's Travel Publications • New York, Toronto, London, Sydney, Auckland
www.fodors.com

Fodor's Sweden

EDITOR: John D. Rambow

Editorial Contributors: Nuha Ansari, Catherine Belonogoff, David Downing, Rob Hincks, Satu Hummasti, David Passey, Helayne Schiff, Mark Sullivan, Chris Swiac, Devin Wilson

Editorial Production: Kristin Milavec

Maps: David Lindroth, Inc., Mapping Specialists, LTD., *cartographers;* Bob Blake and Rebecca Baer, *map editors*

Design: Fabrizio La Rocca, *creative director;* Guido Caroti, *art director;* Jolie Novak, *senior picture editor;* Melanie Marin, *photo editor*

Cover Design: Pentagram

Production/Manufacturing: Angela McLean and Robert B. Shields

Cover Photograph: © Bildhuset AB/Photonica

Copyright

Twelfth Edition

ISBN 0–676–90204–9

ISSN 1528–3070

Important Tip

Although all prices, opening times, and other details in this book are based on information supplied to us at press time, changes occur all the time in the travel world, and Fodor's cannot accept responsibility for facts that become outdated or for inadvertent errors or omissions. So **always confirm information when it matters,** especially if you're making a detour to visit a specific place.

Special Sales

Fodor's Travel Publications are available at special discounts for bulk purchases for sales promotions or premiums. Special editions, including personalized covers, excerpts of existing guides, and corporate imprints, can be created in large quantities for special needs. For more information, contact your local bookseller or write to Special Markets, Fodor's Travel Publications, 280 Park Avenue, New York, NY 10017. Inquiries from Canada should be directed to your local Canadian bookseller or sent to Random House of Canada, Ltd., Marketing Department, 2775 Matheson Boulevard East, Mississauga, Ontario L4W 4P7. Inquiries from the United Kingdom should be sent to Fodor's Travel Publications, 20 Vauxhall Bridge Road, London SW1V 2SA, England.

PRINTED IN THE UNITED STATES OF AMERICA

10 9 8 7 6 5 4 3 2 1

CONTENTS

Maps

ON THE ROAD WITH FODOR'S

The more you know before you go, the better your trip will be. Sweden's most fascinating small museum (or its most elegant design store or best traditional restaurant) could be just around the corner from your hotel, but if you don't know it's there, it might as well be on the other side of the globe. That's where this book comes in. It's a great step toward making sure your next trip lives up to your expectations. As you plan, check out the Web as well. Guidebooks have been helping smart travelers find the special places for years; the Web is one more tool. Whatever reference you consult, be savvy about what you read, and always consider the source. Images and language can be massaged to make places appear better than they are. And one traveler's quaint is another's grimy. Here at Fodor's, and at our on-line arm, Fodors.com, our focus is on providing you with information that's not only useful but accurate and on target. Every day Fodor's editors put enormous effort into getting things right, beginning with the search for the right contributors—people who have objective judgment, broad travel experience, and the writing ability to put their insights into words. There's no substitute for advice from a like-minded friend who has just come back from where you're going, but our writers, having seen all corners of Sweden, are the next best thing. They're the kind of people you'd poll for tips yourself if you knew them.

British journalist **Rob Hincks** updated and expanded most of Sweden. He primarily writes and edits for food and travel magazines in Sweden and England. Rob has lived in Stockholm since 2000, but through his Swedish wife, Mikaela, his associations with the country go back much further.

Our Sweden updater, **Devin Wilson,** is an American journalist, writer, and translator living in Stockholm. Having moved to Sweden four years ago, he has completed a circular journey begun by his great-grandparents, who moved from Sweden to the United States in the early 1900s.

Don't Forget to Write

Your experiences—positive and negative—matter to us. If we have missed or misstated something, we want to hear about it. We follow up on all suggestions. Contact the Scandinavia editor at editors@fodors.com or c/o Fodor's, 280 Park Avenue, New York, New York 10017. And have a fabulous trip!

Karen Cure
Editorial Director

Scandinavia

KEY

--------- Ferry

200 miles

300 km

Barents Sea

TO SVALBARD

North Cape

Vardø
Vadsø
Kirkenes
Hammerfest
Ulsjoki
Ivalo
Inari
Alta
Karasjok
Kautokeino
Enontekiö
Kilpisjärvi
Muonio
Kittilä
Sodankylä
Kemijärvi
Rovaniemi
Tornio
Kemi
Posio
Kuusamo

COMMONWEALTH OF INDEPENDENT STATES (RUSSIA)

Tornjoki

Torniojoki
Torneälv

Suomussalmi
Kuhmo
Nurmes
Petlimo
Joutsijärvi
Pudasjärvi
Oulu
Raahe
Oulujärvi
Kajaani
Oranmäki
Iisalmi
Puolanka
Pulkkila
Karsämäki
Haapajävi
Nivala
Kalajoki
Kokkola
Kyyjärvi

SUOMI (FINLAND)

Kiruna
Jokkmokk
Kalix
Torneå
Arctic Circle

Arvidsjaur
Arjeplog
Piteå
Skellefteå
Umeå

Ångermanälven
Tärnaby
Sorsele
Storuman
Lycksele
Åsele
Strömsund
Mo i Rana
Mosjøen
Sandnessjøen
Brønnøysund
Rørvik
Namsos
Steinkjer
Meråker

SVERIGE (SWEDEN)

Gulf of Bothnia

Tromsø
Hnstad
Narvik
Bodø
Fauske

VESTERÅLEN
LOFOTEN
Vestfjorden

Trondheim

Norwegian Sea

ATLANTIC OCEAN

ISLAND (ICELAND)

TO ICELAND

Arctic Circle

Þingeyri
Ísafjörður
Siglufjörður
Raufarhöfn
Húsavík
Skjálfandi
Bakkaflói
Vopnafjörður
Vopnafjörður
Héraðsflói
Egilsstaðir
Neskaupstaður
Breiðdalsvík
Djúpivogur
Höfn
Hornafjörðaróss
Fagurhólsmýri
Vatnajökull
Kirkjubæjarklaustur
Vík
Myrdalsjökull
Hella
Hveragerði
Hafnarfjörður

Reykjavík

Reykholt
Langjökull
Hofsjökull
Búðir
Stykkishólmur
Búðardalur
Breiðafjörður
Vestfirðir
Hnfflói
Dalvík
Tjörnes
Akureyri

Faxaflói

Westmann Islands

Sweden

ESSENTIAL INFORMATION

AIR TRAVEL

BOOKING

When you book **look for nonstop flights** and **remember that "direct" flights stop at least once.** Try to avoid connecting flights, which require a change of plane. For more booking tips and to check prices and make on-line flight reservations, log on to www.fodors.com.

CARRIERS

All major cities and towns are linked with regular flights by Scandinavian Airlines System (SAS). Malmö Aviation also has service between Stockholm, Göteborg, and Malmö. Most Swedish airports are located a long way from city centers but are served by fast and efficient bus services. From North America, American, Delta, Finnair, Iceland Air, Lufthansa, SAS, United, and other major airlines serve Stockholm's Arlanda International Airport and Göteborg's Landvetter airport. From the United Kingdom, Stockholm and Göteborg are served by SAS, British Airways, and Ryan Air.

➤ AIRLINES AND CONTACTS: **American** (☎ 800/433–7300). **British Airways** (☎ 020/88974000). **Delta** (☎ 800/ 221–1212). **Finnair** (☎ 800/950– 5000). **Iceland Air** (☎ 800/223– 5500). **Lufthansa** (☎ 800/645–3880). **Ryan Air** (☎ 087/03331231 in the U.K.; 0155/202240 in Sweden). **SAS** (☎ 020/727000 or 08/974175 in Sweden; 020/77344020 in the U.K.; 800/433–7300 in the U.S.). **United** (☎ 800/241–6522).

CHECK-IN & BOARDING

Always **ask your carrier about its check-in policy.** Plan to arrive at the airport about 2 hours before your scheduled departure time for domestic flights and 2½ to 3 hours before international flights.

Assuming that not everyone with a ticket will show up, airlines routinely overbook planes. When everyone does, airlines ask for volunteers to give up their seats. In return, these volunteers usually get a certificate for a free flight and are rebooked on the next flight out. If there are not enough volunteers, the airline must choose who will be denied boarding. The first to get bumped are passengers who checked in late and those flying on discounted tickets, so **get to the gate and check in as early as possible,** especially during peak periods.

Always **bring a government-issued photo I.D. to the airport;** even when it's not required, a passport is best.

CUTTING COSTS

Intra-Scandinavian air travel is usually expensive. If you want to economize, look into the Visit Scandinavia Fare offered by SAS. One coupon costs about $85; six about $510, but they vary greatly depending on routing and destination—generally, the cost rises the farther north the destination. The coupons are valid for destinations within Denmark, Norway, and Sweden, and also between Sweden and Finland. They are sold only in the United States and only to non-Scandinavians. Coupons can be used year-round for a maximum of three months and must be purchased in conjunction with transatlantic flights.

The **SAS Visit Scandinavia/Europe Air Pass** offers up to eight flight coupons for one-way travel within and between Scandinavian cities (and participating European cities such as Frankfurt, Paris, and London). Most one-way tickets for domestic travel within each Scandinavian country cost $65; one-way fares between Scandinavian countries are usually $75, unless you are venturing into the far north, Lapland, Iceland, or Greenland (these flights range from $115 to $225). These passes can be bought only in conjunction with a round-trip ticket between North America and Europe on SAS and must be used within three months of arrival. SAS also provides family fares—children between 2 and 17 and a spouse can receive 50% off the full fare of business class tickets with the purchase of one full-fare business class ticket. Contact SAS for information.

The least expensive airfares to Scandinavia must usually be purchased in advance and are nonrefundable. It's smart to **call a number of airlines,** and when you are quoted a good price, **book it on the spot**—the same fare may not be available the next day. Always **check different routings** and look into using different airports. Travel agents, especially low-fare specialists (☞ Discounts & Deals), are helpful.

Consolidators are another good source. They buy tickets for scheduled international flights at reduced rates from the airlines, then sell them at prices that beat the best fare available directly from the airlines, usually without restrictions. Sometimes you can even get your money back if you need to return the ticket. Carefully read the fine print detailing penalties for changes and cancellations, and **confirm your consolidator reservation with the airline.**

➤ CONSOLIDATORS: **Cheap Tickets** (☎ 800/377–1000). **Discount Airline Ticket Service** (☎ 800/576–1600). **Unitravel** (☎ 800/325–2222). **Up & Away Travel** (☎ 212/889–2345). **World Travel Network** (☎ 800/409–6753).

ENJOYING THE FLIGHT

For more legroom, **request an emergency-aisle seat.** Don't sit in the row in front of the emergency aisle or in front of a bulkhead, where seats may not recline. If you have dietary concerns, **ask for special meals when booking.** These can be vegetarian, low-cholesterol, or kosher, for example. On long flights, try to maintain a normal routine, to help fight jet lag. At night, **get some sleep.** By day, **eat light meals, drink water** (not alcohol),

and **move around the cabin** to stretch your legs. For additional jet-lag tips consult *Fodor's FYI: Travel Fit & Healthy* (available at bookstores everywhere).

FLYING TIMES

Flying time from New York to Stockholm is 8 hours. From London's Heathrow Airport, flying time to Stockholm is 2¾ hours. From Sydney and major cities in New Zealand, the flight to any Scandinavian country will be more than 20 hours, and will require at least one transfer.

HOW TO COMPLAIN

If your baggage goes astray or your flight goes awry, complain right away. Most carriers require that you **file a claim immediately.**

➤ AIRLINE COMPLAINTS: U.S. Department of Transportation **Aviation Consumer Protection Division** (✉ C-75, Room 4107, Washington, DC 20590, ☎ 202/366–2220, WEB www.dot.gov/airconsumer). **Federal Aviation Administration Consumer Hotline** (☎ 800/322–7873).

AIRPORTS

Sweden's major gateway, **Arlanda International Airport,** is 41 km (26 mi) north of Stockholm.

➤ AIRPORT INFORMATION: **Arlanda International Airport** (☎ 46/87976100, WEB www.lfv.se/eng/index.asp).

BIKE TRAVEL

Bike rental costs average around SKr 90 per day. Tourist offices and the Swedish Touring Association have information about cycling package holidays that include bike rentals, overnight accommodations, and meals. The Swedish bicycling organization, Cykelfrämjandet (National Cycle Association), publishes a free English-language guide to cycling trips.

➤ CONTACTS: **Cykelfrämjandet** (✉ Thuleg. 43, 113 53 Stockholm, ☎ 08/54591030 Mon.–Thurs. 9–noon, FAX 08/54591039, WEB www.cykelframjandet.a.se). **Swedish Touring Association (STF;** ✉ Box 25, 101 20 Stockholm, ☎ 08/4632200, FAX 08/6781938, WEB www.stfturist.se).

BOAT & FERRY TRAVEL

A rewarding way of seeing Sweden is from the many ferryboats that ply the archipelagos and main lakes. In Stockholm, visitors should buy a special *Båtluffarkort* (Inter Skerries Card, SKr 250) from Waxholmsbolaget. This card allows you unlimited travel on the archipelago ferryboats for a 16-day period. There are excellent links between Harwich, U.K., and Göteborg, and Newcastle, U.K., and Göteborg aboard DFDS Seaways ferries. There are also overnight ferries on Viking Lines and Silja Lines to Helsinki, Finland, both of which offer great bargains for one- and two-day round-trips.

Taking a ferry is not only fun, but often necessary in Scandinavia. Many companies arrange package trips, some offering a rental car and hotel accommodations as part of the deal. The word "ferry" can be deceptive; generally, the ferries are more like small-scale cruise ships, with several dining rooms, sleeping quarters, shopping, pool and sauna, and entertainment.

Ferry crossings often last overnight. The trip between Copenhagen and Oslo, for example, takes approximately 16 hours; most lines leave about 5 PM and arrive about 9 the next morning. The direct cruise between Stockholm and Helsinki takes 12 hours, usually leaving about 6 PM and arriving the next morning at 9. Trips from Germany to Oslo and Helsinki generally take about 20 hours; crossings to Reykjavík from Bergen tend to last about two days (25 hours to the Faroe Islands, and another 24 hours to Iceland). The shortest ferry route runs between Helsingør, Denmark, and Helsingborg, Sweden; it takes only 20 minutes.

CAR FERRIES

Travel by car in Scandinavia often necessitates travel by ferry. Some well-known vehicle and passenger ferries run between Copenhagen, Denmark, and Malmö, Sweden; between Helsingør, Denmark, and Helsingborg, Sweden; between Copenhagen and Göteborg, Sweden; and between Stockholm, Sweden, and Helsinki, Finland. The Helsingør/Helsingborg ferry (ScandLines) takes only 20 minutes; taking a car costs between SKr 255 and SKr 275 (about $24–$26 or £16–£18.50) one-way. Transporting a car between Stockholm and Helsinki costs about € 52 during high season and € 29 during low season (about $47 and $26 or £32 and £18). Round-trip fares are cheaper, and on weekends the Øresund Runt pass (for crossing between Copenhagen and Malmö one way and Helsingborg and Helsingør the other way) costs only SKr 475 (about $45 or £31).

➤ BOAT & FERRY INFORMATION: **Color Line** (✉ Box 30, DK–9850 Hirsthals, Denmark, ☎ 45/99–56–20–00, FAX 45/99–56–20–20; ✉ Hjortneskaia, Box 1422 Vika, N–0115 Oslo, Norway, ☎ 47/22–94–44–00, FAX 47/22–83–04–30; ✉ Color Scandi Line, Torksholmen, S-45 200 Strømstad, Sweden, ☎ 46/52662000, FAX 46/52614669; ✉ Color Line GmbH, Postfach 6080, 24121 Kiel, Germany, ☎ 49/431–7300–300, FAX 49/431–7300–400; WEB www.colorline.no). **ScandLines** (✉ Box 1, DK–3000 Helsingør, Denmark, ☎ 45/33–15–15–15, FAX 45/33–15–10–20; ✉ Knutpunkten 43, S–252 78 Helsingborg, Sweden, ☎ 46/42186100, FAX 46/42186049; WEB www.scandlines.com).

FERRIES FROM ENGLAND

The chief operator between England and many points within Scandinavia, Holland, and Germany is DFDS Seaways, with ships connecting Harwich and Newcastle to Esbjerg, Denmark; Kristiansand, Norway; and Amsterdam. Fjordline offers the only direct service from England to Bergen and northern Norway.

PLYING SCANDINAVIAN WATERS

Connections from Denmark to Norway and Sweden are available through DFDS and the Stena Line. Fjord Line sails along the magnificent west coast of Norway. Connections to the Faroe Islands and Iceland from Norway and Denmark are available through the Smyril Line. Silja Line and Viking Line offer a variety of cruises to Finland, with departures from Stockholm to Mariehamn in the Åland archipelago, Turku (Åbo) and Helsinki (Helsingfors), and a crossing from Umeå to Vaasa.

➤ MAJOR OPERATORS: **DFDS Seaways** (✉ Sankt Annae Plads 30, DK–1295 Copenhagen, Denmark, ☎ 45/33–42–33–42, FAX 45/33–42–33–41; ✉ DFDS Seaways Travel Centre, Scandinavia House, Parkeston, Harwich, Essex CO12 4QG, ☎ 44/8705–333–000, FAX 44/1255–244–382; ✉ DFDS Seaways USA Inc., 6555 NW 9th Ave., Suite 207, Fort Lauderdale, FL 33309, ☎ 800/533–3755, FAX 954/491–7958; ✉ Box 8895, Scandiahamnen, S–402 72 Göteborg, Sweden, ☎ 46/31650610; WEB www.seaeurope.com). **Fjord Line** (✉ Skoltegrunnskaien, Box 7250, N–5020 Bergen, Norway, ☎ 47/55–54–88–00, FAX 47/55–54–86–01; ✉ Tyne Commission Quay, North Shields NE29 6EA, Newcastle, England, ☎ 44/191–296–1313, FAX 44/191–296–1540; WEB www.fjordline.com). **Silja Line** (✉ Mannerheimintie 2, 00100 Helsinki, Finland, ☎ 358/9–18041, FAX 358/9–1804279; ✉ Kungsgatan 2, S–111 43 Stockholm, Sweden, ☎ 46/86663512 or 46/8222140, FAX 46/86119162 or 46/92316066; ✉ c/o DFDS Seaways, Scandinavia House, Parkeston Quay, Harwich, Essex, England CO12 4QG, ☎ 44/1255–240–240, FAX 44/255–244–382; ✉ c/o Norwegian Coastal Voyage, Inc./Bergen Line Service, 405 Park Ave., New York 10022, ☎ 212/319–1300 or 800/323–7436, FAX 212/319–1390; WEB www.silja.com/english). **Smyril Line** (✉ J. Brocksgøta 37, Box 370, FO-110 Tórshavn, Faroe Islands, ☎ 298/34–59–00, FAX 298/34–59–50; ✉ Slottsgate 1, Box 4135 Dreggen, N–5835 Bergen, Norway, ☎ 47/55–32–09–70, FAX 47/55–96–02–72; WEB www.smyril-line.com). **Stena Line** (✉ Trafikhamnen, DK–9900 Frederikshavn, Denmark, ☎ 45/96–20–02–00, FAX 45/96–20–02–80; ✉ PB 764, Sentrum, N–0106 Oslo, Norway, ☎ 47/23–17–91–00, FAX 47/23–17–90–60; ✉ Stena Line AB, S–405 19 Göteborg, Sweden, ☎ 46/ 317040000, FAX 46/31858595; WEB www.stenaline.com). **Viking Line** (✉ Mannerheimintie 14, 00100 Helsinki, ☎ 358/9–12351, FAX 358/9–647075, WEB www.vikingline.fi).

BUSINESS HOURS

BANKS & OFFICES

Banks are officially open weekdays 9:30 AM to 3 PM, but many stay open until 5 on most weekdays and until 6 on Thursday. The bank at Arlanda International Airport is open every day with extended hours, and the Forex and Valuta Specialisten currency-exchange offices also have extended hours.

MUSEUMS & SIGHTS

The opening times for museums vary widely, but most are open from 10 to 4 weekdays and over the weekend but are closed on Monday. Consult the guide in *På Stan,* the entertainment supplement published in *Dagens Nyheter's* Friday edition, or *What's On,* a monthly entertainment listings guide published in Swedish and English by the Swedish tourism authorities. It's available for free at hotels, tourist centers, and some restaurants.

➤ WEB SITES: **På Stan** (WEB www.dn.se/pastan). **What's On** (WEB www.stockholmtown.se).

SHOPS

Shops are generally open weekdays from 9 AM, 9:30 AM, or 10 AM until 6 PM and Saturday from 10 to 1 or 4. Most of the large department stores stay open later in the evening, and some open on Sunday. Several supermarkets open on Sunday, and there are a number of late-night food shops such as the 7-Eleven chain. Systembolaget, Sweden's liquor monopoly and therefore the only place to buy alcohol, is open weekdays from 10 to 6, with extended hours until 7 on Thursday. Many of the larger locations are open on Saturday from 10 to 2.

BUS TRAVEL

There is excellent bus service between all major towns and cities. Consult the Yellow Pages under *Bussresearrangörer* for the telephone numbers of the companies concerned. Recommended are the services offered to different parts of Sweden from Stockholm by Swebus.

➤ BUS INFORMATION: **Interbus** (☎ 08/7279000). **Svenska Buss** (☎ 020/

676767, WEB www.svenskabuss.se).
SwebusExpress (☎ 0200/218218,
WEB www.express.swebus.se).

CAMERAS & PHOTOGRAPHY

The *Kodak Guide to Shooting Great
Travel Pictures* (available at book-
stores everywhere) is loaded with tips.
➤ PHOTO HELP: **Kodak Information
Center** (☎ 800/242–2424).

CAR RENTAL

Major car-rental companies such as
Avis, Bonus, Budget, Europcar, and
Hertz have facilities in all major
towns and cities as well as at airports.
Various service stations also offer car
rentals, including Q8, Shell, Statoil,
and Texaco. See the Yellow Pages
under *Biluthyrning* for telephone
numbers and addresses.

Rates in Stockholm begin at $60 a
day and $175 a week for a manual
economy car without air conditioning
and with unlimited mileage. This does
not include tax on car rentals, which
is 25% in Sweden. A service charge is
usually added, which ranges from
$15 to $25.
➤ MAJOR AGENCIES: **Alamo** (☎ 800/
522–9696; 020/8759–6200 in the
U.K., WEB www.alamo.com). **Avis**
(☎ 800/331–1084; 800/879–2847 in
Canada; 02/9353–9000 in Australia;
09/525–1982 in New Zealand; 0870/
606–0100 in the U.K.; WEB www.avis.
com). **Budget** (☎ 800/527–0700;
0870/156–5656 in the U.K.; WEB
www.budget.com). **Dollar** (☎ 800/
800–6000; 0124/622–0111 in the
U.K., where it's affiliated with Sixt;
02/9223–1444 in Australia; WEB
www.dollar.com). **Hertz** (☎ 800/654–
3001; 800/263–0600 in Canada; 020/
8897–2072 in the U.K.; 02/9669–
2444 in Australia; 09/256–8690 in
New Zealand; WEB www.hertz.com)
National Car Rental (☎ 800/227–
7368; 020/8680–4800 in the U.K.;
WEB www.nationalcar.com).

CUTTING COSTS

To get the best deal, **book through a
travel agent who will shop around.**
Do **look into wholesalers,** companies
that do not own fleets but rent in
bulk from those that do and often
offer better rates than traditional car-
rental operations. Payment must be
made before you leave home.
➤ WHOLESALERS: **Auto Europe** (☎
207/842–2000 or 800/223–5555, FAX
207/842–2222, WEB www.autoeurope.
com). **Europe by Car** (☎ 212/581–
3040 or 800/223–1516, FAX 212/246–
1458, WEB www.europebycar.com).
DER Travel Services (✉ 9501 W.
Devon Ave., Rosemont, IL 60018, ☎
800/782–2424, FAX 800/282–7474 for
information; 800/860–9944 for
brochures, WEB www.dertravel.com).
Kemwel Holiday Autos (☎ 800/678–
0678, FAX 914/825–3160, WEB www.
kemwel.com).

INSURANCE

When driving a rented car you are
generally responsible for any damage
to or loss of the vehicle. Before you
rent, see what coverage your personal
auto-insurance policy and credit cards
provide.

Before you buy collision coverage,
check your existing policies—you
may already be covered. However,
collision policies that car-rental companies sell for European rentals
usually do not include stolen-vehicle
coverage.

REQUIREMENTS & RESTRICTIONS

Ask about age requirements: Several
countries require drivers to be over 20
years old, but some car-rental companies require that drivers be at least 25.
In Scandinavia your own driver's
license is acceptable for a limited
time; check with the country's tourist
board before you go. An International
Driver's Permit is a good idea; it's
available from the American or Canadian Automobile Association, or, in
the United Kingdom, from the Automobile Association or Royal Automobile Club.

SURCHARGES

Before you pick up a car in one city
and leave it in another, **ask about
drop-off charges or one-way service
fees,** which can be substantial. Note,
too, that some rental agencies charge
extra if you return the car before the
time specified in your contract. To
avoid a hefty refueling fee, **fill the
tank just before you turn in the car,**

but be aware that gas stations near the rental outlet may overcharge.

CAR TRAVEL

The Øresundsbron, the new 8-km (5-mi) bridge between Malmö and Copenhagen, simplifies car travel and makes train connections possible between the two countries. Ferry service is cheaper but slower—it takes 45 minutes to make the crossing.

Sweden has an excellent highway network of more than 80,000 km (50,000 mi). The fastest routes are those with numbers prefixed with an E (for "European"), some of which are the equivalent of American highways or British motorways.

Also be aware that there are relatively low legal blood-alcohol limits and tough penalties for driving while intoxicated in Scandinavia; Iceland and Finland have zero-tolerance laws. Penalties include suspension of the driver's license and fines or imprisonment and are enforced by random police roadblocks in urban areas on weekends. In addition, an accident involving a driver with an illegal blood-alcohol level usually voids all insurance agreements, so the driver becomes responsible for his own medical bills and damage to the cars.

In a few remote areas in northern Sweden, road conditions can be unpredictable, and careful planning is required for safety's sake. Several mountain and highland roads in these areas close during winter—when driving in remote areas like these, especially in winter, it is best to let someone know your travel plans. It is also wise to **use a four-wheel-drive vehicle** and to **travel with at least one other car** in these areas.

AUTO CLUBS

➤ IN AUSTRALIA: **Australian Automobile Association** (☎ 02/6247–7311).

➤ IN CANADA: **Canadian Automobile Association** (CAA, ☎ 613/247–0117).

➤ IN NEW ZEALAND: **New Zealand Automobile Association** (☎ 09/377–4660).

➤ IN THE U.K.: **Automobile Association** (AA, ☎ 0990/500–600). **Royal Automobile Club** (RAC, ☎ 0990/722–722 for membership; 0345/121–345 for insurance).

➤ IN THE U.S.: **American Automobile Association** (☎ 800/564–6222).

EMERGENCY SERVICES

The Larmtjänst organization, run by a confederation of Swedish insurance companies, provides a 24-hour breakdown service. Its phone numbers are listed in the Yellow Pages.

GASOLINE

Sweden has some of the highest gasoline rates in Europe, about SKr 10 per liter (about SKr 38 per gallon). Lead-free gasoline is readily available. Gas stations are self-service: pumps marked SEDEL are automatic and accept SKr 20 and SKr 100 bills; pumps marked KASSA are paid for at the cashier; the KONTO pumps are for customers with credit cards.

PARKING

Parking meters and, increasingly, timed ticket machines, operate in larger towns, usually between 8 AM and 6 PM. The fee varies from about SKr 6 to SKr 35 per hour. Parking garages in urban areas are mostly automated, often with machines that accept credit cards; LEDIGT on a garage sign means space is available. Try to avoid getting a parking ticket, which can come with fines of SKr 300 to SKr 700.

ROAD CONDITIONS

All main and secondary roads are well surfaced, but some minor roads, particularly in the north, are gravel.

ROAD MAPS

If you plan on extensive road touring, consider buying the *Vägatlas över Sverige,* a detailed road atlas published by the Mötormännens Riksförbund, available at bookstores for around SKr 270.

RULES OF THE ROAD

Drive on the right, and, no matter where you sit in a car, seat belts are mandatory. You must also have at least low-beam headlights on at all times. Signs indicate five basic speed limits, ranging from 30 kph (19 mph) in school or playground areas to 110 kph (68 mph) on long stretches of *E* roads.

CHILDREN IN SWEDEN

In Sweden children are to be seen *and* heard and are genuinely welcome in most public places.

If you are renting a car, don't forget to **arrange for a car seat** when you reserve. For general advice about traveling with children, consult *Fodor's FYI: Travel with Your Baby* (available in bookstores everywhere).

DISCOUNTS

Children are entitled to discount tickets (often as much as 50% off) on buses, trains, and ferries throughout Scandinavia, as well as reductions on special City Cards. Children under age 12 pay 75% of the adult fare and children under age 2 pay 10% on SAS round-trips. There are no restrictions on the children's fares when booked in economy class. "Family fares," available only in business class, are also worth looking into (☞ Cutting Costs *under* Air Travel).

With the Scanrail Pass (☞ Train Travel)—good for rail journeys throughout Scandinavia—children under age 4 (on lap) travel free; those ages 4–11 pay half fare and those ages 12–25 can get a Scanrail Youth Pass, providing a 25% discount off the adult fare.

FLYING

If your children are age 2 or older, **ask about children's airfares.** As a general rule, infants under 2 not occupying a seat fly at greatly reduced fares or even for free. When booking, **confirm carry-on allowances** if you're traveling with infants. In general, for babies charged 10% of the adult fare you are allowed one carry-on bag and a collapsible stroller; if the flight is full, the stroller may have to be checked or you may be limited to less.

Experts agree that it's a good idea to use safety seats aloft for children weighing less than 40 pounds. Airlines set their own policies: U.S. carriers usually require that the child be ticketed, even if he or she is young enough to ride free, since the seats must be strapped into regular seats. Do **check your airline's policy about using safety seats during takeoff and landing.** And since safety seats are not allowed everywhere in the plane, get your seat assignments early.

When reserving, **request children's meals or a freestanding bassinet** if you need them. But note that bulkhead seats, where you must sit to use the bassinet, may lack an overhead bin or storage space on the floor. For all airlines servicing Scandinavia, it is necessary to reserve children's and baby meals at least 24 hours in advance; travel of an unaccompanied minor should be confirmed at least three days prior to the flight.

LODGING

Most hotels in Scandinavia allow children under a certain age to stay in their parents' room at no extra charge, but others charge for them as extra adults; be sure to **find out the cutoff age for children's discounts.**

SIGHTS & ATTRACTIONS

Places that are especially appealing to children are indicated by a rubber-duckie icon (🦆) in the margin.

CONSUMER PROTECTION

Whenever shopping or buying travel services in Scandinavia, **pay with a major credit card,** if possible, so you can cancel payment or get reimbursed if there's a problem. If you're doing business with a particular company for the first time, **contact your local Better Business Bureau and the attorney general's offices** in your state and (for U.S. businesses) the company's home state as well. Have any complaints been filed? Finally, if you're buying a package or tour, always **consider travel insurance** that includes default coverage (☞ Insurance).

▶ BBBs: **Council of Better Business Bureaus** (✉ 4200 Wilson Blvd., Suite 800, Arlington, VA 22203, ☎ 703/ 276–0100, ℻ 703/525–8277, 🌐 www.bbb.org).

CRUISE TRAVEL

Highly popular four-day cruises are available on the Göta Canal that make use of rivers; lakes; and, on their last lap, the Baltic Sea. This lovely waterway, which links Göteborg on the west coast with Stockholm on the east, has a total of 65 locks, and you travel on fine old steamers, some of which date almost from the canal's opening in 1832. The oldest and most desirable is the *Juno,* built in 1874. Prices start at SKr 5,900 for a bed in a double cabin. For more information, contact the Göta Canal Steamship Company.

To learn how to plan, choose, and book a cruise-ship voyage, check out Cruise How-to's on www.fodors.com.

➤ CRUISE LINES: **Göta Canal Steamship Company** (✉ Box 272, S401 24 Göteborg, ☎ 03/1806315, FAX 03/1158311, WEB www.gotacanal.se).

CUSTOMS & DUTIES

When shopping, **keep receipts** for all purchases. Upon reentering the country, **be ready to show customs officials what you've bought.** If you feel a duty is incorrect or object to the way your clearance was handled, note the inspector's badge number and ask to see a supervisor. If the problem isn't resolved, write to the appropriate authorities, beginning with the port director at your point of entry.

IN AUSTRALIA

Australian residents who are 18 or older may bring home $A400 worth of souvenirs and gifts (including jewelry), 250 cigarettes or 250 grams of tobacco, and 1,125 ml of alcohol (including wine, beer, and spirits). Residents under 18 may bring back $A200 worth of goods. Prohibited items include meat products. Seeds, plants, and fruits need to be declared upon arrival.

➤ INFORMATION: **Australian Customs Service** (Regional Director, ✉ Box 8, Sydney, NSW 2001, Australia, ☎ 02/9213–2000, FAX 02/9213–4000, WEB www.customs.gov.au).

IN CANADA

Canadian residents who have been out of Canada for at least seven days may bring home C$750 worth of goods duty-free. If you've been away fewer than seven days but more than 48 hours, the duty-free allowance drops to C$200; if your trip lasts 24–48 hours, the allowance is C$50. You may not pool allowances with family members. Goods claimed under the C$750 exemption may follow you by mail; those claimed under the lesser exemptions must accompany you. Alcohol and tobacco products may be included in the seven-day and 48-hour exemptions but not in the 24-hour exemption. If you meet the age requirements of the province or territory through which you reenter Canada, you may bring in, duty-free, 1.14 liters (40 imperial ounces) of wine or liquor *or* 24 12-ounce cans or bottles of beer or ale. If you are 19 or older you may bring in, duty-free, 200 cigarettes and 50 cigars. Check ahead of time with the Canada Customs Revenue Agency or the Department of Agriculture for policies regarding meat products, seeds, plants, and fruits.

You may send an unlimited number of gifts worth up to C$60 each duty-free to Canada. Label the package UNSOLICITED GIFT—VALUE UNDER $60. Alcohol and tobacco are excluded.

➤ INFORMATION: **Canada Customs and Revenue Agency** (✉ 2265 St. Laurent Blvd. S, Ottawa, Ontario K1G 4K3, Canada, ☎ 204/983–3500 or 506/636–5064; 800/461–9999 in Canada, WEB www.ccra-adrc.gc.ca).

IN NEW ZEALAND

Homeward-bound residents 17 or older may bring back $700 worth of souvenirs and gifts. Your duty-free allowance also includes 4.5 liters of wine or beer; one 1,125-ml bottle of spirits; and either 200 cigarettes, 250 grams of tobacco, 50 cigars, or a combination of the three up to 250 grams. Prohibited items include meat products, seeds, plants, and fruits.

➤ INFORMATION: **New Zealand Customs** (Custom House, ✉ 50 Anzac Ave., Box 29, Auckland, New Zealand, ☎ 09/300–5399, FAX 09/359–6730, WEB www.customs.govt.nz).

IN SWEDEN

Travelers 21 or older entering Sweden from non-EU countries may import duty-free: 1 liter of liquor and 2 liters of fortified wine; 2 liters of wine or 15 liters of beer; 200 cigarettes or 100 grams of cigarillos or 50 cigars or 250 grams of tobacco; 50 grams of perfume; ¼ liter of aftershave; and other goods up to the value of SKr

1,700. Travelers from the United Kingdom or other EU countries may import duty-free: 1 liter of liquor or 3 liters of fortified wine; 5 liters of wine; 15 liters of beer; 300 cigarettes or 150 cigarillos or 75 cigars or 400 grams of tobacco; and other goods, including perfume and aftershave, of any value.

IN THE U.K.

If you are a U.K. resident and your journey was wholly within the European Union (EU), you won't have to pass through customs when you return to the United Kingdom. If you plan to bring back large quantities of alcohol or tobacco, check EU limits beforehand. From countries outside the European Union, including Iceland and Norway, you may bring home, duty-free, 200 cigarettes or 50 cigars; 1 liter of spirits or 2 liters of fortified or sparkling wine or liqueurs; 2 liters of still table wine; 60 ml of perfume; 250 ml of toilet water; plus £145 worth of other goods, including gifts and souvenirs. If returning from outside the EU, prohibited items include meat products, seeds, plants, and fruits.

➤ INFORMATION: **HM Customs and Excise** (✉ St. Christopher House, Southwark, London, SE1 OTE, U.K., ☎ 020/7928–3344, 🖥 www.hmce. gov.uk).

IN THE U.S.

U.S. residents who have been out of the country for at least 48 hours (and who have not used the $400 allowance or any part of it in the past 30 days) may bring home $400 worth of foreign goods duty-free.

U.S. residents age 21 and older may bring back 1 liter of alcohol duty-free. In addition, regardless of your age, you are allowed 200 cigarettes and 100 non-Cuban cigars. Antiques, which the U.S. Customs Service defines as objects more than 100 years old, enter duty-free, as do original works of art done entirely by hand, including paintings, drawings, and sculptures.

You may also mail or ship packages home duty-free: up to $200 worth of goods for personal use, with a limit of one parcel per addressee per day (except alcohol or tobacco products or perfume worth more than $5); label the package PERSONAL USE and attach a list of its contents and their retail value. Do not label the package UNSOLICITED GIFT or your duty-free exemption will drop to $100. Mailed items do not affect your duty-free allowance on your return.

➤ INFORMATION: **U.S. Customs Service** (✉ 1300 Pennsylvania Ave. NW, Room 6.3D, Washington, DC 20229, 🖥 www.customs.gov; inquiries ☎ 202/354–1000; complaints c/o ✉ 1300 Pennsylvania Ave. NW, Room 5.4D, Washington, DC 20229; registration of equipment c/o Office of Passenger Programs, ☎ 202/927–0530).

DINING

Sweden's major cities offer a full range of dining choices, from traditional to international restaurants. The restaurants we list are the cream of the crop in each price category. Properties indicated by an ✕🏠 are lodging establishments whose restaurant warrants a special trip.

Restaurant meals are a big-ticket item throughout Scandinavia, but there are ways to keep the cost of eating down. Take full advantage of the large buffet breakfast often included in the cost of a hotel room. At lunch, look for the "menu" that offers a set two- or three-course meal for a set price, or limit yourself to a hearty appetizer. Some restaurants now include a trip to the salad bar in the dinner price. At dinner, pay careful attention to the price of wine and drinks, since the high tax on alcohol raises these costs considerably. For more information on affordable eating, *see* Money Matters.

MEALS & SPECIALTIES

The surrounding oceans and plentiful inland lakes and streams provide Scandinavian countries with an abundance of fresh fish and seafood: salmon, herring, trout, and seafood delicacies are mainstays, and are prepared in countless ways. Elk, deer, reindeer, and lamb feed in relatively unspoiled areas in Iceland and northern Norway, Sweden, and Finland, and have the succulent taste of wild game. Berries and mushrooms are still harvested from the forests; sausage appears in a thousand forms, as do potatoes and other root vegetables such as turnips, radishes, rutabaga, and carrots. Some particular northern tastes can seem unusual, such as the fondness for pickled and fermented fish—to be sampled carefully at first—and a universal obsession with sweet pastries, ice cream, and chocolate.

Other novelties for the visitor might be the use of fruit in main dishes and soups, or sour milk on breakfast cereal, or preserved fish paste as a spread for crackers, or the prevalence of tasty, whole-grain crisp breads and hearty rye breads. The Swedish *smörgåsbord* (a kind of buffet meal) is less common these days, but is still the traveling diner's best bet for breakfast. A smörgåsbord usually comes with a wide range of cheeses, fresh fish, and vegetables alongside meat and breads and other starches.

MEALTIMES

Unless otherwise noted, the restaurants listed in this guide are open daily for lunch and dinner.

RESERVATIONS & DRESS

Reservations are always a good idea: we mention them only when they're essential or not accepted. Book as far ahead as you can, and reconfirm as soon as you arrive. We mention dress only when men are required to wear a jacket or a jacket and tie.

WINE, BEER & SPIRITS

Restaurants' markup on alcoholic beverages is often very high in Scandinavia: as much as four times that of a standard retail price.

DISABILITIES & ACCESSIBILITY

Facilities for travelers with disabilities in Scandinavia are generally good, and most of the major tourist offices offer special booklets and brochures on travel and accommodations. Most Scandinavian countries have organizations that offer advice to travelers with disabilities, and can give information on public and local transportation, sights and museums, hotels, and special interest tours. Notify and make all local and public transportation and hotel reservations in advance to ensure a smooth trip.

➤ LOCAL RESOURCES: **DHR De Handikappades Riksförbund** (✉ Box 47305, Katrinebergsvägen 6, 100 74 Stockholm, Sweden, ☎ 46/86858000, WEB www.dhr.se/english.htm).

LODGING

Best Western has properties with wheelchair-accessible rooms in Stockholm. If wheelchair-accessible rooms on other floors are not available, ground-floor rooms are provided.

➤ WHEELCHAIR-FRIENDLY CHAIN: **Best Western** (☎ 800/528–1234).

RESERVATIONS

When discussing accessibility with an operator or reservations agent, **ask hard questions.** Are there any stairs, inside *or* out? Are there grab bars next to the toilet *and* in the shower/tub? How wide is the doorway to the room? To the bathroom? For the most extensive facilities, **opt for newer accommodations.**

SIGHTS & ATTRACTIONS

Although most major attractions in Stockholm present no problems, windy cobblestone streets, especially in the Gamla Stan (Old Town), may be challenging for travelers with disabilities.

TRANSPORTATION

With advance notice, most airlines, buses, and trains can arrange assistance for those requiring extra help with boarding. Contact each individual company at least one week in advance, or ideally at the time of booking.

Confirming ahead is especially important when planning travel to less populated regions. The smaller planes and ferries often used in such areas are not all accessible.

➤ COMPLAINTS: **Aviation Consumer Protection Division** (☞ Air Travel) for airline-related problems. **Civil Rights Office** (✉ U.S. Department of Transportation, Departmental Office of Civil Rights, S-30, 400 7th St. SW, Room 10215, Washington, DC 20590, ☎ 202/366–4648, FAX 202/366–9371, WEB www.dot.gov/ost/docr/index.htm) for problems with surface transportation. **Disability Rights Section** (✉ U.S. Department of Justice, Civil Rights Division, Box 66738, Washington, DC 20035-6738, ☎ 202/514–0301 or 800/514–0301; 202/514–0383 TTY; 800/514–0383 TTY, FAX 202/307–1198, WEB www.usdoj.gov/crt/ada/adahom1.htm) for general complaints.

TRAVEL AGENCIES

In the United States, the Americans with Disabilities Act requires that travel firms serve the needs of all travelers. Some agencies specialize in working with people with disabilities.

➤ TRAVELERS WITH MOBILITY PROBLEMS: **Access Adventures** (✉ 206 Chestnut Ridge Rd., Scottsville, NY 14624, ☎ 716/889–9096, dltravel@prodigy.net), run by a former physical-rehabilitation counselor. **CareVacations** (✉ No. 5, 5110–50 Ave., Leduc, Alberta T9E 6V4, Canada, ☎ 780/986–6404 or 877/478–7827, FAX 780/986–8332, WEB www.carevacations.com), for group tours and cruise vacations. **Flying Wheels Travel** (✉ 143 W. Bridge St., Box 382, Owatonna, MN 55060, ☎ 507/451–5005 or 800/535–6790, FAX 507/451–1685, WEB www.flyingwheelstravel.com).

DISCOUNTS & DEALS

Be a smart shopper and **compare all your options** before making decisions. A plane ticket bought with a promotional coupon from travel clubs, coupon books, and direct-mail offers or on the Internet may not be cheaper than the least expensive fare from a discount ticket agency. And always keep in mind that what you get is just as important as what you save.

DISCOUNT RESERVATIONS

To save money, **look into discount reservations services** with toll-free numbers, which use their buying power to get a better price on hotels, airline tickets, even car rentals. When booking a room, always **call the hotel's local toll-free number** (if one is available) rather than the central reservations number—you'll often get a better price. Always ask about special packages or corporate rates.

When shopping for the best deal on hotels and car rentals, **look for guaranteed exchange rates,** which protect you against a falling dollar. With your rate locked in, you won't pay more, even if the price goes up in the local currency.

➤ AIRLINE TICKETS: ☎ 800/247–4537.

➤ HOTEL ROOMS: **International Marketing & Travel Concepts** (☎ 800/790–4682, WEB www.imtc-travel.com). **Players Express Vacations** (☎ 800/458–6161, WEB www.playersexpress.com). **Steigenberger Reservation Service** (☎ 800/223–5652, WEB www.srs-worldhotels.com). **Travel Interlink** (☎ 800/888–5898, WEB www.travelinterlink.com). **Turbotrip.com** (☎ 800/473–7829, WEB www.turbotrip.com).

PACKAGE DEALS

Don't confuse packages and guided tours. When you buy a package, you travel on your own, just as though you had planned the trip yourself. Fly/drive packages, which combine airfare and car rental, are often a good deal. If you **buy a rail/drive pass,** you may save on train tickets and car rentals. All Eurail- and Europass holders get a discount on Eurostar fares through the Channel Tunnel. Also check rates for Scanrail Passes (☞ Train Travel).

ELECTRICITY

To use electric-powered equipment purchased in the United States or Canada, **bring a converter and adapter.** The electrical current in Scandinavia is 220 volts, 50 cycles alternating current (AC); wall outlets take Continental-type plugs, with two round prongs.

If your appliances are dual-voltage, you'll need only an adapter. Don't use 110-volt outlets marked FOR SHAVERS ONLY for high-wattage appliances such as blow-dryers. Most laptops operate equally well on 110 and 220 volts and so require only an adapter.

EMBASSIES

➤ AUSTRALIA: (✉ Sergels Torg 12, ☎ 08/6132900).

➤ CANADA: (✉ Tegelbacken 4, Box 16129, 10323 Stockholm, ☎ 08/4533000).

➤ UNITED KINGDOM: (✉ Skarpög. 68, 11593 Stockholm, ☎ 08/6713000).

➤ UNITED STATES: (✉ Strandv. 101, 11589 Stockholm, ☎ 08/7835300).

EMERGENCIES

Anywhere in Sweden, dial 112 for emergency assistance.

HOLIDAYS

In general, all Scandinavian countries celebrate New Year's Eve and Day, Good Friday, Easter and Easter Monday, May Day (May 1; celebrated as Labor Day for many of the countries), Midsummer Eve and Day (although its date varies by country), and Christmas (as well as Christmas Eve and Boxing Day, the day after Christmas). In addition, Sweden has the following holidays: Epiphany, Jan. 6; Ascension; Pentecost Monday, All Saint's Day (observed the first Sat. after Oct. 30).

On major holidays such as Christmas, most shops close or operate on a Sunday schedule. On the eves of such holidays, many shops are also closed all day or are open with reduced hours.

On May Day, the city centers are usually full of people, celebrations, and parades. During Midsummer, at the end of June, locals flock to the lakes and countryside to celebrate the beginning of long summer days with bonfires and other festivities.

INSURANCE

The most useful travel-insurance plan is a comprehensive policy that includes coverage for trip cancellation and interruption, default, trip delay, and medical expenses (with a waiver for preexisting conditions).

Without insurance you will lose all or most of your money if you cancel your trip, regardless of the reason. Default insurance covers you if your tour operator, airline, or cruise line goes out of business. Trip-delay covers expenses that arise because of bad weather or mechanical delays. Study the fine print when comparing policies.

If you're traveling internationally, a key component of travel insurance is coverage for medical bills incurred if you get sick on the road. Such expenses are not generally covered by Medicare or private policies. U.K. residents can buy a travel-insurance policy valid for most vacations taken during the year in which it's purchased (but check preexisting-condition coverage). British and Australian citizens need extra medical coverage when traveling overseas.

Always **buy travel policies directly from the insurance company**; if you buy them from a cruise line, airline, or tour operator that goes out of business you probably will not be covered for the agency or operator's default, a major risk. Before making any purchase, **review your existing health and homeowner's policies** to find what they cover away from home.

➤ TRAVEL INSURERS: In the U.S.: **Access America** (✉ 6600 W. Broad St., Richmond, VA 23230, ☎ 800/284–8300, FAX 804/673–1491, WEB www.etravelprotection.com). **Travel Guard International** (✉ 1145 Clark St., Stevens Point, WI 54481, ☎ 715/345–0505 or 800/826–1300, FAX 800/955–8785, WEB www.travelguard.com).

➤ INSURANCE INFORMATION: In the U.K.: **Association of British Insurers** (✉ 51–55 Gresham St., London EC2V 7HQ, U.K., ☎ 020/7600–3333, FAX 020/7696–8999, WEB www.abi.org.uk). In Canada: **RBC Travel Insurance** (✉ 6880 Financial Dr., Mississauga, Ontario L5N 7Y5, Canada, ☎ 905/791–8700; 800/668–4342 in Canada, FAX 905/816–2498, WEB www.royalbank.com). In Australia: **Insurance Council of Australia** (✉ Level 3, 56 Pitt St., Sydney NSW 2000, ☎ 02/9253–5100, FAX 02/9253–5111, WEB www.ica.com.au). In New Zealand: **Insurance Council of New Zealand** (✉ Level 7, 111–115 Customhouse Quay, Box 474, Wellington, New Zealand, ☎ 04/472–5230, FAX 04/473–3011, WEB www.icnz.org.nz).

LANGUAGE

Swedish is closely related to Danish and Norwegian. After "z," the Swedish alphabet has three extra letters, "å," "ä," and "ö," something to bear in mind when using the phone book. Another oddity in the phone book is that *v* and *w* are interchangeable; Wittström, for example, comes before Vittviks, not after. Most Swedes are happy to speak English.

LODGING

The lodgings we list are the cream of the crop in each price category. We always list the facilities that are available—but we don't specify whether they cost extra: when pricing accommodations, always ask what's included and what costs extra.

Sweden offers a variety of accommodations, from simple bed-and-breakfasts, campsites, and hostels to hotels of the highest international standard. In the larger cities, lodging ranges from first-class business hotels run by SAS, Sheraton, and Scandic; to good-quality tourist-class hotels, such as RESO, Best Western, Scandic Budget, and Sweden Hotels; to a wide variety of single-entrepreneur hotels. In the countryside, look for independently run inns and motels, known as guest houses. Farm holidays have also become increasingly available to tourists and Sweden has organizations that can help plan stays in the countryside.

Before you leave home, **ask your travel agent about discounts** (☞ Hotels), including summer hotel checks for Best Western, Scandic, and Inter Nor hotels, and enormous year-round rebates at SAS hotels for travelers over 65. All EuroClass (business class) passengers can get discounts of at least 10% at SAS hotels when they book through SAS.

Two things about hotels usually surprise North Americans: the relatively limited dimensions of Scandinavian beds and the generous size of Scandinavian breakfasts. Scandinavian double beds are often about 60 inches wide or slightly less, close in size to the U.S. queen size. King-size beds (72 inches wide) are difficult to find and, if available, require special reservations.

Older hotels may have some rooms described as "double," which in fact have one double bed plus one foldout sofa big enough for two people. This arrangement is occasionally called a combi-room but is being phased out.

Many older hotels, particularly the country inns and independently run smaller hotels in the cities, do not have private bathrooms. Ask ahead if this is important to you.

Scandinavian breakfasts resemble what many people would call lunch, usually including breads, cheeses, marmalade, hams, lunch meats, eggs, juice, cereal, milk, and coffee. Generally, the farther north you go, the larger the breakfasts become. Breakfast is usually included in hotel rates.

Make reservations whenever possible. Even countryside inns, which usually have space, are sometimes packed with vacationing Europeans.

Ask about high and low seasons when making reservations, since different countries define their tourist seasons differently. Some hotels lower prices during tourist season, whereas others raise them during the same period.

Assume that hotels operate on the **European Plan** (EP, with no meals) unless we specify that they use the **Continental Plan** (CP, with a Continental breakfast), **Modified American Plan** (MAP, with breakfast and dinner), or the **Full American Plan** (FAP, with all meals).

APARTMENT & VILLA RENTALS

With 250 chalet villages with high standards, Sweden enjoys popularity with its chalet accommodations, often arranged on the spot at tourist offices. Many are organized under the auspices of the Swedish Touring Association (STF). DFDS Seaways in Göteborg arranges package deals that combine a ferry trip from Britain across the North Sea and a stay in a chalet village.

➤ RENTAL CONTACTS: **DFDS Seaways** (☎ 031/650600; 191/2936262 within the U.K.). **Swedish Touring Association** (☎ 08/4632200, FAX 08/6781938, WEB www.meravsverige.se).

CAMPING

There are 760 registered campsites nationwide, many close to uncrowded swimming places and with fishing, boating, or canoeing; they may also offer bicycle rentals. Prices range from SKr 70 to SKr 130 per 24-hour period. Many campsites also offer accommodations in log cabins at various prices, depending on the facilities offered. Most are open between June and September, but about 200 remain open in winter for skiing and skating enthusiasts. Sveriges Campingvårdernas Riksförbund (Swedish Campsite Owners' Association or SCR), publishes, in English, an abbreviated list of sites; contact the office for a free copy.

➤ CONTACTS: **Sveriges Campingvårdernas Riksförbund** (⊠ Box 255, 451 17 Uddevalla, ☎ 0522/ 642440, FAX 0522/642430, WEB www. camping.se).

FARM & COTTAGE HOLIDAYS

The old-fashioned farm or country-side holiday, long a staple for Scandinavian city dwellers, is becoming increasingly available to tourists. In general, you can choose to stay on the farm itself, and even participate in daily activities, or you can opt to rent a private housekeeping cottage. Contact the local tourist board or Swedish Farm Holidays for details.

➤ CONTACTS: **Swedish Farm Holidays** (⊠ Box 8, S-668 21 Ed, Sweden, ☎ 46/53412075, FAX 46/53461011, WEB www.bopalantgard.org).

HOME EXCHANGES

If you would like to exchange your home for someone else's, **join a home-exchange organization,** which will send you its updated listings of available exchanges for a year and will include your own listing in at least one of them. It's up to you to make specific arrangements.

➤ EXCHANGE CLUBS: **HomeLink International** (⊠ Box 47747, Tampa, FL 33647, ☎ 813/975–9825 or 800/ 638–3841, FAX 813/910–8144, WEB www.homelink.org; $106 per year). **Intervac U.S.** (⊠ Box 590504, San Francisco, CA 94159, ☎ 800/756–4663, FAX 415/435–7440, WEB www. intervacus.com; $93 yearly fee includes one catalog and on-line access).

HOSTELS

No matter what your age, you can **save on lodging costs by staying at hostels.** In some 4,500 locations in more than 70 countries around the world, Hostelling International (HI), the umbrella group for a number of national youth-hostel associations, offers single-sex, dorm-style beds and, at many hostels, rooms for couples and family accommodations. Membership in any HI national hostel association, open to travelers of all ages, allows you to stay in HI-affiliated hostels at member rates; one-year membership is about $25 for adults (C$26.75 in Canada, £9.30 in the U.K., $30 in Australia, and $30 in New Zealand); hostels run about $10–$25 per night. If a hostel has nearly filled up, members have priority over others; members are also eligible for discounts around the world, even on rail and bus travel in some countries.

➤ ORGANIZATIONS: **Hostelling International—American Youth Hostels** (⊠ 733 15th St. NW, Suite 840, Washington, DC 20005, ☎ 202/783–6161, FAX 202/783–6171, WEB www. hiayh.org). **Hostelling International—Canada** (⊠ 400–205 Catherine St., Ottawa, Ontario K2P 1C3, Canada, ☎ 613/237–7884; 800/663–5777 in Canada, FAX 613/237–7868, WEB www. hostellingintl.ca). **Youth Hostel Association of England and Wales** (⊠ Trevelyan House, 8 St. Stephen's Hill, St. Albans, Hertfordshire AL1 2DY, U.K., ☎ 0870/8708808, FAX 01727/ 844126, WEB www.yha.org.uk). **Youth Hostel Association Australia** (⊠ 10 Mallett St., Camperdown, NSW 2050, Australia, ☎ 02/9565–1699, FAX 02/9565–1325, WEB www.yha. com.au). **Youth Hostels Association of New Zealand** (⊠ Level 3, 193 Cashel St., Box 436, Christchurch, New Zealand, ☎ 03/379–9970, FAX 03/365–4476, WEB www.yha.org.nz).

HOTELS

All hotels listed have private baths unless otherwise noted.

Major hotels in larger cities cater mainly to business clientele and can be expensive; weekend rates are more reasonable and can even be as low as half the normal price. Prices are normally on a per-room basis and include all taxes and service charges and usually breakfast. Apart from the more modest inns and the cheapest budget establishments, private baths and showers are standard.

Whatever their size, almost all Swedish hotels provide scrupulously clean accommodation and courteous service. Since many Swedes go on vacation during July and through early August, make your hotel reservations in advance, especially if staying outside the city areas during that time. Some hotels close during the winter holidays as well; call ahead for information.

Hotels in Sweden offer Inn Checks, or prepaid hotel vouchers, for accommodations ranging from first-class hotels to country cottages. These vouchers, which must be purchased from travel agents or from the Scandinavian Tourist Board before departure, are sold individually and in packets for as many nights as needed and offer savings of up to 50%. Most countries also offer summer bargains for foreign tourists; winter bargains can be even greater. For further information about Scandinavian hotel vouchers, contact the Scandinavian Tourist Board.

ProSkandinavia checks can be used in 400 hotels across Scandinavia (excluding Iceland) for savings up to 50%, for reservations made usually no earlier than 24 hours before arrival, although some hotels allow earlier bookings. One check costs about $35 U.S. Two checks will pay for a double room at a hotel, one check for a room in a cottage. The checks can be bought at many travel agencies in Scandinavia or ordered from **ProSkandinavia** (✉ Nedre Slottsgate 13, N-0157 Oslo, Norway, ☎ 47/22–42–50–06, ℻ 47/22–42–06–57, 𝚆𝙴𝙱 www.proskandinavia.com).

An official annual guide, *Hotels in Sweden*, published by and available free from the Swedish Travel and Tourism Council, gives comprehensive information about hotel facilities and prices. Countryside Hotels comprises 35 select resort hotels, some of them restored manor houses or cen-

turies-old inns. Hotellcentralen is an independent agency that makes advance telephone reservations for any Swedish hotel at no cost. The Sweden Hotels group has about 100 independently owned hotels and its own classification scheme—*A, B,* or *C*—based on facilities.

Major hotel groups like Best Western, Radisson SAS, RESO, Scandic, and Sweden Hotels also have their own central reservations services.

➤ CONTACTS: **Best Western** (☎ 020/792752). **Countryside Hotels** (✉ Box 69, 830 13 Åre, ☎ 06/4751860, ℻ 06/4751920). **Hotellcentralen** (✉ Centralstation, 111 20, ☎ 08/7892425, ℻ 08/7918666). **Radisson SAS** (☎ 02/0797592). **RESO** (☎ 08/4114040). **Scandic** (☎ 08/51751700). **Sweden Hotels** (☎ 020/770000).

➤ TOLL-FREE NUMBERS: **Best Western** (☎ 800/528–1234, 𝚆𝙴𝙱 www.bestwestern.com). **Choice** (☎ 800/221–2222, 𝚆𝙴𝙱 www.choicehotels.com). **Comfort Inn** (☎ 800/228–5150, 𝚆𝙴𝙱 www.comfortinn.com). **Hilton** (☎ 800/445–8667, 𝚆𝙴𝙱 www.hilton.com). **Holiday Inn** (☎ 800/465–4329, 𝚆𝙴𝙱 www.basshotels.com). **Quality Inn** (☎ 800/228–5151, 𝚆𝙴𝙱 www.qualityinn.com). **Radisson** (☎ 800/333–3333, 𝚆𝙴𝙱 www.radisson.com). **Sheraton** (☎ 800/325–3535, 𝚆𝙴𝙱 www.starwoodhotels.com).

MAIL & SHIPPING

POSTAL RATES

Postcards and letters up to 20 grams can be mailed for SKr 5 within Sweden, SKr 7 to destinations within Europe, and SKr 8 to the United States and the rest of the world.

MONEY MATTERS

Prices throughout this guide are given for adults. Substantially reduced fees are almost always available for children, students, and senior citizens. For information on taxes, *see* Taxes.

Sample prices in Sweden include a cup of coffee, SKr 20–SKr 30; a beer, SKr 30–SKr 45; mineral water, SKr 10–SKr 20; cheese roll, SKr 20–SKr 40; pepper steak à la carte, SKr 120–SKr 160; cheeseburger, SKr 60; pizza, starting at SKr 40.

Be aware that sales taxes can be very high, but foreigners can get some refunds by shopping at tax-free stores (☞ Taxes). City cards can save you transportation and entrance fees in many of the larger cities.

You can **reduce the cost of food by planning.** Breakfast is often included in your hotel bill; if not, you may wish to buy fruit, sweet rolls, and a beverage for a picnic breakfast. Electrical devices for hot coffee or tea should be bought abroad, though, to conform to the local current.

Opt for a restaurant lunch instead of dinner, since the latter tends to be significantly more expensive. Instead of beer or wine, **drink tap water—** liquor can cost four times the price of the same brand in a store—but do specify tap water, as the term "water" can refer to soft drinks and bottled water, which are also expensive. Throughout Scandinavia, the tip is included in the cost of your meal.

In most of Scandinavia, liquor and strong beer (over 3% alcohol) can be purchased only in state-owned shops, at very high prices, during weekday business hours, usually 9:30 to 6 and in some areas on Saturday until mid-afternoon. A midsize bottle of whiskey in Sweden, for example, can easily cost SKr 250 (about $35). Weaker beers and ciders are usually available in grocery stores in Scandinavia.

ATMS

The 1,200 or so blue Bankomat cash dispensers nationwide have been adapted to take some foreign cards, including MasterCard, Visa, and bank cards linked to the Cirrus network. You may encounter some complications on remote machines. It's best to use those that are next to major bank offices. For more information, contact Bankomatcentralen in Stockholm or your local bank. American Express has cash and traveler's check dispensers; there's also an office at Stockholm's Arlanda airport.

➤ CONTACTS: **American Express** (✉ Birger Jarlsg. 1, ☎ 020/793211 toll free). **Bankomatcentralen/CEK AB** (☎ 08/7255700).

CREDIT CARDS

Throughout this guide, the following abbreviations are used: **AE,** American Express; **DC,** Diners Club; **MC,** MasterCard; and **V,** Visa.

CURRENCY

The unit of currency is the krona (plural kronor), which is divided into 100 öre and is written as SKr or SEK. Coins come in SKr 1, SKr 5, and SKr 10. Bank notes are at present SKr 20, 50, 100, 500, and 1,000. As of winter 2001, the exchange rate was SKr 11 to the U.S. dollar, SKr 7 to the Canadian dollar, SKr 15 to the pound sterling, SKr 12 to the Irish punt, SKr 6 to the Australian dollar, SKr 4 to the New Zealand dollar, and SKr 1 to the South African rand.

CURRENCY EXCHANGE

Traveler's checks and foreign currency can be exchanged at banks all over Sweden and at post offices displaying the NB EXCHANGE sign. Be sure to have your passport with you when exchanging money at a bank.

OUTDOORS & SPORTS

BOATING & SAILING

Swedes love to be on the water, whether sailing in the Stockholm archipelago or kayaking along the rocky west coast. STF publishes an annual guide in Swedish to all the country's marinas. Svenska Kanotförbundet (Swedish Canoeing Association) publishes a similar booklet. For information on sailing throughout the country contact the Svenska Seglarförbundet (Swedish Sailing Association).

➤ CONTACTS: **Svenska Kanotförbundet** (Swedish Canoeing Association; ✉ Idrotts Hus, 123 87 Farsta, ☎ 08/6056565, 🌐 www.svenskidrott.se/kanot). **Svenska Seglarförbundet** (Swedish Sailing Association; ✉ af Pontins väg 6, 115 21 Stockholm, ☎ 08/4590990, 🌐 www.ssf.se).

GOLF

Sweden has 365 golf clubs; you can even play by the light of the midnight sun at Boden in the far north. Svenska Golfförbundet (the Swedish Golfing Association) publishes an annual guide in Swedish; it costs around SKr 100, including postage.

➤ CONTACTS: **Svenska Golfförbundet** (✉ Box 84, 182 11 Danderyd, ☎ 08/6221500, FAX 08/7558439, WEB www.golf.se).

SKIING

There are plenty of downhill and cross-country facilities in Sweden. The best-known resorts are in the country's western mountains: Åre in the north, with 29 lifts; Idre Fjäll, to the south of Åre, offering accommodations for 10,000; and Sälen in the folklore region of Dalarna. You can ski through May at Riksgränsen in the far north.

TENNIS

Tennis is popular throughout the country, and courts are fairly easy to find. Contact Svenska Tennisförbundet (Swedish Tennis Association) for information.

➤ CONTACTS: **Svenska Tennisförbundet** (✉ Lidingöv. 75, Box 27915, 115 94 Stockholm, ☎ 08/6679770, FAX 08/6646606, WEB www.tennis.se).

PACKING

Check *Fodor's How to Pack* (available in bookstores everywhere) for more tips.

CHECKING LUGGAGE

You are allowed one carry-on bag and one personal article, such as a purse or a laptop computer. Make sure that everything you carry aboard will fit under your seat or in the overhead bin. Get to the gate early, so you can board as soon as possible, before the overhead bins fill up.

PASSPORTS & VISAS

When traveling internationally, **carry your passport** even if you don't need one (it's always the best form of I.D.) and **make two photocopies of the data page** (one for someone at home and another for you, carried separately from your passport). If you lose your passport, promptly call the nearest embassy or consulate and the local police.

ENTERING SCANDINAVIA

All U.S. citizens, even infants, need only a valid passport to enter any Scandinavian country for stays of up to three months.

PASSPORT OFFICES

The best time to apply for a passport or to renew is in fall and winter. Before any trip, check your passport's expiration date, and, if necessary, renew it as soon as possible.

➤ AUSTRALIAN CITIZENS: **Australian Passport Office** (☎ 131–232, WEB www.dfat.gov.au/passports).

➤ CANADIAN CITIZENS: **Passport Office** (☎ 819/994–3500; 800/567–6868 in Canada, WEB www.dfait-maeci.gc.ca/passport).

➤ NEW ZEALAND CITIZENS: **New Zealand Passport Office** (☎ 04/494–0700, WEB www.passports.govt.nz).

➤ U.K. CITIZENS: **London Passport Office** (☎ 0870/521–0410, WEB www.ukpa.gov.uk) for fees and documentation requirements and to request an emergency passport.

➤ U.S. CITIZENS: **National Passport Information Center** (☎ 900/225–5674; calls are 35¢ per minute for automated service, $1.05 per minute for operator service; WEB www.travel.state.gov/npicinfo.html).

SENIOR-CITIZEN TRAVEL

To qualify for age-related discounts, **mention your senior-citizen status up front** when booking hotel reservations (not when checking out) and before you're seated in restaurants (not when paying the bill). When renting a car, ask about promotional car-rental discounts, which can be cheaper than senior-citizen rates.

TRAIN TRAVEL

Seniors over 60 are entitled to discount tickets (often as much as 50% off) on buses, trains, and ferries throughout Scandinavia, as well as reductions on special City Cards. Eurail offers discounts on Scanrail and Eurail train passes (☞ Train Travel).

➤ EDUCATIONAL PROGRAMS: **Elderhostel** (✉ 11 Ave. de Lafayette, Boston, MA 02111-1746, ☎ 877/426–8056, FAX 877/426–2166, WEB www.elderhostel.org).

SHOPPING

Prices in Scandinavia are never low, but quality is high, and specialties are sometimes less expensive here than elsewhere. Scandinavian design in both furniture and glassware is world-renowned. Swedish crystal, Icelandic sweaters, Danish Lego blocks and furniture, Norwegian furs, and Finnish fabrics—these are just a few of the items to look for. Keep an eye out for sales, called *rea* in Swedish.

STUDENTS IN SCANDINAVIA

➤ I.D.s & SERVICES: **Council Travel** (CIEE; ✉ 205 E. 42nd St., 15th floor, New York, NY 10017, ☎ 212/822–2700 or 888/268–6245, FAX 212/822–2699, WEB www.councilexchanges.org) for mail orders only, in the United States. **Travel Cuts** (✉ 187 College St., Toronto, Ontario M5T 1P7, Canada, ☎ 416/979–2406; 800/667–2887 in Canada, FAX 416/979–8167, WEB www.travelcuts.com).

TAXES

VALUE-ADDED TAX

All hotel, restaurant, and departure taxes and V.A.T. (called *moms* all over Scandinavia) are automatically included in prices. V.A.T. is 25%; non EU residents can obtain a 15% refund on goods of SKr 200 or more. To receive your refund at any of the 15,000 stores that participate in the tax-free program, you'll be asked to fill out a form and show your passport. The form can then be turned in at any airport or ferry customs desk. Keep all your receipts and tags; occasionally, customs authorities ask to see your purchases, so pack them where they will be accessible.

Note: Tax-free sales of alcohol, cigarettes, and other luxury goods has been abolished among EU countries, with Sweden, Finland, and Denmark among the last to adopt these regulations. Finland's Åland Islands have some special rights under the EU and therefore allow tax-free sales for ferries in transit through its ports. All Sweden–Finland ferry routes now pass through the islands, de facto continuing the extremely popular tax-free sales for tourists. Air travel to the Scandinavia EU member states (Sweden, Finland, Denmark), as well as Norway, no longer allows tax-free sales.

Global Refund is a V.A.T. refund service that makes getting your money back hassle-free. The service is available Europe-wide at 130,000 affiliated stores. In participating stores, **ask for the Global Refund form** (called a Shopping Cheque). Have it stamped like any customs form by customs officials when you leave the European Union (be ready to show customs officials what you've bought). Then take the form to one of the more than 700 Global Refund counters—conveniently located at every major airport and border crossing—and your money will be refunded on the spot in the form of cash, check, or a refund to your credit-card account (minus a small percentage for processing).

➤ V.A.T. REFUNDS: **Global Refund** (✉ 99 Main St., Suite 307, Nyack, NY 10960, ☎ 800/566–9828, FAX 845/348–1549, WEB www. globalrefund.com).

TELEPHONES

Post offices do not have telephone facilities, but there are plenty of pay phones. Long-distance calls can be made from special telegraph offices called *Telebutik,* marked TELE.

AREA & COUNTRY CODES

Sweden's country code is 46. When phoning Sweden from outside the country, drop the first 0 from the number. Swedish phone numbers vary in their number of digits.

DIRECTORY & OPERATOR ASSISTANCE

➤ CONTACTS: **Directory Assistance** (☎ 118118; ☎ 07977 for international calls). **Operator Assistance** (☎ 90130; ☎ 0018 for international calls).

INTERNATIONAL CALLS

To make an international call, dial 00 followed by the country code, and then your number. Access codes for various international companies are listed below.

LONG-DISTANCE SERVICES

AT&T, MCI, and Sprint access codes make calling long distance relatively convenient, but you may find the local access number blocked in many hotel rooms. First ask the hotel operator to connect you. If the hotel operator balks, ask for an international operator, or dial the international operator yourself. One way to improve your odds of getting connected to your long-distance carrier is to travel with more than one company's calling card (a hotel may block Sprint, for example, but not MCI). If all else fails, call from a pay phone.

➤ ACCESS CODES: **AT&T USADirect** (☎ 020/795611). **MCI Call USA** (☎ 020/795922). **Sprint Express** (☎ 020/799011).

LOCAL CALLS

A local call costs a minimum of SKr 2. For calls outside the locality, dial the area code (see telephone directory). Public phones are of three types: one takes SKr 1 and SKr 5 coins (newer public phones also accept SKr 10 coins); another takes only credit cards; and the last takes only the prepaid *Telefonkort* (telephone card).

MOBILE PHONES

Scandinavia has been one of the world leaders in mobile phone development; almost 50% of the population in Scandinavia owns a cellular phone. Although standard North American cellular phones will not work in Scandinavia, most Scandinavian capitals have several companies that rent cellular phones to tourists. Contact the local tourist offices for details.

PHONE CARDS

A Telefonkort, available at Telebutik, Pressbyrån (large blue-and-yellow newsstands), or hospitals, costs SKr 35, SKr 60, or SKr 100. If you're making numerous domestic calls, the card saves money. Many of the pay phones in downtown Stockholm and Göteborg take only these cards, so it's a good idea to carry one.

TIME

Sweden is one hour ahead of Greenwich Mean Time (GMT) and six hours ahead of Eastern Standard Time (EST).

TIPPING

In addition to the value-added tax, most hotels usually include a service charge of 15%; it is not necessary to tip unless you have received extra services. Similarly, a service charge of 13% is usually included in restaurant bills. It is a custom, however, to leave small change when buying drinks. Taxi drivers and hairdressers expect a tip of about 10%.

TOURS & PACKAGES

Because everything is prearranged on a prepackaged tour or independent vacation, you spend less time planning—and often get it all at a good price.

BOOKING WITH AN AGENT

Travel agents are excellent resources. But it's a good idea to collect brochures from several agencies, as some agents' suggestions may be influenced by relationships with tour and package firms that reward them for volume sales. If you have a special interest, **find an agent with expertise in that area**; the American Society of Travel Agents (ASTA; ☞ Travel Agencies) has a database of specialists worldwide.

Make sure your travel agent knows the accommodations and other services of the place being recommended. Ask about the hotel's location, room size, beds, and whether it has a pool, room service, or programs for children, if you care about these. Has your agent been there in person or sent others whom you can contact?

Do some homework on your own, too: local tourism boards can provide information about lesser-known and small-niche operators, some of which may sell only direct.

➤ TOUR-OPERATOR RECOMMENDATIONS: **American Society of Travel Agents** (☞ Travel Agencies). **National Tour Association** (NTA; ⊠ 546 E. Main St., Lexington, KY 40508, ☎ 859/226–4444 or 800/682–8886, WEB www.ntaonline.com). **United States Tour Operators Association** (USTOA; ⊠ 342 Madison Ave., Suite 1522, New York, NY 10173, ☎ 212/599–6599 or 800/468–7862, FAX 212/599–6744, WEB www.ustoa.com).

BUYER BEWARE

Each year consumers are stranded or lose their money when tour operators—even large ones with excellent reputations—go out of business. So **check out the operator.** Ask several travel agents about its reputation, and try to **book with a company that has a consumer-protection program.** (Look for information in the company's brochure.) In the United States, members of the National Tour Association and the United States Tour Operators Association are required to set aside funds to cover your payments and travel arrangements in the event that the company defaults. It's also a good idea to choose a company that participates in the American Society of Travel Agents' Tour Operator Program (TOP); ASTA will act as mediator in any disputes between you and your tour operator.

Remember that the more your package or tour includes the better you can predict the ultimate cost of your vacation. Make sure you know exactly what is covered, and **beware of hidden costs.** Are taxes, tips, and transfers included? Entertainment and excursions? These can add up.

SIGHTSEEING TOURS

Stockholm Sightseeing runs a variety of sightseeing tours of Stockholm. Also contact local tourist offices.

➤ FEES & SCHEDULES: **Stockholm Sightseeing** (✉ Skeppsbron 22, ☎ 08/ 57814020).

TRAIN TRAVEL

From London, the British Rail European Travel Center can be helpful in arranging connections to Sweden's SJ (Statens Järnvägar), the state railway.

SJ has a highly efficient network of comfortable electric trains. On nearly all long-distance routes there are buffet cars and, on overnight trips, sleeping cars and couchettes in both first and second class. Seat reservations are advisable, and on some trains—indicated with *R, IN,* or *IC* on the timetable—they are compulsory. An extra fee of SKr 15 is charged to reserve a seat on a trip of less than 150 km (93 mi); on longer trips there is no extra charge. Reservations can be made right up to departure time. The high-speed

X2000 train has been introduced on several routes; the Stockholm–Göteborg run takes just under three hours. Travelers younger than 19 years travel at half fare. Up to two children younger than 12 years may travel free if accompanied by an adult.

CUTTING COSTS

SJ cooperates with a number of local traffic systems, allowing you to buy one ticket, called *Tågplusbiljett,* that works on trains, buses, and subways. Speak with the reservations people about what kind of combination you are interested in and where you'd like to travel. The Eurail and InterRail passes are both valid in Sweden. SJ also organizes reduced-cost package trips in conjunction with local tourist offices. Details are available at any railway station or from SJ.

Consider a Scanrail Pass, available for travel in Denmark, Sweden, Norway, and Finland for both first- and second-class train travel: you may have five days of unlimited travel in any two-month period ($276 first class/ $204 second class); 10 days of unlimited travel in two months ($420/ $310); or or 21 consecutive days of unlimited train travel ($486/$360). With the Scanrail Pass, you also enjoy travel bonuses, including free or discounted ferry, boat, and bus travel and a Hotel Discount Card that allows 10%–30% off rates for select hotels June–August.

Passengers ages 12–25 can **buy Scanrail Youth Passes** ($207 first class/$153 second class, five travel days in two months; $315/$233 for 10 travel days in two months; $365/$270 for 21 days of unlimited travel).

Those over age 60 can **take advantage of the Scanrail Senior Pass,** which offers the travel bonuses of the Scanrail Pass and discounted travel ($246 first class/$182 second class, five days; $374/$276 10 days; $432/$321 for 21 consecutive days). Buy Scanrail passes through Rail Europe and travel agents.

For car and train travel, price the Scanrail'n Drive Pass: in 15 days you can get five days of unlimited train travel and two days of car rental (choice of three car categories) with unlimited mileage in Denmark, Norway, and Sweden. You can purchase extra car rental days and choose from first- or second-class train travel. Individual rates for two adults traveling together (compact car $349 first class/$279 second class) are considerably lower (about 25%) than for single adults; the third or fourth person sharing the car needs to purchase only a Scanrail pass.

In Scandinavia, you can **use Eurail-Passes,** which provide unlimited first-class rail travel, in all of the participating countries, for the duration of the pass. If you plan to rack up the miles, get a standard pass. These are available for 15 days ($554), 21 days ($718), one month ($890), two months ($1,260), and three months ($1,558). Eurail- and EuroPasses are available through travel agents and Rail Europe.

If you are an adult traveling with a youth under age 26 and/or a senior, **consider buying a EurailSaver Pass**; this entitles you to second-class train travel at the discount youth or senior fare, provided that you are traveling with the youth or senior at all times. A Saver pass is available for $470 (15 days), $610 (21 days), and $756 (one month); two- and three-month fares are also available.

In addition to standard EurailPasses, **ask about special rail-pass plans.** Among these are the Eurail YouthPass (for those under age 26), a Eurail FlexiPass (which allows a certain number of travel days within a set period), the Euraildrive Pass, and the EuroPass Drive (which combines travel by train and rental car).

Whichever pass you choose, remember that you must **purchase your pass before you leave** for Europe.

Many travelers assume that rail passes guarantee them seats on the trains they wish to ride. Not so. You need to **book seats ahead even if you are using a rail pass**; seat reservations are required on some European trains, particularly high-speed trains, and are a good idea on trains that may be crowded—particularly in summer on popular routes. You will also need a reservation if you purchase sleeping accommodations.

➤ TRAIN INFORMATION: **British Rail European Travel Center** (⊠ Victoria Station, London, ☎ 020/78342345). **DER Travel Services** (☎ 800/782–2424). **Rail Europe** (☎ 800/848–7245). **Statens Järnvägar, or SJ** (⊠ Central Station, Vasag. 1, ☎ 08/7622000 or 020/757575).

➤ WHERE TO BUY RAIL PASSES: **CIT Tours Corp.** (⊠ 342 Madison Ave., Suite 207, New York, NY 10173, ☎ 212/697–2100; 800/248–8687; 800/248–7245 in western U.S., WEB www.cit-tours.com). **DER Travel Services** (⊠ Box 1606, Des Plaines, IL 60017, ☎ 800/782–2424, FAX 800/282–7474, WEB www.dertravel.com). **Rail Europe** (⊠ 226–230 Westchester Ave., White Plains, NY 10604, ☎ 800/438–7245, 914/682–5172, or 416/602–4195; ⊠ 2087 Dundas E, Suite 105, Mississauga, Ontario L4X 1M2, ☎ 800/438–7245, 914/682–5172, or 416/602–4195, WEB www.raileurope.com).

TRAVEL AGENCIES

A good travel agent puts your needs first. Look for an agency that has been in business at least five years, emphasizes customer service, and has someone on staff who specializes in your destination. In addition, **make sure the agency belongs to a professional trade organization.** The American Society of Travel Agents (ASTA)—the largest and most influential in the field with more than 26,000 members in some 170 countries—maintains and enforces a strict code of ethics and will step in to help mediate any agent-client dispute if necessary. ASTA (whose motto is "Without a travel agent, you're on your own") also maintains a Web site that includes a directory of agents. (If a travel agency is also acting as your tour operator, *see* Buyer Beware *in* Tours & Packages.)

➤ LOCAL AGENT REFERRALS: **American Society of Travel Agents** (ASTA; ⊠ 1101 King St., Suite 200, Alexandria, VA 22314, ☎ 800/965–2782 24-hr hot line, FAX 703/739–7642,

WEB www.astanet.com). **Association of British Travel Agents** (✉ 68–71 Newman St., London W1T 3AH, U.K., ☎ 020/7637–2444, FAX 020/7637–0713, WEB www.abtanet.com). **Association of Canadian Travel Agents** (✉ 130 Albert St., Suite 1705, Ottawa, Ontario K1P 5G4, Canada, ☎ 613/237–3657, FAX 613/237–7052, WEB www.acta.net). **Australian Federation of Travel Agents** (✉ Level 3, 309 Pitt St., Sydney NSW 2000, Australia, ☎ 02/9264–3299, FAX 02/9264–1085, WEB www.afta.com.au). **Travel Agents' Association of New Zealand** (✉ Level 5, Paxus House, 79 Boulcott St., Box 1888, Wellington 10033, New Zealand, ☎ 04/499–0104, FAX 04/499–0827, WEB www.taanz.org.nz).

VISITOR INFORMATION

➤ TOURIST INFORMATION: **Stockholm Information Service** at Sweden House (Sverigehuset; ✉ Hamng. 27, Box 7542, 103 93 Stockholm, ☎ 08/7892490). **Swedish Travel and Tourism Council** (✉ 73 Welbeck St., London W15 8AN, ☎ 020/79359784 in the U.K., FAX 020/79355853; ✉ 655 3rd Ave., 18th floor, New York, NY 10017, ☎ 212/885–9700, FAX 212/697–0835; ✉ Box 3030, Kungsg. 36, 103 61 Stockholm, ☎ 08/7255500, FAX 08/7255531).

➤ U.S. GOVERNMENT ADVISORIES: **U.S. Department of State** (✉ Overseas Citizens Services Office, Room 4811 N.S., 2201 C St. NW, Washington, DC 20520, ☎ 202/647–5225 for interactive hot line, WEB travel.state.gov/travel/html); enclose a self-addressed, stamped, business-size envelope.

WEB SITES

Do check out the World Wide Web when planning your trip. You'll find everything from weather forecasts to virtual tours of famous cities. Be sure to **visit Fodors.com** (www.fodors.com), a complete travel-planning site. You can research prices and book plane tickets, hotel rooms, rental cars, vacation packages, and more. In addition, you can post your pressing questions in the Travel Talk section. Other planning tools include a currency converter and weather reports, and there are loads of links to travel resources.

SWEDISH RESOURCES

Swedish Travel & Tourism Council (WEB www.visitsweden.org). **City of Stockholm** (WEB www.stockholm.se/english).

WHEN TO GO

The tourist season runs from mid-May through mid-September; however, many attractions close in late August, when the schools reopen at the end of the Swedish vacation season. The weather can be bright and fresh in the spring and fall (although spring can bring lots of rain), and many visitors prefer sightseeing when there are fewer people around.

CLIMATE

Sweden has typically unpredictable north European summer weather, but, as a general rule, it is likely to be warm but not hot from May until September. In Stockholm, the weeks just before and after Midsummer offer almost 24-hour light, whereas in the far north, above the Arctic Circle, the sun doesn't set between the end of May and the middle of July. Below are average daily maximum and minimum temperatures for Stockholm.

STOCKHOLM

Jan.	30F	-1C	May	57F	14C	Sept.	59F	15C
	23	-5		43	6		48	9
Feb.	30F	-1C	June	66F	19C	Oct.	48F	9C
	23	-5		52	11		41	5
Mar.	37F	3C	July	72F	22C	Nov.	41F	5C
	25	-4		57	14		34	1
Apr.	46F	8C	Aug.	68F	20C	Dec.	36F	2C
	34	1		55	13		28	-2

FESTIVALS & SEASONAL EVENTS

➤ JAN. 13: **Knut** signals the end of Christmas festivities and the "plundering" of the Christmas tree: trinkets are removed from the tree, edible ornaments gobbled up, and the tree itself thrown out.

➤ FEB.: A **market** held in Jokkmokk features both traditional Sámi (Lapp) artifacts and plenty of reindeer. It begins on the first Thursday and runs through Saturday. On **Shrove Tuesday** special buns called *semlor*—lightly flavored with cardamom, filled with almond paste and whipped cream— are traditionally placed in a dish of warm milk, topped with cinnamon, and eaten.

➤ MAR. (FIRST SUN.): The **Vasalopp Ski Race** goes 90 km (56 mi) from Sälen to Mora in Dalarna, and attracts entrants from all over the world.

➤ APR.: On **Maundy Thursday,** which marks the beginning of Easter celebrations, small girls dress up as witches and hand out "Easter letters" for small change or candy. *Påskris,* twigs tipped with brightly dyed feathers, decorate homes. On April 30, for the **Feast of Valborg,** bonfires are lit to celebrate the end of winter. The liveliest celebrations involve the students of the university cities of Uppsala, 60 km (37 mi) north of Stockholm, and Lund, 16 km (10 mi) north of Malmö.

➤ MAY 1: **Labor Day** marches and rallies are held nationwide, and politicians give speeches at the town square. **Tjejtrampet,** one of the world's largest bicycle races for women, takes place in May as well.

➤ JUNE: In early June, the **Restaurant Festival** fills Stockholm's Kungsträdgården with booths offering inexpensive international and Swedish cuisine. Also in June is the **Stockholm Marathon. Midsummer Eve and Day** celebrations are held on the Friday evening and Saturday that fall between June 20 and 26. Swedes raise maypoles decorated with floral garlands and sing, play games, and dance all night long. Traditional celebrations, open to the public, are held every year at Skansen in Stockholm. In mid-June comes the **Hultsfred Festival,** in southern Sweden. It's the country's largest, and wildest, rock festival, with major acts from all over the world.

➤ JUNE 6: **National Day** is celebrated, with parades, speeches, and band concerts nationwide.

➤ JULY: Since 1983 the **Stockholm Jazz Festival** has brought in the world's best jazz and blues musicians for a five-day festival of music and good cheer. It's held on Skeppsholmen, on a stage behind the Moderna Museet.

➤ AUG.: Crayfish are a delicacy in Sweden, and the second Wednesday of August marks the **Crayfish Premiere,** when friends gather to eat them at outdoor parties.

➤ NOV.: The **Stockholm Film Festival** brings world-class films, directors, and actors to the city. The **Stockholm Open** tennis tournament attracts top players for an indoor tournament at the Kungliga Tennishallen. The **Stockholm International Horse Show,** held at the Globen sports center, is a big draw.

➤ NOV. 11: **St. Martin's Day** is celebrated primarily in the southern province of Skåne. Roast goose is served, accompanied by *svartsoppa,* a bisque made of goose blood and spices.

➤ DEC.: For each of the four weeks of **Advent,** which leads up to Christmas, a candle is lit in a four-prong candelabra.

➤ DEC. 10: **Nobel Day** sees the presentation of the Nobel prizes by the king of Sweden at a glittering banquet held in Stadshuset, Stockholm's City Hall.

➤ DEC. 13: On **Santa Lucia Day** young girls are selected to be "Lucias"; they wear candles—today usually electric substitutes—in their hair and sing hymns with their handmaidens and "star boys" at ceremonies around the country.

➤ DEC. 24: **Christmas Eve** is the principal day of Christmas celebration. Traditional Christmas dishes include ham, rice porridge, and lutefisk (dried cod soaked in lye and then boiled).

➤ DEC. 31: **New Year's Eve** is the Swedes' occasion to set off an as-

tounding array of fireworks. Every household has its own supply, and otherwise quiet neighborhood streets are full of midnight merrymakers.

1 DESTINATION: SWEDEN

SWEDISH SPECTACULAR

SWEDEN REQUIRES THE visitor to travel far, in both distance and attitude. Approximately the size of California, Sweden reaches as far north as the Arctic fringes of Europe, where glacier-topped mountains and thousands of acres of pine, spruce, and birch forests are broken here and there by wild rivers, countless pristine lakes, and desolate moorland. In the more populous south, roads meander through mile after mile of softly undulating countryside, skirting lakes and passing small villages with sharp-pointed church spires. Here, the lush forests that dominate Sweden's northern landscape have largely fallen to the plow.

Once the dominant power of the region, Sweden has traditionally looked mostly inward, seeking to find its own Nordic solutions. During the cold war, it tried with considerable success to steer its famous "Middle Way" between the two superpowers, both economically and politically. Its citizens were in effect subjected to a giant social experiment aimed at creating a perfectly just society, one that adopted the best aspects of both socialism and capitalism.

In the late 1980s, as it slipped into the worst economic recession since the 1930s, Sweden made adjustments that lessened the role of its all-embracing welfare state in the lives of its citizens. Although fragile, the conservative coalition, which defeated the long-incumbent Social Democrats in the fall of 1991, attempted to make further cutbacks in welfare spending as the country faced one of the largest budget deficits in Europe. In a kind of nostalgic backlash, the populace voted the Social Democrats back into power in 1994, hoping to recapture the party's policy of cradle-to-grave protection. The world economy didn't exactly cooperate; although Sweden appeared to be crawling toward stability in the mid-1990s, the struggle to balance the budget intensified again by the end of the decade.

Despite those struggles, Sweden took off with the rest of the globe with the explosion of the Internet and new technology. It continues to be one of the world's dominant players in the new information-based economy. Although many start-up companies (and well-established giants such as Ericsson) took their share of economic bumps and bruises in 2001, as a whole there remains a lively entrepreneurial spirit and an intense interest in the business possibilities of the Internet and wireless communications. During the past few years, Sweden has received substantial international press coverage for its innovative technological solutions, new management philosophies, and unique designs for the Web.

New technology is widely used and accepted throughout Sweden. The country has the highest Internet penetration in the world, and more than 50% of the population uses cell phones. If there's an expensive new gadget out on the market, chances are you'll see a stylish Stockholmer using it.

On the social front, an influx of immigrants, particularly from countries outside Europe, is reshaping what was once a homogeneous society. Sweden continues to face political and social difficulties in the areas of immigration and integration, although the tension appears to be fading slightly as more and more artists, musicians, actors, directors, and writers with immigrant backgrounds are receiving national recognition for their work. As considerable public debate about these issues sweeps the country, a society known for its blue-eyed blondes is considering what it means to be a Swede.

Another sign that Swedes seem more willing than ever to refashion their image was Sweden's decision to join the European Union (EU) in January 1995, a move that represented a radical break with its traditional independent stance on international issues. Thus far, the domestic benefits of membership are still debated heavily, but the country's exporting industries have made considerable gains. During the first half of 2001, Sweden held the presidency of the European Union Council of Ministers, the EU's principal decision-making body. This event also marked the first time a sitting president of the United States visited the country, when George W. Bush visited Göteborg for a meeting with EU member states. Perhaps partly due to the lack of concrete results in being part of the EU, the turn of the millennium sees citizens undecided about the value of membership and politicians struggling to demonstrate its importance.

The country possesses stunning natural assets. In the forests, moose, deer, bears, and lynx roam, coexisting with the whine of power saws and the rumble of automatic logging machines. Logging remains the country's economic backbone. Environmental awareness, however, is high. Fish abound in sparkling lakes and tumbling rivers, and sea eagles and ospreys soar over myriad pine-clad islands in the archipelagoes off the east and west coasts.

The country is Europe's fourth largest, 449,963 square km (173,731 square mi) in area, and its population of 8.8 million is thinly spread. If, like Greta Garbo—one of its most famous exports—you enjoy being alone, you've come to the right place. A law called Allemansrätt guarantees public access to the countryside; NO TRESPASSING signs are seldom seen.

Sweden stretches 1,563 km (977 mi) from the barren Arctic north to the fertile plains of the south. Contrasts abound, but they are neatly tied together by a superbly efficient infrastructure, embracing air, road, and rail. You can catch salmon in the far north and, thanks to the excellent domestic air network, have it cooked by the chef of your luxury hotel in Stockholm later the same day.

The seasons contrast savagely: Sweden is usually warm and exceedingly light in summer, then cold and dark in winter, when the sea may freeze and northern iron railway lines may snap. Spring and fall tend to make brief appearances, if any.

Sweden is also an arresting mixture of ancient and modern. The countryside is dotted with runic stones recalling its Viking past: trade beginning in the 8th century went as far east as Kiev and as far south as Constantinople and the Mediterranean, expanded to the British Isles in the 9th through 11th centuries, and settled in Normandy in the 10th century. Small timbered farmhouses and maypoles—around which villagers still dance at Midsummer in their traditional costumes—evoke both the pagan early history and the more recent agrarian culture.

Many of the country's cities are sci-fi modern, their shop windows filled with the latest in consumer goods and fashions, but Swedes are reluctant urbanites: their hearts and souls are in the forests and the archipelagoes, and to there they faithfully retreat in the summer and on weekends to take their holidays, pick berries, or just listen to the silence. The skills of the woodcarver, the weaver, the leather worker, and the glassblower are highly prized. Similarly, Swedish humor is earthy and slapstick. Despite the praise lavished abroad on introspective dramatic artists such as August Strindberg and Ingmar Bergman, it is the simple trouser-dropping farce that will fill Stockholm's theaters, the scatological joke that will get the most laughs.

Although it isn't unusual to see gray-haired men in pastel sweaters playing saxophones on TV, or to warp back to the 1950s in modern concert halls and discos, Sweden's cultural tenor also incorporates a host of global trends. Most radio stations play a mix of Swedish, American, and British hits, and a number of Swedish television programs track international music, art, and culture. Films from all over the world can be seen at the box office, although it's Hollywood that dominates. And when it comes to fashion and design, Stockholm is certainly among the trendiest cities in the world. Glossy magazines like *Wallpaper** seem to be in constant discussion about "cool Stockholm" and the like.

Despite the much-publicized sexual liberation of Swedes, the joys of hearth and home are most prized in what remains in many ways a conservative society. Conformity, not liberty, is the real key to the Swedish character; however, the good of the collective is slowly being replaced by that of the individual as socialism begins to lose its past appeal.

At the same time, Swedes remain devoted royalists and patriots, avidly following the fortunes of King Carl XVI Gustaf, Queen Silvia, and their children in the media, and raising the blue-and-yellow national flag each morning on the flagpoles of their country cottages. Few nations, in fact, make as much of an effort to preserve and defend their natural heritage.

It is sometimes difficult in cities such as Stockholm, Göteborg, or Malmö to realize that you are in an urban area. Right in the center of Stockholm, you can fish for salmon or go for a swim. In Göteborg's busy harbor, you can sit aboard a ship bound for the archipelago and watch fish jump out of the water; in Malmö hares hop around in the downtown parks. It is this pristine quality of life that can make a visit to Sweden a step out of time, a relaxing break from the modern world.

–Updated by Devin Wilson

NEW AND NOTEWORTHY

Scandinavia's largest country had almost always been politically independent and commercially successful. But in the late '80s, Sweden fell into the worst economic recession to hit the country since the 1930s. It was an event that shook the very foundations of Sweden's social structure.

The economy bounced back in the mid-'90s, perhaps due in part to Sweden's entry into the EU in January 1995. The market continued to swell as the country rode the huge wave of the "new economy." But in the first year of the new millennium, Sweden, like the rest of the world, watched as the Internet bubble burst. The country is engaging in watchful waiting.

Known for its leadership as a social welfare state throughout most of the 20th century, the economic crisis of the early 1990s led to a reassessment of its goals. Sweden felt compelled to adopt policies less associated with Social Democracy than with economic rationalism. As a consequence, the safety net that Swedes once relied upon now has a few holes in it. Some experts say that the impact on society is already being felt, with growing stress in areas such as health and education.

The good news is that the slow economy is a boost for foreign tourists, as the weak krona means that Sweden has become a relatively inexpensive place to vacation. Hotel and restaurant prices are still higher than those in the United States, however.

For the first half of 2001, Sweden held the presidency of the European Union. The prime minister at the time, Social Democrat Göran Persson, claimed he would use the time to advance environmental and social causes. But in fact he maintained a conservative and low-key stance. This may be fitting for a country that shows increasing skepticism toward its participation within the EU, including some indecision about when, if ever, it will adopt the euro as its currency.

The year 2001 marked the 100th anniversary of the Nobel Prize, and to celebrate, the Nobel Foundation opened a museum in Stockholm. More than 700 people have been awarded the prize over the years, and to mark the occasion all living Nobel laureates were invited to the 2001 ceremony.

Travel between Arlanda Airport and Stockholm has been greatly improved with the introduction of the Arlanda Express, a high-speed train service that started running in August 1999. The train, which leaves every 15 minutes, travels at speeds of up to 200 kph (135 mph) and completes the trip in just 20 minutes. Tickets cost SKr 140.

Perhaps the most significant event for the South of Sweden in recent times has been the opening of a massive $3 billion bridge over and under the Øresund sea, linking Malmö to Copenhagen in Denmark. Opened to much fanfare in 2000, the bridge allows for both road and train traffic—and a much greater economic exchange between Sweden and Denmark. What it means for tourists is a faster and easier—though somewhat pricey—way to bring a car across the water.

WHAT'S WHERE

In Sweden, streamlined, ultramodern cities give way to lush forests and timbered farmhouses, and modern western European democracy coexists with strong affection for a monarchy. With 449,963 square km (173,731 square mi) for only 8.8 million residents, almost all have room to live as they choose.

Stockholm, one of Europe's most beautiful capitals, is built on 14 small islands. Bustling, skyscraper-lined boulevards are a short walk from twisting medieval streets in this modern yet pastoral city. South of the city, in the densely forested Småland province, are isolated villages whose names are bywords when it comes to fine crystal glassware: Kosta, Orrefors, Boda, and Skruf.

Skåne, the country's southernmost province, and the other southern provinces have a significantly different heritage than the rest of the country. Part of Denmark until 1658, the area still has its own distinct dialect. Known as Sweden's best area for crops, this is a lush, expansive countryside with many farms. It is a place of exceptional beauty, ranging from the coastal headlands of Mölle and the Kullaberg national park, to lovely nature reserves and the urban capital, Malmö. Historic castles abound, reminding you that there has always been an aristocracy in Sweden.

Sweden's second-largest city, Göteborg, is on the west coast. A Viking port in the 11th century, today the city is home to the Scandinavium indoor arena; Nordstan, one of Europe's largest indoor shopping malls; and Liseberg, Scandinavia's largest amusement park. A cruise on the Göta Canal provides a notable coast-to-coast journey through the Swedish countryside.

Dalarna, the central region of Sweden, is considered the most typically Swedish of all the country's 24 provinces, a place of forests, mountains, and red-painted wooden farmhouses and cottages by the shores of pristine, sun-dappled lakes. The north of Sweden, Norrland, is a place of wide-open spaces. Golden eagles soar above snowcapped crags; huge salmon fight their way up wild, tumbling rivers; rare orchids bloom in Arctic heathland; wild rhododendrons splash the land with color. The Bothnian Coast is a rugged, windswept finger of land that runs up the eastern side of Sweden between Stockholm and Norrland. Its grand 19th-century towns and cities testify to the wealth that industry brought in the recent past, and its tiny fishing villages and ancient religious communities point to the more isolated times that preceded it.

PLEASURES AND PASTIMES

Beaches
Beaches in Sweden range from wide, sandy strands to steep, rocky shores, from ocean-front to lakefront, from resorts to remote nature preserves. Beaches are wide and sandy on the western side of the country, steep and rocky on the eastern side. The area most favored for the standard sunbathing and wave-frolicking vacation is known as the Swedish Riviera, on the coast south of Göteborg.

Camping
As soon as the winter frost abates, the Swedes migrate en masse to the country, with camping and sports gear in tow. Of the 760 registered campsites nationwide, many offer fishing, boating, or canoeing, and about 200 remain open in winter for skiing and skating. Many campsites also offer accommodations in log cabins.

Dining
The nation's standard home-cooked meal is basically peasant fare—sausages, potatoes, wild game, fish, and other hearty foods to ward off the winter cold. Yet Sweden has also produced the *smörgåsbord,* a generous and artfully arranged buffet featuring both hot and cold dishes. Fish—fresh, smoked, or pickled—is a Swedish specialty; herring and salmon both come in myriad preparations.

Recently, restaurants in the larger cities have begun offering innovative dishes that combine the ingredients and simplicity of traditional Swedish cuisine with Mediterranean, Asian, and Caribbean influences, a fusion trend that dovetails with an increase in the number of foreign restaurants popping up throughout Sweden. Despite the popularity of such culinary endeavors, it's still easy to find *Husmanskost* (home-cooking) recipes, which are often served in restaurants as a *dagens rätt* (daily special) at lunch. Examples are *pyttipanna* (literally, "bits in the pan"—beef and potato hash topped with a fried egg); pea soup with pancakes, a traditional meal on Thursday; and, of course *köttbullar,* Swedish meatballs, served with lingonberry jam, creamy brown sauce, and mashed potatoes.

Look for *kräftor* (crayfish), boiled with dill, salt, and sugar, then cooled overnight; they are most popular in August. Swedes eat kräftor with hot buttered toast, caraway seeds, and schnapps or beer. Autumn heralds an exotic assortment of mushrooms and wild berries. Trout and salmon are common, as are various cuts of elk and reindeer. To the foreign palate, the best of Norrland's culinary specialties is undoubtedly *löjrom,* pinkish caviar from a species of Baltic herring, eaten with chopped onions and sour cream, and the various desserts made from the cloudberries that thrive here.

CATEGORY	COST*
$$$$	over SKr 370
$$$	SKr 250–SKr 370
$$	SKr 130–SKr 250
$	under SKr 130

*per person for a main course at dinner

Fishing

It is not unusual to see a fisherman landing a thrashing salmon from the quayside in central Stockholm. Outside the city limits, the country is laced with streams and lakes full of fish, and there's excellent deep-sea fishing off the Baltic coast.

Ice-Skating

Sweden produces some of the best hockey players in the world. Just look at Peter Forsberg and Mats Sudin, both stars of the National Hockey League. But there's another, slightly more unusual, type of ice-skating that is also big in Sweden. In *långfärdsskridsåkning* (long-distance skating), extralong skate blades are strapped onto mountaineering boots. This allows the skaters to travel great distances in long, smooth strides. It's especially popular in the Stockholm archipelago when the water between islands is frozen.

Lodging

Service in a Swedish hotel, no matter the price category, is always unfailingly courteous and efficient. Accommodations on the expensive side offer great charm and beauty, but the advantages of location held by less luxurious establishments shouldn't be overlooked. The woodland setting of a camper's *stuga* (small wooden cottage) may be just as desirable and memorable as the gilded antiques of a downtown hotel.

In summer many discounts, special passes, and summer packages are available. Some offer discounts approaching 50%. Weekend rates are also considerably cheaper. Sweden Hotel's ScanPlus Hotel pass costs SKr 90 and gives discounts of 15% to 50%, depending on the hotel. Also if you stay four nights in a row you get a fifth night free.

Vandrarhem (hostels), also scrupulously clean and well run, are more expensive than elsewhere in Europe. The Swedish Touring Club (STF; www.stfturist.se) has 315 hostels and 40 mountain cabins nationwide, most with four- to six-bed family rooms, around 100 with running hot and cold water. They are open to anyone regardless of age. Prices are about SKr 100 per night for members of STF or organizations affiliated with Hostelling International. Nonmembers are charged an additional SKr 35 per night. STF publishes an annual hostel handbook. The Swedish Hostel Association also has a Web site with information in English (www.svif.se).

CATEGORY	COST*
$$$$	over SKr 2,800
$$$	SKr 1,900–SKr 2,800
$$	SKr 1,000–SKr 1,900
$	under SKr 1,000

*All prices are for two people in a standard double room, including breakfast, service charge, and tax.

Sailing

Deep at heart, modern Swedes are still seafaring Vikings. Sweden's cultural dependence on boats runs so deep that a popular gift at Christmas is candles containing creosote, providing the comforting scent of dock and hull for when sailors can't be on their boats—which is most of the year. In summer, thousands of craft jostle among the islands of the archipelago and clog the lakes and rivers. Statistics claim there are more than 250,000 boats in the Stockholm archipelago alone. Boating opportunities are plentiful, from hourly rentals to chartered cruises in anything from kayaks to motor launches to huge luxury ferry liners.

Skiing

Sweden is a skiing nation, with plenty of major mountains for downhill skiing and snowboarding and endless trials for Nordic skiing. The best areas are in the north, with Åre offering the most challenging terrain and Sälen better for families. One of Sweden's legendary sports heroes is Ingemar

Stenmark, the champion downhill skier who dominated the sport in the 1970s. Today, Pernilla Wiberg is the queen of the slopes.

Tennis

When Björn Borg began to win Wimbledon with almost monotonous regularity, Sweden became a force in world tennis. As such, the country is filled with indoor and outdoor courts, and major competitions—notably the Stockholm Open—take place regularly. One of the most unusual is the annual Donald Duck Cup, in Båstad, for children ages 11 to 15; ever since the young Björn won a Donald Duck trophy, the tournament has attracted thousands of youngsters who hope to imitate his success.

GREAT ITINERARIES

Sweden consists of 21 counties. In the southeast is Stockholm county, which includes the capital of the same name. The industrial seaport city of Göteborg and the neighboring west coastal counties of Bohuslän and Halland (the so-called Swedish Riviera) form another region, along with Värmland and Dalsland on the Norwegian border. The southernmost part of Sweden, a lovely mix of farmland, forests, and châteaus, includes Skåne, Småland ("The Kingdom of Glass"), Blekinge, Västergötland, Östergötland, and the island of Öland. Dalarna, the country's heartland, is centered on Lake Siljan and the town of Mora; this is where Swedish folklore and traditions are most visible. To the north of Stockholm is the Bothnian Coast, a land of dramatic cliffs, fjords, and port towns that appear timeless. The northern half of Sweden, called Norrland and including the counties of Lappland and Norrbotten, is a great expanse consisting mostly of mountains and wilderness; here the hardy Sámi (also known as Lapps) herd reindeer. Many hardy visitors come to see the midnight sun.

Sampling all of Sweden's far-flung variety is best suited to a traveler with either no time constraints or an exceedingly generous purse. The few representative stops below, however, can make even a short visit worthwhile.

Numbers in the text correspond to numbers in the margin and black bullets on the maps. We list at least one hotel for each of the towns on the itinerary.

IF YOU HAVE 3 DAYS

Spend two days in the capital city, **Stockholm** ①–㊲; one of these days may be spent on a boat trip in the archipelago or on Lake Mälaren. On the third day either visit **Göteborg** �–㊳—a port town since the Viking era, marked with attractive boulevards, canals, and important museums—by a high-speed train, or fly to **Mora** ㊸, in the heart of Sweden's folklore country, Dalarna. You could also fly to **Gotland** ㊷ for a quick island adventure.

IF YOU HAVE 5 DAYS

Start with two days in **Stockholm** ①–㊲; add a third day for a side trip to **Uppsala** ㊸, Sweden's principal university town, along the banks of the Fyris River. On day four, fly to **Mora** ㊸ and rent a car for a drive around Lake Siljan. On day five, fly to **Göteborg** ㉑–㊳.

IF YOU HAVE 10 DAYS

You can tackle this itinerary using public transportation. Start with three days in **Stockholm** ①–㊲; on day four, take the high-speed train to **Göteborg** ㉑–㊳ and stay two nights; on day six, take the train to **Kalmar** ㊸, with Sweden's best preserved Renaissance castle, via **Växjö** ㊾. From Kalmar, catch the ferry to **Gotland** ㊷. On day eight, return to Stockholm. Spend day nine flying to either **Mora** ㊸ or **Kiruna** ㊸, the northernmost city in Sweden. Return to Stockholm on day ten.

When to Tour Sweden

The official tourist season—when hotel rates generally go down and museum and castle doors open—runs from mid-May through mid-September. This is Sweden's balmiest time of year; summer days are sunny and warm, nights refreshingly cool. (Summer is also mosquito season, especially in the north, but also as far south as Mora.) The colors of autumn fade out as early as September, when the rainy season begins. Winter comes in November and stays through March, and sometimes longer, but winter days can be magnificent when the snow is fresh and the sky is a brilliant Nordic blue. April brings spring, and by the middle of June the whole country goes mad for Midsummer Day.

FODOR'S CHOICE

the loftlike atrium—lends a decidedly modern appeal to this lodging. $

Dining

Wedholms Fisk, Stockholm. The traditional Swedish fare here, especially the fresh fish, is simple but outstanding. $$$–$$$$

Kungstorget, Göteborg. Dishes such as nettle soup with snails and halibut with crispy pigs' feet tempt the adventurous at this stylish eatery with a beautiful location and extensive wine list. $$$

Ulriksdals Wärdshus, Stockholm. The lunchtime smörgåsbord is renowned at this country inn. $$$

Årstiderna i Kockska Huset, Malmö. Inside a building that's been a destination for lovers of fine food since 1524, this restaurants takes traditional Swedish dishes and gives them a vivifying twist. $$–$$$

Örtagården, Stockholm. This vegetarian, no-smoking restaurant has a great buffet and an early 1900s atmosphere. $

Lodging

Berns, Stockholm. Discreet lighting; modern Italian furniture; and swank marble, granite, and wood inlays all work together to bring art-deco style to Bern, where this hotel has been open for business since the days of Strindberg. $$$–$$$$

Elite Plaza, Göteborg. The palatial 1889 exterior encloses a stylish modern hotel with luxury and quiet elegance. All the original details remain, from stucco ceilings to the English mosaic floor. $$

Pärlan, Stockholm. Entering "The Pearl," a bed-and-breakfast on a quiet street in Östermalm, is like walking into a home from the 19th century. $$

Grand Hotel, Mölle. It's not the most plush hotel in the world, but the turreted Grand has a cordial staff, and an unrivaled view of the town below. The hotel's restaurant is also excellent. $–$$

Hotel Continental, Ystad. The Continental is grand inside and out. The remarkable foyer has marble chandeliers and marble pillars and stairs. Every room is bright, modern, and unique. $–$$

Marina Plaza, Helsingborg. The use of space, style, and elegance—especially in

Castles and Churches

Domkyrkan, Lund, the South. A seat of religious power in Sweden beginning in 1103, this monumental cathedral also manages to seem gracious. The astrological clock, with moving mechanical figures, is not to be missed.

Drottningholms Slott, Stockholm. One of the most delightful European palaces is a kind of miniature Versailles full of insights into how mid-18th-century royalty lived.

Kalmar Slott, Småland. Sweden's best-preserved Renaissance castle is set on a commanding site on the Baltic shore. Sections date back 800 years.

Kungliga Slottet, Stockholm. In this magnificent granite edifice, you can tour the State Apartments; the Royal Armory; and the Treasury, where the crown jewels are kept.

Leksands Kyrka, Leksand, Dalarna. Sweden's largest village church is also one of the prettiest. The shaded churchyard opens out onto a stunning view across Lake Silja.

Tjolöholms Slott, Tjolöholm, Swedish Riviera. This eccentric castle, built at the turn of the 20th century by a Scottish manufacturer, has amazing interiors full of "state-of-the-art" touches.

Museums

Carl Larsson Gården, Sundborn. The cottage here contains an exceptional assortment of beautiful rooms and works of art.

The Marinmuseum, Karlskrona. One of the oldest museums in Sweden, the Karlskrona gained a listing as a UNESCO naval history heritage site in 1998 largely because of its world-class naval exhibits. The museum dates from 1752.

Motala Motormuseum. Packed with pristine cars and the paraphernalia of bygone days, the Motor Museum brings the past to life with music and a sense of fun.

Skansen, Stockholm. Farmhouses, windmills, barns, and churches are just some of the buildings brought from around the country for preservation at this museum.

Vasamuseet, Stockholm. The *Vasa*, a warship that sank on its maiden voyage in 1628, was raised nearly intact in 1961, and now has its own museum.

Zorn Museet, Mora. Many fine paintings by Anders Zorn (1860–1920), Sweden's leading impressionist painter, are displayed in this museum next to the beautiful house he built in his hometown.

Special Moments

Cruising on a steamship in the Stockholm archipelago

Happening on the Midsummer celebrations around Lake Silja

Picnicking at sunset on the coastal cliffs beside the mysterious Ales Stones, near Ystad, which mystify archaeologists to this day

2   STOCKHOLM

POSITIONED **WHERE THE WATERS** of Lake Mälaren rush into the Baltic, Stockholm is one of Europe's most beautiful capitals. Nearly 1.6 million people live in the greater Stockholm area, yet it remains a quiet, almost pastoral city.

Built on 14 small islands joined by bridges crossing open bays and narrow channels, Stockholm is a handsome, civilized city filled with parks, squares, and airy boulevards, yet it is also a bustling, modern metropolis. Glass-and-steel skyscrapers abound, but you are never more than a five-minute stroll from twisting medieval streets and waterside walkways.

The first written mention of Stockholm dates from 1252, when a powerful regent named Birger Jarl (d. 1266) built a fortified castle and township here. King Gustav Vasa (1496–1560) took it over in 1523, and King Gustavus Adolphus (1594–1632) made it the heart of an empire a century later.

During the Thirty Years' War (1618–48), Sweden gained importance as a Baltic trading state, and Stockholm grew commensurately. But by the beginning of the 18th century, Swedish influence had begun to wane and Stockholm's development had slowed. It did not revive until the Industrial Revolution, when the hub of the city moved north from Gamla Stan.

Nowadays most Stockholmers live in high-rise suburbs that branch out to the pine forests and lakesides around the capital. They are linked by a highly efficient infrastructure of roads, railways, and one of the safest subway systems in the world. Air pollution is minimal, and the city streets are relatively clean and safe.

EXPLORING STOCKHOLM

Although Stockholm is built on a group of islands adjoining the mainland, the waterways between them are so narrow, and the bridges so smoothly integrated, that the city really does feel more or less continuous. The island of Gamla Stan and its smaller neighbors, Riddarholmen and Helgeandsholmen, form what can be called the town center. South of Gamla Stan, Södermalm spreads over a wide area, where the many art galleries and bars attract a slightly bohemian crowd. North of Gamla Stan is Norrmalm, the financial and business heart of the city. West of Norrmalm is the island of Kungsholmen, site of Stadshuset (City Hall) and most of the city government offices. East of Norrmalm is Östermalm, an old residential neighborhood where many of the embassies and consulates are found. Finally, between Östermalm and Södermalm lies the island of Djurgården, once a royal game preserve, now the site of lovely parks and museums such as Skansen, the open-air cultural heritage park.

Modern Stockholm

The area bounded by Stadshuset, Hötorget, Stureplan, and the Kungliga Dramatiska Teatern (nicknamed Dramaten) is essentially Stockholm's downtown, where the city comes closest to feeling like a bustling metropolis. Shopping, nightlife, business, traffic, dining, festivals—all are at their most intense in this part of town.

A Good Walk

Start at the redbrick **Stadshuset** ①, a powerful symbol of Stockholm. Cross the bridge to Klara Mälarstrand and follow the waterfront to

12

Kommendörsgatan Karlaplan

↑
Millesgården

STERMALM

Narvavägen

Banérgatan

Karlavägen

N. DJURGÅRDEN

Linnégatan

Oxenstiernsgatan

Skeppargatan

Grevgatan

Styrmangatan

Storgatan

Linnégatan

33

Gärdesgatan

Skarpögatan

37 36

..argatan

Oscars
Kyrka

Strandvägen

Strandvägen

Djurgårdsbron

Djurgårdsbrunnsviken

26

27

Rosendalsvägen

32

PPSHOLMEN

22

23

25

31

Alkärret

Hazeliusbacken

DJURGÅRDEN

Sirishovsvägen

Svensksundsvagen

Djurgårdsvägen

29

Falkenb G.

28

Djurgårds
Slätten

Sollidsbacken

Singelbacken

30

Allmänna Gränd

**KASTELL-
HOLMEN**

Baltic →

Saltsjön

BECKHOLMEN

N

KEY

ℹ️ Tourist Information
— Rail Lines

0   500 yards

0   500 meters

Drottninggatan. Take a left, and continue along this popular shop-lined pedestrian street north to the hub of the city, **Sergels Torg** ②. The **Kulturhuset** ③ is in the imposing glass building on the southern side of Sergels Torg. Further north on Drottninggatan is the market-filled **Hötorget** ④. The intersection of Kungsgatan and Sveavägen, where Konserthuset (Concert Hall) stands, is one of the busiest pedestrian crossroads in town.

Head north up Sveavägen for a brief detour to see the spot where Prime Minister Olof Palme was assassinated in 1986. A plaque has been laid on the right-hand side of the street, just before the intersection with Olof Palmes Gata; his grave is in Adolf Fredrik's Kyrkogård, a few blocks farther on. Continue north along Sveavägen, until you reach the large intersection of Odengatan and Sveavägen. On your left is **Stockholms Stadsbiblioteket** ⑤. Go back down Sveavägen and turn right up Tegnérgatan to find **Strindbergsmuseet Blå Tornet** ⑥, where playwright August Strindberg lived from 1908 to 1912. Return to Hötorget by way of Drottninggatan.

Next, walk east along Kungsgatan, one of Stockholm's main shopping streets, to Stureplan. On this street is Sturegallerian, an elegant mall. Head southeast along Birger Jarlsgatan—named for the nobleman generally credited with founding Stockholm around 1252—where there are still more interesting shops and restaurants. When you reach Nybroplan, take a look at the grand **Kungliga Dramatiska Teatern** ⑦.

Heading west up Hamngatan, stop in at **Hallwylska Museet** ⑧ for a tour of the private collection of Countess von Hallwyl's treasures. Continue along Hamngatan to **Kungsträdgården** ⑨, a park since 1562. Outdoor cafés and restaurants are clustered by this leafy spot, a summer venue for public concerts and events. At the northwest corner of the park is Sverigehuset, or Sweden House, the tourist center; on the opposite side of Hamngatan is the NK department store.

TIMING

Allow about 4½ hours for the walk, plus an hour each for guided tours of Stadshuset and Hallwylska Museet (Sept.–June, Sun. only). The Strindbergsmuseet Blå Tornet is closed Monday.

Sights to See

⑧ **Hallwylska Museet** (Hallwyl Museum). This private late-19th-century palace with imposing wood-panel rooms houses a collection of furniture, paintings, and musical instruments in a bewildering mélange of styles. The Countess von Hallwyl left it to the state upon her death. ⊠ *Hamng. 4,* ☎ *08/51955599,* WEB *www.hallwylskamuseet.se.* ⊠ *SKr 65.* ☉ *Guided tours only. Tours in English July and Aug., daily at 1; Sept.–June, Sun. at 1.*

④ **Hötorget** (Hay Market). Once the city's hay market, this is now a popular gathering place with an excellent outdoor fruit and vegetable market. Also lining the square are Konserthuset (Concert Hall), the PUB department store, and a multiscreen cinema Filmstaden Sergel. ⊠ *Just west of Sveaväg.*

NEED A BREAK? Stop at **Kungshallen** (⊠ Hötorget opposite Filmstaden Sergel, ☎ 08/218005) and choose from an array of international goodies. Or, get a window table at the café inside Filmstaden Sergel.

③ **Kulturhuset** (Culture House). Since it opened in 1974, architect Peter Celsing's cultural center, which sits like a glass and stone barn on the south side of Sergels Torg, has become a symbol of Stockholm and of the growth of modernism in Sweden. Stockholmers are divided on the aesthetics of this building—most either love it or hate it. Here there is an array of exhibitions for children and adults, a library, a theater, a cybercafé, a youth center, an exhibition center, and a restaurant. Head to Café Panorama, on the top floor, to savor a jumbo salad and a great view of Sergels Torg down below. ⊠ *Sergels Torg 3,* ☎ *08/508311508,* WEB *www.kulturhuset.stockholm.se.*

❼ Kungliga Dramatiska Teatern (Royal Dramatic Theater). Locally known as Dramaten, the national theater stages works by the likes of Strindberg and other international playwrights in a grand, appealing building whose facade and gilded statuary look out over the city harbor. The theater gave its first performance in 1788, when it was located at Bollhuset on Slottsbacken, next to the Royal Palace. It later moved to Kungsträdgården, spent some time in the Opera House, and ended up at its present location in 1908. Performances are in Swedish. ⊠ *Nybroplan,* ☎ *08/6670680,* WEB *www.dramaten.se.*

❾ Kungsträdgården (King's Garden). This is one of Stockholm's smallest yet most central parks. Once the royal kitchen garden, it now hosts a large number of festivals and events each season. The park has numerous cafés and restaurants, a playground, and an ice-skating rink in winter. ⊠ *Between Hamng. and the Operan.*

❷ Sergels Torg. Named after Johan Tobias Sergel (1740–1814), one of Sweden's greatest sculptors, this busy junction in Stockholm's center is dominated by modern, functional buildings and a sunken pedestrian square with subterranean connections to the rest of the neighborhood.

★ **❶ Stadshuset** (City Hall). The architect Ragnar Östberg, one of the founders of the National Romantic movement, completed Stockholm's City Hall in 1923. Headquarters of the city council, the building is functional but ornate: its immense **Blå Hallen** (Blue Hall) is the venue for the Nobel Prize dinner, Stockholm's principal social event. A trip to the top of the 348-ft tower, most of which can be achieved by elevator, is rewarded by a breathtaking panorama of the city and Riddarfjärden. ⊠ *Hantverkarg. 1,* ☎ *08/50829000,* WEB *www.stockholm.se.* ▨ *SKr 40, tower SKr 15.* ☉ *Guided tours only. Tours in English, June–Aug., daily 10, 11, noon, 2; Sept., daily 10, noon, 2; Oct.–May, daily 10 and noon.*

NEED A
BREAK?

After climbing the Stadshuset tower, relax on the fine grass terraces that lead down to the bay and overlook Lake Mälaren. Or, have lunch in **Stadshuskällaren** (City Hall Cellar; ☎ 08/6505454), where the annual Nobel Prize banquet is held. You can also head a few blocks down Hantverkargatan to find several good small restaurants.

❺ Stockholms Stadsbiblioteket (Stockholm City Library). Libraries aren't always a top sightseeing priority, but the Stockholm City Library is among the most captivating buildings in town. Designed by the famous Swedish architect E. G. Asplund and completed in 1928, the building has a large cylinder in the middle that makes it look a bit like a large birthday cake. Inside is an excellent "information technology" center with free Internet access. And lots of books, too. ⊠ *Sveav. 73,* ☎ *08/50831100,* WEB *www.ssb.stockholm.se,* ☉ *Mon.–Thurs. 10–7, Fri. 10–6, Sat. noon–4.*

❻ Strindbergsmuseet Blå Tornet (Strindberg Museum, Blue Tower). Hidden away over a grocery store, this museum is dedicated to Sweden's most important author and dramatist, August Strindberg (1849–1912), who resided here from 1908 until his death. The interior has been expertly reconstructed with authentic furnishings and other objects, including one of his pens. The museum also houses a library, printing press, and picture archives, and it is the site of literary, musical, and theatrical events. ✉ *Drottningg. 85,* ☎ *08/4115354,* 🕮 *www.strindbergsmuseet.se.* 🎫 *SKr 40.* ☉ *Sept.–May, Tues. 11–7, Wed.–Fri. 11–4, weekends noon–4; June–Aug., Tues.–Fri. 11–4, weekends noon–4.*

Gamla Stan and Skeppsholmen

Gamla Stan (Old Town) sits between two of Stockholm's main islands and is the site of the medieval city. Just east of Gamla Stan is the island of Skeppsholmen, whose narrow, twisting cobble streets are lined with superbly preserved old buildings.

A Good Walk

Start at the waterfront edge of Kungsträdgården and walk across Strömsbron to **Kungliga Slottet** ⑩, where you can see the changing of the guard at noon every day. Walk up the sloping cobblestone drive called Slottsbacken and bear right past the Obelisk to find the main entrance to the palace. Stockholm's 15th-century Gothic cathedral, **Storkyrkan** ⑪, stands at the top of Slottsbacken, but its entrance is at the other end, on Trångsund.

Following Källargränd from the Obelisk or Trångsund from Storkyrkan, you will reach the small square, **Stortorget** ⑫, marvelously atmospheric amid magnificent old merchants' houses. Stockholm's Börshuset (Stock Exchange), which currently houses the **Nobelmuseet** ⑬, fronts the square.

Walk past Svartmangatan's many ancient buildings, including the Tyska Kyrkan, or German Church, with its resplendent oxidized copper spire and airy interior. Continue along Svartmangatan, take a right on Tyska Stallplan to Prästgatan, and just to your left is Mårten Trotzigs Gränd; this lamplit alley stairway leads downhill to Järntorget. From here take Västerlånggatan back north across Gamla Stan, checking out the pricey fashion boutiques, galleries, and souvenir shops along the way.

Cut down Storkyrkobrinken to the 17th-century Dutch baroque **Riddarhuset** ⑭. A short walk takes you over Riddarholmsbron to Riddarholmen—Island of Knights—on which stands **Riddarholmskyrkan** ⑮. Also on Riddarholmen is the white 17th-century palace that houses the **Svea Hovrätt** ⑯. Returning across Riddarholmsbron, take Myntgatan back toward Kungliga Slottet and take a left to cross Stallbron, the bridge. You'll then pass through the refurbished stone **Riksdagshuset** ⑰ on Helgeandsholmen, Holy Ghost Island. Another short bridge returns you to Drottninggatan; take a right onto Fredsgatan and walk until you reach **Medelhavsmuseet** ⑱ on the left, just before Gustav Adolfs Torg. Right there on the square is the **Dansmuseet** ⑲.

The **Operan** ⑳ occupies the waterfront between Gustav Adolfs Torg and Karl XII's Torg (part of Kungsträdgården). A little farther along on Strömgatan, a host of tour boats docks in front of the stately Grand Hotel. Pass the Grand and visit the **Nationalmuseum** ㉑. Cross the footbridge to the idyllic island of Skeppsholmen, the location of the **Östasiatiska Museet** ㉒, with a fine collection of Buddhist art. Also on Skeppsholmen is the **Moderna Museet** ㉓, which is in the same complex that houses the **Arkitekturmuseet.** To the southwest is **Svensk Form** ㉔, a design museum. The adjoining island, Kastellholmen, is a pleasant place for a stroll, especially on a summer evening, with views of the Baltic harbor and Djurgården's lighted parks.

Allow three hours for the walk, and double that if you want to tour the various parts of the palace. The Nationalmuseum and Östasiatiska Museet will take up to an hour each to view. Note that Kungliga Slottet is closed Monday off-season, and Stockholms Leksaksmuseum, Moderna Museet, Nationalmuseum, and Östasiatiska Museet are always closed Monday. The Riddarhuset is open weekdays only; off-season, hit the Riddarholmskyrkan on a Wednesday or weekend.

Sights to See

Arkitekturmuseet. The Museum of Architecture uses models, photos, and drawings to tell the long and interesting story of Swedish architecture. Certain buildings, including the Stockholm Town Hall, Vadstena Castle, and the Helsingborg Concert House, shed light on certain periods. The museum also hosts lectures, debates, and architectural tours of the city. ⊠ *Skeppsholmen,* ☎ *08/58727000,* WEB *www.arkitekturmuseet. se.* ⊠ *SKr 60.* ☉ *Tues. and Thurs. 11–8, Fri.–Sun. 11–6.*

⑲ Dansmuseet (Museum of Dance). Close to the Royal Opera House, the Museum of Dance has a permanent collection that examines dance, theater, and art from Asia, Africa, and Europe. Such artists as Fernand Léger, Francis Picabia, Giorgio de Chirico, and Jean Cocteau are represented in the exhibitions. The Rolf de Maré Study Centre has a vast collection of dance reference materials, including about 4,000 books and 3,000 videos. ⊠ *Gustav Adolfs torg 22–24,* ☎ *08/4417650,* WEB *www. dansmuseet.nu.* ⊠ *SKr 50.* ☉ *Weekdays 11–5, weekends noon–4.*

Järntorget (Iron Square). Named after its original use as an iron and copper marketplace, this square was also the venue for public executions. ⊠ *Intersection of Västerlångg and Österlångg.*

★ **⑩ Kungliga Slottet** (Royal Palace). Designed by Nicodemus Tessin, the Royal Palace was completed in 1760 and replaced the previous palace that had burned here in 1697. Just three weeks later, Tessin—who had also designed the previous incarnation, submitted his drawings for the new palace to the Swedish government. The rebuilding was finally completed, exactly according to Tessin's designs, 60 years later. The four facades of the palace each have a distinct style: the west is the king's, the east the queen's, the south belongs to the nation, and the north represents royalty in general. Watch the changing of the guard in the curved terrace entrance, and view the palace's fine furnishings and Gobelin tapestries on a tour of the **Representationsvän** (State Apartments). To survey the crown jewels, which are no longer used in this self-consciously egalitarian country, head to the **Skattkammaren** (Treasury). The **Livrustkammaren** (Royal Armory) has an outstanding collection of weaponry, coaches, and royal regalia. Entrances to the Treasury and Armory are on the Slottsbacken side of the palace. ⊠ *Gamla Stan,* ☎ *08/4026130 State Apartments; 08/4026130 Treasury; 08/6664475 Royal Armory,* WEB *www.royalcourt.se.* ⊠ *State Apartments SKr 60, Treasury SKr 60, Royal Armory SKr 60; combined ticket for all areas SKr 100.* ☉ *State Apartments and Treasury, May–Aug., daily 10–4; Sept.–Apr., Tues.–Sun. noon–3. Armory, May–Aug., daily 11–4; Sept.–May, Tues.–Sun. 11–4.*

⑬ Medelhavsmuseet (Mediterranean Museum). During the 1700s, this building housed the Royal Courts. Then, in the early 1900s, the vast interior of the building was redesigned to resemble the Palazzo Bevilaqua i Bologna, Italy. The vast collection has a good selection of art from Asia as well as from Ancient Egypt, Greece, and Rome. In the gold room, you can see fine gold, silver, and bronze jewelry from the Far East, Greece, and Rome. ⊠ *Fredsg. 2,* ☎ *08/51955380,* WEB *www.medelhavsmuseet.se.* ✉ *SKr 50.* ⊙ *Tues. 11–8, Wed.–Fri. 11–4, weekends noon–5.*

㉓ Moderna Museet (Museum of Modern Art). Reopened in its original venue on Skeppsholmen, the museum's excellent collection includes works by Picasso, Kandinsky, Dalí, Brancusi, and other international artists. You can also view examples of significant Swedish painters and sculptors and an extensive section on photography. The building itself is striking. Designed by the well-regarded Spanish architect Rafael Moneo, it has seemingly endless hallways of blond wood and walls of glass. ✉ *Skeppsholmen,* ☎ *08/51955200,* WEB *www.modernamuseet.se.* ✉ *SKr 60.* ⊙ *Tues.–Thurs. 11–10, Fri.–Sun. 11–6.*

㉑ Nationalmuseum. The museum's collection of paintings and sculptures is made up of about 12,500 works, including works by Rembrandt and other masters. The print and drawing department is also impressive, with a nearly complete collection of Edouard Manet prints. Art from Sweden and other Nordic countries is emphasized, but other parts of the world are also well represented. ✉ *Södra Blasieholmshamnen,* ☎ *08/51954300,* WEB *www.nationalmuseum.se.* ✉ *SKr 75.* ⊙ *Jan.–Aug., Tues. 11–8, Wed.–Sun. 11–5; Sept.–Dec., Tues. and Thurs. 11–8, Wed., Fri., and weekends 11–5.*

⑬ Nobelmuseet. The Swedish Academy meets at Börshuset (the Stock Exchange) every year to decide the winner of the Nobel Prize for Literature. Until 2004, the building is also the home of the Nobel Museum. Along with exhibits on creativity's many forms, the museum displays scientific models, shows films, and has a full explanation of the process of choosing prizewinners. The museum does a good job covering the controversial selections made over the years. It's a must for Nobel-prize hopefuls and others. ✉ *Börshuset, Stortorget,* ☎ *08/232506,* WEB *www.nobelprize.org/nobelmuseum.* ⊙ *Wed.–Mon. 10–6, Tues. 10–8.*

⑳ Operan (Opera House). Stockholm's baroque Opera House is almost more famous for its restaurants and bars than for its opera and ballet productions, but that doesn't mean that an evening performance should be missed. There's not a bad seat in the house. For just SKr 35, you can even get a listening-only seat (with no view). Still, its food and drink status can't be denied. It has been one of Stockholm's artistic and literary watering holes since the first Operakällaren restaurant opened on the site in 1787. ✉ *Gustav Adolfs Torg,* ☎ *08/248240,* WEB *www.operan.se.*

㉒ Östasiatiska Museet (Museum of Far Eastern Antiquities). If you have an affinity for Asian art and culture, don't miss this impressive collection of Chinese and Japanese Buddhist sculptures and artifacts. Although some exhibits are displayed with little creativity, the pieces themselves are always worthwhile. The more than 100,000 pieces that make up the holdings here include many from China's Neolithic and Bronze ages. ✉ *Skeppsholmen,* ☎ *08/6664250,* WEB *www.mfea.se.* ✉ *SKr 40.* ⊙ *Tues. noon–8, Wed.–Sun. noon–5.*

⑮ Riddarholmskyrkan (Riddarholm Church). Dating from 1270, the Grey Friars monastery is the second-oldest structure in Stockholm and has been the burial place for Swedish kings for more than 400 years. The redbrick structure, distinguished by its delicate iron fretwork spire, is rarely used for services: it's more like a museum now. The most famous figures interred within are King Gustavus Adolphus, hero of the Thirty Years' War, and the warrior King Karl XII, renowned for his daring invasion of Russia, who died in Norway in 1718. The most recent of the 17 Swedish kings to be put to rest here was Gustav V, in 1950. The various rulers' sarcophagi, usually embellished with their monograms, are visible in the small chapels dedicated to the various dynasties. ⊠ *Riddarholmen,* ☎ *08/4026130.* ⚏ *SKr 20.* ☉ *May–Aug., daily 10–4; Sept., weekends noon–3.*

⓮ **Riddarhuset.** Completed in 1674, the House of Nobles was used for parliamentary assemblies and administration during the four-estate parliamentary period that lasted until 1866. Since then, Swedish nobility have continued to meet here every three years for administrative meetings. Hanging from its walls are 2,325 escutcheons, representing all the former noble families of Sweden. Thanks to the building's excellent acoustic properties, Riddarhuset is often used for concerts. ⊠ *Riddarhustorget 10,* ☎ *08/7233990,* [WEB] *www.riddarhuset.se.* ⚏ *SKr 40.* ☉ *Weekdays 11:30 AM–12:30 PM.*

⓱ **Riksdagshuset** (Parliament Building). When in session, the Swedish Parliament meets in this 1904 building. Above the entrance, the architect placed sculptures of a peasant, a burgher, a clergyman, and a nobleman. Take a tour of the building not only to learn about Swedish government but also to see the art within. In the former First Chamber are murals by Otte Sköld illustrating different periods in the history of Stockholm, and in the current First Chamber a massive tapestry by Elisabet Hasselberg Olsson, *Memory of a Landscape,* hangs above the podium. ⊠ *Riksg. 3A,* ☎ *08/7864000,* [WEB] *www.riksdagen.se.* ⚏ *Free.* ☉ *Tours in English late June–late Aug., weekdays 12:30 and 2; late Aug.–late June, weekends 1:30. Call ahead for reservations.*

OFF THE BEATEN PATH **STOCKHOLMS LEKSAKSMUSEUM –** In Södermalm, Stockholm's Toy Museum has a collection of toys and dolls from all over the world, as well as a children's theater with clowns, magicians, storytellers, and puppet shows. The museum is near the Mariatorget subway station, two stops south of Gamla Stan. ⊠ *Mariatorget 1, Södermalm,* ☎ *08/64044492.* ⚏ *SKr 40.* ☉ *Tues.–Fri. 10–4, weekends noon–4.*

⓫ **Storkyrkan.** Swedish kings were crowned in the 15th-century Great Church as late as 1907. Today, its main attractions are a dramatic wooden statue of St. George slaying the dragon, carved by Bernt Notke of Lübeck in 1489, and the *Parhelion* (1520), the oldest-known painting of Stockholm. ⊠ *Trångsund 1,* ☎ *08/7233016.* ☉ *Sept.–Apr., daily 9–4; May–Aug., daily 9–6.*

⓬ **Stortorget** (Great Square). Here in 1520, the Danish king Christian II ordered a massacre of Swedish noblemen. The slaughter paved the way for a national revolt against foreign rule and the founding of Sweden as a sovereign state under King Gustav Vasa, who ruled from 1523 to 1560. One legend holds that if it rains heavily enough on the anniversary of the massacre, the old stones still run red. ⊠ *Near Kungliga Slottet, Gamla Stan.*

NEED A BREAK? As you stroll along the busy shopping street of Västerlånggatan, you may suddenly notice the strong smell of waffles. That would be the fresh waffle-cones being made at **Café Kåkbrinken** (⊠ Västerlång. 41, on the corner of Kåkbrinken near Stortorget), which serves the best (and biggest) ice cream cones in the Old Town.

⓰ **Svea Hovrätt** (Swedish High Court). The Swedish High Court commands a prime site on the island of Riddarholmen, on a quiet and restful quayside. Sit on the water's edge and watch the boats on Riddarfjärden (Bay of Knights) and, beyond it, Lake Mälaren. From here you can see the lake, the stately arches of Västerbron (West Bridge) in the distance, the southern heights, and above all the imposing profile of the City Hall, which appears almost to be floating on the water. At the quay you may see one of the Göta Canal ships. ✉ *Riddarholmen.* ⊙ *Not open to the public.*

㉔ Svensk Form (Swedish Form). This museum emphasizes the importance of Swedish form and design, although international works and trends are also covered. Exhibits include everything from chairs to light fixtures to cups, bowls, and silverware. Find out why Sweden is considered a world leader in industrial design. Every year the museum gives out a prestigious and highly coveted design award called Utmärkt Svenskt Form (Outstanding Swedish Design). The winning objects are then exhibited in the fall. ✉ *Holmamiralens väg 2, Skeppsholmen,* ☎ *08/6443303,* WEB *www.svenskform.se.* ⊙ *Tues. and Thurs. noon–7, Fri.–Sun. noon–5.*

Djurgården and Skansen

Djurgården is Stockholm's pleasure island: on it are the outdoor museum Skansen, the Gröna Lund amusement park, and the *Vasa,* a 17th-century warship raised from the harbor bed in 1961, as well as other delights.

A Good Walk
You can approach Djurgården from the water aboard the small ferries that leave from Slussen at the southern end of Gamla Stan. In summer, ferries also leave from Nybrokajen, or New Bridge Quay, in front of the Kungliga Dramatiska Teatern. Alternatively, starting at the theater, stroll down the Strandvägen quayside—taking in the magnificent old sailing ships and the fine views over the harbor—and cross Djurgårdsbron, or Djurgården Bridge, to the island. Your first port of call should be the **Vasamuseet** ㉕, with a dramatic display of the splendid 17th-century warships. If you have children in tow, be sure to visit **Junibacken** ㉖, just off Djurgårdsbron. Return to Djurgårdsvägen to find the entrance to the **Nordiska Museet** ㉗, worth a visit for an insight into Swedish folklore.

Continue on Djurgårdsvägen to the amusement park **Gröna Lund Tivoli** ㉘, where Stockholmers of all ages come to play. Beyond the park, cross Djurgårdsvägen to **Skansen** ㉙.

From Skansen, continue on Djurgårdsvägen to Prins Eugens Väg, and follow the signs to the beautiful late-19th-century **Waldemarsudde** ㉚. On the way back to Djurgårdsbron, take the small street called Hazeliusbacken around to the charmingly archaic **Biologiska Museet** ㉛. From the museum walk toward Djurgårdsbron and then take a right on Rosendalsvägen. Signs on this street lead to **Rosendals Trädgärder** ㉜, which has beautiful gardens and a delightful café. From here you can stroll back along the water toward the city.

TIMING
Allow half a day for this tour, unless you're planning to turn it into a full-day event with lengthy visits to Skansen, Junibacken, and Gröna Lund Tivoli. The Vasamuseet warrants two hours, and the Nordiska and Biologiska museums need an hour each. Waldemarsudde requires another half hour. Gröna Lund Tivoli is closed from mid-September to late April. The Nordiska Museet closes Monday, and the Biologiska Museet and Waldemarsudde are closed Monday off-season.

Sights to See
☙ **㉛ Biologiska Museet** (Biological Museum). The Biological Museum, in the shadow of Skansen, exhibits preserved animals in various simulated environments. ✉ *Hazeliusporten,* ☎ *08/4428215,* WEB *www.*

skansen.se. ✉ *SKr 30.* ☉ *Apr.–Sept., daily 10–4; Oct.–Mar., Tues.–Sun. 10–3.*

👏 ㉘ **Gröna Lund Tivoli.** Smaller than Copenhagen's Tivoli or Göteborg's Liseberg, this amusement park is a clean, well-organized pleasure garden with a wide range of rides, attractions, and restaurants. If you're feeling especially daring, try the Power Tower. At 80 meters (350 ft) tall, it's Europe's tallest free-fall amusement-park ride. Concerts are held here all summer long, drawing top performers from Sweden and around the world. ✉ *Allmänna Gränd 9,* ☎ *08/58750100,* WEB *www.tivoli.se.* ✉ *SKr 45, not including tickets or passes for rides.* ☉ *Late Apr.–mid-Sept., daily. Hrs vary but are generally noon–11 PM. Call ahead for specific information.*

★ 👏 ㉖ **Junibacken.** In this storybook house, you travel in small carriages through the world of children's book writer Astrid Lindgren, creator of the irrepressible character Pippi Longstocking. Lindgren's tales come alive as various scenes are revealed. It's perfect for children ages 5 and up. ✉ *Galärvarsv.,* ☎ *08/58723000,* WEB *www.junibacken.se.* ☉ *June–Aug., daily 9–6; Sept.–May, Wed.–Sun. 10–5.*

👏 ㉗ **Nordiska Museet** (Nordic Museum). In this elegant late-Victorian structure are peasant costumes from every region of the country and exhibits on the Sámi (pronounced *sah*-mee)—Lapps, the formerly seminomadic reindeer herders who inhabit the far north. Families with children should visit the delightful "village-life" play area on the ground floor. ✉ *Djurgårdsv. 6–16,* ☎ *08/5195600,* WEB *www.nordm.se.* ✉ *SKr 60.* ☉ *Tues. and Thurs. 10–8, Wed. and Fri.–Sun. 10–5.*

㉜ **Rosendals Trädgårder** (Rosendal's Garden). This gorgeous slice of greenery is a perfect place to spend a few hours on a late summer afternoon. When the weather's nice, families and couples flock to the garden café, which is in one of the greenhouses, to enjoy tasty pastries and salads made from the locally grown vegetables. Pick your own flowers from the vast flower beds (paying by weight). ✉ *Rosendalsterrassen 12,* ☎ *08/6622814.* ✉ *Free.* ☉ *May–Sept., daily 11–6; Oct.–Apr., call ahead for hrs.*

★ 👏 ㉙ **Skansen.** The world's first open-air museum, Skansen was founded in 1891 by philologist and ethnographer Artur Hazelius, who is buried here. He preserved examples of traditional Swedish architecture, including farmhouses, windmills, barns, a working glassblower's hut, and churches, brought from all parts of the country. Not only is Skansen a delightful trip out of time in the center of a modern city, but it also provides insight into the life and culture of Sweden's various regions. In addition, the park has a zoo, carnival area, aquarium, theater, and cafés. ✉ *Djurgårdsslätten 4951,* ☎ *08/4428000,* WEB *www.skansen.se.* ✉ *Park and zoo costs vary according to day of week, but are approximately SKr 30 Sept.–Apr. and SKr 60 in May–Aug., aquarium SKr 60.* ☉ *Oct.–Apr., daily 10–4; May, daily 10–8; June–Aug., daily 10–10; Sept., daily 10–5.*

NEED A BREAK?   The **Cirkus Theater** (✉ Djurgårdsslätten, ☎ 08/58798750), on Hazeliusbacken right near the entrance to Skansen, has a lovely terrace café. If you want something a bit more hearty, head to **Hasselbacken Hotel** (✉ Hazeliusbacken 20, ☎ 08/51734300) and dine on its terrace.

★ ㉕ **Vasamuseet** (Vasa Museum). The warship *Vasa* sank on its maiden voyage in 1628, was forgotten for three centuries, located in 1956, and raised from the seabed in 1961. Its hull was found to be largely intact, because the Baltic's brackish waters do not support the worms that can eat through ships' timbers. Now largely restored to her former glory (however short-lived it may have been), the man-of-war resides in a handsome museum. Daily tours are available year-round. ✉ *Galär-varvsv., Djurgården,* ☎ *08/51954800,* WEB *www.vasamuseet.se.* 🖃 *SKr 70.* ☉ *Thurs.–Tues. 10–5, Wed. 10–8.*

③⓪ **Waldemarsudde.** This estate, Djurgården's gem, was bequeathed to the Swedish people by Prince Eugen upon his death in 1947. It maintains an important collection of Nordic paintings from 1880 to 1940, in addition to the prince's own works. ✉ *Prins Eugens väg 6,* ☎ *08/ 54583700,* WEB *www.waldemarsudde.com.* 🖃 *SKr 60.* ☉ *May–Aug., Tues.–Wed. and Fri.–Sun. 11–5, Thurs. 11–8; Sept.–Apr., Tues.–Wed. and Fri. 11–4, Thurs. 11–8, weekends 11–4.*

Östermalm and Kaknästornet

Marked by waterfront rows of Renaissance buildings with palatial rooftops and ornamentation, Östermalm is a quiet, residential section of central Stockholm, its elegant streets lined with museums and fine shopping. On Strandvägen, or Beach Way, the boulevard that follows the harbor's edge from the busy downtown area to the staid diplomatic quarter, you can choose one of three routes. The waterside walk, with its splendid views of the city harbor, bustles with tour boats and sailboats. Parallel to the walk (away from the water) is a tree-shaded walking and bike path. Walk, rollerblade, or ride a bike down the middle and you just might meet the occasional horseback rider, properly attired in helmet, jacket, and high polished boots. Take the route farthest from the water, and you will walk past upscale shops and expensive restaurants.

A Good Walk

Walk east from the Kungliga Dramatiska Teatern in Nybroplan along Strandvägen until you get to Djurgårdsbron, an ornate little bridge that leads to the island of Djurgården. Resist going to the park, and instead turn left up Narvavägen and walk along the right-hand side until you reach Oscars Kyrka. Cross the street and continue up the left side until you reach the **Historiska Museet** ㉝. From here it's only a short walk farther up Narvavägen to Karlaplan, a pleasant, circular park with a fountain. Go across or around the park to find Karlavägen. Heading northwest along this long boulevard, you'll pass by many small shops and galleries. At Nybrogatan, turn left (this intersection is beyond the limits of our map). Be sure to take some time to check out the exclusive furniture stores on your way down to **Östermalmstorg** ㉞, where there's an excellent indoor food market. Cut across the square and take a right down Sibyllegatan to the **Musik Museet** ㉟, installed in the city's oldest industrial building. Within the same block is the **Armémuseum.** Then go back to Nybroplan, where you can catch Bus 69 going east to **Kaknästornet** ㊱ for a spectacular view of Stockholm from the tallest tower in Scandinavia. From here, walk back toward town along Djurgårdsbrunnsvägen until you reach **Tekniska Museet** ㊲.

TIMING

This tour requires a little more than a half day. You'll want to spend about an hour in each of the museums. The bus ride from Nybroplan to Kaknästornet takes about 15 minutes, and the tower merits another half hour. The Historiska and Musik museums are closed Monday, and the Millesgården is closed Monday off-season.

Sights to See

Armémuseum. Reopened in 2000 after a total renovation, the large Military Museum covers everything from Sweden's early might as a kingdom to its unique military position during the 20th century. The castle guards and military band marches from this square every day on its walk to the Royal Palace on Gamla Stan. ⊠ *Riddarg. 13*, ☎ *08/7889560*, WEB *www.armemuseum.org.* ⌨ *SKr 60.* ☉ *Tues. 11–8, Wed.–Sun. 11–4.*

NEED A BREAK?
For the best baguettes and croissants outside Paris, stop by **Riddarbageriet** (⊠ Riddarg. 15), near the Armémuseum. Bread in Stockholm doesn't get any better than this: they deliver to the king and queen and many of the city's best restaurants. You can also get great coffee, sandwiches, and pastries. The bakery is closed in July.

③③ **Historiska Museet** (Museum of National Antiquities). Viking treasures and the Gold Room are the main draw, but well-presented temporary exhibitions also cover various periods of Swedish history. The gift shop here is excellent. ⊠ *Narvav. 13–17*, ☎ *08/5195500*, WEB *www.historiska.se.* ⌨ *SKr 60.* ☉ *Tues.–Wed. and Fri.–Sun. 11–5, Thurs. 11–8.*

③⑥ **Kaknästornet** (Kaknäs TV Tower). The 511-ft-high Kaknäs radio and television tower, completed in 1967, is the tallest building in Scandinavia. Surrounded by an impressive array of satellite dishes, it is also used as a linkup station for a number of Swedish satellite TV channels and radio stations. Eat a meal in a restaurant 426 ft above the ground and enjoy panoramic views of the city and the archipelago. ⊠ *Mörkakroken, off Djurgårdsbrunsv.*, ☎ *08/7892435.* ⌨ *SKr 35.* ☉ *June–Aug., daily 9 AM–10 PM; Sept.–May, daily 10–9.*

OFF THE BEATEN PATH
MILLESGÅRDEN – This gallery and sculpture garden north of the city is dedicated to the property's former owner, American-Swedish sculptor Carl Milles (1875–1955). On display throughout the property are Milles's own unique works, and inside the main building, once his house, is his private collection. On the terrace is the exquisite Anne's House, designed by famous Austrian designer Josef Frank, where Milles spent the final years of his life. The setting is exquisite: sculptures top columns on terraces in a magical garden high above the harbor and the city. Millesgården can be easily reached via subway to Ropsten, where you catch the Lidingö train and get off at Herserud, the second stop. The trip takes about 30 minutes. ⊠ *Carl Milles väg 2, Lidingö*, ☎ *08/4467580*, WEB *www.millesgarden.se.* ⌨ *SKr 70.* ☉ *May–Sept., daily 10–5; Oct.–Apr., Tues.–Fri. noon–4, weekends 11–5.*

☙ ③⑤ **Musik Museet.** Inside what was the military's bread bakery from the 17th century to the mid-1900s, the Music Museum has more than 6,000 instruments in its collection, with the focus on items from 1600 to 1850. Its 18th-century woodwind collection is internationally renowned. The museum also holds jazz, folk, and world music concerts. Children are invited to touch and play some of the instruments, and a motion-sensitive "Sound Room" lets you produce musical effects simply by gesturing and moving around. ⊠ *Sibylleg. 2*, ☎ *08/51955490*, WEB *www.musikmuseet.se.* ⌨ *SKr 40.* ☉ *Tues.–Sun. 11–4.*

③④ **Östermalmstorg.** The market square and its neighboring streets represent old, established Stockholm. **Saluhall** is more a collection of boutiques than an indoor food market; the fish displays can be especially intriguing. At the other end of the square, **Hedvig Eleonora Kyrka,** a church with characteristically Swedish faux-marble painting throughout its wooden interior, is the site of frequent lunchtime concerts in spring and summer. ⊠ *Nybrog. at Humlegårdsg.*

NEED A BREAK?   The little restaurants inside the **Saluhall** (✉ Östermalmstorg) offer everything from take-out coffee to sit-down meals.

Tekniska Museet. Only a 10-minute bus ride from the city, the Museum of Science and Technology has a huge Machinery Hall displaying cars, bicycles, and even airplanes. There are also exhibits on technology in the home and the history of the printed word in Sweden (the first book dates from 1483). Teknorama, the museum's science center, encourages children and young adults to learn more about the natural sciences and technology. There's also a café and gift shop. ✉ *Museiv. 7, Djurgårdsbrunnsv.,* ☎ *08/4505600,* WEB *www.tekmu.se.* 🎫 *SKr 60; free Wed. night.* ☽ *Mon.–Tues. and Thurs.–Fri. 10–5, Wed. 10–9, weekends 11–5.*

Outside the City

There are a number of excellent sites only a short bus or subway ride from the city center, many of which can be combined. Trips to nearly all these places could be done in a morning or afternoon, and even added on to the other walks.

Sights to See

Bergianska Trädgarden. The beautiful Bergianska Botanical Gardens, on a peninsula extending out into the small bay of Brunnsvik, can provide a wonderful break from the city. They are only a short subway ride away. Paths weave along the water in the open park area. Visit Edvard Anderson's modern Växthus (Greenhouse) for its impressive Mediterranean and tropical environments. The century-old Victoriahuset (Victoria House) contains tropical plants as well and has one of the best collections of water plants in the world. ✉ *Frescativ., near the university,* ☎ *08/156545,* WEB *www.bergianska.se.* 🎫 *Park is free, Greenhouse SKr 40, Victoria House SKr 10.* ☽ *Park open daily year-round; Victoria House May–Sept., daily 11–4, weekends 11–5; Greenhouse open daily 11–5.*

Fjärilshuset (Butterfly and Bird House). After a short bus ride and a nice walk through the magnificent Haga Park, you could be in a room filled with hundreds of tropical butterflies. In the bird room, 100 birds of 40 different species fly freely. The Haga Park itself is impressive and worth a lengthy stroll, but be sure to combine it with a trip to this feather-filled oasis. ✉ *Take Bus 515 from the Odenplan subway stop,* ☎ *08/7303981,* WEB *www.fjarilshuset.se.* 🎫 *SKr 60.* ☽ *Apr.–Sept., Tues.–Fri. 10–4, weekends 11–5:30; Oct.–Mar., Tues.–Fri. 10–3, weekends 11–4.*

Naturhistoriska Riksmuseet and Cosmonova (Museum of Natural History). Founded in 1739 by the famous Swedish botanist Linnaeus and his colleagues at the Science Academy, the museum has been in its present location near the university since 1916. The last decade has brought much rebuilding and other improvements. Exhibits include "Life in Water," "Marvels of the Human Body," and "Space Adventure." Cosmonova shows science and nature films in Sweden's only IMAX theater. The subway ride to the Universitet stop takes less than 10 minutes from city center. ✉ *Frescativ. 40,* ☎ *08/51954040,* WEB *www.nrm.se.* 🎫 *SKr 60.* ☽ *Fri.–Wed. 10–7, Thurs. 10–8; Cosmonova mid-May–Sept., Tues.–Sun. (and Mon. June–July) 10–7.*

Tyresö Slottet (Tyresö Castle). After a quick 20-minute bus ride from southern Stockholm, you'll find yourself in the gorgeous Romantic gardens that surround this castle, built in the 1660s. The Nordic Museum led the renovations that restored the grounds to their late-1800s glory. The main building is filled with elaborate salons, libraries, and studies, and the west wing has a nice café and restaurant. Be sure to leave time for both the castle and gardens. ✉ *Take Bus 805 from Gullmarsplan to Tyresö Slott,* ☎ 08/700178, WEB *www.nordm.se/slott.* 🎫 *SKr 50.* ◷ *Sept.–Oct., 11–3; June 22–Aug. 19, Tues.–Sun. 11–4. Tours at noon, 1, and 2.*

Ulriksdals Slottet (Ulriksdals Castle). Construction on the castle began in 1640, but it was during the first half of the 1700s that the castle took on the look that it has today. Built in the Renaissance style, the castle is most associated with King Gustav Adolf and Queen Louise, who in 1923 added a famous living room designed by Carl Malmsten. The Dutch Renaissance chapel from the mid-1800s is still used for mass, weddings, and concerts. ✉ *Take Bus 503 from the Bergshamra subway stop, on the Red Line,* ☎ 08/4026130, WEB *www.royalcourt.se/ulriksdal.* 🎫 *SKr 50.* ◷ *Mid-May–Aug., Tues.–Sun. noon–4; Sept., weekends noon–4.*

DINING

The Stockholm restaurant scene has evolved of late, with new upscale restaurants offering creative menus at trendy, modern locations. The best bring foreign innovations to bear on Sweden's high-quality raw ingredients. The city's top restaurants will charge accordingly, but you aren't likely to leave disappointed. Of course, there are also plenty of less expensive restaurants with traditional Swedish cooking. Among Swedish dishes, the best bets are wild game and fish, particularly salmon, and the smörgåsbord buffet, which usually offers variety at a good price. Reservations are often necessary on weekends.

Downtown Stockholm and Beyond

$$$–$$$$ ✕ **Edsbacka Krog.** In 1626, Edsbacka, just outside town, became
★ Stockholm's first licensed inn. Its exposed rough-hewn beams, plaster walls, and open fireplaces still give it the feel of a country inn for the gentry. Chef Christer Lindström interprets Swedish cuisine creatively. Ease into the meal with seared scallops served with a strawberry gravy and a celery and truffle purée, followed by fillet of baby lamb with glazed vegetables and roasted garlic sauce. ✉ *Sollentunav. 220, Sollentuna,* ☎ 08/963300. AE, DC, MC, V. Closed Sun. and Mon.

$$$–$$$$ ✕ **Wedholms Fisk.** Noted for its fresh seafood dishes, Wedholms Fisk
★ is appropriately set by a bay in Stockholm center. High ceilings, large windows, and tasteful modern paintings from the owner's personal collection create a spacious, sophisticated atmosphere. The traditional Swedish cuisine, which consists almost exclusively of seafood, is simple but outstanding. Try the poached sole in lobster-and-champagne sauce or the Pilgrim mussels Provençal. ✉ *Nybrokajen 17,* ☎ 08/6117874. AE, DC, MC, V. Closed Sun. and July.

$$–$$$$ ✕ **Operakällaren.** Open since 1787, the haughty grande dame of Stockholm is more a Swedish institution than a seat of gastronomic distinction. Thick Oriental carpeting, shiny polished brass, handsome carved-wood chairs and tables, and a decidedly stuffy atmosphere fill the room. The crystal chandeliers are said to be Sweden's finest, and the high windows on the south side face magnificent views of the Royal Palace. The restaurant is famed for its seasonal smörgåsbord, offered from early June through Christmas. Coveted selections include pickled herring, *rollmops* (rolled herring), reindeer and elk in season, and ice cream with cloudberry sauce. In summer, the veranda opens as the Operabryggan Café, facing Kungsträdgården and the waterfront. Around the corner in the same building is the restaurant's *backficka,* a pleasantly active bar/restaurant with a less expensive menu. ✉ *Op-*

A SWEDISH TOAST

From afar, people seem to have a picture of Sweden, conjured in their own, often near-sighted, mind's eye: Nordic woodlands, women with crystalline features, Greta Garbo, bedroom liberty, and a public life lived within rigid, formal constraints. Let's look at formality, for there is some truth in this image.

Please take a seat as an invited guest at the dining table. It is laid with a crisp white cloth, perfect silver, a candelabra, serviettes, and crystal glasses. The wine is chilled and nothing is out of place. Your hostess, a woman of course, is the shimmering image of household perfection.

Nowhere more than at the dining table will you encounter the unspoken truths of Swedish formality, especially in the toast. In Australia or New Zealand it is scarcely de rigueur, and may be accompanied by a drawling, "G'day, mate." In Britain it is all stiff upper lip and chivalry. In the United States the rules are as diverse as the cultures that populate it. But in Sweden, the toast almost defies description. Do not touch your glass yet, even though it is full and you are nervous. Never do this. You must wait until one of the hosts, usually the man, lifts his glass to all. Do not drink. Everyone must reply to the proffered "Skol" (or cheers) with a collective "Skol." Then you will all tilt your glasses to the host and hostess. Delayed eye contact is imperative, before, during and after the measured sip of appreciation. Don't empty the glass. The meal has commenced.

From here on in, the toast will play a vital role but on a personal level. Individuals will toast each other. You are free to toast anyone but the hostess. She can toast anyone she pleases. This is a safeguard against hostess inebriation. The temptation, of course, is for everyone to intermittently toast her in thanks. But this could leave her floundering on the floor, a run in her stockings, and a hand on her husband's best friend's knee. This is not seemly behavior in Swedish society.

The roots of this alcohol-related tradition may lie with the Vikings. They always lived in peril and no one could be trusted. The rule was to toast your "friend" with full eye contact and an arm behind the back to prevent a quick slitting of the throat. Later, state control would become big in Sweden; alcohol was once banned to stop the poor from brewing their potatoes into freedom-inducing alcohol; later it was limited to stave off social and health problems. Even today, you can buy wine and spirits only in government-controlled liquor stores, called Systembolagett. Caution is part of Swedish nature, and alcohol rituals show it.

Back at the dinner table, most of the rules will not be unfamiliar to you, simply practiced in a more accentuated form. I will leave you with your hosts now. You can find your way from here. As a foreigner you will be granted some grace, but whatever you do, do not take the bottle as you leave. From that point, there is certainly no way back.

erahuset, Jakobs Torg 2, ☎ *08/6765800. Reservations essential. Jacket and tie. AE, DC, MC, V. Main dining room closed in July.*

$$–$$$$ ✕ **Restaurangen.** Restaurangen has gained its fine reputation in large
★ part due to its flavor-based menu. Diners build three-, five-, or seven-course meals from 20 different flavors, 15 of which are salty, five of which are sweet. Thus, chili, coriander, and vanilla would result in a chicken spring roll with mint dipping sauce, seafood and tofu with lemongrass juice, and vanilla ice cream with a waffle and fresh strawberries. Each flavor has a letter next to it that corresponds to the wine-list offerings that are recommended to best complement the flavor. The restaurant's interior—a refined but casual atmosphere of blond woods, beige and brown fabrics, and red- and cream-color walls—was created by three students from Stockholm's prestigious Beckman's School of Design. ⊠ *Oxtorgsg. 14,* ☎ *08/220952. AE, DC, MC, V. Closed Sun.*

$$$ ✕ **Bon Lloc.** With an elegant and spacious dining area and a creative, Mediterranean-influenced menu, Bon Lloc has established itself as one of the hottest restaurants in town. The menu uses common ingredients like ham and cod to create dishes that recall Catalonia as much as Sweden. The extensive wine list offers an excellent selection of European wines. The interior's light-brown wood and mosaic tiles allude to Mediterranean styles while still evoking Swedish simplicity, much as the food does. ⊠ *Regeringsg. 111,* ☎ *08/6606060. Reservations essential. AE, DC, MC, V. Closed Sun.*

$$$ ✕ **Fredsgatan 12.** The government crowd files into this funky restaurant at lunch; a more casual, yet stylish, crowd is there at night. In one corner is a group of rainbow-color lounge chairs that contrast nicely with the dark hardwood floors and beautiful table settings. The menu offers creative combinations, such as rabbit *taquitos* (filled tortillas rolled up and deep-fried) or asparagus Caesar salad, with scallops and tiger prawns. When ordering a cocktail, choose a flavor such as mint and sugar or lemon-cherry, and then an alcohol of your choice to mix it with. From the bar, you can get a nice view into the kitchen of this popular restaurant—always a good sign of a place that values its food. ⊠ *Fredsg. 12,* ☎ *08/248052. AE, DC, MC, V. Closed Sun.*

$$$ ✕ **Ulriksdals Wärdshus.** The lunchtime smörgåsbord at this country
★ inn can't be beat. Built in the park of an 18th-century palace in 1868, the traditionally decorated inn overlooks orchards and a peaceful lake in a spectacular countryside setting. This restaurant is among the more exclusive and expensive in Stockholm, but the impeccable service and outstanding cuisine make a splurge here worthwhile. The chilled potato and truffle soup with lobster has an intense, rich flavor. Sea bass served with a ragout of chickpeas, squid, and chorizo stands out, as does the quail with figs, sweet potatoes, and foie gras. ⊠ *Ulriksdals Slottspark, Solna,* ☎ *08/850815. Reservations essential. Jacket required. AE, DC, MC, V. No dinner Sun.*

$$–$$$ ✕ **Stallmästaregården.** A historic old inn with an attractive courtyard and garden, Stallmästaregården is in Haga Park, just north of Norrtull, about 15 minutes by car or bus from the city center. Fine summer meals are served in the courtyard overlooking the waters of Brunnsviken. Specialties include grilled halibut with a ragout of asparagus, potatoes, spring onions, and cherry tomatoes. ⊠ *Norrtull, near Haga; take Bus 52 to Stallmästaregården,* ☎ *08/6101300. AE, DC, MC, V. Closed Sun.*

$–$$$ ✕ **Riche.** This Stockholm establishment was for many years an exclusive club. Today, the elegance and style remain but the diners are from a much broader pool. Eat in the casual glassed-in veranda on wicker chairs, or move inside to the main dining room for more formal dining. For the ultimate in posh tradition, book a table at the Teatergrillen in the back: Madonna's been here a few times and the royal family usually stops by several times a month. All three sections serve Swedish and French cuisine. Upstairs is a chill-out space where DJs play late-night and you can buy simple smørrebrød (open-face sandwiches) until 2 AM. ✉ *Birger Jarlsg. 4,* ☎ *08/6796840. AE, DC, MC, V. Closed Sun.*

$–$$$
★ ✕ **Storstad.** Opened in the summer of 1999, Storstad, or "Big City," quickly established itself among the best of Sweden's restaurants. A lighter and less expensive menu is served in the bar area, which looks out on the street through wide arching windows. In the sparse but inviting dining room in the back you might try the sweet-corn soup with truffle pasta and Parmesan cheese before moving on to meat specialties such as fried duck breast with honey-baked beets, mushroom spring rolls, and port syrup. The wine list is excellent and specializes in French and Californian wines. ✉ *Odeng. 41,* ☎ *08/6733800. Reservations essential. AE, DC, MC, V. No lunch, closed Sun.*

$–$$$ ✕ **Tranan.** There's something about Tranan that makes you want to go back. The food is Swedish with a touch of French, and is consistently some of the best in Stockholm. The stark walls covered with old movie posters and the red-and-white checkered tablecloths are looks to the days when it was a workingman's beer parlor. Try the Biff Rydberg—fillet of beef, fried potatoes, horseradish, and egg yolk: it's a Swedish classic. The bar downstairs has DJs and live music. ✉ *Karlbergsv. 14,* ☎ *08/300765. AE, DC, MC, V. No lunch weekends.*

$$ ✕ **Chiaro.** This elegant, modern restaurant is a short walk from Stureplan. The upstairs dining room, with a large circular central bar, is typically filled with a blend of businesspeople in suits and young hipsters. Downstairs is a bar, where DJs mix the latest releases and up-and-coming artists show their newest works. The menu offers a combination of Swedish, French, Italian, and Asian dishes, from baked salmon to spring rolls. ✉ *Birger Jarlsg. 24,* ☎ *08/6780009. AE, DC, MC, V. Closed Sun.*

$$ ✕ **East.** Just off of Stureplan, East is one of the city's culinary hot spots, offering enticing contemporary pan-Asian fare from Thailand, Japan, Korea, and Vietnam. Order a selection of appetizers to get a sampling of this cross-cultural cooking. East is a perfect spot to have dinner before a night on the town. Try the Luxor: chicken, tiger shrimp, and egg noodles with peanuts, mint leaves, and coconut sauce. The bar area at this vibrant restaurant turns into a miniclub at night, with soul and hip-hop on the turntables. ✉ *Stureplan 13,* ☎ *08/6114959. AE, DC, MC, V.*

$$ ✕ **Halv trappa plus gård.** This hip restaurant is exactly what its name suggests: two half floors, plus a pleasant courtyard. Owned by the same two guys who run Halv Grek Plus Turk (Half Greek plus a Turk), the retro vibe harkens back to the '70s. The menu emphasizes fish, most of it done with a Mediterranean flair. The staff is good-hearted and professional. When possible, the courtyard provides the best bet, but book a table, since there are only 10 out there. ✉ *Lästmakarg. 3,* ☎ *08/6110277. AE, DC, MC, V.* ☉ *Closed Sun., no lunch.*

$$ ✕ **Prinsen.** Situated in the same place at which it opened in 1897, The Prince serves both traditional and modern Swedish cuisine. The interior is rich with mellow, warm lighting; dark wood paneling; and leather chairs and booths. On the walls are black-and-white oil paintings of famous people done by one of the long-serving staff members, as well as paintings done by local artists who used them to settle their tab. The restaurant is known for its scampi salad and wild game dishes. Downstairs is a bar and a space for larger parties. ✉ *Mäster Samuelsg. 4,* ☎ *08/6111331. AE, DC, MC, V. No lunch weekends.*

$$ ✕ **Rolfs Kök.** Small and modern, Rolfs combines an informal atmosphere with excellent Swedish-French cuisine that's served to a nice mix of businesspeople and theater and arts folks. The chairs and the salt and pepper shakers for each table hang on hooks on the wall above each table. Go for the lingonberry-glazed reindeer fillet with cauliflower; root vegetables and smoked chili pepper; or a feta cheese salad with lime, soy, and chili-fried chicken. ⊠ *Tegnérg. 41,* ☏ *08/101696. AE, DC, MC, V. No lunch weekends.*

$$ ✕ **Stockholms Matvarufabriken.** Although it's a bit hard to find, tucked away as it is on a side street and down a small set of stairs, Stockholm's Food Factory is well worth seeking out. The popular bistro restaurant, serving French, Italian, and Swedish cuisine, is packed full on the weekends as young and old come to enjoy the exposed-brick, candlelit dining room and varied menu: here omelets are taken to new levels with ingredients such as truffles and asparagus. For dessert, try the hot banana and kiwi with melted white chocolate and vanilla ice cream. ⊠ *Idung. 12,* ☏ *08/320407. AE, DC, MC, V.*

$$ ✕ **Sturehof.** This complex of a restaurant and two huge bars is a complete social, architectural, and dining experience. Remodeled with wood paneling, leather chairs and sofas, and distinctive lighting fixtures, Sturehof offers a variety of eating and drinking options. There's a bar directly facing Stureplan where you can sit on a summer night and watch Stockholmers gather at the nearby Svampen, a mushroomlike concrete structure that holds pay phones. At the elegant dining room, fine Swedish cuisine is offered. Upstairs is the O-Bar, a dark and smoky lounge filled well into the night with young people and loud music. ⊠ *Stureplan 2,* ☏ *08/4405730. AE, DC, MC, V.*

$$ ✕ **Undici.** First Tomas Brolin was a hero to the Swedish people on the soccer field, now he's a hero on the Stockholm restaurant scene. Undici is one of the city's most popular places to eat and chill. A small seating area in the front is good for finalizing that business deal, while curved leather booths along the wall are better for festive groups of six or seven. The dining room in back is decked out in fine dark woods and white linens and serves a combination of northern Swedish and northern Italian cuisine. Dishes have included such standouts as lamb fillet with canneloni and *rimmat lammlägg* (salt-cured lamb), with goat cheese, spinach, and merguez sausage. Keep an eye out for Mr. Brolin. He likes to hang out with guests and would be happy to autograph your napkin. ⊠ *Stureg. 22,* ☏ *08/6616617. AE, DC, MC, V. No lunch Sat., closed Sun.*

$$ ✕ **Wasahof.** Across the street from Vasaparken, and just a short walk from Odenplan, Wasahof feels like an authentic bistro, but the cooking actually mixes Swedish, French, and Italian recipes. The pleasantly rustic atmosphere and good food has attracted all kinds of culturati— actors, writers, journalists—for some time. Seafood is a specialty here—this is the place for oysters in Stockholm. ⊠ *Dalag. 46,* ☏ *08/ 323440. AE, DC, MC, V. Closed Sun.*

$–$$ ✕ **Dramatenrestaurangen Frippe.** Connected to Lillascenen, the smaller stage that's behind the Royal National Theater, this is the perfect place to grab a bite before a performance. One wall is covered in black-and-white photos of the theater's most famous actors, and posters of major productions line the bar, behind which is the open kitchen. The interior is basic but pleasant and bar stools along the window allow for great people-watching. The food is a sort of gourmet take on *husmanskost,* traditional Swedish cooking. Try the classic Isterband sausage with creamy parsley potatoes. ⊠ *Nybrog./Almlöfsg.,* ☏ *08/6656142. AE, DC, MC, V. No lunch weekends.*

$–$$ ✕ **Kjellsons.** Kjellsons is a bar first and a restaurant second, but this doesn't mean the menu is short on high-caliber dishes (to say nothing of fine drinks). Appetizers include an excellent pea soup (a Swedish tradition) and a delicious avocado and smoked ham salad—most of the fare is traditional Swedish. And be sure and ask for a basket of cracker bread—it comes with a tube of the famous caviar. In summer there's outdoor seating. ⊠ *Birger Jarlsg. 36,* ☎ *08/6110045. AE, DC, MC, V.*

$–$$ ✕ **no 18.** Despite being a high-profile bar and restaurant, no 18 is still able to maintain a certain laid-back atmosphere. Walk in and to your left are tables and low leather chairs across from a bar that curves to a set of stairs. Go up to reach the colorful dining room, which extends farther into a lush courtyard open in summer. In the basement is a large bar and open area for dancing. A less expensive menu has club sandwiches, burgers, and Caesar salad, but if you want to go all the way try the good ol' entrecôte with béarnaise sauce and fries, or a chicken fillet with olive and basil risotto. ⊠ *Linnég. 18,* ☎ *08/6621018. AE, DC, MC, V. Closed Sun.*

$–$$ ✕ **Roppongi.** Although far from downtown, and not exactly in the most happening area, Roppongi's adventurous, creative menu and quality fish make it the best sushi place in Stockholm. This means it's almost always packed, so be ready to share the stripped-down space with other sushi-lovers. The shrimp tempura maki rolls will leave you drooling for more and the tamaki cones are plump and flavor-packed. Try the California temaki cone for a twist on the popular roll of the same name. ⊠ *Hantverkarg. 76,* ☎ *08/6501772. AE, DC, MC, V. No lunch weekends.*

$ ✕ **Il Forno.** You might not expect to find it in Sweden, but Il Forno serves some of the best brick-oven pizza north of the Mediterranean. Choose from more than 25 combinations, all of which use only the freshest ingredients and a tasty, crunchy crust. The kitchen also churns out a number of pasta dishes and sells many varieties of Italian olives, olive oil, and gourmet goods. As much Italian as Swedish is spoken here. Sit outside when possible—the interior can feel a bit stuffy. ⊠ *Atlasg. 9,* ☎ *08/319049. AE, DC, MC, V.*

Gamla Stan and Skeppsholmen

$$$–$$$$ ✕ **Franska Matsalen.** This classic French restaurant in the Grand Hotel
★   serves the best true French cuisine in the city—plus, you can enjoy an inspiring view of Gamla Stan and the Royal Palace across the inner harbor waters. The menu changes five times a year, but the emphasis is always on Swedish ingredients. They're used to create such dishes as medallions of deer with shiitake mushrooms in wild-berry cream sauce. The lofty measure of opulence here is commensurate with the bill. ⊠ *Grand Hotel, Södra Blasieholmsh. 8,* ☎ *08/6793584. Reservations essential. Jacket required. AE, DC, MC, V. Closed weekends.*

$$$–$$$$ ✕ **Pontus in the Green House.** After working for some time under the
★   guidance of the famous chef Erik Lallerstedt—who owned this exquisite restaurant when it was called Eriks—Pontus has taken over operations. You can still count on traditional Swedish fare of the haute school, with a concentration on meat and fish dishes. Everything is well prepared, delicious, and expensive. For a calmer dining experience, choose a corner table upstairs; the ground floor always bustles. You'll be dining among Sweden's rich and famous. For a cheaper menu of traditional Swedish dishes, and slightly less fanfare, sit at the bar downstairs. ⊠ *Österlångg. 17,* ☎ *08/238500. AE, DC, MC, V. ۞ Closed Sun. No lunch on Sat.*

$$–$$$$ ✕ **Den Gyldene Freden.** Sweden's most famous old tavern has been open for business since 1722. Every Thursday, the Swedish Academy meets here in a private room on the second floor. The haunt of bards and barristers, artists and ad people, Freden could probably serve sawdust and still be popular, but the food and staff are worthy of the restaurant's hallowed reputation. The cuisine has a Swedish orientation, bu

Continental influences are spicing up the menu. Season permitting, try the oven-baked fillets of turbot served with chanterelles and crêpes; the gray hen fried with spruce twigs and dried fruit is another good selection. ⊠ *Österlångg. 51,* ☎ *08/109046. AE, DC, MC, V. Closed Sun. No lunch.*

$$–$$$ ✕ **Källaren Diana.** This atmospheric Gamla Stan cellar dates from the Middle Ages. During the first part of the 18th century the building was used as a warehouse and owned by Jonas Alströmer, the scientist who introduced the potato to Sweden—by stealing two bags from England. Today the warehouse is a restaurant that uses the best indigenous ingredients from the Swedish forests and shores. Try the fillet of reindeer with chanterelles, gnocchi, and port wine sauce, or the black-peppered tournedos with artichokes, beets, and a cognac-pepper sauce. ⊠ *Brunnsgränd 2–4,* ☎ *08/107310. AE, DC, MC, V. Closed Sun.*

$–$$$ ✕ **Mårten Trotzig.** This contemporary, functional space is both a dining room and a bar. The short menu demonstrates the chef's imagination, blending multicultural recipes in intriguing ways. Try the yellow- and red-tomato salad with arugula pesto, and move on to the flounder fillet with artichoke hearts, asparagus, and a light grapefruit sauce. In a beautiful plant-lined courtyard, less expensive lunch specials are served. The staff is young, the service professional. ⊠ *Västerlångg. 79,* ☎ *08/4422530. AE, DC, MC, V. Closed Sun.*

$$ ✕ **Grill Ruby.** This American-style barbecue joint (at least as American as you can get in Gamla Stan) is just a cobblestone's throw away from the Saint George–slaying-the-dragon statue. Next door to its French cousin, Bistro Ruby, Grill Ruby skips the escargot and instead focuses on steaks and fish grills. Try the grilled steak with french fries and béarnaise sauce. On Sunday, an American-style brunch is served, where you can enjoy *huevos rancheros* and a big Bloody Mary while blues and country music drifts from the speakers. ⊠ *Österlångg. 14,* ☎ *08/206015. AE, DC, MC, V.*

$$ ✕ **Källaren Aurora.** Elegant, if a little stuffy, this Gamla Stan cellar restaurant is set in a beautiful 17th-century house. Its largely foreign clientele—most often busloads of tourists dropped off for a meal—enjoys top-quality Swedish and international cuisines served in intimate, small rooms. Try charcoal-grilled spiced salmon, veal Parmesan, or orange-basted halibut fillet. ⊠ *Munkbron 11,* ☎ *08/219359. AE, DC, MC, V. No lunch. Closed in July.*

$$ ✕ **Källaren Movitz.** At first glance Movitz looks like nothing more than a typical European pub, which is exactly what it is upstairs. But downstairs it's a luxurious restaurant serving Swedish cuisine with French and Italian influences. The refined table settings and abundant candlelight reflecting off the curves of the light yellow walls of what used to be a potato cellar in the 1600s make this an elegant place to dine. The reindeer steak with mushroom sauce and currant jelly comes highly recommended, as does the pasta stuffed with smoked salmon, shrimp, and ricotta cheese. ⊠ *Tyska Brinken 34,* ☎ *08/209979. AE, DC, MC, V. Closed Sun.*

$ ✕ **Hermitage.** This vegetarian cubbyhole located on one of Gamla Stan's biggest streets is an ideal place to stop and rest while exploring the Old Town. Each day there is a choice of two entrées—one is usually pasta and the other a stew or casserole. If you can't decide on one, go for a combo plate. They also have excellent salads and desserts. The delicious bread, included in the meal along with coffee and tea, is filled with chunks of vegetables. The no-smoking policy here is a welcome respite from the usual smoke-filled cafés in town. ⊠ *Stora Nyg. 11,* ☎ *08/4119500. MC, V.*

Northern Stockholm Dining and Lodging

Södermalm Dining and Lodging

Dining

Gondolen **6**
Hannas Krog **15**
Herman's **9**
Humlehof **10**
Indira **13**
Jeruselum Kebab **1**
Koh Phangan **14**
Opus **12**
Restaurang Ho's **16**

Lodging

Alexandra **11**
Anno 1647 . . . . **5**
Columbus Hotel **7**
Den Röda Båten
Mälaren **3**
Gustav af Klint **8**
Långholmen **17**
Pensionat Oden,
Söder **2**
Scandic Hotel
Slussen **4**

Östermalm

$$$-$$$$ ✕ **Paul & Norbert.** This quaint, romantic restaurant is rustic but re-
★ fined, with fine china and elegant glassware. It's on the city's most im-
pressive avenue, overlooking one of its most charming bays. Indigenous
wild game—reindeer, elk, partridge, and grouse—is prepared with a
French flair; fish dishes are also a draw. Paul & Norbert serves two
main menus, one seven course, one nine course—both of which are more
than SKr 900, but they also serve individual dishes in various combi-
nations. Book ahead; there aren't many tables and the city's elite keep
coming back. ✉ *Strandv. 9,* ☎ *08/6638183. Reservations essential. AE,
DC, MC, V. Closed Sun.*

$-$$$ ✕ **Eriks Bakficka.** A favorite among Östermalm locals, Erik's Bakficka
is a block from the elegant waterside, a few steps down from street
level. Owned by the well-known Swedish chef Erik Lallerstedt (who
also owns Gondolen), the restaurant serves a wide variety of Swedish
dishes, including an innovative seared perch served with scampi ravi-
oli flavored with summer truffles, cream of artichoke, and wasabi. No
smoking is allowed in the main dining room (a policy that's rare in
Stockholm). A lower-priced menu is served in the pub section, where
smoking is still allowed. ✉ *Fredrikshovsg. 4,* ☎ *08/6601599. AE, DC,
MC, V. Closed in July.*

$-$$ ✕ **Il Conte.** The attentive staff at this warm restaurant owned by Emilio
Ingrosso, one of Stockholm's most famous restaurateurs, serves delicious Italian food and wines. The decor is alluring and refined, but at
peak hours the dining room can be quite loud. You can also dine al-
fresco under cast-iron lanterns when the weather cooperates. ✉ *Grevg.
9,* ☎ *08/6612628. Reservations essential. AE, DC, MC, V. No lunch.*

$-$$ ✕ **Sushi Huset** (The Sushi House). Tucked away on a side street just a
short walk down from Östermalmstorg, this minimalist basement
sushi restaurant serves high-quality sushi and Japanese dishes. Even
though it gets crowded on weekends you can usually get a table after
a short wait. Choose from sushi combos of three to 30 pieces, or go
for the bento combo tray with four different mini-dishes. Sit at the small
bar and be friendly with the sushi makers: they might throw a few free
pieces your way while you wait. ✉ *Braheg. 3,* ☎ *08/6634546. AE,
DC, MC, V.*

$ ✕ **Örtagården.** This delightful vegetarian, no-smoking restaurant is lo-
★ cated above the beautiful Östermalm Market Hall. It offers an attractive
all-you-can-eat buffet of soups, salads, hot dishes, and homemade
bread—not to mention a bottomless cup of coffee—in a turn-of-the-
20th-century atmosphere. On Friday nights a jazz club takes over and
turns the once calm location into a swinging bar. ✉ *Nybrog. 31,* ☎
08/6621728. AE, MC, V.

Södermalm

$$-$$$ ✕ **Gondolen.** Suspended like a long train car under the gangway of the
★ Katerina elevator at Slussen square, Gondolen has a magnificent view
over the harbor, Mälaren, and the Baltic. The tenderloin of reindeer
with creamed lace cabbage, asparagus, and a potato terrine is one of
many great dishes. In the summer Erik's Bar serves grilled meat and
seafood out in the open on top of the gangway. ✉ *Stadsgården 6,* ☎
08/6417090. AE, DC, MC, V. Closed Sun.

$-$$$ ✕ **Koh Phangan.** Creative food is served until midnight at this lively
★ Thai restaurant, where you'll be seated in individual "huts," each with
a special name and style. The entire restaurant is decked out in col-
ored lights, fake palm fronds, and trinkets from Thailand. Recorded
jungle sounds play in the background. Sign up for a table on the chalk-

board next to the bar when you arrive. Although you can expect at least an hour-long wait on weekends, the food and surroundings make it well worth a visit. Grilled fish and seafood with extravagant, spicy sauces are the specialty. ⊠ *Skåneg. 57,* ☎ *08/6425040. Reservations not accepted. AE, DC, MC, V.*

$–$$ ✗ **Hannas Krog.** This bohemian neighborhood restaurant is almost always filled with locals. Although it may not be as super-trendy as it was in the early 1990s, it remains a Södermalm hot spot. Guests are serenaded at 10 minutes before the hour by a mooing cow that emerges from the cuckoo clock just inside the door. The dishes—from Caribbean shrimp to Provençal lamb—are all flavorful. Crowds don't slow down the consistent service or detract from the relaxed atmosphere, however. The bar in the basement is loud but pleasant. Local live bands play there on occasion. ⊠ *Skåneg. 80,* ☎ *08/6438225. AE, DC, MC, V. No lunch weekends and July.*

$–$$ ✗ **Humlehof.** If you're feeling extra hungry and a bit tight on funds, go straight to this Bavarian restaurant serving traditional Swedish and Eastern European dishes. Start by ordering an ice-cold Czech or Austrian draft beer; a bowl of what has to be the best goulash in Stockholm; and the *schweizer* (Swiss-style) schnitzel, which is as big as your face and served with salad and fried potatoes. If schnitzel's not your thing, try the pan-fried Haloumi cheese with sundried tomatoes, summer salad, and garlic bread. A TV in the corner above the bar means a sports-bar crowd gathers when a game is on, but it's never out of control and only adds to the restaurant's cheerful atmosphere. ⊠ *Folkungag. 128,* ☎ *08/6410302. AE, DC, MC, V.*

$–$$ ✗ **Opus.** Don't let the stripped-down, albeit charming, small space fool you—Opus's food packs a big-time punch and has earned it a reputation as a top French restaurant in town. Everything is prepared with intense care by the French-born and -trained cook and is served attentively by his Polish wife. Together they own this popular little restaurant, where the sauces are unbeatable. Try the pork fillet with chanterelle sauce or the perch fillet with avocado sauce to find out for yourself. With only 10 tables, be sure to call ahead. ⊠ *Blekingeg. 63,* ☎ *08/6446080. Reservations essential. AE, DC, MC, V. Closed Sun. No dinner Mon.*

$ ✗ **Herman's.** Herman's is a haven for vegetarians out to get the most
★ bang for their kroner. The glassed-in back deck and open garden both provide a spectacular view of the water and Gamla Stan. The food is always served buffet-style and includes various vegetable and pasta salads, warm casseroles, and such entrées as Indonesian stew with peanut sauce and vegetarian lasagna. The fruit pies and chocolate cakes and cookies are delicious. ⊠ *Fjällg. 23A,* ☎ *08/6439480. MC, V.*

$ ✗ **Indira.** This busy Indian restaurant about a block off Götgatanhas has an overwhelming 60 meal choices. The food is cheap and delicious and the service fast. Order as soon as you enter and find a seat at one of the mosaic-coated tables. There are a number of tables in the basement as well, so don't leave right away if it looks packed on the first floor. The chicken *korma*, with raisins and cashews, is fantastic, and the honey-saffron ice cream is a perfect end to the meal. ⊠ *Bondeg. 3B,* ☎ *08/6414046. AE, DC, MC, V.*

$ ✗ **Jerusalem Kebab.** Enter this wild grill and it may be hard to believe you're still in Stockholm. The men behind the counter sing along to the music blaring from the sound system, and the menu is in both Swedish and Arabic. On the walls are surreal landscape paintings, odd sculptures, and loads of hookahs—in fact, there are five or six pipes that the regulars use to smoke their tobacco. Falafel, chicken kebabs, gyros, mixed fried-vegetable plates, lamb fillets—they've got it all, as well as authentic Arabic tea and coffee. Late on weekend nights it's packed with hungry party goers. ⊠ *Hornsg. 92,* ☎ *08/6684131. No credit cards.*

$ ✕ **Restaurang Ho's.** Walk into this hidden gem of a Chinese restaurant and something about it just feels right. Nothing fancy—Ho's lets its authentic, intensely flavored food speak for itself. With more than 100 choices, the menu includes Chinese takes on duck, squid, scallops, pork, chicken, beef, and tofu. The stir-fried squid with green and red pepper in black bean sauce packs a serious punch. Finish with a classic fried banana and ice cream. ⊠ *Hornsg. 151,* ☎ *08/844420. AE, DC, MC, V. Closed Mon.*

LODGING

Although Stockholm has a reputation for prohibitively expensive hotels, great deals can be found during the summer, when prices are substantially lower and numerous discounts are available. More than 50 hotels offer the "Stockholm Package," which includes accommodation for one night, breakfast, and the *Stockholmskortet,* or Stockholm Card, which entitles the cardholder to free admission to museums and travel on public transport. Details are available from travel agents, tourist bureaus, or **Stockholm Information Service** (⊠ Box 7542, 103 93 Stockholm, ☎ 08/7892400, 𝖥𝖠𝖷 08/7892450). Also try **Hotellcentralen** (⊠ Central station, 111 20 Stockholm, ☎ 08/7892425, 𝖥𝖠𝖷 08/7918666); the service is free if you go in person, but a fee applies if you call.

Some hotels close during the winter holidays; call ahead if you expect to travel during that time.

All rooms in the hotels reviewed below are equipped with shower or bath unless otherwise noted.

Downtown Stockholm and Beyond

$$$$ 🏨 **Royal Viking (Radisson SAS).** A few yards from central station, the Royal Viking hotel offers good service, but its rooms tend to be cramped. Nevertheless, rooms do have attractive natural textiles and artwork, sturdy writing desks, separate seating areas, and plush robes in the large bathrooms. Triple-glazed windows and plenty of insulation keep traffic noise to a minimum. The large atrium lobby is spacious, and the split-level lounge is elegant. There is a business-class SAS check-in counter in the lobby. ⊠ *Vasag. 1, 101 24,* ☎ *08/141000,* 𝖥𝖠𝖷 *08/4488355,* 𝖶𝖤𝖡 *www.radissonsas.com. 319 rooms. Restaurant, bar, minibars, no-smoking rooms, indoor pool, sauna, convention center. AE, MC, V.*

$$$$ 🏨 **Sheraton Hotel and Towers.** The Sheraton in Stockholm is nothing less than a business executive's paradise, which means it's also an ideal hotel for the tourist on a generous budget. English is the main tongue at the restaurant and bar, which at night get fairly active once the piano player arrives. The lobby is vast and modern. There's a nice gift shop selling Swedish crystal and international newspapers. Rooms have hardwood floors, leather chairs, thick rugs, and sturdy fine-wood furniture. The big buffet breakfast is not included in room rates. ⊠ *Tegelbackan 6, 101 23,* ☎ *08/4123400,* 𝖥𝖠𝖷 *08/4123409,* 𝖶𝖤𝖡 *www. sheratonstockholm.com. 449 rooms. 2 restaurants, piano bar, sauna, gym, casino. AE, DC, MC, V.*

$$$–$$$$ 🏨 **Berns Hotel.** This cozy, yet subtly ultramodern hotel occupies a
★   mid-19th-century building that received some major modifications in 1999. The restaurant and bar are a joint venture with restaurant entrepreneur and designer Terence Conran. As a result, the building has regained some of the hot-spot status it had at the end of the 19th century.

You can breakfast in the Red Room, immortalized by August Strindberg's novel of the same name: this was one of his haunts. Rates include the use of a nearby fitness center with a pool. ⊠ *Näckströmsg. 8, 111 47,* ☎ *08/56632000,* FAX *08/56632201,* WEB *www.berns.se. 65 rooms, 3 suites. Restaurant, bar, no-smoking rooms, meeting room. AE, DC, MC, V.*

$$$–$$$$ ▥ **Nordic Hotel.** Opened in early 2001 next to central station, this center for the business traveler is actually two hotels—Nordic Light and Nordic Sea—in one. The first focuses on simplicity. Rooms are a mix of dark wood, gray flannel, and black-and-white tile. Adjustable spotlights in the ceiling allow you to change the room's atmosphere. Nordic Sea uses lighter wood with lots of blue fabric and mosaic tiles to create a Mediterranean touch. A huge aquarium in the lobby holds exotic fish. Both are clean and bright and provide excellent service. ⊠ *Vasaplan, 101 37,* ☎ *08/50563000,* FAX *08/50563060,* WEB *www.nordichotels.se. 542 rooms. 2 bars, 2 lounges, meeting rooms. AE, DC, MC, V.*

$$$–$$$$ ▥ **Scandic Hotel Anglais.** This '60s hotel, directly across from the Royal Library and the tree-filled Humlegården, is popular among North American business travelers and tourists. It's in the center of almost everything—shopping, sightseeing, and major businesses. The clean, pleasant rooms have wall-to-wall carpeting and furniture. An agreement with Sturebadet, Stockholm's most exclusive bathhouse, gives guests access to its excellent facilities, which include tiled pools from the turn of the last century. At night in Scandic's piano bar you'll hear more English than anything else. ⊠ *Humlegårdsg. 23,* ☎ *08/51734000,* FAX *08/51734011,* WEB *www.scandichotels.se. 212 rooms. 2 restaurants, piano bar, meeting rooms. AE, DC, MC, V.*

$$$–$$$$ ▥ **Sergel Plaza.** The lobby in this stainless-steel-paneled hotel is welcoming, with cane chairs set up in a pleasant, skylit seating area. The bright rooms are practical but tend to lack the luxury that the price tag may lead you to expect. In fact, the decor can be a bit disappointing, with run-of-the-mill furnishings and a tad too much gray. But its central location on the main pedestrian mall makes it a good base for exploring Stockholm. In the morning, choose between an international buffet or a Japanese breakfast; the Anna Rella Restaurant serves innovative Swedish and international dishes. At night the piano bar behind the lobby fills with guests. ⊠ *Brunkebergstorg 9, 103 27,* ☎ *08/226600,* FAX *08/215070,* WEB *www.scandic-hotels.se. 405 rooms. Restaurant, bar, no-smoking rooms, sauna, shops, casino, convention center. AE, DC, MC, V.*

$$$ ▥ **Adlon.** Although in a building dating from 1884, the Adlon considers itself a high-tech business hotel. All rooms, which are clean and fresh but rather undistinguished, offer Internet connections. The hotel's proximity to downtown Stockholm and central station make it ideal for the business traveler hoping to find some time to explore while in town. Despite traffic, rooms on the street remain quiet. Rates are cheaper if rooms are booked via the Web. ⊠ *Vasag. 42, 111 20,* ☎ *08/4026500,* FAX *08/208610,* WEB *www.adlon.se. 78 rooms, 65 singles. Breakfast room, no-smoking rooms, meeting rooms. AE, DC, MC, V.*

$$$ ▥ **Amaranten.** Although it's on the island of Kungsholmen and therefore a bit out of the way, this large, modern hotel is just a few minutes' walk from Stockholm's central train station. Rooms are contemporary, with satellite television and complimentary movie channels. Fifty rooms (which cost extra) have air-conditioning and soundproofing. ⊠ *Kungsholmsg. 31, Box 8054, 104 20,* ☎ *08/6925200,* FAX *08/6526248,* WEB *www.firsthotels.com. 410 rooms. Restaurant, brasserie, piano bar, no-smoking rooms, indoor pool, sauna, meeting room. AE, DC, MC, V.*

$$$ 🏨 **Lydmar Hotel.** Just opposite Humlegården, the beautiful park in the center of Stockholm that holds the Royal Library, stands this modern hotel. Only a 10-minute walk from the downtown hub of Sergels Torg and a stone's throw from Stureplan, the epicenter of Stockholm's nightlife, the Lydmar is more than just a hotel, it's also one of the trendiest bars in town. Even if you don't stay here, be sure to take a ride in the elevator, in which you can choose from eight different kinds of quality (believe it or not) elevator music. The lobby lounge is alive on weekends with jazz and with DJs spinning the latest club music. ✉ *Stureg. 10, 114 36,* ☎ *08/56611300,* FAX *08/56611301,* WEB *www.lydmar.se. 61 rooms, 5 suites. AE, DC, MC, V.*

$$$ 🏨 **Radisson SAS SkyCity Hotel.** Right in the center of Arlanda Airport's SkyCity complex, this hotel is equipped and furnished in a variety of tasteful styles. If your room faces the runway, you can watch the planes take off and land (the extensive soundproofing makes them seem to do so quietly). When you're flying out very early in the morning, or stuck with a layover in Stockholm, it's the ideal airport hotel. ✉ *Arlanda Airport, 190 45,* ☎ *08/59077300,* FAX *08/59378100,* WEB *www.radissonsas.com. 230 rooms. Restaurant, bar, no-smoking rooms, gym, meeting room. AE, DC, MC, V.*

$$$ 🏨 **Scandic Hotel Continental.** In city center across from the train station, the Continental is a reliable hotel that's especially popular with Americans. Rooms have a minibar, trouser press, and satellite television. An extravagant Scandinavian buffet is served in the Gustavian breakfast rooms. ✉ *Klara Vattugränd 4, 101 22,* ☎ *08/51734200,* FAX *08/517342311,* WEB *www.scandic-hotels.com. 268 rooms. Restaurant, bar, no-smoking rooms, sauna, meeting room. AE, DC, MC, V.*

$$–$$$ 🏨 **Birger Jarl.** Renovations have turned Birger Jarl into a "design" hotel. The entire hotel was revamped (when the owners realized that room 247 had been overlooked, they decided to leave it as a memorial to times past). Each of seven rooms were remodeled by one of the country's top designers: it costs extra to stay in one of these. The majority of the rooms are not large but are well furnished and have nice touches, such as heated towel racks in the bathrooms; all double rooms have bathtubs. Four family-style rooms have extra floor space and sofa beds. You can choose your breakfast from an extensive buffet just off the lobby, but room service is also available. ✉ *Tuleg. 8, 104 32,* ☎ *08/6741000,* FAX *08/6737366,* WEB *www.birgerjarl.se. 225 rooms. Coffee shop, no-smoking rooms, sauna, meeting room. AE, DC, MC, V.*

$$–$$$ 🏨 **Crystal Plaza Hotel.** Housed in one of Stockholm's oldest hotel buildings (1895), the Crystal Plaza, with a circular tower and peach walls, is sure to catch the eye of anyone walking down Birger Jarlsgatan. Most of the rooms have a mix of birch wood furniture, hardwood floors with small rugs, and the requisite hotel artwork on the walls. Rooms facing the inner courtyard can be a bit quieter than those on the street. If you want only the best, throw down a little extra money for one of the circular tower rooms, two of which have balconies. The hotel's location, just a stone's throw from the hip bars of Stureplan and downtown shopping, makes it an ideal place for folks looking to have quick access to a good time in the city. ✉ *Birger Jarlsg. 35, 111 45,* ☎ *08/4068800,* FAX *08/241511,* WEB *www.crystalplaza.aos.se. 112 rooms. Restaurant, bar, breakfast room. AE, DC, MC, V.*

$$–$$$ 🏨 **Stockholm Plaza Hotel.** On one of Stockholm's foremost streets for shopping and entertainment, and only a short walk from the city's nightlife and business center, this hotel is ideal for the traveler who wants a central location. The building was built in 1884 and was nearly torn down in 1979 before the Stockholm City Museum stepped in and stopped the destruction. The Elite hotel chain took over in 1984. Rooms are

furnished in an elegant, old-world manner and are reasonably sized. ✉ *Birger Jarlsg. 29, 103 95,* ☎ *08/56622000,* FAX *08/56622020,* WEB *www.elite.se. 151 rooms. Restaurant, bar, meeting rooms. AE, DC, MC, V.*

$$ 🏠 **Arcadia.** On a hilltop near a large waterfront nature preserve, this converted dormitory is within 15 minutes of downtown by bus or subway, or 30 minutes on foot along pleasant shopping streets. Rooms are furnished in a spare, neutral style, with plenty of natural light. The adjoining restaurant serves meals on the terrace in summer. To get here, take Bus 43 to Körsbärsvägen. ✉ *Körsbärsv. 1, 114 89,* ☎ *08/ 56621500,* FAX *08/56621501,* WEB *www.arcadia.elite.se. 82 rooms. Restaurant. AE, DC, MC, V.*

$$ 🏠 **August Strindberg.** A narrow, frescoed corridor leads from the street to the flagstone courtyard, into which the hotel's restaurant expands in summer. Parquet flooring and high ceilings distinguish the rooms, which are otherwise plainly furnished. Kitchenettes are available; some rooms can be combined into family apartments. The four floors have no elevator. ✉ *Tegnérg. 38, 113 59,* ☎ *08/325006,* FAX *08/ 209085. 19 rooms. Restaurant, kitchenettes (some). AE, DC, MC, V.*

$$ 🏠 **Central Hotel.** Less than 300 yards from central station, this practical hotel is a good option for both business and pleasure travelers. The rooms are fairly small, but all face a pleasant, quiet courtyard. And, thanks to extra sound insulation, the chaos of Vasagatan remains outside the room. Bathrooms have a shower only. ✉ *Vasag. 38, 101 20,* ☎ *08/56620800,* FAX *08/247573,* WEB *www.centralhotel.se. 93 rooms. In-room data ports, no-smoking rooms, meeting room. AE, DC, MC, V.*

$$ 🏠 **City.** This large, modern-style hotel is near the city center and Hötorget market, making it ideal for shopping and sightseeing (or movie watching, since it's also close to a movie complex). Rooms are filled with modern, no-frills furniture. Some have hardwood floors. Breakfast is served in the atrium Winter Garden restaurant. ✉ *Slöjdg. 7, 111 81,* ☎ *08/7237200,* FAX *08/7237209,* WEB *www.rica.cityhotels.se. 293 rooms. Restaurant, no-smoking rooms, sauna, meeting room. AE, DC, MC, V. BP.*

$$ ✕🏠 **Claes på Hörnet.** This may be the most exclusive—and smallest—
★ hotel in town, with only 10 rooms in a former 1739 inn. The rooms, comfortably furnished with period antiques, go quickly (book three or so months in advance, especially around Christmas). The restaurant ($$) is worth visiting even if you don't spend the night: its old-fashioned dining room serves Swedish and Continental dishes such as outstanding *strömming* (Baltic herring) and cloudberry mousse cake. Reservations are essential, as are a jacket and tie. Note that the restaurant (but not the hotel) is closed in July. ✉ *Surbrunnsg. 20, 113 48,* ☎ *08/165130,* FAX *08/6125315. 10 rooms. Restaurant. AE, DC, MC, V.*

$$ 🏠 **Hotel Gustav Wasa.** The Gustav Wasa, named after the first king of Sweden, is right next to Openplan square. The hotel is in a 19th-century residential building and has fairly large, bright rooms with herringbone hardwood floors, original trim and details along the ceilings, and a funky blend of antiques and more-modern furniture. Ask for a room with a window out to the street in order to get a direct view of the grand Gustav Wasa Church and the Odenplan. The other available view, of the inner courtyard, is much less exciting. The downtown location and lower prices make this an excellent place for budget travelers who prefer a friendly hotel that feels slightly lived in. ✉ *Västmannag. 61, 113 25,* ☎ *08/343801,* FAX *08/307372,* WEB *www.hotel. wineasy.se/gustav.vasa. 33 rooms. AE, DC, MC, V.*

$$ 🏨 **Tegnérlunden.** A quiet city park fronts this modern hotel, a 10-minute walk along shop-lined Sveavägen from the downtown hub of Sergels Torg. Although the rooms are small and sparsely furnished, they are clean and well maintained. The lobby is bright with marble, brass, and greenery, as is the sunny rooftop breakfast room. ✉ *Tegnérlunden 8, 113 59,* ☎ *08/54545550,* FAX *08/54545551,* WEB *www.swedenhotels.se. 103 rooms. Breakfast room, no-smoking rooms, sauna, meeting room. AE, DC, MC, V.*

$ 🏨 **Bema.** This small hotel is relatively central, on the ground floor of an apartment block near Tegnérlunden park. Room decor is Swedish modern, with beechwood furniture. One four-bed family room is available. Breakfast is served in your room. Given the price, it's difficult to beat. ✉ *Upplandsg. 13, 111 23,* ☎ *08/232675,* FAX *08/205338. 12 rooms. AE, DC, MC, V.*

Gamla Stan and Skeppsholmen

$$$$ 🏨 **Grand Hotel.** The city's showpiece hotel is an 1874 landmark on the quayside at Blasieholmen, just across the water from the Royal Palace. Visiting political dignitaries, Nobel Prize winners, and movie stars come to enjoy the gracious old-world atmosphere, which extends to the comfortable, well-furnished rooms. One of the hotel's most alluring features is a glassed-in veranda overlooking the harbor, where an excellent smörgåsbord buffet is served. Guests have access to the high-class Sturebadet Health Spa nearby. Franska Matsalen, the hotel's main restaurant, serves French cuisine and is ranked as one of the best in the city. ✉ *Södra Blasieholmshamnen 8, Box 16424, 103 27,* ☎ *08/ 6793500,* FAX *08/6118686,* WEB *www.grandhotel.se. 307 rooms, 20 suites. 2 restaurants, bar, no-smoking rooms, sauna, shops, meeting room. AE, DC, MC, V.*

$$$–$$$$ 🏨 **Radisson SAS Strand Hotel.** This old-world yellow-brick hotel, built in 1912 for the Stockholm Olympics, has been completely and tastefully modernized. It's on the water across from the Royal Dramatic Theater, directly in front of the quay where many of the boats leave for the archipelago. It's also only a short walk from the Old Town and the museums on Skeppsholmen. No two rooms are alike, but all are furnished with antiques and have such rustic touches as flowers painted on woodwork and furniture. The Piazza restaurant has an outdoor feel to it: Italian cuisine is the specialty, and the wine list is superb. An SAS check-in counter for business-class travelers adjoins the main reception area. ✉ *Nybrokajen 9, Box 16396, 103 27,* ☎ *08/50664000,* FAX *08/6112436,* WEB *www.radissonsas.com. 148 rooms. Restaurant, no-smoking rooms, sauna, meeting room. AE, DC, MC, V.*

$$$ 🏨 **Lady Hamilton.** As charming as its namesake, Lord Nelson's mis-
★ tress, the Lady Hamilton opened in 1980 as a modern hotel inside a 15th-century building. Swedish antiques accent the light, natural-tone decor in all the guest rooms and common areas. Romney's "Bacchae" portrait of Lady Hamilton hangs in the foyer, where the Lady also supports the ceiling in the form of a large, smiling figurehead from an old ship. The breakfast room, furnished with captain's chairs, looks out onto the lively cobblestone street, and the subterranean sauna rooms, in whitewashed stone, provide a secluded fireplace and a chance to take a dip in the building's original, medieval well. The honeymoon suite is impeccable. ✉ *Storkyrkobrinken 5, 111 28,* ☎ *08/234680,* FAX *08/ 4111148,* WEB *www.lady-hamilton.se. 34 rooms. Bar, breakfast room, no-smoking rooms, sauna, meeting room. AE, DC, MC, V.*

$$$ 🏨 **Reisen.** This 17th-century hotel on the waterfront in Gamla Stan has
★ been open since 1819. A 2000 renovation modernized the hotel while preserving its history and old-world charm. The rooms looking out over

the water are fantastic, and for a surprisingly small amount of extra money you can get a room with a private sauna and Jacuzzi. There's a fine Italian restaurant with a grill, tea and coffee service in the library, and what is reputed to be the best piano bar in town. A small swimming pool, dominated by businessmen cooling off after the sauna, is built under the medieval arches of the foundations. ☒ *Skeppsbron 12–14, 111 30,* ☎ *08/223260,* ℻ *08/201559,* WEB *www.firsthotels.com. 144 rooms. Restaurant, piano bar, no-smoking floor, indoor pool, sauna, meeting room. AE, DC, MC, V.*

$$$ 🏨 **Victory.** Slightly larger than its brother and sister hotels, the Lord Nelson and Lady Hamilton, this extremely atmospheric Gamla Stan building dates from 1640. The decor is nautical, with items from the HMS *Victory* and Swedish antiques. Each room is named after a 19th-century sea captain. The noted Lejontornet restaurant keeps an extensive wine cellar. ☒ *Lilla Nyg. 5, 111 28,* ☎ *08/143090,* ℻ *08/202177,* WEB *www.victory-hotel.se. 48 rooms. Restaurant, bar, no-smoking floor, 2 saunas, meeting room. AE, DC, MC, V.*

$$–$$$ 🏨 **Lord Nelson.** The owners of the Lady Hamilton and the Victory run this small hotel with a nautical atmosphere right in the middle of Gamla Stan. Rooms are only a touch larger than cabins—but service is excellent. Noise from traffic in the pedestrian street outside can be a problem during the summer. ☒ *Västerlångg. 22, 111 29,* ☎ *08/232390,* ℻ *08/101089,* WEB *www.lord-nelson.se. 31 rooms. Café, no-smoking room, sauna, meeting room. AE, DC, MC, V.*

$$–$$$ 🏨 **Mälardrottningen.** One of the more unusual establishments in Stockholm, Mälardrottningen, a Sweden Hotels property, was once Barbara Hutton's yacht. Since 1982, it has been a quaint and pleasant hotel, with a crew as service-conscious as any in Stockholm. Tied up on the freshwater side of Gamla Stan, it is minutes from everything. The small suites are suitably decorated in a navy-blue and maroon nautical theme. Some of the below-deck cabins are a bit stuffy, but in summer you can take your meals out on deck. The ship's chief assets are novelty and absence of traffic noise. ☒ *Riddarholmen 4, 111 28,* ☎ *08/54518780,* ℻ *08/243676. 59 cabins. Restaurant, bar, grill, no-smoking rooms, sauna, meeting room. AE, DC, MC, V.*

$$ 🏨 **Gamla Stan.** This quiet, cozy hotel is tucked away on a narrow street in one of the Gamla Stan's 17th-century houses. All rooms are decorated in the Gustavian style with hardwood floors, Oriental rugs, and antique furniture. A short walk from the Gamla Stan metro stop, it's a perfect home base for later exploring. ☒ *Lilla Nyg. 25,* ☎ *08/7237250,* ℻ *08/7237259,* WEB *www.rica.cityhotels.se. 51 rooms. No-smoking floor, meeting room. AE, DC, MC, V.*

Östermalm

$$$ 🏨 **Castle Hotel.** On a back street just off Birgar Jarlsgatan, this centrally located hotel has been in operation since the 1930s. The owners are great jazz enthusiasts, and the hotel has hosted such jazz greats as Dizzy Gillespie, Chet Baker, and Benny Carter. Rooms are done with art deco furnishings but are on the diminutive side. Following the jazz theme, the two suites are named "Suite Georgia Brown" and "Suite Lorraine." ☒ *Riddarg. 14, 114 35,* ☎ *08/6795700,* ℻ *08/6112022,* WEB *www.castle-hotel.se. 50 rooms, 2 suites. Restaurant, meeting room. AE, DC, MC, V.*

$$$ 🏨 **Diplomat.** Within easy walking distance of Djurgården, this elegant hotel is less flashy than most in its price range. The building is a turn-of-the-20th-century town house that housed foreign embassies in the 1930s and was converted into a hotel in 1966. Rooms have thick carpeting and high ceilings; those in the front, facing the water, have

magnificent views over Stockholm Harbor. The T-Bar, formerly a rather staid tearoom and restaurant, is now one of the trendiest bars among the city's upper crust. The second-floor bar is ideal for a break from sightseeing. ✉ *Strandv. 7C, 104 40,* ☎ *08/4596800,* FAX *08/ 4596820. 133 rooms. Restaurant, bar, no-smoking room, sauna, meeting room. AE, DC, MC, V.*

$$$ ⊞ **Hotel Esplanade.** Right on the water and only a few buildings down from Stockholm's Royal Dramatic Theater, Hotel Esplanade is a beautiful hotel with a real touch of old Stockholm. Originally a guest house operated by an elderly woman, the inn's current owners have sought to maintain the hominess—you'll probably be offered a glass of fine brandy in the lounge when you check in. Rooms are individually decorated with antiques and some offer water views. Breakfast is served in the original art nouveau–style breakfast room. Be sure to call well ahead to book a room, since many regulars return every year. ✉ *Strandv. 7A, 114 56,* ☎ *08/6630740,* FAX *08/6625992,* WEB *www.hotelesplanade.se. 34 rooms. Breakfast room, lobby lounge, sauna. AE, DC, MC, V.*

$$$ ⊞ **Mornington.** Just off the main square of Östermalm, the Mornington is close to both the nightlife of Stureplan and the downtown business district. Renovations in 2000 significantly modernized the lobby, bar, and restaurant, making the area a rather hip place to relax. It also resulted in the addition of a nice little library— more than 4,000 books (mostly in Swedish) are spread throughout the lobby and are available to read during your stay. All rooms have hardwood floors and nice furniture, but ask for a renovated room on the sixth or seventh floor— the older rooms are a bit worn out. ✉ *Nybrog. 53, 102 44,* ☎ *08/ 50733000,* FAX *08/50733039,* WEB *www.mornington.se. 140 rooms. Restaurant, bar, no-smoking rooms, sauna, steam room, solarium, meeting room. AE, DC, MC, V.*

$$ ⊞ **Örnsköld.** Just behind the Royal Dramatic Theater in the heart of
★ the city, this hidden gem has the atmosphere of an old private club, with a brass-and-leather lobby and Victorian-style furniture in the moderately spacious, high-ceiling rooms. Rooms over the courtyard are quieter, but those facing the street—not a particularly busy one— are sunnier. The hotel is frequented by actors appearing at the Royal Theater. ✉ *Nybrog. 6, 114 34,* ☎ *08/6670285,* FAX *08/6676991. 30 rooms. AE, MC, V.*

$$ ⊞ **Pärlan.** The name of this hotel means "The Pearl" and that's ex-
★ actly what it is. Located on the second floor of an early-19th-century building on a quiet street, the Pärlan is a friendly alternative to the city's bigger hotels. Furniture throughout is a mix of fine antiques and flea market bargains, making it quirky and homey. A balcony looking out over the inner courtyard is a perfect spot for eating breakfast, which is served buffet-style in the kitchen every morning. Be sure to admire the ultra-Swedish tile oven in the corner of the dining room. If you want to get a feel for what it's like to really live in this neighborhood, this is your best bet. Book far in advance, since the rooms are almost always full. ✉ *Skepperg. 27, 114 52,* ☎ *08/6635070,* FAX *08/6677145. 9 rooms with bath. AE, MC, V.*

$$ ⊞ **Wellington.** From the outside the building resembles the Industri-
★ huset (Industry House) across the street, but inside is a delightful hotel with polite, professional staff and quality service. It's in a quiet residential area in Östermalm near the Hedvig Eleonora Church and cemetery, a calm home base from which to enjoy the city. Rooms are modern and fresh with hardwood floors. Rooms facing the inner courtyard have balconies. Ask for a room on the top floor for a great view of the neighborhood's rooftops. The breakfast buffet is top-notch, serving all the Swedish classics, including pickled herring. ✉ *Storg. 6, 114 51,* ☎ *08/*

6670910, FAX 08/6671254, WEB *www.wellington.se. 60 rooms. Bar, break-fast room, in-room data ports, sauna, meeting rooms. AE, MC, V.*

Södermalm

$$$ 🏨 **Scandic Hotel Slussen.** Working with what appears to be a dubious location (atop a tunnel above a six-lane highway), the Scandic has pulled a rabbit out of a hat. Built on special noise- and shock-absorbing cushions, the hotel almost lets you forget about the highway. The intriguing labyrinth of levels, separate buildings, and corridors is filled with such unique details as a rounded stairway lighted from between the steps. The guest rooms are exquisitely designed and modern, with plenty of stainless steel and polished wood inlay to accent the maroon color scheme. The Eken restaurant and bar serves food indoors and out. If you eat or drink too much, there's a gym with excellent facilities. The hotel is at Slussen, easily accessible from downtown. ⊠ *Guldgränd 8, 104 65,* ☎ *08/51735300,* FAX *08/51735311,* WEB *www.scandic.se. 264 rooms. 2 restaurants, piano bar, no-smoking rooms, indoor pool, hair salon, sauna, gym, meeting room. AE, DC, MC, V.*

$$ 🏨 **Alexandra.** This economy hotel is a five-minute walk from the subway and only a few stops from the city center. Rooms are clean and fairly big, although the decor is a reminder that most of the renovations here took place during the late '80s. There are a number of cheaper rooms, adjacent to the parking garage, without windows. ⊠ *Magnus Ladulåsg. 42, 118 27,* ☎ *08/840320,* FAX *08/7205353. 68 rooms, 5 two-room suites. Breakfast room, no-smoking rooms, sauna. AE, DC, MC, V.*

$$ 🏨 **Anno 1647.** Named for the date the building was erected, this
★ small, pleasant hotel is three stops on the subway from the city center. Rooms vary in shape, but all have original, well-worn pine floors with 17th-century–style appointments. There's no elevator in this four-story building. The bar and café are a rather popular hangout. The menu is international. Guest DJs control the sound waves. ⊠ *Mariagränd 3, 116 41,* ☎ *08/4421680,* FAX *08/4421647. 42 rooms, 30 with bath. Snack bar. AE, DC, MC, V.*

$-$$ 🏨 **Columbus Hotel.** Just a few blocks from busy Götgatan, the Columbus
★ is an oasis of calm and Swedish history. Built in 1780, it was originally a brewery, then a jail, then a hospital, then a temporary housing area. Since 1976, the beautiful building, with its large, tranquil inner courtyard, has been a hotel. Rooms have wide-beam, polished hardwood floors, antique furniture, and wallpaper and fabrics that feel authentic, and comfortable. Many look out over the courtyard, others on the nearby church. In summer, breakfast is served outside. The peace and quiet this hotel provides, even though it's close to all the action, makes it ideal for a vacation. ⊠ *Tjärhovsg. 11, 116 21,* ☎ *08/6441717,* FAX *08/7020764,* WEB *www.columbus.se. 64 rooms, 36 with bath. Bar, café. AE, MC, V.*

$-$$ 🏨 **Pensionat Oden, Söder.** Clean, inexpensive, and centrally located, this bed-and-breakfast is on the second floor of a 19th-century building. Hornsgatan, the street it's on, is Södermalm's busiest and filled with pubs, restaurants, and shops. Rooms have hardwood floors, Oriental rugs, and an odd blend of new and old furniture. A kitchen is available for use. The hotel is popular with parents visiting their children in college, academics traveling on a budget, and backpackers. Book rooms well in advance, especially during the holidays. ⊠ *Hornsg. 66B,* ☎ *08/6124349,* FAX *08/6124501,* WEB *www.pensionat.nu. 35 rooms, 8 with bath. No-smoking rooms. AE, MC, V.*

Youth Hostels

Don't be put off by the "youth" bit: there's actually no age limit. The standards of cleanliness, comfort, and facilities offered are usually extremely high. Hostels listed are on Skeppsholmen and Södermalm.

$–$$ 🚢 ***Den Röda Båten Mälaren*** (The Red Boat). Built in 1914, the *Mälaren* originally traveled the waters of the Göta Canal under the name of *Sätra.* Today she has to settle for sitting still in Stockholm as a youth hostel. The hostel cabins are small but clean and have bunk beds. There are also four "hotel" rooms with private bath and nicer furniture and details. In the summer, the restaurant offers great views of Stockholm along with basic, traditional Swedish food. Breakfast costs an additional 45 SKr, but sheets are included in your rate. ⊠ *Södermälarstrand kajplats 6, 116 21,* ☎ *08/6444385,* FAX *08/6413733,* WEB *www.rodabaten.nu. 35 rooms, 4 with bath. MC, V.*

$ 🚢 ***af Chapman.*** This circa-1888 sailing ship, permanently moored in Stockholm Harbor just across from the Royal Palace, is a landmark in its own right. Book early—the place is so popular in summer that finding a bed may prove difficult. Breakfast (SKr 45) is not included in the room rate; there are no kitchen facilities. ⊠ *Västra Brobänken, Skeppsholmen 111 49,* ☎ *08/4632266,* FAX *08/6119875,* WEB *www.stfchapman.com. 136 beds, 2- to 6-bed cabins. Café.* ☉ *Mid-Jan.–mid-Dec. DC, MC, V.*

$ 🏠 ***Bosön.*** Out of the way on the island of Lidingö, this hostel is part of the Bosön Sports Institute, a national training center pleasantly close to the water. You can rent canoes on the grounds and go out for a paddle. Breakfast is included in the room rate. There are laundry facilities and a kitchen you can use. All rooms are clean and fresh. ⊠ *Bosön, 181 47 Lidingö,* ☎ *08/6056600,* FAX *08/7671644. 70 beds. Cafeteria, sauna, boating, coin laundry. MC, V. BP.*

$ 🏠 ***City Backpackers.*** You won't find cheaper accommodations closer to central station than City Backpackers, which has 65 beds. The 19th-century building typifies the European youth hostel, and this one is clean and well run. Guests have access to a common kitchen, a lounge with cable TV, recently renovated showers, and a courtyard. The seven-person apartment, with its own kitchen and bathroom, is ideal for a group of young backpackers or an adventurous, large family. ⊠ *Upplandsg. 2A,* ☎ *08/206920,* FAX *08/100464,* WEB *www.citybackpackers.se. 15 rooms. MC, V.*

$ 🏠 ***Gustav af Klint.*** A "hotel ship" moored at Stadsgården quay, near Slussen subway station, the *Gustav af Klint* harbors 120 beds in its two sections: a hotel and a hostel. The hostel section has 18 four-bunk cabins and 10 two-bunk cabins; a 14-bunk dormitory is also available from May through mid-September. The hotel section has four single-bunk and three two-bunk cabins with bedsheets and breakfast included. The hostel rates are SKr 120 per person in a four-bunk room, and SKr 140 per person in a two-bunk room; these do not include bedsheets or breakfast, which are available at an extra charge. All guests share common bathrooms and showers. There is a cafeteria and a restaurant, and you can dine on deck in summer. ⊠ *Stadsgårdskajen 153, 116 45,* ☎ *08/ 6404077,* FAX *08/6406416. 7 hotel cabins, 28 hostel cabins, 28 dormitory beds, all without bath. Restaurant, cafeteria. AE, MC, V.*

$ 🏠 ***Långholmen.*** This former prison, built in 1724, was converted into a combined hotel and hostel in 1989. The hotel rooms are made available as additional hostel rooms in the summer. Rooms are small and windows are nearly nonexistent—you *are* in a prison—but that hasn't stopped travelers from flocking here. Each room has two to five beds, and all but 10 have bathrooms with shower. The hostel is on the island of Långholmen, which has popular bathing beaches and a Prison

Museum. The Inn, next door, serves Swedish home cooking, the Jail Pub offers light snacks, and a garden restaurant operates in the summer. ✉ *Långholmen, Box 9116, 102 72,* ☎ *08/6680500,* 🖷 *08/ 7208575,* 🌐 *www.langholmen.se. 254 beds June–Sept., 26 beds Sept.– May. Restaurant, cafeteria, sauna, beach, coin laundry. AE, DC, MC, V.*

$ 🖼 **Skeppsholmen.** This former craftsman's workshop in a pleasant and quiet part of the island was converted into a hostel for the overflow from the *af Chapman,* an anchor's throw away. Breakfast costs an additional SKr 45. ✉ *Skeppsholmen, 111 49,* ☎ *08/4632266,* 🖷 *08/6117155. 155 beds, 2- to 6-bed rooms. Café, coin laundry. DC, MC, V.*

Camping

You can camp in the Stockholm area for SKr 80–SKr 130 per night. **Bredäng Camping** (✉ 127 31 Skärholmen, ☎ 08/977071), has camping and a youth hostel. Its facilities are excellent and include a restaurant and bar. Fifteen kilometers (9 mi) from Stockholm, in Huddinge, is **Stockholm SweCamp Flottsbro** (✉ 141 25 Huddinge, ☎ 08/4499580), where you can camp, play golf, rent canoes and bikes, and hang out on a beach. At **Rösjöbaden Camping** (✉ 192 56 Sollentuna, ☎ 08/ 962184), a short drive north of town, you can fish, swim, and play minigolf and volleyball.

NIGHTLIFE AND THE ARTS

Stockholm's nightlife can be broken up into two general groups based on their geography. First, there's Birger Jarlsgatan, Stureplan, and the city end of Kungsträdgården, which are more upscale and trendy, and thus more expensive. At the bars and clubs in this area, it's not unusual to wait in line with people who look like they just stepped off the pages of a glossy magazine. To the south, in Södermalm, things are a bit looser and wilder, but that doesn't mean the bars are any less hip. At night Söder can get pretty crazy—it's louder and more bohemian, and party goers walk the streets.

In general, on weekends, clubs and bars are often packed with tourists and locals, and you might have to wait in line. It's also sometimes hard to distinguish between a bar and nightclub, since many bars turn into clubs late at night. Many establishments will post and enforce a minimum age requirement, which could be anywhere from 18 to 30, depending on the clientele they wish to serve, and they may frown upon jeans and sneakers. Your safest bet is to wear dark clothes. Most places are open until around 3 AM.

The tourist guide *What's On* (www.stockholmtown.com) is available free of charge at most hotels, tourist centers, and some restaurants. It lists the month's events in both English and Swedish. The Thursday editions of the daily newspapers *Dagens Nyheter* (www.dn.se) and *Svenska Dagbladet* (www.svd.se) carry current listings of events, films, restaurants, and museums in Swedish. There's also a monthly guide called *Nöjesguiden* (the Entertainment Guide; www.nojesguiden.se), which has listings and reviews in Swedish.

Nightlife

Bars and Nightclubs

Go to Stureplan (at one end of Birger Jarlsgatan) on any given weekend night and you'll see crowds of people gathering around *Svampen* (the Mushroom), a concrete structure that's a roof over pay phones. It's *the* meeting place for people getting ready to go out in this area.

Berns Salonger (✉ Berns Hotel, Berzelii Park, ☎ 08/56632000) has three bars—one in old-world, 19th-century style, and two modern rooms—plus a huge veranda that's spectacular in the summer. Music here gets so thumping you can hear it down the street. **Folkhemmet** (✉ Renstiernas Gata 30, ☎ 08/6405595), marked by a blue "F" imitating the "T" for the subway, is a longtime favorite of the artsy locals. The atmosphere is friendly and inviting, but be prepared for lots of smoke and a crowded bar. Close to the Mushroom is the casually hip **Lydmar Bar** (✉ Stureg. 10, ☎ 08/56611300), with black leather couches and chairs and a small stage for bands and DJs. Most people here are in the music business. **Mosebacke Etablissement** (✉ Mosebacke Torg 3, ☎ 08/6419020) is a combined indoor theater, comedy club, and outdoor café with a spectacular view of the city. The crowd here leans toward over-30 hipsters. The **O-bar** (✉ Stureplan 2, ☎ 08/4405730), located upstairs through the restaurant Sturehof, is where the downtown crowd gathers for late-night drinks and music ranging from bass-heavy hip-hop to hard rock. The **Sturehof** itself is a prime location for evening people-watching. The outdoor tables are smack dab in the middle of Stureplan. For what has to be Stockholm's biggest rum collection (more than 64 varieties), slide into **Sjögräs** (Sea Grass; ✉ Timmermansg. 24, ☎ 08/841200), where the drinks go down smoothly to the sounds of reggae. Wander along Götagatan with its lively bars and head for **Snaps/Rangus Tangus** (✉ Medborgarplatsen, ☎ 08/6402868), an India-inspired eatery and cellar lounge/bar in a 300-year-old building. There is live music here, and the latest DJs spin here as well. **Sophie's Bar** (✉ Biblioteksg. 5, ☎ 08/6118408) is another one of Stockholm's major celebrity hangouts. It can be a bit elitist and uptight, but that didn't stop Madonna from checking it out when she was in town. From Sophie's Bar it's a short walk to **Spy Bar** (✉ Birger Jarlsg. 20, ☎ 08/6118408), one of Stockholm's most exclusive clubs. It's often filled with local celebrities and lots of glitz and glamour. The **T-Bar** (✉ Strandv. 7C, ☎ 08/4596802) used to be the quaint tea bar at the Diplomat Hotel. You can still drink afternoon tea (or cocktails) there, but today it's a hangout for the city's ultracool. **Tiger** (✉ Kungsg. 18, ☎ 08/244700) is a multilevel club and restaurant with a Latin touch. On the first floor it's all about salsa and *mojitos* (Cuban cocktails made with rum and mint). On the huge second floor, the music is anything from hip-hop to house music. Always expect a line and two tough doormen. At Odenplan, the basement bar of **Tranan** (✉ Karlbergsv. 14, ☎ 08/300765) is a fun place to party in semidarkness to anything from ambient music to hard rock. Lots of candles, magazines, and art are inside. A trendy, youngish crowd props up the long bar at **WC** (✉ Skåneg. 51, ☎ 08/7022963), with ladies' drink specials on Sunday. Luckily, the only thing that'll remind you of the name (which stands for "water closet," or bathroom) are the holes in the middle of the bar stools.

Stockholm can also appease your need for pub-style intimacy. Guinness, ale, and cider enthusiasts rally in the tartan-clad **Bagpiper's Inn** (✉ Rörstrandsg. 21, ☎ 08/311855), where you can get a full range of bar food. **The Dubliner** (✉ Smålandsg. 8, ☎ 08/6797707), probably Stockholm's most popular Irish pub, serves up pub food and hosts live folk music on stage. It's not unusual to see people dancing on the tables. As green as a four-leaf clover, **Limerick** (✉ Tegnérg. 10, ☎ 08/6731902) is a popular Hibernian watering hole. The very British **Tudor Arms** (✉ Grevg. 31, ☎ 08/6602712) is just as popular as when it opened in 1969. Brits who are missing home cooking will be relieved when they see the menu. **Wirströms Pub** (✉ Stora Nyg. 13, ☎ 08/212874) shows its setting in labyrinthine, 17th-century cellars to advantage. Expect lots of smoke, live acoustic music, mostly anglophone patrons, and lots of beer. There are also 130 whiskeys available.

Cabaret

Börsen (⌧ Jakobsg. 6, ☎ 08/7878500) offers high-quality international cabaret shows. Tucked behind the Radisson SAS near Nybroplan is **Wallmans Salonger** (⌧ Teaterg. 3, ☎ 08/6116622), where singing and dancing waitstaff and talented stage performers entertain until midnight.

Casinos

Many hotels and bars have a roulette table and sometimes blackjack; games operate according to Swedish rules that are designed to limit the amount you can lose.

Dance Clubs

Café Opera (⌧ Operahuset, ☎ 08/6765807), at the waterfront end of Kungsträdgården, is a popular meeting place for young and old alike. It has the longest bar in town, fantastic 19th-century ceilings and details, plus dining and roulette, and major dancing after midnight. The kitchen offers a night menu until 2:30 AM. **Daily News Café** (⌧ Kungsträdgården, ☎ 08/215655), a glitzy nightclub near Sweden House, is returning to its 1980s popular glory. The crowd here varies depending on the night, with lots of late-night stragglers looking for fun before going home. Up near Cityterminalen, is **Heaven** (⌧ Kungsg. 65, ☎ 08/54516000), a popular nightclub in a great location. On Friday it's taken over by 18- and 19-year-olds—Saturday it's for 20-somethings. Södermalm's **Mälarsalen** (⌧ Torkel Knutssonsg. 2, ☎ 08/6581300) caters to the nondrinking jitterbug and fox-trot crowd. **Penny Lane** (⌧ Birger Jarlsg. 29, ☎ 08/201411) is a soft-disco nightclub specifically for a 30- and 40-something crowd.

Gay Bars

Patricia (⌧ Stadsgården, Berth 25, ☎ 08/7430570) is a floating restaurant, disco, and bar right next to Slussen. And don't worry, the boat doesn't rock enough to make you sick. All are welcome at **TipTop** (⌧ Sveav. 57, ☎ 08/329800) but most of the clientele is gay. Men and women dance nightly to '70s disco and modern techno. Hidden down behind the statue of Saint George and the dragon on Gamla Stan, **Mandus Bar och Kök** (⌧ Österlangg. 7, ☎ 08/206055) is a warm and friendly restaurant and bar perfect for drinking and talking late into the night.

Jazz Clubs

The best and most popular jazz venue is **Fasching** (⌧ Kungsg. 63, ☎ 08/216267), where international and local bands play year-round. The classic club **Nalens** (⌧ Regeringsg. 74, ☎ 08/4533434), which was popular back in the '50s and '60s, is back on the scene with major performances throughout the year. There are three different stages. **Stampen** (⌧ Stora Nyg. 5, ☎ 08/205793) is an overpriced, but atmospheric, club in Gamla Stan with traditional jazz nightly. Get there early for a seat.

Piano Bars

Piano bars are part of Stockholm's nightlife. The **Anglais Bar** at the Hotel Anglais (⌧ Humlegårdsg. 23, ☎ 08/6141600) is popular on weekends. Most people there are English-speaking international travelers staying at the hotel. The **Clipper Club** at the Hotel Reisen (⌧ Skeppsbron 1214, ☎ 08/223260) is a pleasant, dark-wood, dimly lit bar on Gamla Stan.

Rock Clubs

Pub Anchor (⌧ Sveav. 90, ☎ 08/152000), on Sveavägen's main drag, is the city's downtown hard-rock bar. **Krogen Tre Backar** (⌧ Tegnérg.

12–14, ☎ 08/6734400) is as popular among hard-rock fans as the Pub Anchor is. It's just off Sveavägen. International rock acts often play at **Klubben** (✉ Hammarby Frabriksv. 13, ☎ 08/4622200), a small bar and club in the Fryshuset community center south of town.

The Arts

Stockholm's theater and opera season runs from September through May. Both Dramaten and Operan shut down in the summer months. When it comes to popular music, big-name acts such as Neil Young, U2, and Eminem frequently come to Stockholm during the summer while on their European tours. Artists of this type play at Globen sports arena. For tickets to theaters and shows try **Biljettdirekt** (☎ 077/1707070) at Sweden House or any post office.

Classical Music

International orchestras perform at **Konserthuset** (✉ Hötorget 8, ☎ 08/102110), the main concert hall. The **Music at the Palace** series (☎ 08/102247) runs June through August. Off-season, there are weekly concerts by Sweden's Radio Symphony Orchestra at **Berwaldhallen** (Berwald Concert Hall; ✉ Strandv. 69, ☎ 08/7845000). After Konserthuset, the best place for classical music is at **Nybrokajen 11** (✉ Nybrokajen 11, ☎ 08/071700), where top international musicians perform in relatively small listening halls.

Dance

When it comes to high-quality, international dance in Stockholm, there's really only one place to go. **Dansenshus** (✉ Barnhusg. 12–14, ☎ 08/57890040), which celebrated its 10th anniversary in 2001, hosts the best Swedish and international acts, with shows ranging from traditional Japanese dance to street dance and modern ballet. You can also see ballet at the Royal Opera house.

Film

Stockholm has an abundance of cinemas, all listed in the Yellow Pages under *Biografer.* Current billings are listed in evening papers, normally with Swedish titles; call ahead if you're unsure. Foreign movies are subtitled, not dubbed. Most, if not all, cinemas take reservations over the phone: popular showings can sell out ahead of time. Cinemas are either part of the SF chain, or **SandrewMetronome**. Listings for each can be found on the wall at the theater or in the back of the culture pages of the daily newspapers. **Filmstaden Sergel** (✉ Hötorget, ☎ 08/56260000), is a 14-screen complex at one end of Hötorget. **Biopalatset** and **Filmstaden Söder** (✉ Medborgarplatsen, ☎ 08/6443100 or 08/56260000) are on the south side of town and have many films to choose from. If you are interested in smaller theaters with a bit more character, try the **Grand** (✉ Sveav. 45, ☎ 08/4112400), a nice little theater with two small screens and not a bad seat in the house. **Röda Kvarn** (✉ Biblioteksg. 5, ☎ 08/7896073) is a beautiful old movie theater right near Stureplan. **Zita** (✉ Birger Jarlsg. 37, ☎ 08/232020) is a one-screen theater that shows foreign films. A small restaurant is in the back.

Opera

It is said that Queen Lovisa Ulrika began introducing opera to her subjects in 1755. Since then, Sweden has become an opera center of standing, a launch pad for such names as Jenny Lind, Jussi Björling, and Birgit Nilsson. **Operan** (The Royal Opera House; ✉ Jakobs Torg 2, ☎ 08/248240), dating from 1898, is now the de facto home of Sweden's operatic tradition. **Folkoperan** (✉ Hornsg. 72, ☎ 08/6160750) is a modern company with its headquarters in Södermalm. Casting traditional presentation and interpretation of the classics to the wind, the company stages productions that are refreshingly new.

Theater

Kungliga Dramatiska Teatern (Royal Dramatic Theater, called Dramaten; ✉ Nybroplan, ☎ 08/6670680) sometimes stages productions of international interest, in Swedish, of course. The exquisite **Drottningholms Slottsteater** (Drottningholm Court Theater; ✉ Drottningholm, ☎ 08/6608225) presents opera, ballet, and orchestral music from May to early September; the original 18th-century stage machinery is still used in these productions. Drottningholm, the royal residence, is reached by subway and bus or by a special theater-bus (which leaves from the Grand Hotel or opposite the Central Train Station). Boat tours run here in summer.

OUTDOOR ACTIVITIES AND SPORTS

Stockholmers, and Swedes in general, love the outdoors and spend a great deal of time doing outdoor sports and activities. Because the city is spread out on a number of islands, one is almost always close to the water. The many large parks, including Djurgården and Haga Park, allow people to quickly escape the hustle and bustle of downtown.

The most popular summertime activities in Stockholm are golf, biking, rollerblading, tennis, and sailing. In the winter people like to ski and ice skate.

Beaches

The best bathing places in central Stockholm are on the island of Långholmen and at Rålambshov at the end of Norr Mälarstrand. Both are grassy or rocky lakeside hideaways. Topless sunbathing is virtually de rigueur.

Biking and Rollerblading

Stockholm is laced with bike paths, and bicycles can be taken on the commuter trains (except during peak traveling times) for excursions to the suburbs. The bike paths are also ideal for rollerblading. You can rent a bike for between SKr 150 and SKr 250 per day. Rollerblades cost between Skr 80 and SKr 120. Most places require a deposit of a couple thousand kronor. **Cykelfrämjandet** (✉ Thuleg. 43, 113 53, ☎ 08/54591030, WEB www.cykelframjandet.a.se), a local bicyclists' association, publishes an English-language guide to cycling trips. City and mountain bikes can be rented from **Cykel & Mopeduthyrning** (✉ Strandv. at Kajplats 24, ☎ 08/6607959), for SKr 170. Also try **Skepp & Hoj** (✉ Galärvarvsv. 2, ☎ 08/6605757), pronounced "ship ahoy," which has nice city cruisers for SKr 250 per day.

Boating

Boating in Stockholm's archipelago is an exquisite summertime activity. From May to September sailboats large and small and gorgeous restored wooden boats cruise from island to island. Both types of boats are available for rental. Walk along the water on Strandvägen, where many large power yachts and sailboats (available for charter) are docked. Sea kayaking has also become increasingly popular and is a delightful way to explore the islands.

Contact **Svenska Seglarförbundet** (Swedish Sailing Association; ✉ af Pontins väg 6, 115 21, ☎ 08/4590990, WEB www.ssf.se) for information on sailing, and the **Svenska Kanotförbundet** (Swedish Canoeing Association; ⊠ Idrotts Hus, 123 87 Farsta, ☎ 08/6056565, WEB www.svenskidrott.se/kanot) for more information on canoeing and kayaking. **Capella Skärgårdscatering** (⊠ Zirocco, Strandv. Kajplats 20, ☎ 08/7326850) has a large power yacht available for afternoon and overnight charters for groups of up to 40 people. At the end of Strandvägen, before the bridge to Djurgården, is **Tvillingarnas Båtuthyrning** (⊠ Djurgårdsbron, ☎ 08/6633739), which has large and small motorboats and small sailboats. **Point 65 N** (⊠ Styrmansg. 23), a short walk up from Strandvägen, has high-quality sea kayaks for rent. Its staff will help you get them down and back from the water if it's a two- or three-day rental.

Fitness Centers

Health and fitness is a Swedish obsession. The **Sports Club Stockholm** (City Sports Club; ⊠ Birger Jarlsg. 6C, ☎ 08/6798310; Atlanta Sports Club; ⊠ St. Eriksg. 34, ☎ 08/6506625) chain has women's and mixed gym facilities for SKr 90 a day. For a relatively inexpensive massage, try the **Axelsons Gymnastiska Institut** (⊠ Gästrikeg. 1012, ☎ 08/54545900). **Friskis & Svettis** (⊠ St. Eriksg. 54, ☎ 08/4297000) is a local chain of indoor and, in summer, outdoor gyms specializing in aerobics; branches are scattered throughout the Stockholm area. Monday through Thursday at 6 PM, from the end of May into late August, it hosts free aerobic sessions in Rålambshovs Park.

Golf

There are numerous golf courses around Stockholm. Greens fees run about SKr 450 to SKr 650, depending on the club. Contact **Sveriges Golfförbund** (⊠ Kevingestrand 20, Box 84, 182 11 Danderyd, ☎ 08/7315370, WEB sfg.golf.se), which is just outside Stockholm, for information. **Stockholms Golfklubb,** which has a midlevel 18-hole course, is located there as well. **Lidingö Golfklubb** (⊠ Kyttingev. 2, Lidingö, ☎ 08/7317900) has an 18-hole, forest-and-park course. It's about a 20-minute drive from the city center. **Ingarö Golfklubb** (⊠ Fogelvik, Ingarö, ☎ 08/57028244), which has two 18-hole courses—one midlevel, one difficult—is also about 20 minutes away.

Running

Numerous parks with footpaths dot the central city area, among them **Haga Park** (which also has canoe rentals), **Djurgården,** and the wooded **Liljans Skogen.** A very pleasant public path follows the waterfront across from Djurgården, going east from Djurgårdsbron past some of Stockholm's finest old mansions and the wide-open spaces of Ladugårdsgärdet, a park that's great for a picnic or flying a kite.

Skiing

The **Excursion Shop** (⊠ Sweden House, Kungsträdgården, Stockholm, ☎ 08/7892415) has information on skiing as well as other sport and leisure activities and will advise on necessary equipment.

Spectator Sports

The ultramodern, 281-ft **Globen** (⊠ Box 10055, 121 27, Globentorget 2, ☎ 08/7251000), the world's tallest spherical building, hosts such sports as ice hockey and equestrian events. It has its own subway station. Inside the same sports complex as Globen is **Söderstadion** (⊠ Box 10055, 121 27, Globentorget 2, ☎ 08/7251000), the open-air stadium where the Hammarby soccer team plays professional soccer. North of the city is **Råsunda Stadion** (✉ Box 1216, Solnav. 51, 171 23 Solna, ☎ 08/7350935), Stockholm's largest soccer stadium and host to the biggest games between the city's teams.

Swimming

In town center, **Centralbadet** (✉ Drottningg. 88, ☎ 08/242403) has an extra-large indoor pool, whirlpool, steam bath, and sauna. **Eriks-dalsbadet** (✉ Hammarby Slussv. 20, ☎ 08/50840250) underwent huge renovations in 2000 and is now the city's largest swimming complex. At Stureplan, the slightly exclusive **Sturebadet** (✉ Sturegallerian, ☎ 08/54501500) offers a swimming pool, aquatic aerobics, and a sauna.

Tennis

With stars such as Björn Borg and Stefan Edberg, it's impossible for tennis not to be huge in Stockholm. Contact **Svenska Tennisförbundet** (✉ Lidingöv. 75, Box 27915, 115 94 Stockholm, ☎ 08/6679770, FAX 08/6646606, WEB www.tennis.se) for information. Borg once played at **Kungliga Tennishallen** (Royal Tennis Hall; ✉ Lidingöv. 75, ☎ 08/4591500), which hosts the Stockholm Open every year. **Tennisstadion** (✉ Fiskartorpsv. 20, ☎ 08/215454) has well-maintained courts.

SHOPPING

If you like to shop 'til you drop, then charge on down to any one of the three main department stores in the central city area, all of which carry top name brands from Sweden and abroad for both men and women. For souvenirs and crafts, peruse the boutiques and galleries in Västerlånggatan, the main street of Gamla Stan. For jewelry, crafts and fine art, hit the shops that line the raised sidewalk at the start of Hornsgatan on Södermalm. Drottninggatan, Birger Jarlsgatan, Biblioteksgatan, Götgatan, and Hamngatan also offer some of the city's best shopping.

Department Stores and Malls

Sweden's leading department store is **NK** (✉ Hamng. 18–20, across the street from Kungsträdgården, ☎ 08/7628000); the initials, pronounced enn-*koh*, stand for *Nordiska Kompaniet*. You pay for the high quality here. **Åhléns City** (✉ Klarabergsg. 50, ☎ 08/6766000) has a selection similar to NK with slightly better prices. Before becoming a famous actress, Greta Garbo used to work at **PUB** (✉ Drottningg. 63 and Hötorget, ☎ 08/4021611), with 42 independent boutiques. Garbo fans will appreciate the small exhibit on level H2—an array of photographs begins with her employee ID card.

Gallerian (✉ Hamng. 37, ☎ 08/7877899), in the city center just down the road from Sergels Torg, is a large indoor mall closely resembling those found in the United States. Toys, shoes, music, a hardware store, designer clothes, and food are among the wares. **Sturegallerian** (✉ Grev Tureg. 9, ☎ 08/6114606), is a midsize department store on Stureplan that carries mostly exclusive clothes, bags, and accessories.

Markets

At **Hötorget** there's a lively outdoor market every day, where you can buy fresh fruit and vegetables at prices well below those at grocery stores. It's open from 9 to 6. For a good indoor market hit **Hötorgshallen** (✉ Hötorget), located directly under Filmstaden. The market is filled with butcher shops, coffee and tea shops, and fresh fish markets. It closes at 6 PM. If you're interested in high-quality Swedish food, try the classic European indoor market **Östermalms Saluhall** (⊠ Östermalmstorg).

The best areas for bric-a-brac and antiques are **Odengatan** and **Roslagsgatan**; take the subway to the Odenplan station.

Specialty Stores

Auction Houses

Perhaps the finest auction house in town is **Lilla Bukowski** (⊠ Strandv. 7, ☎ 08/6140800), in its elegant quarters on the waterfront. **Auktions Kompaniet** (⊠ Regeringsg. 47, ☎ 08/235700) is next to NK downtown. **Stockholms Auktionsverk** (⊠ Jakobsg. 10, ☎ 08/4536700) is under the Gallerian shopping center.

Books

Akademibokhandeln has a wide variety of books in English (⊠ Mäster Samuelsg. 32, ☎ 08/6136100, WEB www.akademibokhandeln.se).

If you don't find what you need at Akademibokhandeln, **Hedengrens** (⊠ Stureplan 4/Sturegallerian, ☎ 08/6115132) is also well stocked, especially with fiction and poetry. **Hemlins** (⊠ Västerlångg. 6, Gamla Stan, ☎ 08/106180) carries foreign titles and antique books.

Gifts

Swedish pottery, jewelry, kitchen items, wooden toys, linens, and cookbooks from all over the country are available at **Svensk Hemslöjd** (⊠ Sveav. 44, ☎ 08/232115). Though prices are high at **Svenskt Hantwerk** (⊠ Kungsg. 55, ☎ 08/214726), so is the quality of gift items and souvenirs.

Glass

Kosta Boda and Orrefors produce the most popular and well-regarded lines of glassware. The **Crystal Art Center** (⊠ Tegelbacken 4, ☎ 08/217169), near central station, has a great selection of smaller glass items. **Duka** (⊠ Sveav. 24–26, ☎ 08/104530) specializes in crystal and porcelain at reasonable prices. **NK** carries a wide, representative line of Swedish glasswork in its Swedish Shop downstairs. **Nordiska Kristall** (⊠ Kungsg. 9, ☎ 08/104372), near Sturegallerian, has a small gallery of one-of-a-kind art-glass sculptures as well as plates, vases, glasses, bowls, ashtrays, and decanters. **Svenskt Glas** (⊠ Birger Jarlsg. 8, ☎ 08/6797909), near the Royal Dramatic Theater, carries a decent selection of quality Swedish glass, including bowls from Orrefors.

Interior Design

Sweden is recognized globally for its unique design sense and has contributed significantly to Scandinavian design in general. All of this makes Stockholm one of the best cities in the world for shopping for furniture and home and office accessories.

On the corner of Östermalmstorg, in the same building as the marketplace, is **Bruka** (⊠ Humlegårdsg. 1, ☎ 08/6601480), which has a wide selection of creative kitchen items as well as wicker baskets and chairs. In Söder **CBI/Klara** (⊠ Nytorgsg. 36, ☎ 08/6949240) sells furniture, kitchen items, and other funky things for the home—all made by Swedish and international designers. **David Design** (⊠ Nybrog. 7, ☎ 08/6119855), which opened in 2001, sells fine furniture, rugs, mirrors, and decorative items for the house. **DIS** (⊠ Humlegårdsg. 19, ☎ 08/6112907) sells heavy, dark-wood furniture that has an Asian flair. The rugs and pillowcases are also stunning.

For high-minded, trendy furniture that blends dark woods, stainless steel, and colorfully dyed wools, head to **House** (⊠ Humlegårdsg. 14, ☎ 08/6611100). There's also a nice assortment of vases and glassware. If you're after the *best* of Scandinavian design (and the most expensive), try **Nordiska Galleriet** (⊠ Nybrog. 11, ☎ 08/4428360). It has everything from couches and chairs to tables and vases. Slightly out of the way in the Fridhemsplan neighborhood in western Stockholm, **R.O.O.M.** (⊠ Alströmerg. 20, ☎ 08/6925000) has an impressive assortment of Swedish and international tables, chairs, rugs, pillows, beds—the list goes on. It also has a great book selection, lots of nice ceramic bowls and plates, and many decorations and utensils for the kitchen and bathroom. For elegant home furnishings, affluent Stockholmers tend to favor **Svenskt Tenn** (⊠ Strandv. 5A, ☎ 08/6701600), best known for its selection of designer Josef Franck's furniture and fabrics.

Men's Clothing

Swedish designer Claes Bondelid makes rugged, stylish clothes for men, which he sells at **Bondelid** (⊠ Götg. 40, ☎ 08/4620068). His sweaters and jackets are especially nice. **Brothers** (⊠ Drottningg. 53, ☎ 08/4111201) sells relatively inexpensive Swedish clothes that are often inspired by the more expensive international brands. For suits and evening suits for both sale and rental, **Hans Allde** (⊠ Birger Jarlsg. 58, ☎ 08/207191) provides good, old-fashioned service. For the latest line of fine men's clothing, go to the **Hugo Boss Shop** (⊠ Birger Jarlsg. 6, ☎ 08/6110750). **J. Lindeberg** (⊠ Grev Tureg. 9, ☎ 08/6786165) has brightly colored clothes in many styles. The golf line has been made famous by Swedish golfer Jesper Parnevik. A great spot for trendy Swedish designs is **Mr. Walker** (⊠ Regeringsg. 42, ☎ 08/7966096). The threads here are fabulous, but be prepared to part with some serious crowns—it's hard to walk out empty-handed. Top men's fashions can be found on the second floor of **NK** (⊠ Hamng. 18–20, ☎ 08/7628000), which stocks everything from outdoor gear and evening wear to swimsuits and work-out clothes. The Swedish label **Tiger** (☎ 08/7628772), with a section inside NK, sells fine suits, shoes, and casual wear.

Paper Products

For unique Swedish stationery and office supplies in fun colors and styles, go to **Ordning & Reda** (⊠ NK, Hamng. 18–20, ☎ 08/7628462).

Women's Clothing

Swedish designer **Anna Holtblad** (⊠ Grev Tureg. 13, ☎ 08/54502220) sells her elegant designs at her own boutique. She specializes in knitted clothes. **Champaigne** (⊠ Biblioteksg. 2, ☎ 08/6118803) has European and Swedish designs that are often discounted. **Flippa K** (⊠ Grev Tureg. 18, ☎ 08/54588888) has quickly become one of Sweden's hottest designers. Her stores are filled with young women grabbing the latest fashions. The clothes at **Indiska** (⊠ Drottningg. 53 and elsewhere, ☎ 08/109193) are inspired by the bright colors of India. **Kookai** (⊠ Biblioteksg. 5, ☎ 08/6119730) carries trendy, colorful European designs for young women. For lingerie and fashionable clothing at a decent price go to **Twilfit** (⊠ Nybrog. 11, ☎ 08/6637505; ⊠ Sturegallerian 16, ☎ 08/6110455; ⊠ Gamla Brog. 3638, ☎ 08/201954). **Hennes & Mauritz** (H & M; ⊠ Hamng. 22; Drottningg. 53 and 56; Sergelg. 1 and 22; and Sergels Torg 12, all ☎ 08/7965500) is one of the few Swedish-owned clothing stores to have achieved international success. Here you can find updated designs at great prices. **Polarn & Pyret** (⊠ Hamng. 10, Gallerian, Drottningg. 29, ☎ 08/6709500) carries high-quality Swedish children's and women's clothing. For the modern rebel look, go to **Replay** (⌂ Kungsg. 6, ☎ 08/231416), where the collection covers everything from jeans to underwear. One department store with almost every style and type of clothing and apparel is **NK** (⌂ Hamng. 18–20, ☎ 08/7628000).

STOCKHOLM A TO Z

To research prices, get advice from other travelers, and book travel arrangements, visit www.fodors.com.

AIRPORTS AND TRANSFERS

Initially opened in 1960 solely for international flights, Stockholm's Arlanda International Airport now also contains a domestic terminal. The airport is 42 km (26 mi) from the city center; a freeway links them. The airport is run by Luftfartsverket, a state-owned company.

➤ AIRPORT INFORMATION: **Arlanda International Airport** (☎ 08/7976000, FAX 08/7978600, WEB www.arlanda.lfv.se).

AIRPORT TRANSFERS

Travel between Arlanda International Airport and Stockholm has been greatly improved with the completion of the Arlanda Express, a high-speed train service. The yellow-nose train leaves every 15 minutes, travels at a speed of 200 kph (125 mph), and completes the trip from the airport to Stockholm's central station in just 20 minutes; single tickets cost SKr 140.

Flygbussarna, "flight buses," leave both the international and domestic terminals every 10 to 15 minutes from 6:30 AM to 11 PM and make a number of stops on the way to their final destination at the Cityterminalen at Klarabergsviadukten, next to the central railway station. The trip costs SKr 70 and takes about 35 minutes.

A bus-taxi combination package is available. The bus lets you off by the taxi stand at Haga Forum, Jarva Krog, or Cityterminalen and you present your receipt to the taxi driver, who takes you to your final destination. A trip will cost between SKr 160 and SKr 220, depending on your destination.

For taxis, be sure to ask about a *fast pris* (fixed price) between Arlanda and the city. It should be between SKr 350 and SKr 435, depending on final destination. The best bets for cabs are Taxi Stockholm, Taxi 020, and Taxikurir. All major taxi companies accept credit cards. Watch out for unregistered cabs, which charge high rates and won't provide the same service.

➤ TAXIS AND SHUTTLES: **Arlanda Express** (☎ 020/222224, WEB www.arlandaexpress.com). **Flygbussarna** (☎ 08/6001000, WEB www.flygbussarna.com). **Taxi 020** (☎ 020/939393). **Taxikurir** (☎ 08/300000). **Taxi Stockholm** (☎ 08/150000).

BIKE TRAVEL

One of the best ways to explore Stockholm is by bike. There are bike paths and special bike lanes throughout the city, making it safe and enjoyable. Bike rentals will be about SKr 90 per day. One of the best places to ride is on Djurgården. Cykel & Mopeduthyrning and Skepp & Hoj both service that area.

➤ BIKE INFORMATION: **Cyke & Mopeduthyrning** (Bike and Moped Rentals; ⌂ Standv. kajplats 24, ☎ 08/6607959). **Skepp & Hoj, Djurgårdsbron** (bike rentals; ⌂ Galärvarvsv. 2, ☎ 08/6605757).

BOAT AND FERRY TRAVEL

Waxholmsbolaget (Waxholm Ferries), offers the *Båtluffarkortet* (Inter-Skerries Card), a discount pass for its extensive commuter network of archipelago boats; the price is SKr 250 for 16 days of unlimited travel. The Strömma Kanalbolaget operates a fleet of archipelago boats that provide excellent sightseeing tours and excursions.

➤ BOAT AND FERRY INFORMATION: **Strömma Kanalbolaget** (☎ 08/58714000). **Waxholmsbolaget** (☎ 08/6795830).

BUS TRAVEL TO AND FROM STOCKHOLM

All the major bus and coach services, including Flygbussarna, Swebus Express, Svenska Buss, and Interbus, arrive at Cityterminalen (City Terminal), next to the central railway station. Reservations to destinations all over Sweden can be made by calling Swebus.

➤ BUS INFORMATION: **Cityterminalen** (✉ Karabergsviadukten 72, ☎ 08/7005140). **Interbus** (☎ 08/7279000, WEB www.interbus.se). **Swebus Express** (☎ 0200/218218, WEB www.express.swebus.se). **Svenska Buss** (☎ 020/676767, WEB www.svenskabuss.se).

BUS TRAVEL WITHIN STOCKHOLM

Late-night bus service connects certain stations when trains stop running. The comprehensive bus network serves out-of-town points of interest, such as Waxholm and Gustavsberg.

CAR RENTAL

Rental cars are readily available in Sweden and are relatively inexpensive. Because of the availability and efficiency of public transport, there is little point in using a car within the city limits. If you are traveling elsewhere in Sweden, you'll find that roads are uncongested and well marked but that gasoline is expensive (about SKr 10 per liter/or SKr 40 per gallon). All major car-rental firms are represented, including Avis, Budget, Hertz, and National. Statoil gas stations also rent out cars, as do local Swedish companies such as Berras and Auto, which can sometimes have better prices than the major companies.

➤ MAJOR AGENCIES: **Auto** (✉ Östgötg. 75, ☎ 08/6428040). **Avis** (✉ Ringv. 90, ☎ 08/6449980). **Berras** (✉ Skepparg. 74, ☎ 08/6611919). **Budget** (✉ Klarabergsviadukten 92, ☎ 020/787787). **Hertz** (✉ Vasag. 26, ☎ 08/240720). **National** (✉ Klarabergsg. 33, ☎ 08/242655). **Statoil** (☎ 020/252525 throughout Sweden; ✉ Vasag. 16, ☎ 08/202064; ✉ Birger Jarlsg. 68, ☎ 08/211593).

CAR TRAVEL

Approach the city by either the E20 or E18 highway from the west, or the E4 from the north or south. The roads are clearly marked and well sanded and plowed during winter. Signs for downtown read CENTRUM.

Driving in Stockholm is often deliberately frustrated by city planners, who impose many restrictions to keep traffic down. Keep an eye out for bus lanes marked with "Buss" on the pavement. Driving in that lane can result in a ticket. Get a good city map, called a Trafikkarta, available at most service stations for around SKr 75.

EMBASSIES

➤ AUSTRALIA: (✉ Sergels Torg 12, ☎ 08/6132900).
➤ CANADA: (✉ Tegelbacken 4, ☎ 08/4533000).
➤ NEW ZEALAND: Consulate-General (✉ Nybrog. 34, ☎ 08/6600460).
➤ UNITED KINGDOM: (✉ Skarpög. 68, ☎ 08/6713000).
➤ UNITED STATES: (✉ Strandv. 101, ☎ 08/7835300).

EMERGENCIES

Dial 112 for emergencies—this covers police, fire, ambulance, and medical help, as well as sea and air rescue services. Private care is available via CityAkuten. Hospitals are called *sjukhus,* literally "sick house," in Swedish, and regular doctors' offices are called *Läkerhuset.* Dentists are listed under under *tandläkare,* or *tandvård.* There is a 24-hour national health service via the emergency number listed below.

➤ DOCTORS AND DENTISTS: **Folktandvården** (national dental service; ☎ 020/6875500). **Läkerhuset Hörtorgscity** (☒ Sveav. 13–15, ☎ 08/243800). **Läkerhuset Riddargatan 12** (☒ Riddarg. 12, ☎ 08/6797900).

➤ EMERGENCY SERVICES: **CityAkuten** (Emergency Medical Care; ☒ Apelbergsg. 48, ☎ 08/4122961). **CityAkuten Tandvården** (Emergency Dental Care; ☒ Olof Palmesg. 13A, ☎ 08/4122900).

➤ HOSPITALS: **Ersta Sjukhus** (☒ Fällg. 44, ☎ 08/7146100). **Karolinska Sjukhuset** (☒ Solna [just north of Stockholm], ☎ 08/51770000). **Södersjukhuset** (☒ Ringv. 52, ☎ 08/6161000). **St. Görans Sjukhus** (☒ Sankt Göransplan 1, ☎ 08/58701000).

➤ POLICE: **Polisen** (Stockholm Police Headquarters; ☒ Norra Agneg. 33-37, ☎ 08/4010000).

➤ 24-HOUR PHARMACIES: **C. W. Scheele** (☒ Klarabergsg. 64, ☎ 08/4548130).

ENGLISH-LANGUAGE MEDIA

BOOKS

Many bookshops stock English-language books. Akademibokhandeln has a wide selection of English books, with an emphasis on reference titles. Hedengren's has the best and most extensive selection of English- and other foreign-language books, from fiction to nonfiction, photography to architecture. NK has a large bookstore with an extensive English-language section.

➤ BOOKSTORES: **Akademibokhandeln** (☒ Mäster Samuelsg. 32, near the city center, ☎ 08/6136100). **Hedengrens** (☒ Stureplan 4, Sturegallerian shopping complex, ☎ 08/6115132). **NK** (☒ Hamng. 18–20, ☎ 08/7628000).

RADIO

There are two major radio stations with English-language programming in Stockholm. Radio Sweden, part of the state-owned radio company, has news about Sweden in English, daily and weekly English programs, as well as many shows from National Public Radio in the United States, and the BBC in England. You can pick up Radio Sweden at 89.6 FM.

SUBWAY TRAVEL

The subway system, known as T-banan (*Tunnelbanan,* with stations marked by a blue-on-white T), is the easiest and fastest way to get around. Servicing more than 100 stations and covering more than 96 km (60 mi) of track, trains run frequently between 5 AM and 3 AM.

TAXIS

Stockholm's taxi service is efficient but overpriced. If you call a cab, ask the dispatcher to quote you a *fast pris* (fixed price), which is usually lower than the meter fare. Reputable cab companies are Taxi 020, Taxi Stockholm, and Taxikurir. Taxi Stockholm has an immediate charge of SKr 25 whether you hail a cab or order one by telephone. A trip of 10 km (6 mi) should cost about SKr 97 between 6 AM and 7 PM, SKr 107 at night, and SKr 114 on weekends.

➤ TAXI COMPANIES: **Taxi 020** (☎ 020/939393). **Taxikurir** (☎ 08/300000). **Taxi Stockholm** (☎ 08/150000).

TOURS

BOAT TOURS

Strömma Kanalbolaget runs a variety of sightseeing tours of Stockholm. Boats leave from the quays outside the Royal Dramatic Theater, Grand Hotel, and City Hall. Stockholm Sightseeing, which leaves from Skeppsbron in front of the Grand, has four different tours, including an "Under the Bridges" tour and a "Historical Canal" tour. Trips range from one to four hours and cost from SKr 90 to SKr 260.

➤ FEES AND SCHEDULES: **City Hall** (late May–early Sept., ⊠ Hantverkarg. 1, ☎ 08/5082900). **Stockholm Sightseeing** (⊠ Skeppsbron 22, ☎ 08/57814020, WEB www.stockholmsightseeing.com). **Strömma Kanalbolaget** (⊠ Skeppsbron 22, ☎ 08/58714000).

BUS TOURS

Open Top Tours offers a bus tour in eight different languages, using individual headphones. The tour, which covers all the main points of interest, leaves each day at 9:20 AM from the tourist center at Sweden House. More comprehensive tours, taking in museums, Gamla Stan, and City Hall, are available through City Sightseeing.

➤ FEES AND SCHEDULES: **City Sightseeing** (⊠ Skeppsbron 11, ☎ 08/58714030 or 08/4117023, WEB www.citysightseeing.com). **Open Top Tours** (⊠ Hamng. 27, ☎ 08/6860612). **Sweden House** (⊠ Hamng. 27, Box 7542, 103 93 Stockholm, ☎ 08/7892490).

PRIVATE GUIDES

You can hire your own guide from Stockholm Information Service's Guide Centralen. In summer, be sure to book guides well in advance.

➤ CONTACTS: **Guide Centralen** (⊠ Sweden House, Hamng. 27, Box 7542, ☎ 08/7892490, FAX 08/7892491).

WALKING TOURS

City Sightseeing runs several tours, including the "Romantic Stockholm" tour of the cathedral and City Hall; the "Royal Stockholm" tour, which features visits to the Royal Palace and the Treasury; and the "Old Town Walkabout," which strolls through Gamla Stan in just over one hour.

➤ FEES AND SCHEDULES: **City Sightseeing** (☎ 08/4117023).

TRAIN TRAVEL

Both long-distance and commuter trains arrive at Stockholm central station on Vasagatan, a main boulevard in the heart of the city. For train information and ticket reservations 6 AM–11 PM, call the SJ number below. There is a ticket and information office at the station where you can make reservations. Automated ticket-vending machines are also available.

➤ TRAIN INFORMATION: **Central Station** (⊠ Vasag., ☎ 08/7622000). **Citypendeln** (Commuter Train; ☎ 08/6001000, WEB www.citypendeln.se). **SJ** (State Railway Company; ⊠ central station, ☎ 020/757575, WEB www.sj.se).

TRANSPORTATION AROUND STOCKHOLM

The cheapest way to travel around the city by public transport is to purchase the Stockholmskortet (Stockholm Card). In addition to unlimited transportation on city subway, bus, and rail services, it offers free admission to more than 60 museums and several sightseeing trips. The card costs SKr 220 for 24 hours, SKr 380 for two days, and SKr 540 for three days; you can purchase the card from the tourist center at Sweden House on Hamngatan, from the Hotellcentralen accommodations bureau at central station, and from the tourist center at Kaknäs Tower.

Stockholm has an excellent bus system, which is operated by SL, the state train company. In 2000, the subway system was bought from SL by Connex, the same company that runs the subways in Paris and London. Tickets for subways and buses are interchangeable. Maps and timetables for all city transportation networks are available from the SL information desks at Sergels Torg, central station, Slussen, and online.

Bus and subway fares are based on zones. All trips in downtown will be SKr 16. As you travel farther out of downtown, zones are added to the fare in increments of SKr 8. Each ticket is good for one hour on both buses and the subway. Single tickets are available at station ticket counters and on buses, but it's cheaper to buy an SL Tourist Card from one of the many Pressbyrån newsstands. There's also a pass called a Rabattkupong, valid for both subway and buses, that costs SKr 110 and is good for 10 trips downtown (fewer if you travel in more zones) within the greater Stockholm area during an unlimited period of time. If you plan to travel within the greater Stockholm area extensively during a 24-hour period, you can purchase a 24-hour pass for SKr 70; a 72-hour pass costs SKr 135. The 24-hour pass includes transportation on the ferries between Djurgården, Nybroplan, and Slussen. The 72-hour pass also entitles the holder to admission to Skansen, Gröna Lund Tivoli, and Kaknäs Tower. People under 18 or over 65 pay SKr 36 for a one-day pass and SKr 72 for a two-day pass.

➤ CONTACTS: **Connex** (☎ 08/60010000, WEB www.connex.nu). **SL** (☎ 08/6001000, WEB www.sl.se).

TRAVEL AGENCIES

For a complete listing of travel agencies, see the Yellow Pages under *Resor-Resebyråer,* or contact American Express. For air travel, contact SAS. SJ, the state railway company, has its main ticket office at central station.

➤ LOCAL AGENT REFERRALS: **American Express** (✉ Birger Jarlsg. 1, ☎ 08/6795200; 020/793211 toll free). **SAS** (✉ Klarabergsviadukten 72, accessible from central station, ☎ 020/727000). **SJ** (Statens Järnvägar; ✉ Vasag. 1, ☎ 020/757575).

VISITOR INFORMATION

➤ TOURIST INFORMATION: **City Hall** (June–Aug., ✉ Hantverkarg. 1, ☎ 08/5082900). **Fjäderholmarna** (☎ 08/7180100). **Kaknästornet** (Kaknäs TV Tower, ✉ Ladugårds-gärdet, ☎ 08/7892435). **Stockholm Central Station** (✉ Vasag., ☎ 020/757575). **Stockholm Information Service** (Sweden House, ✉ Hamng. 27, Box 7542, 103 93 Stockholm, ☎ 08/7892490). **Swedish Travel and Tourism Council** (✉ Box 3030, Kungsg. 36, 103 61 Stockholm, ☎ 08/7255500, FAX 08/7255531).

3 SIDE TRIPS FROM STOCKHOLM

S URROUNDING STOCKHOLM is a latticework of small, historic islands, most of them crowned with castles straight out of a storybook world. Set aside a day for a trip to any of these; half the
pleasure of an island outing is the leisurely boat trip to get there. (Note
that the castles can all be reached by alternative overland routes, if you
prefer the bus or train.) Farther afield is the island of Gotland, whose
medieval festival, Viking remains, and wilderness preserves will take
you back in time. The university town of Uppsala is another popular
day-trip destination; its quiet atmosphere and Gothic cathedral provide an edifying contrast to Stockholm's more energetic character.

Drottningholm

38 *1 km (½ mi) west of Stockholm.*

★ Occupying an island in Mälaren (Sweden's third-largest lake) some 45
minutes from Stockholm's center, **Drottningholms Slott** (Queen's Island
Castle) is a miniature Versailles dating from the 17th century. The royal
family once used this property only as a summer residence, but, tiring of
the Royal Palace back in town, they moved permanently to one wing of
Drottningholm in the 1980s. Designed and built by the same father-and-
son team of architects that built Stockholm's Royal Palace, the castle began
to be constructed in 1662 on the orders of King Karl X's widow, Eleonora.
Today it remains one of the most delightful of European palaces, reflecting
the sense of style practiced by mid-18th-century royalty. The interiors,
dating from the 17th, 18th, and 19th centuries, are a rococo riot of decoration with much gilding and trompe l'oeil. Most sections are open to
the public. ⊠ *Drottningholm,* ☎ *08/4026280.* ⌧ *SKr 50.* ⊗ *May–
Aug., daily 10–4:30; Sept., daily noon–3:30; guided tours in summer only.*

The lakeside gardens of Drottningholms Slott are its most beautiful asset,
containing **Drottningholms Slottsteater,** the only complete theater to survive from the 18th century anywhere in the world. Built by Queen Lovisa Ulrika in 1766 as a wedding present for her son Gustav III, the
Court Theater fell into disuse after his assassination at a masked ball
in 1792 (dramatized in Verdi's opera *Un Ballo in Maschera*). In 1922,
the theater was rediscovered; there is now a small theater museum here
as well, where you can sign up for a backstage tour and see the original backdrops and stage machinery and some amazing 18th-century
tools used to produce such special effects as wind and thunder. To get
performance tickets, book well in advance at the box office; the season runs from late May to early September. A word of caution: the seats
are extremely hard—take a cushion. ⊠ *Drottningholm,* ☎ *08/7590406,
08/6608225 box office.* ⌧ *SKr 50.* ⊗ *May–Aug., daily noon–4:30; Sept.,
daily 1–3:30. Guided tours in English at 12:30, 1:30, 2:30, 3:30, and
4:30. Closed for 10 days at beginning of July.*

Arriving and Departing

Boats bound for Drottningholms Slott leave from Klara Mälarstrand,
a quay close to Stadshuset (City Hall). Call **Strömma Kanalbolaget** (☎
08/58714000) for schedules and fares. Alternatively you can take the
T-bana (subway) to Brommaplan, and buses 177, 301–23, or 33
from there. Call **Stockholms Lokal Trafik** (☎ 08/6001000) for details.

Mariefred

39 *63 km (39 mi) southwest of Stockholm.*

The most delightful way to experience the true vastness of Mälaren
the trip to Mariefred—an idyllic little town of mostly timber houses–

Side Trips from Stockholm

aboard the coal-fired steamer of the same name, built in 1903 and still going strong. The town's winding, narrow streets, pretty, ancient squares, and wooded lakeside paths are all perfect for walking. The **Mariefred Tourist Office** has maps and information about tours.

Mariefred's principal attraction is **Gripsholm Slott.** Built in the 1530s by Bo Johansson Grip, the Swedish high chancellor, the castle contains fine Renaissance interiors, a superbly atmospheric theater commissioned in 1781 by the ill-fated Gustav III, and Sweden's royal portrait collection. ☎ *0159/10194.* 🎟 *SKr 50.* 🕐 *May–Aug., daily 10–4; Sept., Tues.–Sun. 10–3; Oct.–Apr., weekends noon–3; guided tours only.*

An old converted barn across from Gripsholm Slott houses **Grafikens Hus** (Graphic House), a center for contemporary graphic art. Visitors can see various exhibitions or take part in workshops covering all aspects of graphic art. There is also a good coffee shop and a gift shop that sells artwork. ✉ *Mariefred, 647 21,* ☎ *0159/23160.* 🎟 *SKr 50.* 🕐 *May–Aug., daily 11–5; Sept.–Apr., Tues. 11–8, Wed.–Sun. 11–5.*

The **S.S. Mariefred** departs from Klara Mälarstrand, near Stadshuset, Stockholm's City Hall. The journey takes 3½ hours each way, and there is a restaurant on board. ☎ *08/6698850.* 🎟 *SKr 170 round-trip.* 🕐 *Departures at 10 AM: May, weekends only; mid-June–late Aug., Tues.–Sun. Return trip departs from Mariefred at 4:30.*

You can also travel by narrow-gauge steam railway from Mariefred to a junction on the main line to Stockholm, returning to the capital by ordinary train. Contact the **Mariefred Tourist Office** for details.

Dining and Lodging

$$ ✕🏠 **Gripsholms Värdshus & Hotel.** At the oldest inn in Sweden (and the only one in Mariefred), guests get a sense of the real Sweden. Lovingly restored and luxuriously appointed, this yellow wood hotel stands on the site of an old monastery. Rooms are large and airy, with wooden floors and highlights of bright yellow and sky blue. The whole hotel is full of delightful art and artifacts, including some wonderful old Swedish tile fireplaces. The restaurant ($$) serves elegant food in a wood-paneled dining room. Local produce is used in such dishes as lightly salted North Sea cod with mussels and glazed fillet of veal with sweetbreads. ⊠ *Kykog. 1, 647 23,* ☎ *0159/34750,* ⅎ˟ *0159/34777. 45 rooms, 44 with bath, 10 suites. Restaurant, bar, no-smoking rooms, sauna. AE, DC, MC, V. BP.*

Visitor Information

The **Mariefred Tourist Office** (☎ 0159/29790) is open only in the summer; the rest of the year, call **Mälarturism** (☎ 0152/29690) for information for all of Lake Mälaren.

Sigtuna

40 *48 km (30 mi) northwest of Stockholm.*

An idyllic town situated on a northern arm of Lake Mälaren, Sigtuna was the principal trading post of the Svea, the tribe that settled Sweden after the last Ice Age; its Viking history is still apparent in the many runic stones preserved all over town. Founded in 980, Sigtuna is Sweden's oldest town and as such it's not surprising that it has Sweden's oldest street, Stora Gatan. After it was ransacked by Estonian pirates, its merchants went on to found Stockholm sometime in the 13th century. Little remains of Sigtuna's former glory, beyond parts of the principal church. The town hall dates from the 18th century, and the main part of town dates from the early 1800s. There are two houses said to date from the 15th century.

About 20 km (12 mi) northeast of Sigtuna and accessible by the same ferryboat is **Skokloster Slott,** an exquisite Baroque castle. Commissioned in 1654 by a celebrated Swedish soldier, Field Marshal Carl Gustav Wrangel, the castle is furnished with the spoils of Wrangel's successful campaigns. ⊠ *Bålsta,* ☎ *018/386077.* ⅎ *SKr 60.* ☉ *Daily noon–6.*

Dining and Lodging

$$ ✕⍟ **Sigtuna Stadshotell.** Near the lake shore, this beautifully restored hotel was built in 1909 and soon after became a central gathering place among locals—despite the fact that at the time it was considered one of the ugliest buildings in all of Sigtuna. In its early days the hotel had Sigtuna's first cinema, and in the cellar the state liquor store operated an inn. Today's hotel rooms have hardwood floors, high ceilings, and interesting little nooks and angles. The restaurant ($–$$) offers a great view of the water and is elegantly decorated. The traditional Swedish menu emphasizes herring dishes. Bread and ice cream are both made on the premises. ⊠ *Stora Nyg. 3, 193 22,* ☎ *08/59250100,* ⅎ˟ *08/ 59251587. 24 rooms. Restaurant, no-smoking rooms, meeting rooms. AE, DC, MC, V. BP.*

Arriving and Departing

From June to mid-August Sigtuna can be reached by boat from the quay near Stockholm's City Hall (Strömma Kanalbolaget, ☎ 08/58714000) round-trip fare is SKr 140. Another option is to take a commuter train from Stockholm's central station to Märsta, where you change to Bus 570 or 575.

Vaxholm and the Archipelago

㊹ *32 km (20 mi) northeast of Stockholm.*

Skärgården (the archipelago) is Stockholm's greatest natural asset: more than 25,000 islands and skerries, many uninhabited, spread across an almost tideless sea of clean, clear water. The islands closer to Stockholm are larger and more lush, with pine tree–covered rock faces and forests. There are also more year-round residents on these islands. But as you move away from the mainland, the islands become smaller and more remote as you encounter rugged, rocky islets. To sail lazily among these islands aboard an old steamboat on a summer's night is a timeless delight, and all throughout the warmer months Swedes flee the chaos of the city for quiet weekends on the waters.

For the tourist with limited time, one of the simplest ways to get a taste of the archipelago is the one-hour ferry trip to Vaxholm, an extremely pleasant, though sometimes crowded, mainland seaside town of small, red-painted wooden houses. Guarding what was formerly the main sea route into Stockholm, Vaxholm's fortress now houses the small **Vaxholms Fästnings Museum** (Vaxholm Fortress Museum), which documents the defense of Stockholm over the centuries. The museum contains military memorabilia and tells how the imposing stone castle helped defend against the Danes and Russians in the 17th and 18th centuries. You can reach the fortress by taking a small boat from the town landing, in front of the tourist office; a discounted combination ticket includes the boat fare and entrance to the museum. ☎ *08/54172157.* ⊠ *SKr 30.* ⊙ *Mid-May–Aug., daily noon–4. Group admission at other times by appointment.*

An even quicker trip into the archipelago is the 20-minute ferry ride to **Fjäderholmarna** (the Feather Islands), a group of four secluded islands. In the 19th-century the islands were the last chance for a refreshment stop for archipelago residents rowing into Stockholm to sell their produce. After 50 years as a military zone, the islands were opened to the public in the early 1980s. Today they are crammed with arts-and-crafts studios, shops, an aquarium, a small petting farm, a boat museum, a large cafeteria, an ingenious "shipwreck" playground, and even a smoked-fish shop.

Although it's situated on the mainland, **Saltsjöbaden** is far enough out into the wilds to be considered the archipelago. Construction of the seaside town started in 1891. Designed from the beginning to be a community for the affluent, Saltsjöbaden was based partly on the suburban communities springing up at the same time in the United States. By 1893, the railway had been extended to Saltsjöbaden and the town was one of the first in Sweden to have electric street lights. Today, the town has within it some of the grand architecture of the 19th century, having been built by some of Europe's leading contemporary architects. The best way to reach the town is by train. SJ runs a regular service from central Stockholm.

If you are interested in a longer voyage out into the islands, there are several possibilities. Contact the Sweden House and ask for the "Destination Stockholm Archipelago" catalog, which lists more than 350 holiday homes for rent. For accommodations bookings, contact **Hotellcentralen** (☎ 08/7892425). The representatives at the Sweden House can also help you plan a customized trip.

One of the most popular excursions is to **Sandhamn,** the main town on the island of Sandön—south of Stockholm and home to about 100 permanent residents. The journey takes about three hours by steamship, but there are faster boats available. This is a sailing paradise; the Royal Swedish Yacht Club was founded here 100 years ago. Its fine-sand beaches make it an ideal spot for swimming. You can also give scuba diving a try—introductory lessons are available; ask at the Sweden House for details. Explore the village of Sandhamn and its narrow alleys and wooden houses, or stroll out to the graveyard outside the village where tombstones bear the names of sailors from around the world.

Another popular island is **Utö**, which contains Sweden's oldest iron mine (ca. AD 1100–1200). A number of the miners' homes from the 18th century have been restored. About 200 people live year-round on the island, which has a number of cafés, camping sites, and swimming spots. You can also rent bicycles from a shop near the ferry landing. The boat trip to the island takes about three hours. Utö is particularly known for its bread. *Utö limpa,* a slightly sweetened and spiced sandwich bread, is to be found only on the island and is considered a high delicacy. Many of the thousands of people who go sailing in the archipelago every year make a special detour to stock up on the bread, partly because of its exquisite taste and partly because of its long-keeping properties.

A little bit closer to Stockholm is the island of **Grinda,** long a popular recreation spot among Stockholmers. Rental cabins from the '40s have been restored to their original condition; there are about 30 of these available through **Din Skärgård** (☎ 08/54249072). The **Grinda Wärdshus** (☎ 08/54249491), a still-functioning inn from the turn of the 20th century, is one of the largest stone buildings in the archipelago. Since a number of walking paths cut through the woods and open fields, it takes just 15 minutes to walk from one end of Grinda to the other, and exploring is easy. The trip to the island takes about two hours.

At the far southern tip of Stockholm's archipelago lies **Trosa,** a town full of wooden houses that's right on the Baltic Sea. The tiny river that runs through the middle of the town is flanked by beautiful villas painted white, red, yellow, and mint-green—a reflection of Trosa's heritage as a seaside retreat for stressed, wealthy Stockholmers. Around the small, cobbled town square is an array of small arts and crafts shops and market stalls selling fish, fruit, and vegetables.

Five kilometers (three miles) to the north of Trosa is the impressive **Tullgarns Slott,** the royal summer palace. Built in the early 1700s, the palace was turned into a playful summer retreat in 1772 by King Gustaf's younger brother, Fredrik Adolf. The grounds include sculptured parks and gardens, an orangery, and a theater. The palace's interiors are full of ornate plasterwork, paintings of royals and landscapes, and much of the original, French-influenced furnishings. ⊠ *Trosa,* ☎ *08/55172011.* ☜ *SKr 50.* ☉ *May–Sept., daily 11–4.*

If you'd prefer to stay on board a boat and simply cruise around the islands, seek out the **Blidösund.** A coal-fired steamboat built in 1911 that has remained in almost continuous service, the *Blidösund* is now run by a small group of enthusiasts who take parties of around 250 on evening music-and-dinner cruises. The cruises depart from a berth close to the Royal Palace in Stockholm. ⊠ *Skeppsbron, Stockholm,* ☎ *08/4117113.* ☜ *SKr 120.* ☉ *Departures early May–late Sept., Mon.–Thurs. 7 PM (returns at 10:45).*

Among the finest of the archipelago steamboats is the **Saltsjön,** which leaves from Nybrokajen, close to the Strand Hotel. Tuesday through Thursday evenings you can take a jazz-and-dinner cruise for SKr 120; weekends from late June to late August, pay SKr 175 to go to Utö, an attractive island known for its bike paths, bakery, and restaurant. In December, there are three daily Julbord cruises, serving a Christmas smörgåsbord. ⊠ *Strömma Kanalbolaget, Skeppsbron 22, Stockholm,* ☎ *08/58714000.* ⊙ *Departures July–early Aug. and Dec.*

Dining

$$$ ✕ **Fjäderholmarnas Krog.** A crackling fire on the hearth in the bar area welcomes the sailors who frequent this place. In case you don't travel with your own sailboat, you can time your dinner to end before the last ferry returns to the mainland. The food here is self-consciously Swedish: fresh, light, and beautifully presented; the service is professional, the ambience relaxed. It's a great choice for a relaxed, special night out. ⊠ *Fjäderholmarna,* ☎ *08/7183355. AE, DC, MC, V. Closed Oct.–Apr.*

$$$ ✕ **Sandhamns Värdshus.** Built in 1672 as a guest house and restaurant for tired sailors, the bright yellow Sandhamn Inn is now a delightful place to stop for meal. A terrace provides a view over the colorful seaside town below, and in the summer there's outdoor seating on a large veranda. The menu is rooted in Swedish traditions with a focus on local seafood. Try the seafood stew spiced with saffron and served with freshly baked bread and aioli. The grilled calf's liver with fried sage and apple chips is also a worthy choice. ⊠ *Sandhamn,* ☎ *08/57153051. AE, DC, MC, V.*

$$ ✕ **Dykarbaren.** The idea for this old wooden harborside restaurant came from similar cafés in Brittany, France. Simple local dishes, mostly of fish, are served up in an informal wooden tabled dining area. Originally just catering for local divers, Dykarbaren now serves everyone. ⊠ *Strandpromenaden, Sandhamn,* ☎ *08/57153554. AE, DC, MC, V.*

$ ✕ **Gröna Caféet.** A grassy garden terrace and an appealing selection of fresh open sandwiches on hearty brown bread make this small, old-fashioned café a hit. It's on Rådhusgatan, by the town square. ⊠ *Rådhusg. 26, Vaxholm,* ☎ *08/5413151. No credit cards.*

$ ✕ **Tre Små Rum.** The old mint-green, red-roofed house that contains "Three Small Rooms" is the fitting place for simple, light lunches. The sandwiches (made from freshly baked bread) are delicious at this lunch-only café. There's also a handsome array of cakes and pastries: at least 40 types daily. If you don't want to sit in one of the rooms, there is a small outside seating area. ⊠ *Östra Långg., Trosa,* ☎ *0156/ 12151. MC, V. Closed dinner.*

Lodging

Lodging options in the archipelago vary from island to island. The larger, more inhabited islands often have at least one decent hotel, if not a few, whereas some of the smaller more deserted islands have only an inn or two or camping facilities. Hostels are available at low cost on some islands and some private homes rent out rooms and offer B&B accommodations. It's also possible to rent small cabins. Details are available from the Sweden House.

$$$ ✕🖫 **Radisson SAS Grand Hotel.** Many say that this is the only reason to come to the beautiful but quiet town of Saltsjöbaden. Next to the sea and the surrounding countryside, the hotel is one of the most breathtaking in the whole archipelago. Built in 1893, it's a castlelike concoction of white stone, arched windows, and towers. The huge rooms are filled with colorful period furniture that is set off perfectly against the plain stone fireplaces and pastel walls. The restaurant ($$$) is a grand, gilt, pillared, and mirrored affair with crisp linens, fine crystal, and a very well-prepared classic French menu. ⊠ *113 83 Saltsjöbaden,* ☎ *08/50617000,* 🖷 *08/50617025. 105 rooms, 85 with bath, 10 suites. Restaurant, bar, minibars, no-smoking rooms, room service, saltwater pool, sauna, spa, miniature golf, 2 tennis courts, jogging, ice-skating. AE, DC, MC, V. BP.*

$$ ☷ **Bomans.** Right on the water and brimming with old-world charm, this family-run hotel is more than 100 years old. The bedrooms are stuffed with floral patterns, iron bedsteads, feather quilts, lace, and linen. Downstairs there is a small bar and a very good restaurant. Lace tablecloths, chandeliers, and tangerine linens and fabrics help create a warm mood in the restaurant ($$), where you can also dine outside in the summer months. The menu is unashamedly Swedish, with high-quality versions of such classic dishes as meatballs, salmon, and elk with lingonberries. ✉ 619 30 Trosa, ☎ 0156/52500, FAX 0156/52510, WEB www.bomans.se. 31 rooms, 2 with bath, 2 suites. Restaurant, bar, no-smoking rooms, meeting rooms. AE, DC, MC, V. BP.

$$ ☷ **Grinda Wärdshus.** Housed in one of the archipelago's largest stone buildings, this 19th-century villa has homey rooms and bright, comfortable public areas. Since the hotel is right on the water, you may wish to take a refreshing dip in the sea before tackling the sumptuous breakfast buffet of Scandinavian classics. ✉ Södra Bryggan, 100 05 Grinda, ☎ 08/54249491, FAX 08/54249497, WEB www.grindawardshus.se. 34 rooms without bath. Restaurant, in-room VCRs. AE, DC, MC, V. BP.

$$ ☷ **Sandhamn Hotel and Conference.** Built in the "archipelago" style, the Sandhamm overlooks the local harbor. Rooms have light-wood accents with pale white and blue furnishings. The curtains are linen. The recreational area has an indoor and outdoor pool as well as a gym. Live music is often played on the grounds in summer. The hotel adjoins the Seglarrestaurangen, which also looks out over the water and serves traditional Swedish cuisine with a French influence. ✉ 130 30 Sandhamn, ☎ 08/57153170, FAX 08/57450450. 81 rooms, 3 suites. Restaurant, bar, indoor-outdoor pool, sauna, gym, meeting room. AE, DC, MC, V.

$$ ☷ **Utö Värdshus.** The rooms are large and well furnished here, with traditional furniture resembling that found in a Swedish farmhouse. Choose between a room in the sprawling white main hotel or 1 of the 30 that are in a cabin on the grounds. The restaurant ($$) has a grand wooden ceiling lit with chandeliers. The food is eclectic, ranging from salmon with Champagne sauce to tandoori lamb with noodles. ✉ Gruvbryggan, 130 56 Utö, ☎ 08/50420300, FAX 08/50420301, WEB www.uto-vardshus.se. 75 rooms without bath. Restaurant, bar, no-smoking rooms, sauna. AE, DC, MC, V. BP.

$$ ☷ **Waxholms Hotell.** Perched directly on Vaxholm's harbor, Waxholm's is a stone's throw from where the ferries land. Rooms in this excellent little hotel are clean and bright, and most offer a view of the water and the fortress that sits in the harbor. The restaurant and bar are the best in town, and the wraparound dining room provides great views of the boats on the water. The varied menu has everything from Thai spring rolls to Greek salad to clams poached in white wine and garlic. ✉ Hamng. 2, 185 21, ☎ 08/54130150, FAX 08/54131376. 32 rooms. Restaurant, bar, no-smoking rooms, meeting room. AE, DC, MC, V.

$ ☷ **Rum i Backen.** Built at the turn of the 20th century on Vaxholm's main street, this house was originally used as a meeting place for dances and gatherings. Today it's a lovely and quite affordable B&B. There's just one room. Since it's in an annex to the house, it's a sort of self-contained apartment, with a shower, kitchen, and small veranda. The breakfast, which you make yourself, is included. ✉ Kungsg. 14, 185 34 Vaxholm, ☎ 08/314021, FAX 08/54133315. 1 room. No credit cards. CP.

Outdoor Activities and Sports

A visit to the islands is one of the finest opportunities you can get in Sweden to take a bracing dip in the fresh, clean waters of the sea. Sometimes surprisingly warm, mostly heart-racingly chilly, but always memorable, a quick dip in these waters will set you up for the day. There are literally thousands of great swimming spots, but Sandhamn and Utö have the sandy beaches and rocky outcrops that keep them among the best.

Vaxholm and the Archipelago A to Z

To research prices, get advice from other travelers, and book travel arrangements, visit www.fodors.com.

BOAT AND FERRY TRAVEL

Regular ferry services to the archipelago depart from Strömkajen, the quayside in front of the Grand Hotel. Cruises on a variety of boats leave from the harbor in front of the Royal Palace or from Nybrokajen, across the road from the Royal Dramatic Theater. Ferries to the Feather Islands run almost constantly all day long in the summer (Apr. 29–Sept. 17), from Slussen, Strömkajen, and Nybroplan. Contact Strömma Kanalbolaget, Waxholmsbolaget, or Fjäderholmarna.

An excellent way to see the archipelago is to purchase an **Inter Skerries Card,** which costs SKr 250 and allows for unlimited boat travel throughout the islands for 16 days. Use the card for day trips from Stockolm, or go out for longer excursions and bounce around from island to island. You can also purchase the **See Sea Card,** which costs SKr 440 and allows unlimited travel in Stockholm, Åland, and the Åbo (Finland) archipelago. Both cards are available at the tourist center at the Stockholm Information Service.

➤ BOAT AND FERRY INFORMATION: **Fjäderholmarna** (☎ 08/7180100). **Stockholm Information Service** (Sweden House, ✉ Hamng. 27, Box 7542, 103 93 Stockholm, ☎ 08/7892490). **Strömma Kanalbolaget** (☎ 08/58714000). **Waxholmsbolaget** (☎ 08/6795830).

TRAIN TRAVEL

There are regular train services to Saltsjöbaden from Stockholm. The journey takes about 20 minutes. To get to Trosa, take a 1-hour train ride from Stockholm to Vagnhärad, where there is a bus waiting to take the 10-minute trip to Trosa.

➤ TRAIN INFORMATION: **SJ** (☎ 020/757575).

TOURS

A great way to discover the remote, less visited parts of the archipelago is to go out with Sandhamnsguiderna, a tour group that operates out of Sandhamn. Experienced guides will take you on tailor-made excursions, in small or large groups, to explore the outer reaches of the deserted archipelago. Prices for the tours depend on number of people, and length.

➤ FEES AND SCHEDULES: **Sandhamnsguiderna** (☎ 08/6408040).

VISITOR INFORMATION

The Vaxholms Tyristbyrå (Vaxholm Tourist Office) is in a large kiosk at the bus terminal, adjacent to the marina and ferry landing. Hours are daily 10–5. Sandhamn Turisbyrå (Sandhamn Tourist Office) is in the town center at Sandhamns Hamnservices. The Utö Turisbyrå (Utö Tourist Bureau) is near the ferry landing. More information on Grinda is available from the Sweden House.

➤ TOURIST INFORMATION: **Sandhamn Turisbyrå** (☎ 08/57153000). **Sweden House** (✉ Hamng. 27, Box 7542, 103 93 Stockholm, ☎ 08/7892490). **Trosa Turisbyrå** (☎ 0156/52222). **Utö Turisbyrå** (☎ 08/50157410). **Vaxholms Tyristbyrå** (✉ Söderhamnen, 185 83 Vaxholm, ☎ 08/54131480).

Gotland

 85 km (53 mi) southwest of Stockholm.

Gotland is Sweden's main holiday island, a place of wide, sandy beaches and wild cliff formations called *raukar.* Measuring 125 km (78 mi) long and 52 km (32 mi) at its widest point, Gotland is where Swedish sheep-farming has its home. In its charming glades, 35 different varieties of wild orchids thrive, attracting botanists from all over the world.

The first record of people living on Gotland dates from around 5,000 BC. By the Iron Age, it had become a leading Baltic trading center. When the German marauders arrived in the 13th century, they built most of its churches and established close trading ties with the Hanseatic League in Lübeck. They were followed by the Danes, and Gotland finally became part of Sweden in 1645.

Gotland's capital, **Visby,** is a delightful, hilly town of about 20,000 people. Medieval houses, ruined fortifications, churches, and cottage-lined cobbled lanes lend Visby its fairy-tale atmosphere. Thanks to a very gentle climate, the roses that grow along many of the town's facades bloom even in November.

In its heyday Visby was protected by a wall, of which 3 km (2 mi) survive today, along with 44 towers and numerous gateways. It is considered the best-preserved medieval city wall in Europe after that of Carcassonne in southern France. Take a stroll to the north gate for an unsurpassed view of the wall.

Visby's cathedral, **St. Maria Kyrka,** is the only one of the town's 13 medieval churches that is still intact and in use. Built between 1190 and 1225 as a place of worship for the town's German parishioners, few of the original fittings remain due to the extensive and sometimes clumsy restoration work done over the years. That said, the sandstone font and the unusually ugly angels decorating the pulpit are both original features worth a look.

Burmeisterska Huset, the home of the Burmeister—or principal German merchant—organizes exhibitions displaying the works of artists from the island and the rest of Sweden. Call the tourist office in Visby to arrange for viewing. ⊠ *Strandg. 9,* ☎ *no phone.* ☜ *Free.*

The **Fornsalen** (Fornsal Museum) contains examples of medieval artwork, prehistoric gravestones and skeletons, and silver hoards from Viking times. Be sure to also check out the ornate "picture stones" from AD 400–600, which depict ships, people, houses, and animals. ⊠ *Mellang. 19,* ☎ *0498/292700.* ☜ *SKr 30.* ۞ *Mid-May–Sept., daily 11–6; Oct.–mid-May, Tues.–Sun. noon–4.*

The **Visby Art Museum** has some innovative exhibitions of contemporary painting and sculpture. On the first floor is the permanent display, which is mostly uninspiring, save for a beautiful watercolor by local artist Axel Lindman from 1917. It shows Visby from the beach, in all its splendid medieval glory. ⊠ *St. Hansg. 21.* ☜ *SKr 30.* ۞ *May–Sept., daily 10–5.*

Medieval activities are re-created at **Kapitelhusgården.** Families can watch and take part in metal and woodworking skills, coin making, dressmaking, archery, and hunting. ⊠ *Drottensg. 8,* ☎ *0498/292700.* ☜ *SKr 40.* ۞ *June–Aug., daily noon–6.*

The 4 km (2½ mi) of stalactite caves at **Lummelunda,** about 18 km (11 mi) north of Visby on the coastal road, are unique in this part of the world and are worth visiting. The largest was discovered in 1950 by three boys out playing. ⊠ *Lummelunds Bruk,* ☎ *0498/273050.* ⌦ *SKr 50.* ⊙ *May–Sept., daily 9–5.*

A pleasant stop along the way to Lummelunda is the **Krusmyntagården** (☎ 0498/296900), a garden with more than 200 herbs, 8 km (5 mi) north of Visby.

There are approximately 100 old churches on the island that are still in use today, dating from Gotland's great commercial era. **Barlingbo,** from the 13th century, has vault paintings, stained-glass windows, and a remarkable 12th-century font. The exquisite **Dalhem** was constructed in about 1200. **Gothem,** built during the 13th century, has a notable series of paintings of that period. **Grötlingbo** is a 14th-century church with stone sculptures and stained glass (note the 12th-century reliefs on the facade). **Öja,** a medieval church decorated with paintings, houses a famous holy rood from the late 13th century. The massive ruins of a Cistercian monastery founded in 1164 are now called the **Roma Kloster Kyrka** (Roma Cloister Church). **Tingstäde** is a mix of six building dating from 1169 to 1300.

Curious rock formations dot the coasts of Gotland, remnants of reefs formed more than 400 million years ago, and two **bird sanctuaries, Stora** and **Lilla Karlsö,** stand off the coast south of Visby. The bird population consists mainly of guillemots, which look like penguins. Visits to these sanctuaries are permitted only in the company of a recognized guide. ☎ *0498/241113 or 0498/241139.* ⌦ *SKr 180 for guided tour of both sanctuaries.* ⊙ *May–Aug., daily.*

Dining

$$ ✕ **Clematis.** This campy restaurant is one of the most popular in Visby—guests are thrown back a few centuries to the Middle Ages for an authentic night of food, song, and dance. Here you'll dine from a flat slab of bread instead of a plate, your only utensil a knife. The staff don period attire and are known to break into a tune while delivering food to tables. Traditional Swedish fare is served, with a focus on meats and island ingredients. Drinks are served in stone goblets. ⊠ *Strandg. 20,* ☎ *0498/292727. AE, DC, MC, V.* ⊙ *No lunch.*

$$ ✕ **Donners Brunn.** Set in a beautiful orange brick house, on a small square in Visby, the chef proprietor of this restaurant, Bo Nilsson, was once chef at the renowned Operakällaren in Stockholm. The menu uses excellent local ingredients to make French-influenced dishes that are reasonably priced, given their quality. The house specialty of Gotland lamb with fresh asparagus and hollandaise sauce is delicious. ⊠ *Donners Plats 3,* ☎ *0498/271090. Reservations essential. AE, DC, MC, V.*

$$ ✕ **Gutekällaren.** Despite the name, the "Gotlander cellar" is above ground in a 12th-century building. Mediterranean dishes, including fish and shellfish stew with coconut and lemongrass and fillet of lamb with salad of red beets, asparagus, and Parmesan, are the draw. The striking interior includes primary-color leather chairs and coffee-color walls. ⊠ *Stora Torget 3,* ☎ *0498/210043. DC, MC.*

$$ ✕ **Krusmyntagården.** This marvelous little garden-café opened in the late '70s and has passed down through several owners. The garden now has more than 200 herbs and other plants, all of them grown organically. Most are used in such traditional Gotland dishes as tender grilled lamb (served on Tuesday and Thursday nights). ⊠ *Brissund,* ☎ *0498/ 296900. AE, DC, MC, V.*

$–$$ ✕ **Björklunda Värdshuset.** An old stone farmhouse is the setting for the small restaurant, run by a husband and wife team. You can have a predinner drink in the apple orchard before tucking into local salmon, lamb, and pork dishes of ample proportions. ⊠ *Björklunda, Burgsvik,* ☎ *0498/497190. AE, DC, MC, V.*

$–$$ ✕ **Konstnärsgården.** Hans and Birgitta Belin run a wonderful establishment in the tiny village of Ala. He is an artist, she a chef. As you eat your lovingly prepared food in this old manor house restaurant, you can view and buy the work of Hans as well as that of other artists. The venison that's often on the menu is raised on the premises, and in the summer months whole lambs are spit-roasted outdoors in the orchard gardens. ⊠ *30 km (19 mi) southeast of Visby, Ala,* ☎ *0498/55055. MC, V.*

Lodging

$$ 🏨 **Hotell Solhem.** A small, fresh, hotel resembling a beach-house, the Solhem offers wonderful views of Visby harbor and the sea beyond. The rooms and public areas are small, but the hotel is very bright and simply furnished, making the lack of size acceptable. ⊠ *Solhemsg. 3, 621 58,* ☎ *0498/279070. 94 rooms, 1 with bath. Bar, sauna. AE, DC, MC, V. BP.*

$$ 🏨 **Strand Hotel.** An environmentally conscious hotel with efficient heating and cooling systems, the Strand may ease your conscience with its approach. In any case, the lap pool, sauna, and the bright, comfortable rooms will ease your spirit. The clubby, relaxing bar has large leather sofas and a smoking area in an adjoining library. All things considered, the Strand is a good deal. ⊠ *Strandg. 34, 621 56,* ☎ *0498/ 258800,* 𝐅𝐀𝐗 *0498/258811,* 𝐖𝐄𝐁 *www.strandhotel.net. 110 rooms, 2 with bath, 6 suites. Restaurant, bar, indoor lap pool, sauna. AE, DC, MC, V. BP.*

$$ 🏨 **Toftagården.** Nestled among the trees near the Gotland coast about 20 km (12 mi) from Visby, the placid, verdant grounds here are ideal for strolling, lazing about, and reading in the shade. The long, sandy beach in Tofta is also nearby, as is the Kronholmen golf course. Most of the brightly furnished rooms, all on the ground floor, have their own terrace. There are also a number of cottages with kitchens—a two-night minimum stay is required for these. If the sea water at the beach is too cold, take a dip in the outdoor heated pool. The restaurant serves very good regional fare. ⊠ *Toftagården, 621 98,* ☎ *0498/297000,* 𝐅𝐀𝐗 *0498/ 265666. 50 rooms, 15 cottages. Restaurant, kitchenettes (some), pool, sauna. AE, DC, MC, V. BP.*

$$ 🏨 **Wisby Hotell.** The tall, thin building that's now the Wisby dates from the 1200s and is at the junction of two narrow streets. A hotel since 1855, the ochre-color walls, light floral patterned fabrics, dark wood, and vaulted ceilings give it old European grandeur. There are two excellent bars in the hotel, one a glassed-in courtyard that serves cocktails, and the other a cozy pub with a good beer selection. ⊠ *Strandg. 6, 621 24,* ☎ *0498/257500,* 𝐅𝐀𝐗 *0498/257550,* 𝐖𝐄𝐁 *www.wisbyhotell.se. 134 rooms, 94 with bath, 10 suites. Restaurant, 2 bars, no-smoking rooms. AE, DC, MC, V. BP.*

$ 🏨 **Hotel St. Clemens.** Four buildings make up the St. Clemens, in Visby's Old Town. They range in age from the 1940s all the way back to the 1600s. Rooms are simple and modern with private baths; some have small kitchens. There are two gardens on the property, one of which is shared with the St. Clemens church, one of Visby's oldest. ⊠ *Smedjeg. 3, 621 55,* ☎ *0498/219000,* 𝐅𝐀𝐗 *0498/279443. 32 rooms. Breakfast room, kitchenettes (some), sauna. AE, DC, MC, V. CP.*

$ 🏨 **Kronholmens Gård.** This charming little complex has its own small beach a short walk from Kronholmen's acclaimed 27-hole golf course. There are two cabins. One has four rooms with five small beds apiece. Inside the other is a common kitchen and living room that all the guests share. For families hoping to save a little money and who enjoy cooking for themselves, this is a great spot on the island. Weekly discounts are available. ✉ *Västergarn, 620 20 Klintehamn,* ☎ *0498/245004,* ℻ *0498/245023. 1 4-bedroom cabin. Sauna. AE, DC, MC, V.*

$ 🏠 **Villa Alskog.** A short drive from the sandy beaches to the south of
★ Gotland, Villa Alskog is a delightful inn surrounded by beautiful open spaces, stone fences, and small groves of trees. The building dates to 1840 and was originally a residence for the local priest. Today its 10 guest rooms have been renovated into bright, simply furnished living spaces with hardwood floors. Most of the cozy rooms have their own bath. The location is ideal for swimming, hiking, and horseback riding. ✉ *620 16 Alskog,* ☎ *0498/491188,* ℻ *0498/491120. 10 rooms, 7 with bath. Restaurant, café, sauna, meeting room. AE, DC, MC, V. BP.*

Nightlife and the Arts

Medeltidsveckan (Medieval Week), celebrated in early August, is a citywide festival marking the invasion of the prosperous island by the Danish King Valdemar on July 22, 1361. Celebrations begin with Valdemar's grand entrance parade, and continue with jousts, an open-air market on Strandgatan, and a variety of street-theater performances re-creating the period.

The ruin of **St. Nicolai,** the old dilapidated church in Visby, holds regular concerts throughout the summer months. Everything from folk to rock to classical is available. The tourist office has details.

There are many bars and drinking establishments on Gotland, but the best are in Visby. **Skeppet** (✉ Strandv., ☎ 0498/210710), a lively bar playing both live and recorded rock music, attracts a frantic young crowd.

Graceland (☎ 0498/215500) is on a boat moored in Visby's harbor. As the name suggests, it's a mecca for Elvis fans. The 35-and-over crowd fills its Priscilla Bar and dances to the King's finest until 2 AM.

Outdoor Activities and Sports

Bicycles, tents, and camping equipment can be rented from **Gotlands Cykeluthyrning** (✉ Skeppsbron 2, ☎ 0498/214133). **Gotlandsleden** is a 200-km (120-mi) bicycle route around the island; contact the tourist office for details.

For an aquatic adventure, **Gotlands Havskajakcenter** (☎ 0498/223012, 🖾 Kr 150 for three hours) will rent you a canoe and a life jacket from their center at Valleviken, on the northeast coast of the island. From here you can explore the 15 uninhabited islands nearby. Many have beautiful rock formations.

If you do nothing else on Gotland, you must go for a swim. The island has miles and miles of beautiful, golden beaches, and unusually warm water for this part of the world. The best and least crowded beaches are at Fårö and Själsö to the north of the island.

Shopping

Barbro Sandell (✉ Längsv. 146, Norrlanda, ☎ 0498/39075) is a bright shop with one of the island's best selections of fabrics printed with local patterns.

G.A.D (Good Art and Design; ✉ Södra Kyrkog. 16, ☎ 0498/249410) sells stunningly simple, modern furniture that has been designed and made on Gotland. Just as at its shop in Stockholm, the firm sells high-end pieces with a cosmopolitan flair.

Gotland A to Z

To research prices, get advice from other travelers, and book travel arrangements, visit www.fodors.com.

BOAT AND FERRY TRAVEL

Car ferries sail from Nynäshamn, a small port on the Baltic an hour by car or rail from Stockholm; commuter trains leave regularly from Stockholm's central station for Nynäshamn. Ferries depart at 11:30 AM year-round. From June through mid-August there's an additional ferry at 12:30 PM. A fast ferry operates from mid-April until mid-September, departing three times a day. The regular ferry takes about five hours; the fast ferry takes 2½ hours. Boats also leave from Oskarshamn, farther down the Swedish coast and closer to Gotland by about an hour. Call Gotland City Travel for more information.

➤ BOAT AND FERRY INFORMATION: **Gotland City Travel** (✉ Kungsg. 57, ☎ 08/4061500; ✉ Nynäshamn, ☎ 08/5206400; ✉ Visby, ☎ 0498/ 247065).

CAR RENTAL

➤ AGENCIES: **Biltjänst** (✉ Endrev. 45, Visby, ☎ 0498/218790). **Budget** (✉ Visby, ☎ 0498/279396).

CONTACTS AND RESOURCES

➤ DOCTORS AND DENTISTS: **Visby Hospital** (☎ 0498/268009).

TOURS

Guided tours of the island and Visby, the capital, are available in English by arrangement with the tourist office.

VISITOR INFORMATION

The main tourist office is Gotlands Turistservice at Österport in Visby. You can also contact Gotland City Travel in Stockholm for lodging or ferry reservations.

➤ TOURIST INFORMATION: **Gotland City Travel** (☎ 08/4061500). **Gotlands Turistservice** (☎ 0498/203300, FAX 0498/249059).

Uppsala

❸ *67 km (41 mi) north of Stockholm.*

Sweden's principal university, Uppsala has only one rival for the title: Lund, to the south. August Strindberg, the nation's leading dramatist, studied here—and by all accounts hated the place. Ingmar Bergman, his modern heir, was born in town. It is also a historic site where pagan (and extremely gory) Viking ceremonies persisted into the 11th century. Uppsala University, one of the oldest and most highly respected institutions in Europe, was established in 1477 by Archbishop Jakob Ulfson. As late as the 16th century, nationwide *tings* (early parliaments) were convened here. Today it is a quiet home for about 170,000 people. Built along the banks of the Fyris River, the town has a pleasant jumble of old buildings that is dominated by its cathedral, which dates from the early 13th century.

The last day of April never fails to make the town become one big carnival—the Feast of Valborg. To celebrate the arrival of spring (and the end of the school year), students of the university don sailorlike hats and charge down the hill from the university library (try not to get in their way). The university chorus then sings traditional spring songs on the steps of the main building. And finally the whole town slips into mayhem. Thousands descend upon the city as the streets are awash in Champagne and celebrations. It's an age-old custom worth seeing, but it's not for the fainthearted.

Ideally you should start your visit with a trip to **Gamla Uppsala** (Old Uppsala), 5 km (3 mi) north of the town. Here under three huge mounds lie the graves of the first Swedish kings—Aun, Egil, and Adils—of the 6th-century Ynglinga dynasty. Close by in pagan times was a sacred grove containing a legendary oak from whose branches animal and human sacrifices were hung. By the 10th century, Christianity had eliminated such practices. A small church, which was the seat of Sweden's first archbishop, was built on the site of a former pagan temple.

Today the archbishopric is in Uppsala itself, and **Gamla Uppsala Kyrka,** the former seat, is largely kept up for the benefit of tourists. The whitewashed walls and simple rows of enclosed wooden pews make the church plain but calming. The tomb of Anders Celsius, the inventor of the temperature scale that bears his name, is about the only other thing to look at inside.

NEED A BREAK? To sample a mead brewed from a 14th-century recipe, stop at the **Odinsborg Restaurant** (☎ 018/323525), near the Gamla Uppsala burial mounds.

The Gamla Uppsala **Historiskt Center** (Historical Center) contains exhibits and archaeological findings from the Viking burial mounds that dominate the local area. Just opened in 2000, the museum distinguishes between the myth and legends about the area and what is actually known about its history. Next to Gamla Uppsala Church, the ultramodern building made of wood and copper will change color as it ages. Its aggressive design has stirred up a wide range of both affection and dislike among the somewhat settled population. ☎ 018/239300. ⌷ SKr 50. ☉ May–Sept., daily 10–5; Oct.–Apr., Tues.–Sun. 10–5.

Back in Uppsala, your first visit should be to **Uppsala Domkyrka** (Uppsala Cathedral). Its 362-ft twin towers—whose height equals the length of the nave—dominate the city. Work on the cathedral began in the early 13th century; it was consecrated in 1435 and restored between 1885 and 1893. Still the seat of Sweden's archbishop, the cathedral is also the site of the tomb of Gustav Vasa, the king who established Sweden's independence in the 16th century. Inside is a silver casket containing the relics of St. Erik, Sweden's patron saint. ☎ 018/187177. ⌷ Free. ☉ Daily 8–6.

The **Domkyrka Museet** in the north tower has arts and crafts, church vestments, and church vessels on display. ☎ 018/187177. ⌷ SKr 20. ☉ May–Aug., daily 9–5; Sept.–Apr., Sun. 12:30–3.

Gustav Vasa began work on **Uppsala Slott** (Uppsala Castle) in the 1540s. He intended the building to symbolize the dominance of the monarchy over the church. It was completed under Queen Christina nearly a century later. Students gather here every April 30 to celebrate the Feast of Valborg and optimistically greet the arrival of spring. Call the tourist center for information. ⌷ Castle SKr 40. ☉ Guided tours of castle mid-Apr.–Sept., daily at 11 and 2 (additional tours late June–mid-Aug., weekends at 10 and 3).

In the excavated Uppsala Slott ruins, the **Vasa Vignettes,** scenes from the 16th century, are portrayed with effigies, costumes, light, and sound effects. ⌷ SKr 40. ☉ Mid-Apr.–Aug., daily 11–4; Sept., weekends 10–5.

One of Uppsala's most famous sons, Carl von Linné, also known as Linnaeus, was a professor of botany at the university during the 1740s. He created the Latin nomenclature system for plants and animals. The **Linné Museum** is dedicated to his life and works. ✉ Svartbäcksg. 27, ☎ 018/136540. ⌷ SKr 20. ☉ Late May and early Sept., weekends noon–4; June–Aug., Tues.–Sun. 1–4.

The botanical treasures of Linnaeus's old garden have been re-created and are now on view in **Linnéträdgården.** The garden's orangery houses a pleasant cafeteria and is used for concerts and cultural events. ⊠ *Svartbäcksg. 27,* ☎ *018/109490.* ⊠ *SKr 20.* ☉ *May–Aug., daily 9–9; Sept.–Apr., daily 9–7.*

Uppsala Universitetet (Uppsala University; ☎ 018/4710000), founded in 1477, is known for the **Carolina Rediviva** university library, which contains a copy of every book published in Sweden, in addition to a large collection of foreign works. Two of its most interesting exhibits are the *Codex Argentus,* a Bible written in the 6th century, and Mozart's original manuscript for his 1791 opera *The Magic Flute.*

Completed in 1625, the **Gustavianum,** which served as the university's main building for two centuries, is easy to spot by its remarkable copper cupola, now green with age. The building houses the ancient anatomical theater—one of only seven in the world to function on natural light—where human anatomy lectures and public dissections took place. The Victoria Museum of Egyptian Antiquities is in the same building. ⊠ *Akademig. 3,* ☎ *018/4717571.* ⊠ *SKr 40.* ☉ *June–Aug., daily 11–3; Anatomical Theater also Sept.–May, weekends noon–3.*

Dining and Lodging

\$\$–\$\$\$ ✕ **Domtrappkällaren.** In a 14th-century cellar near the cathedral, Domtrappkällaren serves excellent French and Swedish cuisines. Game is the specialty, and the salmon and reindeer are delectable. ⊠ *Sankt Eriksgränd 15,* ☎ *018/130955. Reservations essential. AE, DC, MC, V.*

\$\$ ✕ **Hambergs Fisk.** As the name suggests, this is a fish restaurant, the one slightly odd concession to nonfish eaters being several dishes made from goose liver. Since the restaurant is really one part of a food court, you can sample the wonderful menu and then head to the deli counter to bring away fresh fish, pâtés, and other fine foods. ⊠ *Fyris Torg 8,* ☎ *018/710050. AE, DC, MC, V.*

\$–\$\$ ✕ **Katalin.** You can eat and watch the trains rattle by in this converted warehouse behind the main station. Just as the interior is simple and modern, Katalin serves classic versions of such Swedish favorites as salmon and meatballs. There is often a jazz band in the evenings and on weekends the bar is one of the most popular in town. ⊠ *Östra Station,* ☎ *018/140680. AE, DC, MC, V.*

\$–\$\$ ✕ **Svenssons Restaurang.** With one end of the large, semicircular room given over to a floor-to-ceiling window, Swenssons has a great view of the river Fyris, which courses through the center of town. Set on top of the town's old food hall, the restaurant is furnished tastefully and simply with blond wood and primary colors. The French menu emphasizes grilled meats and fish, all of them done with a Mediterranean touch. Try the lamb with rosemary and sweet peppers or the sole with lobster sauce. ⊠ *Saluhallen, St. Eriks Torg 8,* ☎ *018/150150. Reservations essential. AE, DC, MC, V.*

\$ ✕ **Café Alma.** A huge hit with local students, this lunch-only Mediterranean restaurant is in the basement of the main university building. The delicious and varied buffet (SKr 60) has such dishes as spicy chicken kebabs, roast peppers and eggplant, and mozzarella and tomato salad. Everything's made in-house by the two wonderfully friendly owners. No à la carte is offered. ⊠ *Övre Slottsg.,* ☎ *018/4712330. MC, V. No dinner.*

\$\$\$ ⯐ **Gillet.** Operated by the Sweden Hotels group, Uppsala's largest hotel first opened in 1971. Rooms are bright and large, with pleasant watercolors, soft furnishings, and hardwood floors. The hotel is only a short walk from Uppsala's most famous buildings. The public areas are a little bland and standardized, but very comfortable. ⊠ *Dragar-*

VALBORG EVE

The streets of Uppsala, this ancient university town, are awash with humanity. Across the urban landscapes the people stream, apparently without aim. There is joy in the air and beer on the doorsteps. It is April 30, the day of Valborg Eve. Summer is on the cusp and this is a contemporary interpretation of the traditional mass in honor of St. Valborg, the daughter of an Anglo-Saxon king and a nun who lived from 710 to 799. Near Willibald and Wunnibald in Germany she became mother superior to a monastery founded by her brothers; a spirit of God on earth.

Such noble origins are far from the minds of the masses today. Revelry is the theme. The day began early with Champagne breakfasts and by midday the park outside Europe's oldest university, founded in 1477, is crowded with picnickers. Most are adorned in their (high school) graduation caps, and all are full of whiskey and song. The chancellor gives his speech. The choirs sing. Like a shotgun spray, the people disperse to the parks. Everything feels possible today.

Although Valborg has religious roots, its meaning has evolved over the centuries. From something that centered on the village church, it developed an agrarian theme. In these harsh climes, the farmers and their families would shrug their cares away and feel the release from the long winter. The sun shone, the animals were out of their barns, and the fields were being planted. The cycle of nature had begun again. It is a moment very closely linked to the seasons, which the Swedes, given their trying winters, are very sensitive to.

One of the great rituals of Valborg Eve is the nighttime bonfire. It owes its origins not to God but to paganism and stems from the terrible otherworldly fears that people then held, surely metaphoric tales that encoded the tribulations of the human condition. The bonfire was believed to deliver protection from the spiritual realm. It was said to haunt the evil spirits themselves and chase away dangerous animals. Today it is, in a sense, a time in which people destroy the results of their spring cleaning. All the collected rubbish and pruned trees are used to build the pile and then torched. Those who have shown great stamina or restraint during the day will be present at the huge bonfire that sparkles to the heavens and lights the night. It is a big social occasion, accompanied by traditional foods, the herring and the schnapps. Here, you, too, can fly like an eagle on the wings of collective elation. Valborg in Uppsala was one of the most extraordinary events of unshackled human release that I have ever seen. It may not be the Rio carnival, but Uppsala is not Brazil, either, and the Swedish will always have their own ways.

brunnsg. 23, 751 42, ☎ *018/155360,* FAX *018/153380. 160 rooms, 48 with bath. 2 restaurants, pool. AE, DC, MC, V. BP.*

$$ 🏨 **Grand Hotel Hörnan.** An old-world hotel (1906), the Hörnan's city-center location means that it's near the train station and has views of both the castle and the cathedral. The rooms are spacious and have cozy lighting and homey furnishings. ⊠ *Bandgårdsg. 1, 753 20,* ☎ *018/ 139380,* FAX *018/120311. 37 rooms. AE, DC, MC, V. BP.*

$$ 🏨 **Scandic Hotel Uplandia.** This branch of the giant Nordic chain has the usual modern comforts and high-tech amenities expected of an international business hotel. There's also the pleasing design that's found in the best Scandinavian hotels. Blond wood accented with moss-green and aquamarine fabrics give the decor a sophisticated edge. ⊠ *Dragarbrunnsg. 32, 751 40,* ☎ *018/4952600,* FAX *018/4952611,* WEB *www. scandic.se. 133 rooms, 93 with bath, 2 suites. Restaurant, bar, in-room data ports, no-smoking rooms, room service, sauna, meeting rooms. AE, DC, MC, V. BP.*

$ 🏨 **First Hotel Linné.** The namesake of this white stone town-house hotel would be likely to appreciate its lush gardens and a warm atmosphere. The hotel's interior is in harmony with the gardens outside: soft floral prints and warm reds dominate. In winter, a huge open fire is lit. Rooms are done in a bright modern Scandinavian design, with earth and red tones. Floors and furniture are primarily wood. ⊠ *Skolg. 45, 750 02,* ☎ *018/102000,* FAX *018/137597. 116 rooms, 28 with bath, 6 suites. Restaurant, bar, minibars, no-smoking rooms, sauna. AE, DC, MC, V. BP.*

Nightlife and the Arts

Svenssons (⊠ Sysslomansg. 15, ☎ 018/553310) is Uppsala's most popular nightspot. The two-floor building houses a bar, a restaurant, and a nightclub. The restaurant (not to be confused with the Svenssons on St. Eriks Torg, which has the same owner) is nothing to speak of. But after 9, when food is no longer being served, on come the '80s tunes and out comes the roulette table. Downstairs are two more bars, with loads of chrome, mirrors, and people, all of them gyrating to contemporary dance music. Arrive early to avoid lines. For a relaxed evening, head to **Alex Vinbar** (⊠ Skolg. 45, ☎ 018/102000), a dark, comfortable wine bar that sells many wines by the glass and plays mainly jazz. **Uppsala Stadsteater** (town theater; ⊠ Kungsg. 53, ☎ 018/ 160300) is a local theater known for its high-quality productions, many directly from Stockholm and a fair number in English.

Shopping

Saluhallen (⊠ St. Eriks Torg 8, ☎ 018/711840) is a beautiful 19th-century food hall that's perched right on the river. There is a very wide selection of exotic and local produce to choose from, or just look at. The cheese choices are great. **Trolltyg** (⊠ Östra Åg. 25, ☎ 018/146304) has an exclusive selection of the sort of clean-line clothes and household furnishings that Scandinavian design is known for. The shop is wonderfully laid out and is a joy to explore, especially the fabrics section. Out in Old Uppsala, **Gamla Uppsala Keramik** (Gamla Uppsala Pottery; ⊠ Ulva Kvam, ☎ 018/322060) makes all its own pottery and china, many with ancient local designs from Viking graves and stone carvings.

Uppsala A to Z

To research prices, get advice from other travelers, and book travel arrangements, visit www.fodors.com.

ARRIVING AND DEPARTING

Trains between Stockholm and Uppsala run every hour, throughout the day, all year-round. The cost of a one-way trip is SKr 70. For timetables and train information contact SJ.

➤ Train Information: **SJ** (☎ 020/757575).

TOURS

You can explore Uppsala easily by yourself, but English-language guided group tours can be arranged through the Uppsala Guide Service.

➤ Fees and Schedules: **Uppsala Guide Service** (☎ 018/274818).

VISITOR INFORMATION

The main tourist office is in the town center; in summer, a small tourist information office is also open at Uppsala Castle.

➤ Tourist Information: **Main Tourist Office** (✉ Fyris Torg 8, ☎ 018/274800). **Information Office at Uppsala Castle** (☎ 018/554566).

4 THE BOTHNIAN COAST

NDENTED WITH SHIMMERING FJORDS, peppered with pine-clad islands, and lined with dramatically tall cliffs, the Bothnian Coast is a dramatic sliver of land on Sweden's east coast.

Its history and prosperity both come from the sea. This is as true of the grand 19th-century stone houses built from the profits of international sea trading as it is of the ancient fishing villages, which are now used mainly as holiday homes for urban Swedes. The Bothnian Coast has both kinds of dwellings in abundance. In the north of the region you can see traces of the religious fervor that took hold in past centuries, evident in the small religious communities and the many ancient, well-preserved churches and artifacts in towns such as Umeå and Skellefteå.

Many of the original wood cottages that dotted this coastline have been destroyed by fires over the years. The worst damage, caused by Russia's many incursions through the area in the 18th century, prompted many of the towns along the coast to rebuild themselves in grand styles more befitting a capital than a local fishing town. Aided by the burgeoning shipping trade in the 1800s, port towns such as Gävle, Sundsvall, and Umeå created cities of wide boulevards, huge central squares, and monumental stone buildings partly to discourage future fires from spreading.

Gävle

44 *180 km (111 mi) north of Stockholm (via E4).*

Gävle, the capital of the county (*land* in Swedish) Gästrikland, is considered by many Swedes a gateway to the northern wildernesses. The town was granted its charter in 1446. This great age is not evident in the mix of grand 19th-century boulevards and parks and modern, bland shopping centers that make up much of the small downtown area. The original town was destroyed in a great fire in the mid-1800s, and the only part that survives today was the small enclave that lay south of the river, which kept the flames away. The grand architectural style of much of the town reflects the wealth it once enjoyed as a major trading port. Today it is better known as home to Gevalia, Sweden's largest coffee producer, a fact that is evident on the days when the town fills with the heavenly smell of roasting beans drifting from the factory chimneys.

The **Joe Hill Museet,** dedicated to the Swedish emigrant who went on to become America's first well-known protest singer and union organizer, is in Hill's former home in the oldest section of Gävle. Once a poor, working-class district, this is now the most highly sought-after residential part of town, with art studios and crafts workshops nearby. The museum—furnished in the same style as when Hill lived there— contains very few of his possessions but does display his prison letters. The house itself bears witness to the poor conditions that forced so many Swedes to emigrate to the United States (an estimated 850,000 to 1 million between 1840 and 1900). Hill, whose original Swedish name was Joel Hägglund, became a founder of the International Workers of the World and was executed for the murder of a Salt Lake City grocer in 1914. He maintained his innocence right up to the end. ⊠ *Nedre Bergsg. 28,* ☎ *02/6613425.* ⊡ *Free.* ☉ *June–Aug., daily 11–3.*

The **Skogsmuseet Silvanum** (Silvanum Forestry Museum) is on the west end of town, by the river. Silvanum, Latin for "Forest," was inaugurated in 1961; it was the first such museum in the world and is one of the largest. The museum provides an in-depth picture of the forestry

The Bothnian Coast

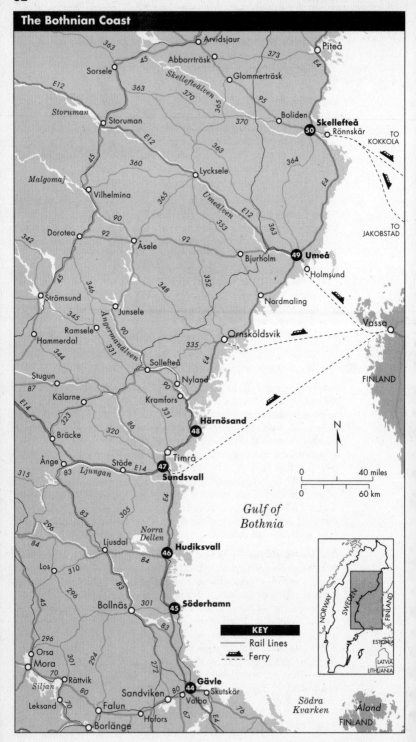

Arvidsjaur

Piteå

363

Sorsele

45

Abborrträsk

373

E4

Skellefteälven

Glommerträsk

E12

363

370

95

Storuman

370

Boliden

Storuman

365

Skellefteå

E12

363

50 Rönnskär

TO KOKKOLA

Malgomaj

360

Lycksele

364

Vilhelmina

365

Umeälven

E4

90

E12

353

Dorotea

92

Åsele

92

363

TO JAKOBSTAD

342

45

Bjurholm

49 Umeå

346

352

Holmsund

Strömsund

345

Junsele

348

Nordmaling

Vassa

Ramsele

90

Ångermanälven

Ornsköldsvik

Hammerdal

344

331

335

FINLAND

Stugun

Sollefteå

E4

87

Kälarne

90

Nyland

323

331

Kramfors

Bräcke

320

86

48 Härnösand

Ånge

Stöde

E14

Timrå

N

315

83

Ljungan

47 Sundsvall

83

305

E4

Gulf of Bothnia

Los

310

Norra Dellen

0   40 miles

0   60 km

84

Ljusdal

84

46 Hudiksvall

45

296

Bollnäs

301

45 Söderhamn

296

301

294

83

KEY

Orsa

Mora

— Rail Lines

70

Rättvik

301

272

- - - Ferry

Siljan

80

44 Gävle

NORWAY SWEDEN FINLAND

Leksand

70

Sandviken

80

Valbo

Skutskär

Södra Kvarken

Åland

ESTONIA

Falun

67

FINLAND

LATVIA

Hofors

76

LITHUANIA

Borlänge

E4

industry in Sweden, still the backbone of the country's industrial wealth: trees cover more than 50% of Sweden, and forest products account for 20% of national exports. Silvanum includes a forest botanical park and an arboretum that contains an example of every tree and bush growing in Sweden. ⊠ *Kungsbäcksv. 32*, ☎ *02/6614100.* ⌨ *Free.* ☉ *Tues. 10–2, Wed. 10–7, Thurs.–Fri. 10–4, weekends 1–5.*

For a glimpse of Gävle's past, go to the **Länsmuseet** (County Museum). Inside this impressive redbrick building is a museum celebrating the history of the town and area. On the ground floor are changing exhibits on local artists and photographers. Upstairs there are old farm implements, clothes, and re-creations of local house interiors that extend from the 12th century on through the 1930s. The largest part of the museum is dedicated to the town's maritime history and includes model ships as well as trinkets and treasures brought back from sea voyages long ago. ⊠ *Strandg. 20*, ☎ *02/6655635.* ⌨ *SKr 30.* ☉ *Tues.–Sun. noon–4.*

Housed in what used to be the local train storage shed, the **Sveriges Järnvägsmuseum** (Swedish Railway Museum) displays a wide range of engines and coach cars. The royal hunting car from 1859 is thought to be the world's oldest. ⊠ *Rälsg. 1*, ☎ *02/6106448.* ⌨ *SKr 40.* ☉ *Tues.–Sun. 10–4.*

Dining and Lodging

$$ ✕ **Johansson's.** Good local fish dishes and an extensive wine list make this restaurant something of a gourmet treat in Gävle. The interior of dark wood and white tablecloths appears somewhat flat and sober at first, but the warm, friendly staff and elegant service will add a brighter dimension to your dining experience. ⊠ *Nyg. 7*, ☎ *02/6100734. AE, DC, MC, V.*

$$ ✕ **Söderhjelmska Gården.** This classic Swedish wooden house dates from 1773 and stands out from the rest of mostly modern Gävle. The interior, furnished in traditional white wood and blue linen, is split into the same small rooms that existed when it was still a residence. In summer you can also eat in the tree-lined garden. The traditional Swedish menu emphasizes fish, and the specialty of the house is perch with beets. ⊠ *S. Kungsg. 23*, ☎ *02/6613393. Reservations essential. AE, DC, MC, V.*

$ ✕ **Järnvägsrestaurangen.** Very good daily lunch specials and a simple, home-cooked selection in the evening are what the Railway Restaurant has to offer. The restaurant is in the old railway station building, which adjoins the current one. A large glass veranda in front is the perfect place to sit and watch Gävle go by. On weekend evenings the restaurant doubles as a lively bar and music venue. ⊠ *Stora Esplanadg.*, ☎ *02/6514495. AE, DC, MC, V.*

$$ ▥ **Hotel Winn.** What this hotel in the city center lacks in charm and design, it makes up for in facilities. Aimed at convention goers, the Winn has very large rooms with every convenience. The leisure facilities are also excellent. ⊠ *Norra Slottsg. 9, 801 38*, ☎ *02/6647000,* FAX *02/6647009. 200 rooms, 6 suites, 20 rooms with bath. Restaurant, bar, in-room data ports, in-room fax, in-room safes, minibars, no-smoking rooms, room service, indoor pool, sauna, gym, laundry service, concierge, meeting rooms, parking (fee). AE, DC, MC, V.*

$$ ▥ **Scandic Hotel Grand.** Built in 1836, this is Gävle's best attempt to re-create the glories of yesteryear. Behind the imposing stone facade are pleasing turn-of-the-20th-century and art-deco features, including a sweeping lobby bar with huge chandeliers. The bedrooms have decor that is a little stale, but they are comfortable and of a good size. ⊠ *Nyg. 45, 801 04*, ☎ *02/6129060,* FAX *02/6124499. 220 rooms, 7 suites,*

95 rooms with bath. Restaurant, bar, sauna, gym, convention center. AE, DC, MC, V.

Shopping

The beautiful furniture, clothes, and kitchenware at the **Gefle Design Forum** (✉ Drottningg. 25, ☎ 02/6188008) come from Stockholm Design House, the capital's well-known design group. It's also a good place to pick up fun gift items. For something classic, head to **Prylboden** (✉ Norra Kungsg. 11, ☎ 02/6189761) a small, friendly shop selling 19th- and 20th-century antiques, especially housewares. Drink trays, coffee cups, and large furniture pieces all vie to catch the attention of the nostalgic.

Nightlife and Arts

In the small park between Norra Rådmansgatan and Norra Kungsgatan is the grand stone building that contains **Gävle Teatren** (Gävle Theater; ✉ Norra Råmansg. 23, ☎ 02/6129200). Its beautiful gilded auditorium was built in the late 1800s. Many of the plays it stages are in English. For a raucous night out, head to **O'Learys** (✉ Södra Kungsg. 31, ☎ 02/6183020), an Irish pub that's also a sports bar. Catch the latest soccer or baseball game while sampling some of the excellent beers available. Friday and Saturday nights, the place becomes a disco and the most popular nightspot in town. **Heartbreak Hotel** (✉ Norra Strandg. 15, ☎ 02/6183020) is a bar and nightclub with a 1950s American rock-and-roll theme. Memorabilia of Elvis and others is plastered on the walls. If you're lucky, you may catch one of the many Elvis impersonators, who perform periodically.

Söderhamn

45 *75 km (47 mi) north of Gävle (via E4).*

Söderhamn is a town with a lot of space. Besides the extensive open countryside that borders the town, the center is awash with parks, gardens, and wide boulevards. In summer, Swedes come from all over to enjoy the pretty public spaces. The many trees help to remove air pollution, making sitting in an open-air café here exceptionally pleasing. The town's architecture is a mix of monumental 18th-century buildings, erected through fortunes made by fishing, and modern shopping precincts built to replace areas devastated by numerous fires. This coastal town is also close to one of the finest archipelagos in the region: more than 500 islands, islets, and skerries are near.

For stunning panoramic views of the town and the surrounding forest and sea, climb **Oscarborg**, a 75-ft tower at the edge of town. Built in 1895, the white tower and attached building resemble a Disneyesque fairy-tale castle.

Dating back to the 1600s, **Smedjan** (Blacksmiths) is a living, working museum, where you can watch craftsmen use traditional methods to make horseshoes and other items. ✉ *Kungsgården,* ☎ *02/7035031.* ☞ *Free.* ⊙ *June–Aug., Mon. and Thurs. 2–8. All other times by appointment.*

Dining and Lodging

$$ ✕ **Restaurang Albertina.** This converted red wooden barn is situated on the water's edge, just north of Söderhamn, in the old fishing village of Skärså. Inside, scrubbed wooden walls and beamed ceilings blend with the crisp, white table linen. Fish is a must here. The locally caught salmon that's served is among the best in the region. ✉ *Skärså,* ☎ *02/ 7032010. AE, MC, V.*

$ ✕ **RådhusKonditoriet.** Inside an uninspiring building is a restaurant that doubles as one of the few photographic galleries in the north of Swe-

den. The gallery and the excellent selection of sandwiches, sp
teas, and light meals make it worth the trip. ⊠ *Kykog. 10,* ☏
7012457. AE, MC, V. Closed Sun.

$$ 🏨 **First Hotell Statt.** The oldest hotel in town is also the most luxu
ous. All the rooms are individually furnished and have wooden floor
and a comfortable mix of blond wood and pastel furnishings. The pub
lic areas have their original chandeliers, stucco-work ceilings, and
large open fireplaces, giving the hotel a feel of old luxury. ⊠ *Oxtorgsg.*
17, 826 22, ☏ *02/7073570,* ⅏ *02/7013524. 78 rooms without bath.*
Restaurant, bar, sauna, nightclub, convention center. AE, DC, MC, V.

$ 🏨 **Centralhotellet.** As the name suggests, it's the central location that
makes this hotel worth the stay. The rooms are quite dark and small,
but are well furnished with antique-style fittings and wooden floors.
⊠ *Rådhustorget, 826 32,* ☏ *02/7070000,* ⅏ *02/7016060. 13 rooms,*
none with bath. Restaurant, bar, nightclub. AE, DC, MC, V.

Nightlife and the Arts

Inside the Folkets Hus (People's House), a 1950s building built for town
gatherings, **Café August** (⊠ Rådhusparken, ☏ 06/5038450) is a lively
nightspot. Although the building isn't glamorous, the interior has orig-
inal paintings on the walls and a pleasingly quiet color scheme through-
out. As night falls the place comes alive with two floors of modern dance
music, live bands, and an outdoor bar area for cooling off. **Pub Tre Bockar**
(⊠ Bankgränd 1, ☏ 06/5099994) is a traditional English pub. The dark
wood interior is jammed with people on weekend evenings. They all
want to sample the live music, disco sound, and good beer.

Outdoor Activities and Sports

Söderhamn is the perfect place for a boat trip out to the nearby
archipelago. The **MS Sandskär** (☏ 02/7012254) is one of many boats
that offers day trips with fishing and swimming. For an energetic in-
land-water adventure, there are myriad lakes and rivers around Söder-
hamn that are perfect for canoeing. For more information contact
Fritidskontoret (leisure office; ☏ 02/7075000).

Shopping

There are real bargains to be found at **Albert and Herbert** (⊠ Sanna-
hedsv. 11, ☏ 06/5017777), an outlet store that sells clothes, house-
hold items, and furniture. The range is huge, and the quality is excellent.

Hudiksvall

46 *60 km (37 mi) north of Söderhamn via E4.*

Granted its town charter in 1582, Hudiksvall's history is bound up with
the sea. Having been partially destroyed by fire 10 times, Hudiksvall
is now an interesting mix of architectural styles. The small section of
the old town that remains is built around a central harbor and con-
tains some fine examples of flower-strewn courtyards and traditional
wood-panel buildings built along narrow, cobbled streets.

The **Fiskarstan** (Fishertown) neighborhood is tightly packed with strik-
ing streets of fishermen's huts and houses and boardwalks of wooden
fish stores that hang precariously over the water. Lilla Kyrkogatan, the
oldest street in town, leads to Hudiksvall's Church, which is still
marked by cannonballs from a Russian invasion in 1721. Guided
tours, maps, and information can be arranged through the town's
tourist office (☏ 06/5019100).

Inside a former bank building in the middle of town, the **Hälsinglands**
Museum offers insight into the development of Hudiksvall and the sur-
rounding region. Furniture, house reconstructions, religious artifacts,

extiles, and art are all organized and displayed thoughtfully. It's ealing picture of life in the area. ☒ *Storg. 31*, ☎ *06/5019600.* 🖃 *kr 20.* ☉ *Mon. noon–6, Tues.–Thurs. 9–4, weekends 11–3.*

Dining and Lodging

$$ ✕ **Bruns VS.** This very relaxed, informal restaurant offers a wildly diverse choice of foods, from traditional Swedish to Polynesian and beyond. There's a pub area, for those seeking only liquid refreshment, and in the summer there's a huge terrace for outside dining. ☒ *Brunnsg. 2*, ☎ *06/5010402. AE, DC, MC, V.*

$$ ✕ **Gretas Krog.** Long ago discovered, this restaurant, built right by the fishing docks, is rarely empty and seldom disappoints. The interior trades predictably on fishing history through sepia photographs of weatherbeaten fishermen and old nets strung from the ceiling, but there is something undeniably cozy about it all. The menu is packed with good local specialties and traditional Swedish cuisine. ☒ *Västra Tväkajen*, ☎ *06/5096600. Reservations essential.*

$$ 🏨 **First Hotell Statt.** From the outside, the grand 19th-century yellow stone facade of this hotel, with its pillars and arches, looks like a typical Swedish town hall. Once you've gone inside, the more familiar marble floor and pastel shades confirm that you have arrived at your hotel. Rooms here are large and nicely decorated with navy and russet tones, wood floors, and Persian rugs. Those with a sea view cost just a little more and are worth it. ☒ *Storg. 36, 824 22*, ☎ *06/5015060,* 🖷 *06/5096095. 106 rooms, 26 with bath, 8 suites, 2 with sauna. Restaurant, pub, pool, sauna, gym, nightclub, convention center. AE, DC, MC, V. BP.*

Outdoor Activities and Sports

Hudiksvall's archipelago is centered around the peninsula of **Hornslandet,** just north of the town. As well as the usual fishing, swimming, and boating, the peninsula is home to Europe's second-largest system of mountain caves, which can be explored by experts and beginners alike. Call **Alf Siden** (☎ *06/5070492*), who arranges and conducts official tours of the caves.

Shopping

Slöjd i Sjöboden (☒ Möljen, ☎ *06/5012041*) is a series of old fishing huts now housing stalls where 15 local craftspeople sell their wares. Locally inspired textiles, jewelry, ceramics, and glassware can all be bought at very good prices.

Sundsvall

🔄 *80 km (50 mi) north of Hudiksvall via E4.*

Sundsvall also goes by the name of *Stenstan* (Stone Town), and rightly so. When the town was razed by fire in 1888, it was rebuilt entirely out of stone, which is atypical for this part of Sweden. The new design added more parks and widened roads in order to help keep any later fires from spreading. Sundsvall's wide boulevards and parks, lined by the impressive limestone and brick buildings, make it resemble Sweden's largest cities, Stockholm and Göteborg.

The best place to get a feel for the city and its history is at the **Kulturmagasinet** (Culture Warehouse), a series of four 19th-century waterfront warehouses that now include a museum, library, archives, a children's culture center, art exhibitions, and street music. The museum, which traces the town's history, is built over an old street, where tram tracks and cobbles are still in place. It gives a good sense of what Sundsvall was like when it was still a busy trading port. ☒ *Packhusg.*

8, ☎ 06/0191803. ⊡ June–Aug. SKr 20, Sept.–May free. ⊙ Mon.–Thurs. 10–7, Fri. 10–6, weekends 11–4.

Sundsvall is a good city to walk around, as most of the points of interest are woven into the streets, boulevards, and squares of **Storgatan** and **Stora Torget.** History comes to life here with churches, the town hall, and grand porticoed, stone buildings all flexing their architectural muscles. Guided tours and maps can be arranged through the tourist office (☎ 06/0610450).

Gustav Adolfs kyrka, at the far end of Storgatan, is Sundsvall's main church. In keeping with much of the city, it's a 19th-century, grand affair that's built of red brick. There is a pleasing order about the interior, its vaults and pillars all constructed from smooth, square stones that look like children's building blocks.

Dining and Lodging

$$ ✕ **Restaurang Grankotten.** The food here, modern Swedish with a French influence, has won praise from all over. Dishes such as veal with truffles and anything that uses the delicious local elk are worth traveling for. The views of Sundsvall from the turn-of-the-19th-century building are stunning, especially if you dine outside in the summer. ⊠ *Norra Stadsberget, ☎ 06/0614222. Reservations essential. AE, DC, MC, V. Closed Sun.*

$$ ✕ **Skeppsbrokällaren.** Classic Swedish design and furnishings and good Scandinavian cuisine are the main attractions at this quiet basement restaurant, on the site of the original boat entrance to the city. For a more calming dining experience book a table in the Röda Rummet (Red Room), a smaller darkened dining area at the back of the restaurant. ⊠ *Sjög. 4, ☎ 06/0173660. Reservations essential. AE, DC, MC, V.*

$$ ⌂ **Comfort Hotel Sundsvall.** Grand stone arches and portals give an impression of stately luxury to this centrally located hotel. The interior doesn't quite live up to its original promise, but the rooms are large, comfortable, individually furnished in earth and red tones, and have wooden floors. ⊠ *Sjög. 11, 852 34, ☎ 06/0150720, FAX 06/0123456, 52 rooms, 3 with bath. Restaurant, bar, sauna, pool. AE, DC, MC, V.*

$$ ⌂ **First Hotel Strand.** The 1960s exterior to this hotel is wholly disappointing, given the grandeur of Sundsvall that surrounds it. Inside, however, it's a different story. The rooms are large and well equipped; leisure facilities are second to none; and the breakfast buffet, famous in these parts, will keep you going 'til dinner. ⊠ *Strandg. 10, 851 06, ☎ 06/0121800, FAX 06/0619202. 203 rooms, 30 with bath, 6 suites. Restaurant, bar, pool, sauna, nightclub, business services, convention center. AE, DC, MC, V. BP.*

Nightlife and the Arts

Bars and pubs provide the best source of evening entertainment in Sundsvall. **Spegelbaren** (⊠ Nybrog. 10, ☎ 06/0156006) with its large mirrors, glass ceilings, and 19th-century paintings, is one of the best. If you have spare vacation money to use up, then head for **Casino Cosmopol** (⊠ Södermalmsg. 7, ☎ 06/0156289). Housed in the old railway station, built in 1875, it is Sweden's oldest international-style casino. The **Kulturmagasinet** (⊠ Packhusg. 8, ☎ 06/0191803) is a museum with art exhibitions (mostly of Swedish artists); a children's theater; and live music, readings, and debates.

Outdoor Activities and Sports

The nearby river of Ljungan is an excellent spot for rafting. Tours include one hour of white-water rafting, beautiful scenery, and lunch on a small island. Contact the tourist office (☎ 06/0616767) for more information.

Shopping

Northern Sweden's largest shopping mall, **Ikano Huset,** is 8 km (5 mi) north of Sundsvall, along Route E4. Shops include everything from large international brands such as IKEA, to local handicraft stores. **Sköna Ting** (✉ Nybrog. 15, ☎ 06/0170501), meaning "beautiful things," is a crafts store selling gifts and trinkets: dolls, linen and lace, and hand-blown glass. Everything is locally made and of good quality.

Härnösand

48 *40 km (25 mi) north of Sundsvall via E4.*

Dating from 1585, Härnösand is a town rich in history. Narrow, ancient streets lined with wood-panel houses contrast with 18th- and 19th-century boulevards and squares. The town has a long history as an administrative center for local government, a history hinted at in its orderly layout and infrastructure as well as the grandness of its buildings. In the center of town is Sweden's smallest—and only— white cathedral.

With works by both Chagall and Matisse on display, **Härnösands Konsthall** is an art museum of considerable note. The museum has works by many of Sweden's prominent painters and sculptors and puts on around 20 exhibitions per year. ✉ *Stora Torget 2,* ☎ *06/11348142.* ☞ *Free.* ☉ *Tues.–Fri. 11–3, weekends noon–3.*

Länsmuseet Västernorrland is an excellent, well-thought-out history museum that covers Härnösand and the surrounding area. The museum also has one of the country's largest collections of weapons. ✉ *Murberget,* ☎ *06/1188600.* ☞ *Free.* ☉ *Daily 11–5.*

Dining and Lodging

$$ ✗ **Highlander.** At this Scottish/Irish theme pub all the requisite details are in place—even a staff dressed in kilts. There's Irish beer and a good selection of wines. The food is hearty and filling with lots of beef and other meat dishes on the menu. ✉ *Nybrog. 5,* ☎ *06/11511170. AE, MC, V. Closed Sun.*

$$ ✗ **Spjutegården.** Stark-white walls are broken up by small local paintings at this very traditional restaurant in a building from the early 1800s. The floor and ceiling are both made of white wood, and a huge, open fireplace makes the room cozy. The menu consists of very good traditional Swedish food with international touches. As in most Swedish restaurants, the fish dishes are worth a try. ✉ *Murberget,* ☎ *06/11511090. Reservations essential. AE, MC, V.*

$$ ▥ **First Hotel.** Of the three hotels in Härnösand, this is the best choice. Large, functional rooms in cream, green, and purple all have wooden floors, armchairs, a desk, and generally very good views of the harbor. ✉ *Skeppsbron 9, 871 30,* ☎ *06/11554440,* FAX *06/11554447. 95 rooms with bath, 7 suites. Restaurant, bar, pub, sauna, gym, meeting room. AE, DC, MC, V.*

Nightlife and the Arts

The place to be seen in Härnösand is **Apoteket** (✉ Köpmang. 5, ☎ 06/11511717), a nightclub and bar popular with those 25 years and over. Modern hits are mixed with classics in this darkened lounge. When you can dance no more, the bar does great cocktails.

Shopping

Hantverksboden (✉ Järnvägsg., ☎ 06/1188140) is an old wooden building next to the water where local craftsmen rent stalls to sell their wares. Silverware, jewelry, handicrafts, glassware, and pottery are all in abundance.

Umeå

⑭ *225 km (140 mi) north of Härnösand (via E4).*

Built on the River Ume, Umeå is the largest city in northern Sweden. Since it's a university town with the youngest average population of anywhere in the country, there are many bars, restaurants, festivals, and cultural events to visit.

Aside from taking a walk around the city's open squares and wide boulevards, the best way to get to know Umeå is by visiting **Gammlia,** a series of museums that focus on the city and surrounding area. The open-air museum has a living village made up of farmhouses and working buildings. Actors in period costumes demonstrate how people lived hundreds of years ago. You can wander by farm animals and learn about baking bread, preserving meat, and harvesting grain. There is also a church and historic gardens. The indoor museums feature exhibitions on Umeå's history, a fishing and maritime museum, the Swedish ski museum, and a modern art museum that shows work from major Swedish and international artists. A sort of intellectual theme park, Gammlia can take the better part of a day to see everything. ⊠ *Gammliav.,* ☎ *09/0171800.* ⊡ *Free.* ☉ *Daily 10–5.*

OFF THE BEATEN PATH

NORBYSKÄ – Around 1800, this island had Europe's largest sawmill, and an ambitious group of Swedes attempted to set up a utopian commune around this industry. The attempt at good living didn't work, and the commune broke up around 1830. However, much of what they built remains today as a monument to their dreams. By walking around the island you can see the remains of the houses, school, and work buildings the commune created. The island is also perfect for picnics, fishing, swimming, and safaris to view the local seal population. Norbyskä is a 15-minute boat trip from Umeå. For details and prices contact the Umeå tourist office (☎ 09/0161616).

Dining and Lodging

$$ ✕ **Greta & Co.** Housed inside a somewhat indifferent hotel, Gretas is a must for those seeking out authentic regional specialities. Food from around northern Sweden is served in a dining room of simple, classic Swedish design. The reindeer, rabbit, and salmon are exceptional. ⊠ *Skolg. 62,* ☎ *09/0100730. AE, DC, MC, V.*

$$ ✕ **Il Fratello.** A bistro that's classically Italian in both decor and food, Il Fratello operates as a pub at lunch. But at night, the candles are lit in the wine bottles and the gingham cloths come out. The menu emphasizes dishes made of garlic, veal, olives, tomatoes, and pasta. ⊠ *Nyg. 22,* ☎ *09/0129551. AE, DC, MC, V.*

$ ✕ **Grottan.** This restaurant and bar is very popular with the local student population and comes alive at night. The decor is basic, with redchecked tablecloths and plain wood chairs. The simple menu is well executed and full of café classics such as lasagna, beef bourguignonne, and steaks. ⊠ *Axtorpsv.,* ☎ *09/0779600. AE, DC, MC, V.*

$$ ⊞ **Hotel Winn.** The beautiful powder-blue clapboard exterior of this hotel encloses a modern, officelike reception area, but one that is comfortable and welcoming nonetheless. Rooms are very stylishly furnished with paintings and lots of dark wood and asymmetrical fittings. The Mucky Duck, a classic English-style pub on the premises, serves roughly 40 types of beer and is always busy in the evening. ⊠ *Vasaplan, 901 06,* ☎ *09/0711100,* FAX *09/0711150. 87 rooms, 5 with bath, 5 suites. Bar, pub, no-smoking rooms, sauna. AE, DC, MC, V.*

$$ ⊞ **Scandic Hotel Plaza.** A clean modern glass and brick structure dominating the city skyline, the Scandic is one of the most stylish hotels in the region. The huge open lobby has a staircase of marble and steel, copper-toned pillars, and tile floors. A lounge, restaurant, bistro, and bar all lead off from the lobby. At the very top of the hotel is a luxury health suite and spa, which has exceptional views of the city. Rooms are large, well equipped, and decorated in pastel shades. ⊠ *Storg. 40, 903 04,* ☎ *09/02056300,* FAX *09/02056311. 196 rooms, 58 with bath, 1 suite. 2 restaurants, bar, lounge, minibars, no-smoking rooms, sauna, spa, gym, convention center. AE, DC, MC, V.*

$ ⊞ **Strand Hotell.** Although this hotel is a severe, redbrick blob from the '70s, it's very central, right on the water, and well priced. The rooms are large and basically furnished with notably comfortable beds. ⊠ *Västra Strandg. 11, 903 26,* ☎ *09/070400,* FAX *09/0704090. 41 rooms, 15 with bath. Restaurant, bar, meeting rooms. AE, DC, MC, V.*

Nightlife and the Arts

Being a student town, Umeå is never short of a good night out. The nightlife scene here, as in many Swedish towns, revolves around bars and pubs. The stylish **Blå** (⊠ Rådhusesplanden, ☎ 09/0135660) is full of chrome, glass, and people with attitude. It's the place to see and be seen in town. For an informal night out try **Rex** (⊠ Rådhustorget, ☎ 09/0126050), a friendly and popular haunt that attracts a young crowd. For those who prefer something a little more sedate and traditional, **Äpplet** (⊠ Vasaplan, ☎ 09/0156200) puts on fox-trot, cha-cha, and tango for all comers.

Shopping

Designers Guild (⊠ Kungsg. 49, ☎ 09/0131300), the fabric and print shop started by English designer Patricia Guild, sells beautiful English-, French-, and Italian-inspired fabrics, clothes, and household goods.

Skellefteå

🔟 *140 km (87 mi) northeast of Umeå via E4.*

In 1324 King Magnus Eriksson invited anyone who believed in Jesus Christ, or anyone who wanted to convert to Christianity, to settle a town near the river Skellefte. Thus Skellefteå was born, and for hundreds of years it was a devout Christian township. In recent times, the town has made a living from the electronics and computer industries, and from nearby gold and silver mining.

The focus of the town's religious beliefs still stands today, in the form of **Skellefteå Landskyrka.** Inside the area known as Bonnstan—a 400-room "village" built to house traveling churchgoers in the 17th century when attendance was compulsory—the striking neoclassical Skellefteå County Church has a dome roof. It's home to some exquisite medieval sculptures, including an 800-year-old walnut wood carving of the Virgin Mary, one of the few Romanesque Maria carvings left anywhere in the world.

One of the very few art museums in the world dedicated to women artists, **Anna Nordlander Museum** displays about 80 of this Swedish painter's portraits and landscapes. Born in 1843, success came quickly and increased steadily until her death from tuberculosis at the age of 36. ⊠ *Kanalg. 73,* ☎ *09/10736100.* 🎫 *Free.* ☉ *Daily 10–5.*

Dining and Lodging

$$ ✕ **Kriti.** An authentic Greek restaurant in the north of Sweden is not what you may expect, but you won't be disappointed. Garish yellow tablecloths with red napkins, rickety wooden chairs, white concrete walls, and a small tile roof over the bar make this the real deal. Huge

portions of good meat and fish dishes leave most people quite satisfied. ⊠ *Kanalg. 51,* ☎ *09/10779535. AE, DC, MC, V.*

$$ ✕ **Värdshuset Disponenten.** This beautiful green colonial-style wooden mansion has wrought-iron balconies and ivy creepers on the walls. The smörgåsbord that's offered here is generous and well prepared. Cold and hot fish, meat, and vegetable dishes are almost all made using local ingredients—some as local as the kitchen garden. ⊠ *Skelleftehamnsv. 63,* ☎ *09/1030930. Reservations essential. AE, DC, MC, V. Closed Sat. dinner.*

$$ 🏨 **Rica Hotel.** Each room is individually furnished in this modern hotel. The building's low light, candles, and dark furnishings are very restful. ⊠ *Torget 2, 931 31,* ☎ *09/10732500,* 𝔽𝔸𝕏 *09/10732529. 123 rooms, 25 with bath, 2 suites. Restaurant, bar, in-room data ports, sauna. AE, DC, MC, V.*

$$ 🏨 **Scandic Hotel.** This modern building is shaped like an upturned boat, half of which is made of glass. This huge glassed portion is the Winter Garden, which houses the lobby, lounges, restaurants, and an extraordinary collection of huge trees, tropical palms, and flowers. The large rooms are furnished in blond wood and come with all the modern additions you would expect of an international hotel. ⊠ *Kanalg. 75, 931 78,* ☎ *09/10752400,* 𝔽𝔸𝕏 *09/10752411. 111 rooms without bath, 4 suites. 2 restaurants, bar, pool, sauna, gym, convention center. AE, DC, MC, V.*

Nightlife and the Arts

Underbar (⊠ Torget, ☎ 09/10732500) means wonderful, and if you asked the locals that's exactly how most would describe this dark and smoky nightclub. The three underground floors become unbelievably packed on weekends. There are two bars and dance floors, a disco, and a stage where live bands play the very popular local punk-pop sound known as *Skelleftepop.*

Locally sponsored and managed **Pinkerton** (⊠ Magasingränd 3, ☎ 091085060) has the promotion of Skellefteå music very much on its mind. The dark, cool club serves up cold beer, snacks, and lots of local pop, blues, jazz, and rock bands.

Shopping

The market stalls arranged under the large roof of the **Handelsgården** (⊠ Storg. 46, ☎ 09/10779924) mean that the place offers one-stop shopping for ceramics, glass, jewelry, woodwork, woven textiles, prints and artwork, and delicatessen foods.

The Bothnian Coast A to Z

To research prices, get advice from other travelers, and book travel arrangements, visit www.fodors.com.

AIR TRAVEL
CARRIERS

The only carrier to Sundsvall Airport is SAS, which operates nine flights a day from Stockholm.

➤ AIRLINES AND CONTACTS: **SAS** (☎ 02/0727727).

AIRPORTS

Sundsvall Airport (20 km/12 mi west of Sundsvall) is the area's main airport. Local flight connections can be made to Umeå and Skellefteå. A bus service to Sundsvall runs in connection with arriving and departing SAS flights and costs SKr 60. A taxi will cost SKr 250–SKr 300.

➤ AIRPORT INFORMATION: **Sundsvall Airport** (☎ 06/06088000). **Taxi Västernorrland** (☎ 06/0199000).

BUS TRAVEL

Swebus operates a twice-daily service from Stockholm to Gävle. Y-Buss operates a daily service from Stockholm to Hudiksvall, Sundsvall, Härnösand, and Umeå.

➤ Bus Information: **Swebus** (☎ 02/00218218). **Y-Buss** (☎ 02/00334444).

CAR RENTAL

Avis and Hertz have offices in Gävle, Sundsvall, and Umeå. Europcar has offices in Gävle and Umeå.

➤ Major Agencies: **Avis** (✉ Gävle, ☎ 02/6186880; ✉ Sundsvall, ☎ 06/0570210; ✉ Umeå, ☎ 09/0131111). **Europcar** (✉ Gävle, ☎ 02/6621095; ✉ Umeå, ☎ 09/0153960). **Hertz** (✉ Gävle, ☎ 02/6644938; ✉ Sundsvall, ☎ 06/0669080; ✉ Umeå, ☎ 09/0177140).

CAR TRAVEL

From Stockholm take E4 directly north 174 km (108 mi) to Gävle. From Göteborg, take E20 284 km (177 mi) to Örebro, Route 60 north 164 km (102 mi) to Borlänge and Route 80 west 70 km (43 mi) to Gävle. From Gävle the E4 runs the entire length of the Bothnian coast, through every major town, north to Skellefteå.

EMERGENCIES

For emergencies dial ☎ 112. There are several hospitals in the area and emergency dental care is available at Sundsvall and Umeå. There are late-night pharmacies in Gävle and Sundsvall that stay open until 11.

➤ Hospitals: **Gävle Hospital** (☎ 02/6154000). **Hudiksvall Hospital** (☎ 06/5092000). **Söderhamn Hospital** (☎ 02/7077000). **Umeå Hospital** (☎ 09/07850000).

➤ Dental Care: ✉ Sundsvall, ☎ 06/0613135; ✉ Umeå, ☎ 07/03992480.

➤ Late-Night Pharmacies: ✉ Gävle, ☎ 02/6149200; ✉ Sundsvall, ☎ 06/0181117.

TOURS

The Bothnian coast covers many miles, and tours of the entire area are not available. Individual towns and cities usually offer their own tour, either of the town or points of interest in the surrounding area. Details of tours can be obtained from an individual town's tourist information offices.

➤ Contacts: **Gävle City Tour** (☎ 02/6147430). **Hudiksvall Town Walk** (☎ 06/5019100). **Skellefteå Countryside Tours** (☎ 09/10711210). **Umeleden Way** (waterside cycling path with many stops, including Europe's largest hydroelectric power station; ☎ 09/0161616).

TRAIN TRAVEL

SJ operates hourly train services from Stockholm to Gävle, Söderhamn, Hudiksvall, Sundsvall, and Härnösand. Tågkompaniet operates a night train from Stockholm to Umeå, with connections to Skellefteå.

➤ Contacts: **SJ** (☎ 02/0757575). **Tågkompaniet** (☎ 02/0444111).

VISITOR INFORMATION

➤ Tourist Information: **Gävle** (✉ Drottningg. 37, ☎ 02/6147430). **Härnösand** (✉ Järnvägsg. 2, ☎ 06/1188140). **Hudiksvall** (✉ Möljen, ☎ 06/5019100). **Skellefteå** (✉ Trädgårdsg., ☎ 09/10736020). **Söderhamn** (✉ Resecentrum, ☎ 02/7075353). **Sundsvall** (✉ Stora Torget, ☎ 06/0610450). **Umeå** (✉ Renmarkstorget 15, ☎ 09/0161616).

5 GÖTEBORG

IF YOU ARE PASSING THROUGH GÖTEBORG (Gothenburg) on the way to your coastal vacation spot, do try to spend a day or two exploring this attractive port. A quayside jungle of cranes and warehouses attests to the city's industrial might, yet within a 10-minute walk of the waterfront is an elegant, modern city of broad avenues, green parks, and gardens. This is not to slight the harbor along both banks of the Göta Älv (river): it comprises 22 km (14 mi) of quays with warehouses and sheds covering more than 1.5 million square ft, making Göteborg Scandinavia's largest port. The harbor is also the home of Scandinavia's largest corporation, the automobile manufacturer Volvo (which means "I roll" in Latin), as well as of the roller-bearing manufacturer SKF and the world-renowned Hasselblad camera company.

Historically, Göteborg owes its existence to the sea. Tenth-century Vikings sailed from its shores, and a settlement was founded here in the 11th century. Not until 1621, however, did King Gustav II Adolf grant Göteborg a charter to establish a free-trade port on the model of others already thriving on the Continent. The west-coast harbor would also allow Swedish shipping to avoid Danish tolls exacted for passing through Öresund, the stretch of water separating the two countries. Foreigners were recruited to realize these visions: the Dutch were its builders—hence the canals that thread the city—and many Scotsmen worked and settled here, though they have left little trace.

Today Göteborg resists its second-city status by being a leader in attractions and civic structures. The Scandinavium was until recently Europe's largest indoor arena; the Ullevi Stadium stages some of the Nordic area's most important concerts and sporting events; Nordstan is one of Europe's biggest indoor shopping malls; and Liseberg, Scandinavia's largest amusement park in the area, attracts some 2.5 million visitors a year. Above the Göta River is Älvsborgsbron, at 3,060 ft the longest suspension bridge in Sweden, and under a southwestern suburb runs the Gnistäng Tunnel, which at 62 ft claims the odd distinction of being the world's widest tunnel cut through rock for motor vehicles.

EXPLORING GÖTEBORG

Göteborg is an easy city to explore: most of the major attractions are within walking distance of one another, and the streetcar network is excellent—in summer you can take a sightseeing trip on an open-air streetcar. The heart of Göteborg is Kungsportsavenyn (more commonly referred to as Avenyn, "the Avenue"), a 60-ft-wide, tree-lined boulevard that bisects the city along a northwest-southeast axis. Avenyn links Göteborg's cultural heart, Götaplatsen, at the southern end, with the main commercial area, now dominated by the modern Nordstan shopping center. Beyond lies the waterfront, busy with all the traffic of the port, as well as some of Göteborg's newer cultural developments.

To the west are the Haga and Linné districts. Once home to the city's dockyard, shipping and factory workers, these areas are now alive with arts and crafts galleries, antiques shops, boutiques selling clothes and household goods, and small street cafés and restaurants. Most of these shops are inside original wood and brick cottages, which line the narrow streets.

Cultural Göteborg

A pleasant stroll will take you from Götaplatsen's modern architecture along the Avenyn—the boulevard Kungsportsavenyn, lined with elegant shops, cafés, and restaurants—and across the Rosenlunds and Hamn canals to finish at Kungsportsplats. At the square the street becomes Östra Hamngatan and slopes gently up from the canal.

A Good Walk

Start your tour in **Götaplatsen** ⑤, a square dominated by a fountain statue of Poseidon; behind him is the **Konstmuseet** ⑤. Stroll downhill past the cafés and restaurants along Avenyn to the intersection with Vasagatan. A short way to the left down Vasagatan, at the junction with Teatergatan, you can visit the **Röhsska Museet** ⑤, one of the few galleries dedicated to Swedish design.

Continue down Vasagatan. If the weather's good, have a look in at the Vasa Parken, or Vasa Park. Then turn right to go north on Viktoriagatan, cross the canal, and then make an immediate left to visit one of the city's most peculiar attractions, **Feske Körkan** ⑤, an archaic spelling of *Fisk Kyrkan*, the Fish Church. It is actually an indoor fish market.

You may now feel inspired to visit the city's principal place of worship, **Domkyrkan** ⑤. Follow the canal eastward from Feske Körkan and turn left onto Västra Hamngatan; walk about four blocks to the church. Continue northward on Västra Hamngatan and cross the canal to get to Norra Hamngatan, where you'll find the **Stadsmuseet** ⑥, housed in the 18th-century Swedish East India Company.

TIMING

Depending on how much time you want to spend in each museum, this walk may take anywhere from a couple of hours to the better part of a day. Note that many sites close Monday off-season.

Sights to See

⑤ **Domkyrkan** (Göteborg Cathedral). The cathedral, in neoclassic yellow brick, dates from 1802, the two previous cathedrals on this spot having been destroyed by fire. Though disappointingly plain on the outside, the interior is impressive. Two glassed-in verandas, originally used for the bishop's private conversations, run on each side of the cathedral's length. The altar is impressively ornate and gilt. Next to it stands a post-Resurrection cross, bare of the figure of Jesus and surrounded by his gilded burial garments strewn on the floor. ⊠ *Kungsg. 20,* ☎ *031/7316130.* ☉ *Weekdays 8–5, Sat. 8–3, Sun. 10–3.*

⑤ **Feske Körkan** (Fish Church). Built in 1872, this fish market gets its nickname from its Gothic-style architectural details. The beautiful arched and vaulted wooden ceiling covers rows and rows of stalls, each offering silvery, slippery goods to the shoppers who congregate in this vast hall. ⊠ *Fisktorget, Rosenlundsg.*

OFF THE
BEATEN PATH

FISKHAMNEN – An excellent view of Älvsborgsbron (Älvsborg Bridge), the longest suspension bridge in Sweden, is available from Fiskhamnen, the Fish Docks, west of Stigbergstorget. Built in 1967, the bridge stretches 3,060 ft across the river and is built high so that ocean liners can pass beneath. The government plans to turn part of the harbor into a scenic walkway with parks and cafés. The work is set to be finished in 2002. Also look toward the sea to the large container harbors: Skarvikshamnen; Skandiahamnen (where boats depart for England); and Torshamnen, which welcomes most of the cargo and passengers to the city today.

★ ⑤ **Götaplatsen** (Göta Place). This square was built in 1923 in celebration of the city's 300th anniversary. In the center is the Swedish-American sculptor Carl Milles fountain statue of Poseidon choking an

Göteborg

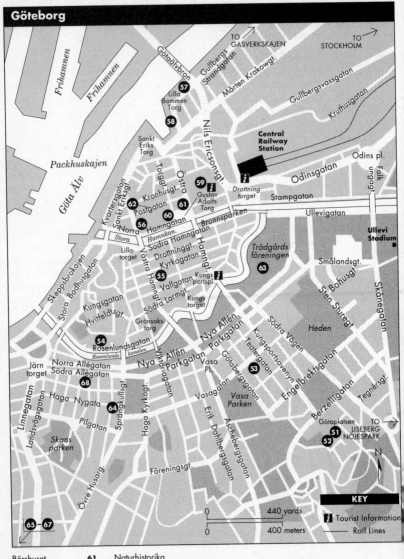

enormous shark. Behind the statue stands the Konstmuseet, flanked by the **Konserthuset** (Concert Hall) and the **Stadsteatern** (Municipal Theater), three contemporary buildings in which the city celebrates its important contribution to Swedish cultural life. The **Stadsbiblioteket** (Municipal Library) maintains a collection of more than half a million books, many in English.

52 Konstmuseet (Art Museum). This impressive collection of the works of leading Scandinavian painters and sculptors encapsulates some of the moody introspection of the artistic community in this part of the world. The museum's Hasselblad Center devotes itself to showing the progress in the art of photography. The Konstmuseet's holdings include works by Swedes such as Carl Milles, Johan Tobias Sergel, the impressionist Anders Zorn, the Victorian idealist Carl Larsson, and Prince Eugen. The 19th- and 20th-century French art collection is the best in Sweden, and there's also a small collection of old masters. ⊠ *Göta-platsen*, ☎ *031/612980.* 🎫 *SKr 35.* ☉ *Mon.–Tues. and Thurs.–Fri. 11–4, Wed. 11–9, weekends 11–5. Closed Mon. Sept.–May.*

OFF THE BEATEN PATH	**LISEBERG NÖJESPARK** – Göteborg proudly claims Scandinavia's largest amusement park. The city's pride is well earned: Liseberg is one of the best-run, most efficient parks in the world. In addition to a wide selection of carnival rides, Liseberg also has numerous restaurants and theaters, all set amid beautifully tended gardens. It's about a 30-minute walk east from the city center or a 10-minute ride by bus or tram; in summer a vintage open streetcar makes frequent runs to Liseberg from Brunnsparken in the middle of town. ⊠ *Örgrytev.,* ☎ *031/400100.* 🎫 *SKr 45.* ☉ *Late Apr.–June and late Aug., daily 3–11; July–mid-Aug., daily noon–11; Sept., Sat. 11–1 and Sun. noon–8.*

53 Röhsska Museet (Museum of Arts and Crafts). Fine collections of furniture, books and manuscripts, tapestries, and pottery are on view. Artifacts date back as far as 1,000 years, but it's the 20th-century gallery, with its collection of many familiar household objects, that seems to provoke the most enjoyment. ⊠ *Vasag. 37–39,* ☎ *031/613850.* 🎫 *SKr 35.* ☉ *Year-round, weekends noon–5; May–mid-June, weekdays noon–4; mid-June–Aug., Mon. and Wed.–Fri. noon–6, Tues. noon–9; Apr. and Sept., Tues. noon–9, Wed.–Fri. noon–4.*

56 Stadsmuseet (City Museum). Once the warehouse and auction rooms of the Swedish East India Company, a major trading firm founded in 1731, this palatial structure dates from 1750. Today it contains exhibits on the Swedish west coast, with a focus on Göteborg's nautical and trading past. One interesting exhibit deals with the East India Company and its ship the *Göteborg*. On its 1745 return from China, she sank just outside the city while members of the crew's families watched from shore. ⊠ *Norra Hamng. 12,* ☎ *031/612770.* 🎫 *SKr 40.* ☉ *Weekdays noon–6, weekends 11–4. Closed Mon. Sept.–Apr.*

NEED A BREAK?	In the cellar of Stadsmuseet, the **Ostindiska Huset Krog & Kafé** (☎ 031/135750) re-creates an 18th-century pub. The *dagenslunch*, priced at SKr 65, is available from 11:30 to 2.

Commercial Göteborg

Explore Göteborg's portside character, both historic and modern, at the waterfront development near town center, where an array of markets and boutiques keep you busy for hours.

A Good Walk

Begin at the harborside square known as Lilla Bommen Torg, where the **Utkiken** ㊼ offers a bird's-eye view of the city and harbor. The waterfront development here includes the training ship **Viking,** the Opera House, and the **Maritima Centrum** ㊽.

From Lilla Bommen Torg, take the pedestrian bridge across the highway to **Nordstan** ㊾. Leave the mall at the opposite end, which puts you at Brunnsparken, the hub of the city's streetcar network. Turn right and cross the street to Gustav Adolfs Torg, the city's official center, dominated by **Rådhuset** ㊿. On the north side of the square is **Börshuset** ㉑, built in 1849.

Head north from the square along Östra Hamngatan and turn left onto Postgatan to visit **Kronhuset** ㉒, the city's oldest secular building, dating from 1643. Surrounding the entrance to Kronhuset are the **Kronhusbodarna,** carefully restored turn-of-the-20th-century shops and arts and crafts boutiques.

Return to Gustav Adolfs Torg and follow Östra Hamngatan south over the Stora Hamnkanal to Kungsportsplats, where the Saluhall, or Market Hall, has stood since 1888. A number of pedestrian-only shopping streets branch out through this neighborhood on either side of Östra Hamngatan. Crossing the bridge over Rosenlunds Kanalen from Kungsportsplats brings you onto Kungsportsavenyn and the entrance to **Trädgårn** ㉓.

TIMING

The walk itself will take about two hours; allow extra time to explore the sites and to shop. Note that Kronhuset is always closed weekends, and Utkiken is closed weekdays off-season. The Kronhusbodarna is closed Sunday. Trädgårn is closed Monday off-season.

Sights to See

㉑ **Börshuset** (Stock Exchange). Completed in 1849, the former Stock Exchange building houses city administrative offices as well as facilities for large banquets. The fabric of the large, opulent banqueting halls and blue stucco anterooms is under considerable strain through age. Although not officially open to the public staff can sometimes be persuaded to let you in to look around. If you can get in, you won't be disappointed. ✉ *Gustav Adolfs Torg 5.*

OFF THE BEATEN PATH — **GASVERKSKAJEN –** For an interesting tour of the docks, head northeast from Lilla Bommen about 1½ km (1 mi) along the riverside to the Gas Works Quay, just off Gullbergsstrandgatan. Today, this is the headquarters of a local boating association, its brightly colored pleasure craft contrasting with the old-fashioned working barges either anchored or being repaired at Ringön, just across the river.

Kronhusbodarna (Historical Shopping Center). Glassblowing and watchmaking are among the arts and crafts offered in this area of shops, which adjoin the Kronhuset. There is also a nice, old-fashioned café. ✉ *Kronhusg. 1D.* ☺ *Closed Sun.*

㉒ **Kronhuset** (Crown House). The city's oldest secular building, dating from 1643, was originally the city's armory. In 1660 Sweden's Parliament met here to arrange the succession for King Karl X Gustav, who died suddenly while visiting the city. ✉ *Postg. 68,* ☎ *031/7117377.* 🎫 *SKr 30.* ☺ *Weekends 11–4.*

㊽ **Maritima Centrum** (Marine Center). Here modern naval vessels, including a destroyer, submarines, lightship, cargo vessel, and various tugboats, provide insight into Göteborg's historic role as a major port. The main attraction is the huge naval destroyer, complete with a medical room where mannequins are shown in the middle of performing a leg amputation. ✉ *Packhuskajen,* ☎ *031/105950.* 💳 *SKr 50.* 🕐 *May–June, daily 10–6; July–Aug., daily 10–9; Mar.–Apr. and Sept.–Nov., daily 10–4.*

OFF THE BEATEN PATH
NYA ELFSBORGS FÄSTNING – Boats leave regularly from Lilla Bommen to the Elfsborg Fortress, built in 1670 on a harbor island to protect the city from attack. ✉ ☎ *031/609660.* 💳 *SKr 65.* 🕐 *6 departures daily early May–Aug., daily; Sept., weekends.*

59 **Nordstan.** Sweden's largest indoor shopping mall—open daily—comes replete with a huge parking garage, 24-hour pharmacy, post office, several restaurants, entertainment for children, the department store Åhlens, and a tourist information kiosk. ✉ *Entrances on Köpmansg., Nils Ericsonsg., Kanaltorgsg., and Östra Hamng.*

60 **Rådhuset.** Though the Town Hall dates from 1672, when it was designed by Nicodemus Tessin the Elder, its controversial modern extension by Swedish architect Gunnar Asplund is from 1937. The building therefore offers two architectural extremes. One section has the original grand chandeliers and trompe l'oeil ceilings; the other has glass elevators, mussel-shape drinking fountains, and vast expanses of laminated aspen wood. Together they make a fascinating mix. ✉ *Gustav Adolfs Torg 1.*

OFF THE BEATEN PATH
SJÖFARTSMUSEET & AKVARIET – This museum combines maritime history with an aquarium. The museum has model ships, cannons, a ship's medical room, and a collection of figureheads. The adjacent aquarium contains a good selection of Nordic marine life and a more exotic section with, among other animals, two alligators and some piranhas. ✉ *Karl Johansg. 1, 2 km (1 mi) west of the city center,* ☎ *031/612901.* 💳 *SKr 35.* 🕐 *Weekdays 9–5, weekends 10–5.*

63 **Trädgårn** (Botanic Gardens). Here you'll find beautiful open green spaces, a magnificent Rose Garden with more than 3,000 varieties; a Butterfly House; and the Palm House, whose design echoes that of London's Crystal Palace. ✉ *Just off Kungsportsavenyn,* ☎ *031/611911 for Butterfly House.* 🕐 *Park 7AM–8PM; Palm House 10–4; Butterfly House Oct.–Mar., Tues.–Sun. 10–3; Apr., Tues.–Sun. 10–4; May and Sept., daily 10–4; June–Aug., daily 10–5.*

57 **Utkiken** (Lookout Tower). This red-and-white-stripe skyscraper towers 282 ft above the waterfront, offering an unparalleled view of the city and skyscrapers from the viewing platform at the top. ✉ *Lilla Bommen.* 💳 *SKr 25.* 🕐 *May–Aug., daily 11–7; Oct.–Apr., weekends 11–4.*

OFF THE BEATEN PATH
VIKING – This four-masted schooner, built in 1907, was among the last of Sweden's sailing cargo ships. The Hotel and Restaurant School of Göteborg opened a hotel and restaurant inside the ship in February 1995. Those not staying at the hotel or eating at the restaurant are also welcome. ✉ *Lilla Bommen,* ☎ *031/635800.* 💳 *SKr 25.* 🕐 *9–7 daily.*

Haga and Linné Districts

Just west of the main city, these two areas are at the forefront of the new, cosmopolitan Göteborg. Once so run-down that they were scheduled for demolition, they now make up one of the city's most attractive areas. A stroll through the close network of cobbled streets will take you past wood and stone artisans' houses. Once home to the city's poor, the buildings now contain expensive cafés and boutiques where Göteborg's wealthy young elite go to see and be seen.

A Good Walk

Set off from the east end of **Haga Nygatan** ⑥ and stroll west past the busy cafés and boutiques selling art-deco light fixtures and antique kitchenware. Turn left onto Landsvägsgatan and walk up to join Linnégatan, the Dutch-inspired street that's now considered Göteborg's "second Avenyn." There is an air of quiet sophistication about Linnégatan, with small antique and jewelry shops competing for attention against secluded street cafés and high-end design and crafts shops.

Walk south along Linnégatan for five minutes to get to **Slottskogen** ⑥. If relaxing is your thing, you can spend some time lounging in this huge, tranquil expanse of parkland. Alternatively, you can make use of your time here and visit the **Naturhistorika Museet** ⑥, Göteborg's oldest museum, or the **Botaniska Trädgården** ⑥, on the south side of the park.

Depart the park the same way you came in, and wind your way north up Nordenhemsgatan. At the end of this road, turn right onto Första Långgatan and then onto Södra Allégatan. Here you can find the beautiful and tranquil oasis of the **Haga Badet** ⑥, a superbly renovated bathhouse.

TIMING

At a gentle pace, the walk alone will take about one hour. If you allow yourself to be tempted by the great shopping, superb cafés, and both museums, you could spend nearly a whole day in this part of the city.

Sights to See

⑥ **Botaniska Trädgården** (Botanical Gardens). With 1,200 plant species this is Sweden's largest botanical gardens. Herb gardens, bamboo groves, a Japanese valley, forest plants, and tropical greenhouses are all on display. ⊠ *Slotskoggen,* ☎ *031/7411101.* 🎟 *SKr 20.* ☉ *Daily 9–6.*

⑥ **Haga Badet.** This stunning bathhouse was built at the end of the 19th century by the Swedish philanthropist Sven Renström. Originally used by local dock and factory workers, it now plays host to Göteborg's leisure hungry elite. It's well worth a visit. The pretty pool is art nouveau, with wall paintings, an arched ceiling, and lamps with a diving-lady motif. The Roman baths and the massage and spa area all exude relaxation, but the architecture alone is worth a look, even if you don't intend to take the plunge. ⊠ *Södra Allég. 4,* ☎ *031/600600.* 🎟 *SKr 150 to use facilities, otherwise free.* ☉ *Weekdays 7–9:30, Sat. 11:30–3, Sun. 10–5.*

⑥ **Haga Nygatan.** The redbrick buildings that line this street were originally poorhouses donated by the Dickson family, the city's British industrialist forefathers. ROBERT DICKSON can still be seen carved into the facades of these buildings. The buildings' ground floors were made of stone in order to prevent the spread of fire (the upper floors are wood). The Dickson family's impact on the architecture of the west of Sweden can also be seen in Robert's grandson James's impressive, fanciful mansion in Tjolöholm, to the south of Göteborg. ⊠ *Haga Nyg.*

⑥ **Naturhistorika Museet.** Although the Natural History Museum has a collection containing more than 10 million preserved animals, you may be disappointed to discover that the majority are tiny insects that sit unnoticed in rows of drawers. It's worth a visit to see the world's only stuffed blue whale. Harpooned in 1865, the whale now contains a Victorian café, complete with red-velvet sofas; the top half of the creature is secured to its underside by hinges. This bizarre café is now open only during election years, which includes 2002. (The Swedish word for election, *val,* is the same as that for whale.) ⊠ *Slottskogen,* ☎ *031/7752400.* 🎟 *SKr 40.* ☉ *Daily 11–5.*

OFF THE
BEATEN PATH
SKANSEN KRONAN – To the south of Haga is one of Göteborg's two surviving 17th-century fortress towers. Built on a raised mound of land, the tower houses the military museum, containing displays of weapons dating back to the Middle Ages, and Swedish uniforms from the 19th and 20th centuries. The museum's presentations can be a little dry at times, and is probably only for the true enthusiast of military history. But the view northward across the city makes the journey worthwhile.

65 **Slottskogen.** Spend some time in this stunning area of parkland containing cafés, farm animals, a seal pond, Sweden's oldest children's zoo, and many birds, including even pink flamingos in summer. Slottskogen is one of the best parts of the city in which to take a break. ⊠ *South of Linnég.* ☉ *Daily, dawn–dusk.*

OFF THE
BEATEN PATH
VOLVO MUSEUM – In Arendal, 8 km (5 mi) west of the city center, the Volvo Museum pays homage to the car company that in one way or another helps support 25% of Göteborg's population. Not surprisingly, exhibits include most of Volvo's cars over the years as well as some prototypes, the first electric car, and an early jet engine, the first one used by the Swedish Air Force. A 20-minute film helps to put the whole history into perspective at this rather well put together museum. ⊠ *Avd. 1670 ARU,* ☎ *031/664814.* ☑ *SKr 30.* ☉ *June–Aug., Tues.–Fri. 10– 5, weekends 11–4; Sept.–May, Tues.–Fri. noon–5, weekends 11–4.*

DINING

You can eat well in Göteborg, but expect to pay dearly for the privilege. Fish dishes are the best bet here. Call ahead to be sure restaurants are open, as many close for a month in summer.

$$$–$$$$ ✕ **28+.** Step down from the street into this former wine and cheese
★ cellar to find an elegant restaurant owned by two of the best chefs in Göteborg. Finely set tables, flickering candles, and country-style artwork evoke the mood of a rustic French town. Italian and American flavors blend their ways into the French dishes; choose a five- or seven-course meal, or take your pick à la carte. Note that one of the best wine cellars in Sweden is at your disposal. ⊠ *Götaborgsg. 28,* ☎ *031/ 202161. Jacket required. AE, DC, MC, V. Closed Sun.*

$$$ ✕ **Kungstorget.** This stunning restaurant is in the heart of the city, flanked
★ by Rosenlunds Kanalen on one side and Saluhallen, a beautiful Victorian food market, on the other. Inside, the wooden floors and terracotta walls create a feeling of simplicity and warmth. The menu offers classic French-style cuisine with a modern twist. For the truly adventurous diner, dishes such as nettle soup with snails or halibut with crispy pigs' feet may be too tempting to pass up. The selection of wines is excellent, as are the 400-year-old cellars in which it is kept (a visit to the cellars can be arranged through the cooperative sommelier). To finish your dining experience, try one of the impressive digestives and brandies available—some more than 100 years old. ⊠ *Kungstorget 14,* ☎ *031/ 7110022. AE, DC, MC, V. Closed Sun.*

$$$ ✕ **Le Village.** Ever been to a restaurant with tables and chairs you liked so much that you wished you could take them home? What about the lamps or the paintings on the wall? Well, at Le Village that's exactly what you can do. Everything in this restaurant, and the connected antiques shop (☎ 031/143833), is for sale. The food is exceptional, especially the seasonal meat dishes. Try the smaller dining room if you want to avoid some of the prices in the main room. ⊠ *Tredje Läng. 13,* ☎ *031/242003, AE, DC, MC, V. Closed Sun.*

Göteborg Dining and Lodging

Dining

A Hereford
Beefstouw **16**
Amanda Boman . . . **12**
Cyrano **18**
Den Lilla Taverna . . **19**
Fiskekrogen **8**
Gabriel **15**
Kafe Kakel **7**
Kungstorget **13**
Le Village **17**
Noon **26**
Palace **6**

Pharmacy **10**
Plus (+) **24**
Räkan **33**
Restaurang
Frågetecken **34**
Sjömagasinet **20**
Smaka **27**
The Place **30**
Trägårn **11**
28+ **28**
Westra Piren
Restaurant **21**

Lodging

Eggers **2**
Elite Plaza **9**
Europa **3**
Excelsior **29**
Göteborgs
Vandrarhem **38**
Lilton **25**
Liseberg Heden . . . **36**
Novotel **23**
Opalen **35**

Panorama **37**
Park Avenue
(Radisson SAS) . . . **31**
Partille
Vandrarhem **1**
Quality Hotel 11 . . **22**
Radisson SAS
Scandinavia **5**
Riverton **14**
Royal **4**
Rubinen **32**

KEY

🛈 Tourist Information

Rail Lines

$$$ ✕ **Noon.** Swedish and Asian styles fuse to produce innovative, quality seafood and noodle dishes that are served in a simple, modern setting. Try a few of the smaller, less expensive appetizers or go all out with the flounder in lemon ginger sauce with saffron dumplings. ⊠ *Viktoriag. 2,* ☎ *031/138800. AE, DC, MC, V.*

$$$ ✕ **The Place.** Possibly Göteborg's finest dining establishment, the Place
★ offers a warm, intimate atmosphere created by terra-cotta ceilings, pastel-yellow walls, and white linen tablecloths. A wide selection of exotic dishes, from smoked breast of pigeon to beef tartare with caviar, are prepared with quality ingredients. This is also the home of one of the best wine cellars in Sweden, with Mouton Rothschild wines dating from 1904. An outdoor terrace is open during summer. ⊠ *Arkivg. 7,* ☎ *031/160333. Reservations essential. AE, DC, MC, V.*

$$$ ✕ **Räkan.** This informal and popular place makes the most of an unusual gimmick: the tables are arranged around a long tank, and if you order shrimp, the house specialty, they arrive at your table in radio-controlled boats you navigate yourself. ⊠ *Lorensbergsg. 16,* ☎ *031/ 169839. Reservations essential. AE, DC, MC, V. No lunch weekends.*

$$$ ✕ **Sjömagasinet.** Seafood is the obvious specialty at this waterfront restaurant. In a 200-year-old renovated shipping warehouse, the dining room has views of the harbor and the suspension bridge. An outdoor terrace opens up in summer. ⊠ *Klippans Kulturreservat,* ☎ *031/ 7755920. Reservations essential. AE, DC, MC, V.*

$$$ ✕ **Smaka.** Deep-blue walls and ambient music create Smaka's mellow mood, a perfect backdrop for sampling what the chef calls "modernized" Swedish cuisine. Göteborg's younger crowd tends to stay here for a few extra drinks after eating. ⊠ *Vasaplatsen 3,* ☎ *031/132247. AE, DC, MC, V.*

$$$ ✕ **Trägårn.** Spicy, Asian-influenced cuisine stands out against linen tablecloths in this earth-tone restaurant; the vegetarian menu is extensive. A wall of glass in the two-story dining hall affords a view of Göteborg's beautiful Trägårnpark; another wall is covered in blond-wood paneling, a contrast to the black slate floor. ⊠ *Nya Allén,* ☎ *031/102080. AE, DC, MC, V. Closed Sun.*

$$–$$$ ✕ **A Hereford Beefstouw.** Probably as close as Sweden gets to an American steak house, this restaurant has gained popularity in a town controlled by fish restaurants. Chefs grill beef selections in the center of the three dining rooms, one of which is set aside for nonsmokers. Thick wooden tables, pine floors, and landscape paintings give the place a rustic touch. ⊠ *Linnég. 5,* ☎ *031/7750441. AE, DC, MC, V. No lunch weekends or July.*

$$–$$$ ✕ **Palace.** In the center of Brunnsparken, the Palace is one of Göteborg's most popular summer spots for eating, dancing, and drinking. Live bands and DJs play the '70s and '80s favorites of the well-dressed fortysomethings who frequent the restaurant and nightclub. The extensive single-malt whiskey collection is known around town: call ahead to arrange a tasting. The menu of mostly traditional Swedish cuisine is extensive. ⊠ *Brunnsparken,* ☎ *031/802100. AE, DC, MC, V. Closed Sun.*

$$–$$$ ✕ **Westra Piren Restaurant.** Across the river from central Göteborg lies Eriksberg, where former dockyards mix with modern buildings. Perched at the end of a pier that juts out into the harbor, this restaurant has a main dining hall in an elegant triangular room on the second floor and a less expensive brasserie on the first floor; contemporary French-inspired Swedish fare is on the menu at both. In summer food is served on an outdoor patio. Finding the pier by car can prove difficult; consider taking a ferry from the city side of the river. ⊠ *Dockepiren, Eriksberg,* ☎ *031/519555. Reservations essential. Jacket and tie. AE, DC, MC, V. Main dining hall closed Sun.*

$–$$$ ✕ **Fiskekrogen.** The Fish Inn has more than 30 fish and seafood dishes from which to choose. Lunches are particularly good, ideal if you're coming from the Stadsmuseet across the canal. ✉ *Lilla Torget 1,* ☎ *031/101005. AE, DC, MC, V. Closed Sun.*

$$ ✕ **Plus (+).** This relaxing restaurant recalls the Sweden of the past. The restaurant is inside a ramshackle early 1900s wooden house whose foundations are attached to the bedrock on which the city was built. (As you travel through town, you may see some of this rock poking up through the modern sidewalks and streets.) Eat well-prepared fish and meat dishes with a varied international flavor at polished wood tables, all the while sitting beneath antique chandeliers. ✉ *Linnég. 32,* ☎ *031/ 240890. AE, DC, MC, V.*

$$ ✕ **Restaurang Frågetecken.** With a name that translates to "Restaurant Question Mark," this spot has attracted a good deal of curiosity. Its location, just a minute's walk from Götaplatsen, also makes it popular with locals and visitors alike. Eat in the busy, bright conservatory in summer, or in the relaxing interior, which is decorated in neutral colors. If you don't mind the noise and the hectic pace, dine in the open kitchen to watch the chefs carefully preparing their Balkan-influenced food. Anything with duck is delicious, but also pricey. Pasta dishes are homey, comforting, and a little easier on the pocket. ✉ *Södra Vägan 20,* ☎ *031/160030. Reservations essential. AE, DC, MC, V.*

$–$$ ✕ **Cyrano.** A little piece of southern France in Sweden, this superb, au-
★ thentically Provençal bistro is an absolute must. Inside, the tables are crammed close together, French art hangs on the walls, and French touches extend throughout. Highlights include a sumptuously creamy fish soup, sardines with garlic, and grass-fed lamb with tomatoes and sweet peppers. A laid-back atmosphere and friendly, helpful service combine to create the great buzz that continues to draw in the trendier citizens of Göteborg. Cyrano also does the best wood-fire-cooked pizzas in the city. ✉ *Prinsg. 7,* ☎ *031/143110. Reservations essential. AE, DC, MC, V.*

$–$$ ✕ **Kafe Kakel.** Inside a late-18th-century building, this café is perfect for a relaxing, inexpensive lunch or a drink. It's centered around a bright indoor courtyard that is filled with buffet tables offering soups, salads, and sandwiches. ✉ *Kyrkog. 33,* ☎ *031/7115920. MC, V. No dinner Sun.*

$–$$ ✕ **Pharmacy.** An average interior of ubiquitous blond wood is given an edge with the addition of a medical theme; pill bottles line up with wine bottles and forceps with knives and forks. A well-accomplished, if a little short, menu mixes Swedish classics with Italian twists. Keep an eye out for lamb meatballs with olive mashed potatoes, and anything with the delicious local pork. ✉ *Västra Hamng. 15,* ☎ *031/ 7014947. AE, MC, V. Closed Sun.*

$ ✕ **Amanda Boman.** This little restaurant in one corner of the market hall at Kungsportsplats keeps early hours, so unless you eat an afternoon dinner, plan on lunch instead. The cuisine is primarily Swedish, including fish soup and gravlax. ✉ *Saluhallen,* ☎ *031/137676. AE, DC, MC, V. Closed Sun. No dinner.*

$ ✕ **Den Lilla Taverna.** A very good, lively, and popular Greek restaurant, with paper tablecloths and Greek mythological scenes painted on the walls. Live bouzouki music on Wednesday and Saturday evenings gives the place an authentic feel. ✉ *Oliver Dahlsg. 17,* ☎ *031/1128805. AE, DC, MC, V.*

$ ✕ **Gabriel.** A buffet of fresh shellfish and the fish dish of the day draw crowds to this restaurant on a balcony above the fish hall. You can watch all the trading as you eat lunch. ✉ *Feske Körkan,* ☎ *031/ 139051. AE, DC, MC, V. Closed Sun. and Mon. No dinner.*

LODGING

$$$$ 🏨 **Park Avenue (Radisson SAS).** Though this modern luxury hotel sorely lacks much character, all the facilities are in place, including an SAS check-in counter. The well-equipped rooms are decorated in earth tones and have good views of the city. ✉ *Kungsportsavenyn 36–38, Box 53233, 400 16,* ☎ *031/176520,* FAX *031/169568. 318 rooms with bath. 2 restaurants, bar, 2 no-smoking floors, indoor pool, sauna, meeting room. AE, DC, MC, V. BP.*

$$$$ 🏨 **Radisson SAS Scandinavia.** Across Drottningtorget from the central train station, the Radisson SAS is Göteborg's most modern and spectacular international hotel. The attractive atrium lobby is home to two restaurants: Frascati, which serves international cuisine, and the Atrium piano bar with a lighter menu. Rooms are large and luxurious and decorated in pastels. Guests receive a 20% discount at the well-appointed health club on the premises. ✉ *Södra Hamng. 59–65, 401 24,* ☎ *031/806000,* FAX *031/159888. 344 rooms with bath. Restaurant, piano bar, no-smoking rooms, hair salon, health club, shops, casino, convention center, travel services. AE, DC, MC, V. BP.*

$$$ 🏨 **Eggers.** Dating from 1859, Best Western's Eggers has more old-world ★ character than any other hotel in the city. It is a minute's walk from the train station and was probably the last port of call in Sweden for many emigrants to the United States. Rooms vary in size, and all are beautifully appointed, often with antiques. Only breakfast is served. ✉ *Drottningtorget, Box 323, 401 25,* ☎ *031/806070,* FAX *031/154243. 65 rooms. No-smoking rooms, meeting room. AE, DC, MC, V. BP.*

$$$ 🏨 **Europa.** Large and comfortable, this hotel is part of the Nordstan ★ mall complex, very close to the central train station. The rooms are airy and colorful with a very modern feel. There are also special rooms with Internet hookups. Service throughout is deft and courtly. ✉ *Köpmansg. 38, 401 24,* ☎ *031/801280,* FAX *031/154755. 475 rooms, 5 suites. Restaurant, piano bar, no-smoking floor, indoor pool, sauna, convention center, parking. AE, DC, MC, V. BP.*

$$$ 🏨 **Liseberg Heden.** Not far from the famous Liseberg Amusement Park, Liseberg Heden is a popular family hotel. Each of the modern rooms has light-color walls, a satellite television, a minibar, and a large desk, and most have wood floors. Perks include a sauna and a very good restaurant. ✉ *Sten Stureg., 411 38,* ☎ *031/7506900,* FAX *031/ 7506930. 160 rooms. Restaurant, minibars, no-smoking rooms, sauna, meeting room. AE, DC, MC, V. BP.*

$$$ 🏨 **Opalen.** If you are attending an event at the Scandinavium, or if you have children and are heading for the Liseberg Amusement Park, this RESO hotel is ideally located. Rooms are bright and modern. ✉ *Engelbrektsg. 73, Box 5106, 402 23,* ☎ *031/7515300,* FAX *031/7515311. 241 rooms. Restaurant, bar, 2 no-smoking floors, sauna. AE, DC, MC, V. BP.*

$$$ 🏨 **Panorama.** Within reach of all downtown attractions and close to Liseberg, this Best Western hotel is a quiet, relaxing place to stay. The rooms have dark walls in reds and other earth tones, dark wood floors, large wall mirrors, and fabrics done in light pastel colors. ✉ *Eklandag. 51–53, Box 24037, 400 22,* ☎ *031/7677000,* FAX *031/7677070. 339 rooms. Restaurant, lounge, no-smoking floor, hot tub, sauna, meeting room, free parking. AE, DC, MC, V. BP.*

$$$ 🏨 **Quality Hotel 11.** Situated on the water's edge in Eriksberg, Hotel 11 combines the warehouse style of the old waterfront with a modern interior of multitier terraces. Commonly used by large companies for business conferences, the hotel also welcomes families who want to stay across the harbor from downtown Göteborg. The rooms are clean, bright, and modern; some offer panoramic views of the harbor. Next door is Eriksbergshallen, a theater and conference hall that hosts international performances. ⊠ *Masking. 11, 417 64 Eriksberg,* ☎ *031/ 7791111,* FAX *031/7791110. 133 rooms. Restaurant, bar, no-smoking rooms, sauna, meeting room. AE, DC, MC, V. BP.*

$$$ 🏨 **Riverton.** Convenient for people arriving in the city by ferry, this hotel is close to the European terminals and overlooks the harbor. Built in 1985, it has a glossy marble floor and reflective ceiling in the lobby. Rooms are decorated with abstract-pattern textiles and whimsical prints. ⊠ *Stora Badhusg. 26, 411 21,* ☎ *031/7501000,* FAX *031/ 7501001. 190 rooms. Restaurant, bar, no-smoking rooms, hot tub, sauna, meeting room, free parking. AE, DC, MC, V. BP.*

$$$ 🏨 **Royal.** Göteborg's oldest hotel, built in 1852, is small, family-
★ owned, and traditional. Rooms, most with parquet floors, are individually decorated with reproductions of elegant Swedish traditional furniture. The Royal is in the city center a few blocks from the central train station. ⊠ *Drottningg. 67, 411 07,* ☎ *031/806100,* FAX *031/156246. 82 rooms. Breakfast room, no-smoking floor. AE, DC, MC, V. BP.*

$$$ 🏨 **Rubinen.** The central location on Avenyn is a plus, but this Scandic hotel can be noisy in summer. Rooms aren't especially notable, but the location of this hotel makes it a great spot if you want to be in the middle of the action. ⊠ *Kungsportsavenyn 24, Box 53097, 400 14,* ☎ *031/ 7515400,* FAX *031/7515400. 185 rooms. Restaurant, bar, no-smoking rooms, meeting room. AE, DC, MC, V. BP.*

$$ 🏨 **Elite Plaza.** A five-minute walk from the central station, the Plaza
★ is one of the smartest hotels in the city. The palatial building, an architectural attraction in itself, dates from 1889. In 2000 the building was modernized with care to give it an air of grandeur, quality, and restfulness. All original features are untouched, from the stucco ceilings to the English mosaic floors, and are tastefully matched with modern art and up-to-date guest facilities. Rooms are decorated in earth tones and dark wood, and offer all modern facilities, including Internet hookups. The hotel restaurant, Swea Hoff, has very high standards, offering international cuisine, Swedish specialties, seafood, and a fine wine list. ⊠ *Västra Hamng. 3, Box 110 65, 404 22,* ☎ *031/7204000,* FAX *031/7204010. 144 rooms, 87 with bath, 5 suites. Restaurant, bar, pub, no-smoking rooms, convention center. AE, DC, MC, V. BP.*

$$ 🏨 **Excelsior.** A shabbily stylish 1880 building in a road of classic Göteborg houses, this is a place to come for character and history. The Excelsior has been in operation since 1930, and offers rooms that are full of homey comfort and faded grandeur. Greta Garbo and Ingrid Bergman both stayed here as, more recently, did musician Sheryl Crow. Classic suites—Garbo's was number 535—with splendid 19th-century features cost no more than ordinary rooms. ⊠ *Karl Gustavsg. 7, 411 25,* ☎ *031/175435,* FAX *031/175439. 62 rooms without bath, 3 suites. Restaurant, bar. AE, DC, MC, V. BP.*

$$ 🏨 **Novotel.** The redbrick industrial-age architecture of this old brewery belies a mishmash of architectural styles inside. Situated just west of the city on the Göta Älv, the top floors afford spectacular views of Göteborg. There's a very big central atrium, complete with obligatory fake foliage, and an expensive restaurant, Carnegie Kay, attached. ⊠ *Klippan 1, 414 51,* ☎ *031/149000,* FAX *031/422232. 148 rooms, 50 with bath, 5 suites. Restaurant, bar, no-smoking rooms, sauna, free parking. AE, DC, MC, V. BP.*

$ 🏨 **Göteborgs Vandrarhem.** This hostel is 5 km (3 mi) from the train station, in a modern apartment block. Rooms are contemporary, with Swedish-designed furnishings. Breakfast (SKr 40) is not included in the rates. ⊠ *Mejerig. 2, 412 76,* ☎ *031/401050,* FAX *031/401151. 250 beds, 6- to 8-bed apartments. MC, V. Closed Sept.–May.*

$ ⊞ **Lilton.** This unobtrusive bed-and-breakfast-style hotel is inside a small, ivy-covered brick building. Rooms are simple and comfortable, the service friendly and unfussy. ⊠ *Föreningsg. 9, 411 27,* ☎ *031/828808,* FAX *031/822184. 14 rooms without bath. Breakfast room, no-smoking. AE, DC, MC, V. CP.*

$ ⊞ **Partille Vandrarhem.** This hostel is in a pleasant old house 15 km (9 mi) outside the city, next to a lake for swimming. Rooms have harmonious light- and dark-blue fabrics, simple wood furniture, and rich watercolors of local scenes. You can order meals or prepare them yourself in the guest kitchen. ⊠ *Landvetterv., Box 214, 433 24, Partille,* ☎ *031/446501,* ☎ FAX *031/446163. 120 beds, 2- to 6-bed rooms. No credit cards.*

Camping

Fine camping sites are at **Uddevalla** (Hafstens Camping, ☎ 0522/644117), **Göteborg** (Kärralund, ☎ 031/840200, FAX 031/840500), and **Askim** (Askim Strand, ☎ 031/286261, FAX 031/681335).

NIGHTLIFE AND THE ARTS

Music, Opera, and Theater

Home of the highly acclaimed Göteborg Symphony Orchestra, **Konserthuset** (⊠ Götaplatsen, ☎ 031/615310) has a mural by Sweden's Prince Eugen in the lobby. **Operan** (⊠ Packhuskajen, ☎ 031/131300), where Göteborg's Opera Company performs, incorporates a 1,250-seat auditorium with a glassed-in dining area overlooking the harbor. **Stadsteatern** (⊠ Götaplatsen, Box 5094, ☎ 031/615050 tickets; 031/615100 information) puts on high-quality productions of classics by such playwrights as Shakespeare, Molière, and Ibsen. Most of its plays are performed in Swedish.

Nightlife

Bars

If, like many Göteborgers, you have a penchant for all things British, head for **Beefeater Inn** (⊠ Plantageg. 1, ☎ 031/426092), where the staff dresses in tartan kilts, red phone boxes are against the walls, and there's a good selection of English beers. As its name implies, **The Dubliner** (⊠ Ösra Hamng. 50, ☎ 031/139020) is a brave attempt at re-creating what the locals imagine to be old Irish charm. If you're looking for an urbane bar, try **Niva** (⊠ Kungsportsavenyn 9, ☎ 031/7018090), a popular bar with a stylish tile interior and a crowd to match. **Harley's** (⊠ Kungsportsavenyn 10, ☎ 031/137565) attracts a very young, very loud crowd. **Napoleon** (⊠ Vasag. 11, ☎ 031/137550) is a dark, mellow hangout, crowded with oddities. Even the exterior walls are covered in paintings.

Discos and Cabaret

One of the city's liveliest haunts is **Trägårn** (⊠ Nya Allen, ☎ 031/102080), a complex of five bars, a disco, and show bands housed in a strange building resembling a half-built sauna. **Bubbles Nightclub** (⊠ Kungsportsavenyn 8, ☎ 031/105820) is big and brash, attracting mainly people in their thirties. Chrome, mirrors, and a white-tile ceiling like those found in offices make this a memorable place for a drink. At **Rondo** (⊠ Liseberg, ☎ 031/3351033), you can dance the night away on Sweden's largest dance floor while surrounded by people of all ages. There's always a friendly atmosphere, as well as a live band. The **Cabaret Lorensberg** (⊠ Park Avenue Hotel, Kungsportsavenyn 36,

☎ 031/206058) plays traditional and contemporary music and has song and dance performances by gifted artists.

Jazz Clubs
Modern jazz enthusiasts usually head for **Neffertiti** (✉ Hvitfeldtsplatsen 6, ☎ 031/7111533), the trendy, shadowy club where the line to get in is always long. Performers at **Jazzhuset** (✉ Eric Dahlbergsg. 3, ☎ 031/133544) tend to play traditional, swing, and Dixieland jazz.

Film
As in all Swedish cinemas, the ones in Göteborg show mostly English-language films. They're subtitled, never dubbed. The strangest movie theater in town is **Bio Platset** (✉ Kungstorget), a converted meat market turned into a 10-screen cinema. The walls are in various clashing fruit colors, and the floodlit foyer has sections scooped out to reveal Göteborg's natural rock. **Hagabion** (✉ Linnég. 21, ☎ 031/428810) is a good art-house cinema housed in an old ivy-covered school.

OUTDOOR ACTIVITIES AND SPORTS

Beaches

There are several excellent local beaches. The two most popular—though they're rarely crowded—are Askim and Näset. To reach Askim take the Express Blå bus from the central station bus terminal. It's a 10 km (6 mi) journey south of the city center. For Näset catch Bus 19 from Brunnsparken for the 11 km (7 mi) journey southwest of Göteborg.

Diving

The water on the west coast of Sweden, although colder than that on the east coast, is a lot clearer: it's great for diving around rocks and wrecks. Wrap up warmly and bring your diving certificate. Among the many companies offering diving is **Aqua Divers** (☎ 031/220030).

Fishing

Mackerel fishing is popular here. The **M.S. Daisy** (☎ 031/963018 or 010/2358017), which leaves from Hjuvik on the Hisingen side of the Göta River, takes expeditions into the archipelago. With plenty of salmon, perch, and pike, the rivers and lakes in the area have much to offer. For details call Göteborg's **fishing information line** (☎ 031/7730700).

Golf

There are many good golf clubs surrounding Göteborg. **Göteborgs Golfklubb** (✉ Kungsbacka, ☎ 0300/566354) and **Chalmers Golfklubb** (✉ Landvetter, ☎ 031/918430), both 18-hole, are two of the best. All players are welcome, but as with all Swedish courses, you must have a handicap certificate to play.

Indoor Swimming

Vatten Palatset (✉ Häradsvägen 3, Lerum, ☎ 0302/17020) is a decent indoor pool. As well as regular swimming, this huge complex offers indoor and outdoor adventure pools, water slides, water jets, wave pools, bubble pools, and saunas.

Running

Many running tracks wind their way around Göteborg, but to reach the most beautiful one, hop on the number 28 bus from Gamelstad-

storget to Angered Centrum. Here the **Angered and Lärjeåns Dalgång**
winds its way through 8 km (5 mi) of leafy forests and undulating pas-
tures.

SHOPPING

Department Stores

Åhléns (☎ 031/800200) is in the Nordstan mall. Try the local branch
of **NK** (⊠ Östra Hamng. 42, ☎ 031/107000) for men's and women's
fashions and excellent household goods.

Specialty Stores

Antiques

Antikhallarna (Antiques Halls; ⊠ Västra Hamng. 6, ☎ 031/7111324)
has one of Scandinavia's largest antiques selections. Sweden's leading
auction house, **Bukowskis** (⊠ Kungsportsavenyn 43, ☎ 031/200360),
is on Avenyn. For a memorable antiques-buying experience, check out
Auction House (⊠ Trådje Långg. 9, ☎ 031/124430). There's a large
amount of very good silver, porcelain, and jewelry hidden among the
more trashy items. Viewings on Monday and Tuesday 9–noon precede
the auctions on Wednesday and Thursday 9–3.

Crafts

Excellent examples of local arts and crafts can be bought at **Bohuss-
löjden** (⊠ Kungsportsavenyn 25, ☎ 031/160072). If you are looking
to buy Swedish arts and crafts and glassware in a suitably atmospheric
setting, visit the various shops in **Kronhusbodarna** (⊠ Kronhusg. 1D,
☎ 031/7110832). As they have since the 18th century, the sheds and
stalls at **Crown House** (⊠ Postg. 6–8), sell traditional, handcrafted quality goods, including silver and gold jewelry, watches, and handblown
glass.

Men's Clothing

The fashions at **Gillblads** (⊠ Kungsg. 44, ☎ 031/108846) suit a young
and trendy customer. **Ströms** (⊠ Kungsg. 27–29, ☎ 031/177100) has
occupied its street-corner location for two generations, offering clothing of high quality and good taste.

Women's Clothing

Gillblads (⊠ Kungsg. 44, ☎ 031/108846) has the most current fashions. **H & M** (Hennes & Mauritz; ⊠ Kungsg. 55–57, ☎ 031/7110011)
sells stylish, affordable clothes. **Ströms** (⊠ Kungsg. 27–29, ☎ 031/
177100) offers clothing of high quality and mildly conservative style.

Food Markets

There are several large food markets in the city area, but the most impressive is **Salluhallen** (⊠ Kungstorget). Built in 1889, the barrel-roof
wrought-iron, glass, and brick building stands like a monument to industrial architecture. Everything is available here, from fish, meat,
and bakery products to deli foods, herbs and spices, coffee, cheese, and
even just people watching.

GÖTEBORG A TO Z

*To research prices, get advice from other travelers, and book travel ar-
rangements, visit www.fodors.com.*

AIR TRAVEL TO AND FROM GÖTEBORG

CARRIERS

Among the airlines operating to and from Göteborg are Air France, British Airways, Lufthansa, and SAS.

➤ AIRLINES AND CONTACTS: **Air France** (☎ 031/941180). **British Airways** (☎ 020/781144). **Lufthansa** (☎ 031/941325 or 020/228800). **SAS** (☎ 031/942000 or 020/727727).

AIRPORTS AND TRANSFERS

Landvetter airport is approximately 26 km (16 mi) from the city.

➤ AIRPORT INFORMATION: **Landvetter Airport** (☎ 031/941100).

AIRPORT TRANSFERS

Landvetter is linked to Göteborg by freeway. Buses leave Landvetter every 15 to 30 minutes and arrive 30 minutes later at Nils Ericsonsplatsen by the central train station, with stops at Lisebergsstationen, Korsvägen, the Radisson SAS, and Kungsportsplatsen; weekend schedules include some nonstop departures. The price of the trip is SKr 50. For more information, call GL (Göteborg Bus and Tram).

The taxi ride to the city center should cost no more than SKr 250. A shared SAS limousine for up to four people to the same address costs SKr 215.

➤ TAXIS AND SHUTTLES: **GL** (☎ 031/801235). **SAS Limousine Service** (☎ 031/7942424).

BOAT AND FERRY TRAVEL

Traveling the entire length of the Göta Canal by passenger boat to Stockholm takes between four and six days. For details, contact the Göta Canal Steamship Company. For information about sailing your own boat on the Göta Canal, contact AB Göta Kanalbolaget.

➤ BOAT AND FERRY INFORMATION: **AB Göta Kanalbolaget** (☎ 0141/53510). **Göta Canal Steamship Company** (✉ Hotellplatsen 2, Box 272, 401 24 Göteborg, ☎ 031/806315; ✉ N. Riddarholshamnen 5, 111 28 Stockholm, ☎ 08/202728).

BUS TRAVEL TO AND FROM GÖTEBORG

All buses arrive in the central city area. The principal bus company is Swebus.

➤ BUS INFORMATION: **Swebus** (☎ 0200/218218).

CAR RENTAL

Avis has offices at the airport and the central railway station. Hertz has an office in town also.

➤ MAJOR AGENCIES: **Avis** (☎ 031/946030 or 031/805780; at the central railway station ☎ 031/946030 or 031/805780). **Hertz** (✉ Spannmålsg. 16, ☎ 031/946020).

CAR TRAVEL

Göteborg is reached by car either via the E20 or the E4 highway from Stockholm (495 km/307 mi) and the east, or on the E6/E20 coastal highway from the south (Malmö is 290 km/180 mi away). Markings are excellent, and roads are well sanded and plowed in winter.

CONSULATES

➤ CANADA: (✉ Sydatlanten, Scandiahamnen, ☎ 031/645580).
➤ UNITED KINGDOM: (✉ Drottningg. 63, ☎ 031/131327).

EMERGENCIES

Dial 112 for emergencies anywhere in the country, or dial the emergency services number listed below day or night for information on medical services. Emergencies are handled by the Mölndalssjukhuset,

Östrasjukhuset, and Sahlgrenska hospitals. There is a private medical service at CityAkuten weekdays 8–6. There is a 24-hour children's emergency service at Östrasjukhuset as well.

The national dental-service emergency number and the private dental-service number are listed below. Both are available 8 AM–9 PM only; call the dental emergency number for after-hours emergencies.
➤ DOCTORS AND DENTISTS: **Dental-Service Emergencies** (☎ 031/807800). **Private Dental-Services** (☎ 031/800500).
➤ EMERGENCY SERVICES: **Medical Services Information (SOS Alarm)** (☎ 031/7031500).
➤ HOSPITALS: **After hours emergencies** (☎ 031/7031500). **CityAkuten** (✉ Drottningg. 45, ☎ 031/101010). **Mölndalssjukhuset** (☎ 031/861000). **Östrasjukhuset** (☎ 031/374000). **Sahlgrenska Hospital** (☎ 031/601000).
➤ 24-HOUR PHARMACIES: **Vasen** (✉ Götg. 12, in Nordstan shopping mall, ☎ 031/804410).

ENGLISH-LANGUAGE MEDIA
BOOKS
Nearly all bookshops stock English-language books. The broadest selection is at Eckersteins Akademibokhandeln.
➤ BOOKSTORES: **Eckersteins Akademibokhandeln** (✉ Södra Larmg. 11, ☎ 031/171100).

TAXIS
To order a taxi, call Taxi Göteborg.
➤ TAXI COMPANIES: **Taxi Göteborg** (☎ 031/650000; for advance reservations, call ☎ 031/500504).

TOURS
BOAT TOURS
For a view of the city from the water and an expert commentary on its sights and history in English and German, take one of the Paddan sightseeing boats. *Paddan* means "toad" in Swedish, an apt commentary on the vessels' squat appearance. The boats pass under 20 bridges and take in both the canals and part of the Göta River.
➤ FEES AND SCHEDULES: **Paddan** (✉ Kungsportsbron, ☎ 031/133000, ▣ SKr 70).

BUS TOURS
A 90-minute bus tour and a two-hour combination boat-and-bus tour of the chief points of interest leave from outside the main tourist office at Kungsportsplatsen every day from mid-May through August and on Saturday in April, September, and October. Call the tourist office for schedules.

TRAIN TRAVEL
There is regular service from Stockholm, taking a little over 4½ hours, as well as frequent high-speed (X2000) train service, which takes about three hours. All trains arrive at the central train station in Drottningtorget, downtown Göteborg. For schedules, call SJ. Streetcars and buses leave from here for the suburbs, but the hub for all streetcar traffic is a block down Norra Hamngatan, at Brunnsparken.
➤ TRAIN INFORMATION: **Central Train Station** (☎ 031/805000). **SJ** (☎ 031/104445 or 020/757575).

TRANSPORTATION AROUND GÖTEBORG
Stadstrafiken is the name of Göteborg's excellent transit service. Transit brochures, which are available in English, explain the various discount passes and procedures; you can pick one up at a TidPunkten office.

The best bet for the tourist is the Göteborg Card, which covers free use of public transport, various sightseeing trips, and admission to Liseberg and local museums, among other benefits. The card costs SKr 75 for one day, SKr 125 for two days, and SKr 225 for three days; there are lower rates for children younger than 18 years from mid-June to mid-September. You can buy the Göteborg Card as well as regular tram and bus passes at Pressbyrån shops, camping sites, and the tourist information offices.

➤ CONTACTS: **TidPunkten** (✉ Drottningtorget, Brunnsparken, Nils Ericsonsplatsen, and Folkungabron, ☎ 031/801235).

TRAVEL AGENCIES
See the Yellow Pages under *Resor-Resebyråer.*
➤ LOCAL AGENT REFERRALS: **STF** (✉ Drottningtorget 6, Box 305, 401 24, ☎ 031/150930). **Ticket Travel Agency** (✉ Östra Hamng. 35, ☎ 031/176860).

VISITOR INFORMATION
The main tourist office is Göteborg's Turistbyrå. There are also offices at the Nordstan shopping center and in front of the central train station at Drottningtorget.

A free visitor's guide called *Göteborgarn* is available in English during the summer; you can pick it up at tourist offices, shopping centers, and some restaurants, as well as on the streetcars.

The Friday edition of the principal morning newspaper, *Göteborgs Posten,* includes a weekly supplement called "Aveny"—it's in Swedish but is reasonably easy to decipher.

➤ TOURIST INFORMATION: **Göteborg's Turistbyrå** (✉ Kungsportsplatsen 2, 411 10 Göteborg, ☎ 031/612500, FAX 031/132184). **Nordstan shopping center** (✉ Nordstadstorget, 411 05 Göteborg, ☎ 031/615371).

6 SIDE TRIPS FROM GÖTEBORG

BOHUSLÄN

T HE BOHUSLÄN COASTAL REGION NORTH of Göteborg, with its
indented, rocky coastline, provides a foretaste of Norway's fjords
farther north. It was from these rugged shores that the 9th- and
10th-century Vikings sailed southward on their epic voyages. Today
small towns and attractive fishing villages nestle among the distinctively
rounded granite rocks and the thousands of skerries (rocky isles or reefs)
and larger islands that form Sweden's western archipelago. The ideal
way to explore the area is by drifting slowly north of Göteborg, taking full advantage of the uncluttered beaches and small rustic fishing
villages. Painters and sailors haunt the region in summer.

Kungälv

15 km (9 mi) north of Göteborg.

Strategically placed at the confluence of the two arms of the Göta River,
Kungälv was an important battleground in ancient times. Though
today it is something of a bedroom community for Göteborg, the
town still has several ancient sights, including a white wooden church
dating from 1679, with an unusual baroque interior, and narrow cobbled streets full of ancient, leaning, wooden houses.

For a sense of Kungälv's military past, visit the ruins of **Bohus Fästning,** a fortress built by the Norwegians in 1308; it was the site of many
battles between Swedish, Norwegian, and Danish armies. ⊠ *Kungälv,*
☎ *0303/99200.* ≊ *SKr 25.* ☉ *May–June and Aug., daily 10–7; July,
daily 10–8; Sept., weekends 11–5.*

Outdoor Activities and Sports

The tiny village of Rönang, on the island of Tjörn, offers excellent **deep-
sea fishing**; mackerel and cod are among the prized catch. There are
several companies that can take you out, usually in a boat of 12 people. One of the best is **Havsfiske med Hajen** (⊠ Hamnen, Marstrand,
☎ 0304/672447). Prices range between SKr 100 and SKr 350, depending
on how far you go out. All equipment and tackle is included in the price
and you can keep whatever you catch. Most boats leave twice daily.
To get to Tjörn, drive over the road bridge from Stenungsund, just north
of Kungälv on the E6.

Marstrand

69 *17 km (11 mi) west of Kungälv (via Route 168).*

Unusually high stocks of herring used to swim in the waters around
Marstrand, which is on an island of the same name. The fish made the
town extremely rich. But after the money came greed and corruption:
Marstrand soon became known as the most immoral town in Scandinavia, a problem that culminated in the murder of a town cleric in 1586.
Soon after this the town burned down and the fish disappeared. As
Göteborg and Kungälv became major trade centers in the early 19th
century, Marstrand was forced to abandon its hopes of regaining the
prosperity it once had, and turned to tourism instead. By 1820, all the
town's wooden herring salting houses had been turned into fashionable and lucrative bathhouses.

Marstrand is still a place where people come to take to the clear, blue
waters and swim, sail, and fish. But the main draw is **Carlstens Fästning,** the huge stone-walled castle that stands on the rock above the

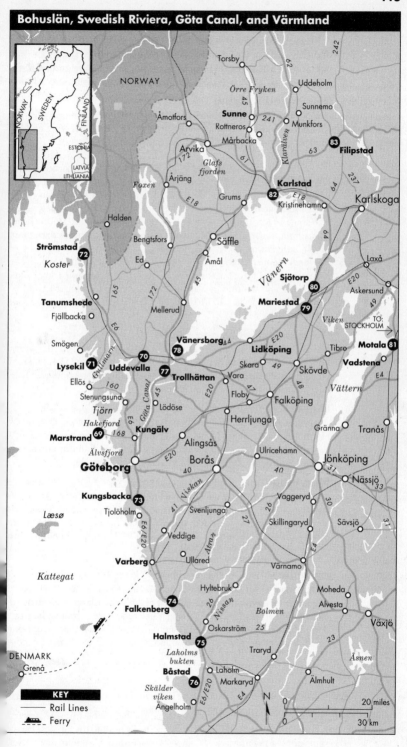

town. Tours of Carlstens Fortress are not completely in English, but most guides are more than willing to translate. The tours include a morbidly fascinating look at the castle's prison cells, where you can see drawings done in blood and hear tales of Carlsten's most famous prisoner, Lasse-Maja—he dressed up as a woman to seduce and then rob local farmers. ☎ 030/360265. 🎫 SKr 25. ⊙ June–Sept., daily 11–6.

Dining and Lodging

$$ ✕🏨 **Grand Hotell Marstrand.** History and luxury abound in this tile-roof hotel, which resembles a French château. Large balconies and verandas open onto a small park, beyond which lies the ocean. Inside, the hotel is stylishly simple, with bold colors and clean Scandinavian furniture. The rooms are equally light and airy, and the bathrooms have white tiles and brass fittings. A windowed sauna in one of the towers looks out over the harbor. The traditional restaurant ($$) serves excellent local seafood specialties: the garlic-marinated langoustine is a standout. ⊠ *Rådhusg. 2, 440 30,* ☎ *0303/60322,* FAX *0303/60053,* WEB *www.grandmarstrand.se. 22 rooms with bath, 6 suites. Restaurant, bar, sauna, convention center. AE, DC, MC, V. BP.*

$ 🏨 **Hotell Nautic.** This basic but good hotel is right on the harbor. The rooms are quite plain but functional, with wood floors and a small desk and chair. The building is a classic white clapboard construction. ⊠ *Långg. 6, 440 35,* ☎ *0303/61030,* FAX *0303/61200. 29 rooms without bath. AE, DC, MC, V. BP.*

Outdoor Activities and Sports

The coastline around Marstrand looks most beautiful from the water. **Boat Charter - After Work** (⊠ Södra Strandg., ☎ 0303/61584) will rent you a boat, complete with captain, for cocktails, sightseeing, and fishing. It costs about SKr 500 an hour.

Nightlife

Among the usual peppering of provincial drinking places, **Oscars** (⊠ Hamng. 11, ☎ 0303/61554) stands out as one of the best. Sweden's first disco (1964) has retained its silver and wood glamour and serves up good music at weekends and great beer all the time.

Shopping

The center of Marstrand is full of ancient cobbled streets, pastel-painted wooden houses, and arts and crafts shops selling locally inspired paintings, handicrafts, and ceramics. Two to look out for are **Mary Carlsson** (⊠ Kungsg. 2–4, ☎ 0708/960459) and **Lankilde Boa** (⊠ Boa Myren 29, ☎ 0703/965131).

OFF THE BEATEN PATH   **GULLHOLMEN –** North of Marstrand, along Route 160, is the town of Ellös, on the island of Orust. A short, frequent ferry from here will take you to the windswept, rugged cliff tops of the small island of Gullholmen. In its 13th-century fishing village, tiny red-painted wooden houses huddle together around a large church. The rest of Gullholmen is set aside as a nature reserve, which supports bird life of all kinds.

Uddevalla

❼⓪ *64 km (40 mi) north of Kungälv, 79 km (49 mi) north of Göteborg.*

A former shipbuilding town located at the head of a fjord, Uddevalla is best known for a 1657 battle between the Danes and the Swedes. Heavy rains doused the musketeers' tinderboxes, effectively ending hostilities.

The history of the whole Bohuslän region can be seen at the **Bohusläns Museum.** Exhibitions reflect the local culture, countryside, and industries, including, of course, fishing. The museum also traces the history of local inhabitants over the 10,000 years since people first settled this part of Sweden. ⊠ *Museeg. 1,* ☎ *0522/656500.* ⌑ *Free.* ☉ *Mon.–Thurs. 10–8, Fri.–Sun. 10–4.*

OFF THE BEATEN PATH

GUSTAVBERG – Adjoining Uddevalla to the west, Gustavberg lays claim to being Sweden's oldest seaside resort, having been mentioned by the botanist Linnaeus in a book he wrote in 1746. There is little left to see of the resort now, save the richly ornamented wooden Society House, but there is a beautiful little park that leads down to the water's edge, a perfect place for a refreshing swim.

Lodging

$$ 🏨 **Bohusgården.** This modern concrete-block hotel's cliff-top location has stunning views of the sea. But even though the rooms are comfortable, they're not that inspiring. The plain, cold, and basic furnishing makes them livable, but not very welcoming. It is the spa that attracts people here. Pampering treatments include facials, mineral-water baths, massage, and more opulent services. ⊠ *Nordens Väg 6, 451 43,* ☎ *0522/36420,* FAX *0522/34472,* WEB *www.bohusgarden.se. 97 rooms, 25 with bath. Restaurant, bar, pool, spa. AE, DC, MC, V. BP.*

$$ 🏨 **Carlia.** A hotel by this name has been in Uddevalla for more than 100 years in one form or another. In its latest guise it has large comfortable rooms with furnishings and fabrics that are a touch on the floral side; a homey bar; and a well-equipped reading area with books, newspapers, and periodicals. All the suites have Jacuzzis. ⊠ *N. Drottningg. 22, 451 16,* ☎ *0522/14140,* FAX *0522/17081. 114 rooms, 9 with bath, 7 suites. Bar, breakfast room, sauna, library. AE, DC, MC, V. BP.*

Lysekil

❼ *30 km (19 mi) west of Uddevalla via E6 and Route 161.*

Perched on a peninsula at the head of Gullmarn Fjord, Lysekil has been one of Sweden's most popular summer resorts since the 19th century, when the wealthiest citizens of Sweden would come to take the therapeutic waters. Back then, the small resort was made up mainly of fancy villas painted mustard and brown. Today, you can still see the original houses, but among them are now such modern devices of "healing" as amusement arcades and cotton-candy stalls.

The surrounding coastline has great, rugged walking trails. These trails offer stunning views of the undulating skerries and islets that dot the water below. Guided botanical and marine walks can be organized by the **tourist office** (☎ 0523/13050).

Take any of the many flights of steps that start from Lysekil's main seafront road to get to **Lysekil Kyrka.** Probably the town's most impressive landmark, Lysekil Church is carved from the pink granite of the area and has beaten copper doors. Its windows were painted by Albert Eldh, the early 20th-century artist. ⊠ *Stora Kyrkog.*

Havets Hus (House of the Sea) concentrates on the fish and other sea life found in local waters. The giant aquariums contain everything from near microscopic lifeforms to giant cod and even a small but menacing shark. The tour ends with a walk through a 26-ft glass tunnel that has fish swimming above and around you. The in-house café has a hole in the floor that looks down into the water above the glass tunnel. As you sip your coffee, you can watch with amusement as the slightly befuddled people wander below you and parents try to stop their children from throwing their cakes in to feed the fish. ⊠ *Strandv.,* ☎ *0523/ 16530.* ⌑ *SKr 10.* ☉ *Daily 10–6.*

Twenty minutes north of Lysekil on Route 162 is **Nordens Ark.** A cut above the usual safari parks, Nordens Ark is a sanctuary for endangered animals. This haven of tranquility is home to red pandas, lynxes, snow leopards, and arctic foxes. The best way to see the elusive wild animals is to follow the small truck that delivers their food at feeding times. ⊠ Åby säteri, Hunnebostrand, ☎ 0523/79590.

<table>
<tr><td>OFF THE
BEATEN PATH</td><td>SMÖGEN – Situated at the very tip of a westerly outcrop of land, Smögen is an ideal point for a quick stop-off. To get here, head north on Route 162 and then head west on Route 171 'til it stops. The small village's red fishing huts; crystal blue water; and pretty, scrubbed boardwalks appear on many postcards of Bohuslän. Down on the main boardwalk a stop at the Bageri Skäret (⊠ Hamnen 1, ☎ 0523/32317) is a must. As well as having a great ocean view from the upstairs veranda, this small café and bar makes exquisite cakes and bread.

FJÄLLBACKA – Twenty-seven kilometers (sixteen miles) north of Lysekil, directly along the coast route, is this picture-perfect village, with pastel wooden houses nestled in the rock. Fjällbacka was home to actress Ingrid Bergman's summerhouse. In the square named after her, you can see her statue peering out over the water where her ashes were scattered, to the distant islands where her house was. Behind the square is a dramatic ravine known as Kungskliftan (King's Cliff) where, among many others added since, you can find King Oscar II's name, which he etched into the rock in 1887.</td></tr>
</table>

Dining and Lodging

$$ ✕ **Brygghuset.** A short boat ride and a walk through a stunning hilltop fishing village on the island of Fiskebäckskil will bring you to this lovely little restaurant. The interior is rustic, with wood beams and plain wooden tables. Here you watch the chefs in the open kitchen as they prepare excellent local fish dishes. In the summer there is outdoor eating, or you can just choose a glass of wine from the excellent wine list and watch the boats sail by. The ferry *Carl Wilhelmsson* leaves from outside the tourist office in Lysekil every half hour, bringing you to the restaurant 20 minutes later. ⊠ *Fiskebäckskil*, ☎ 0523/22222. *Reservations essential. AE, DC, MC, V.*

$–$$ ✕ **Pråmen.** This modern-looking restaurant has large windows and is on legs that allow it to jut out over the water. The view is great; with the windows open you can smell the sea. You can feast on good portions of simply cooked local fish and wash it down with cold beer. ⊠ *Södra Hamng.*, ☎ 0523/13452. *AE, DC, MC, V.*

$$ ▥ **Lysekil Havshotell.** This tall, narrow hotel has stunning views from atop a cliff. Stripped wood floors and a miscellany of furnishings and fabrics create relaxed surroundings. Many rooms have sofas and include bathrobes. Only breakfast is served, and there's a stocked bar (done on the honor system) in each room. For breathtaking views across the water, reserve Room 18, which costs SKr 200 extra. ⊠ *Turistg. 13, 453 30*, ☎ 0523/79750, ℻ 0523/14204. *19 rooms without bath, 2 suites. Breakfast room. AE, MC, V. BP.*

$ ▥ **Strand Vandrarhem.** This hostel is on the seafront and offers simple, friendly accommodations. Unless you stipulate otherwise and pay an additional fee, you may find yourself sharing the room with another guest (the rooms are outfitted with bunk beds). The welcome here is warm, and the breakfast (SKr 45 extra) is excellent. ⊠ *Strandv. 1, 453 30*, ☎ 0523/19751, ℻ 0523/12202, ☒☒ *www.svif.se/083.htm. 12 rooms without bath. AE, DC, MC, V.*

Nightlife and the Arts

During the month of July, Lysekil comes alive to the sounds of the annual **Lysekil Jazz Festival.** Various big-name Swedish, and some international, jazz musicians play in open air concerts and in bars and restaurants. Contact **Lysekil Turistbyrån** (tourist office; ☎ 0523/13050) for details of planned events.

Outdoor Activities and Sports

For a taste of the sea air, and a great look at some local nature, take one of the regular seal safaris. Boat trips to view these fascinating, wallowing, slimy-looking mammals leave from the main harbor three times daily between June and August, cost SKr 120, and take about two hours. Details and times are available from Lysekil Turistbyrån (☎ 0523/13050).

Tanumshede

45 km (28 mi) north of Lysekil (via Route 161 and E6).

From roughly 4000 to 3000 BC, Tanumshede was a coastal settlement. Now it's 5 km (3 mi) from the sea, since sea level is now 50 ft lower than it was then. Although the town itself is not extraordinary, it does hold the largest single collection of Bronze Age rock carvings in Europe. A UNESCO World Heritage site since 1994, people flock from all over the world to see the rudimentary scrapings that depict battles, hunting, and fishing.

Most of the carvings are within a short distance of the road, etched onto the weather-worn rocks that were picked up and deposited around the countryside by retreating Ice Age glaciers, but the ones that are farther out, carved onto the largest rocks, are best reached by bicycle. Bikes can be rented from **Westmans** (✉ Riksv. 67, ☎ 0525/20100), for SKr 20 per day.

Named European museum of the year in 1999 and heralded for its fantastic architecture, the **Vitlycke Museet** tells the story of the area's famous rock carvings and tries to show what life would have been like between 1500 and 500 BC. It also makes some amusing and seemingly random attempts at decoding the messages held in the stones. ✉ *Tanumshede,* ☎ *0525/20950.* ☞ *SKr 50.* ⊙ *Apr.–Sept., daily 10–6; Oct.–Dec., daily 11–5; Jan.–Mar., by appointment only.*

Strömstad

72 *90 km (56 mi) northwest of Uddevalla, 169 km (105 mi) north of Göteborg.*

This popular Swedish resort claims to have more summer sunshine than any other town north of the Alps. Formerly Norwegian, it has been the site of many battles between warring Danes, Norwegians, and Swedes. A short trip over the Norwegian border takes you to Halden, where Sweden's warrior king, Karl XII, died in 1718.

The **Strömstad Museum,** housed in a beautiful 18th-century redbrick mansion, has thoughtful, informative displays on the town's history and the importance of fishing as a local industry. Attached to the museum is a good town archive that includes old pictures showing how life was lived here. ✉ *Södra Hamng. 26,* ☎ *0562/10275.* ☞ *SKr 25.* ⊙ *May–Sept., weekdays 11–4, weekends 11–2.*

Although it is of no particular historical importance, **Strömstad Kyrka** is well worth a visit just to marvel at its interior design. The Strömstad Church's seemingly free-form decoration policy throws together wonderfully detailed, crowded frescoes; overly ornate gilt chandeliers; brass lamps from the 1970s; and model ships hanging from the roof. In the graveyard you can find the stone of Adolf Fritiof Cavalli-Holmgren, the eccentric jeweler's son who went on to become a financier and Sweden's richest man for a brief period around 1900. He was responsible for the design of the grand, copper-roof town hall in the middle of Strömstrad. He never actually got to see it, or live in its specially created penthouse apartment, since he fell out with the local council over the design. ⊠ *S. Kyrkog. 10,* ☎ *0526/10029.*

The open air museum **Fiskartorpet,** with its collection of small houses and farm buildings and domestic and working animals, gives an insightful look into the local farming community of 150 years ago. ⊠ *Karlsg. 45,* ☎ *0526/61753.* 🎦 *Free.* ☉ *May–Aug., daily 11–7.*

OFF THE
BEATEN PATH

KOSTER ISLANDS – There are regular ferryboats from Strömstad to the Koster Islands, Sweden's two most westerly inhabited islands and a perfect place to escape to tranquility. With no motorized vehicles allowed, the two islands are ideal for biking around. Bikes can be rented for SKr 50 at the spot where you disembark from the boat. Most of the island is a sanctuary for wildlife, so that the only sounds you hear as you bike through the meadows are bird cries. You will come across the occasional café or coffee shop, usually in small red wooden houses. The prawn sandwiches are always superb.

Dining and Lodging

$ ✕ **Göstases.** Somewhat resembling the interior of a wooden boat, this restaurant, perched right on the quayside, specializes in locally caught fish and seafood. Inside, knots, ropes, life preservers, stuffed fish, and similar paraphernalia abound. But it all pales when you see the low prices for fresh lobster, crab, prawns, and fish, all of which can be washed down with equally affordable cold beer. There is outside seating in the summer, so you can sit and watch the fishing boats bring in your catch and the pleasure boats float by. ⊠ *Strandpromenaden,* ☎ *0526/10812. MC, V.*

$$ ✕🏨 **Laholmen.** This huge, sprawling hotel and restaurant offers goodquality food and excellent accommodation on a grand scale. The rooms are a bit garish, with overly vivid color schemes, but they are large and well equipped. The restaurant ($$) has a good buffet and an intriguing menu of local dishes, including exquisite prawn sandwiches at lunch. The restaurant as well as most bedrooms have views looking out across the pretty harbor and the water beyond, which is scattered with skerries. ⊠ *Badhusg., 452 30,* ☎ *0526/197000,* 𝔽𝔸𝕏 *0526/ 10036. 123 rooms without baths, 10 suites. Restaurant, bar, lounge, sauna, convention center. AE, DC, MC, V. BP.*

Bohuslän A to Z

To research prices, get advice from other travelers, and book travel arrangements, visit www.fodors.com.

BUS TRAVEL
Buses leave from behind the central train station in Göteborg; the main bus lines are Bohus Trafiken and GL. The trip to Strömstad takes between two and three hours.
➤ Bus Information: **Bohus Trafiken** (☎ 0522/14030). **GL** (☎ 031/ 801235).

CAR TRAVEL

The best way to explore Bohuslän is by car. The E6 highway runs the length of the coast from Göteborg north to Strömstad, close to the Norwegian border, and for campers there are numerous well-equipped and uncluttered camping sites along the coast's entire length.

TRAIN TRAVEL

Regular service along the coast connects all the major towns of Bohuslän. The trip from Göteborg to Strömstad takes about two hours, and there are several trains each day. For schedules, call SJ.
➤ TRAIN INFORMATION: SJ (⊠ Göteborg, ☎ 031/103000 or 020/757575).

VISITOR INFORMATION

➤ TOURIST INFORMATION: **Göteborg Turistbyrå** (⊠ Kungsportsplatsen 2, 411 10 Göteborg, ☎ 031/612500, FAX 031/132184). **Kungälv** (⊠ Fästningsholmen, ☎ 0303/99200). **Kungshamn** (⊠ Hamng. 6, ☎ 0523/37150). **Lysekil,** (⊠ Södra Hamng. 6, ☎ 0523/13050). **Marstrand** (⊠ Hamng., ☎ 0303/60087). **Strömstad** (⊠ Tullhuset, Norra Hamnen, ☎ 0526/62330). **Tanumshede** (⊠ Stora Oppen 5, ☎ 0525/20400). **Uddevalla** (⊠ Kampenhof, ☎ 0522/97700).

SWEDISH RIVIERA

The coastal region south of Göteborg, Halland—locally dubbed the Swedish Riviera—is the closest that mainland Sweden comes to having a resort area. Fine beaches abound, and there are plenty of sporting activities that can be done in the area. But Halland's history is dark, since it was the frontline in fighting between Swedes and Danes. Evidence of such conflicts can be found in its many medieval villages and fortifications. The region stretches down to Båstad in the country's southernmost province, Skåne.

Kungsbacka

73 *25 km (15 mi) south of Göteborg.*

This bedroom community of Göteborg holds a market on the first Thursday of every month. A break in a high ridge to the west, the **Fjärås Crack,** offers a fine view of the coast. Formed by melting ice 13,000 years ago, the ridge made a perfect transport route for nomadic tribes of 10,000 years ago, who used it to track the retreating ice northward to settle their new communities. Some important archaeological discoveries have been made here, and much of the information learned is on display on signs dotted along the ridge. The signs act as a sort of self-guided outdoor museum, dealing with the geological and anthropological history of the ridge.

★ At Tjolöholm, 12 km (7 mi) down the E6/E20 highway from Kungsbacka, is **Tjolöholms Slott** (Tjolöholm Castle), a manor house built by James Dickson, a Scottish merchant and horse breeder. (He was also the grandson of Robert Dickson, the philanthropist and founder of the Swedish East India trade company.) The English Tudor–style house, constructed at the beginning of the 20th century, contains many fascinating elements. By and large, they become a tribute to Dickson's passion for all things modern, including an early version of a pressurized shower and a horse-drawn vacuum cleaner with a very long hose to reach up through the house windows. Dickson died of lead poisoning before the house was completed—he cut his finger while opening a bottle of Champagne and wrapped the lead foil wrapper around the cut. The house he left behind offers much insight into one man's dream.

⊠ *Fjärås,* ☎ *0300/544200.* ⌦ *SKr 50.* ⊗ *June–Aug., daily 11–4; Sept. and Apr.–May, weekends 11–4; Oct., Sun. 11–4.*

Near Tjolöholm is the tiny 18th-century village of Äskhult, the site of an open-air museum, the **Gamla By.** When land reforms forced farmers to combine patches of land into large estates, the four farmers living in Äskhult refused, and kept their land separate. This refusal left the village unable to expand while both of the neighboring areas became towns. And so it stayed that way, until the last inhabitants moved out in the middle of the 19th century. Today you can wander through the houses and farm buildings to get a glimpse of what life was like for 18th-century peasant farmers. ☎ *0300/542159.* ⌦ *SKr 20.* ⊗ *May–Aug., daily 10–6; Sept., weekends 10–6.*

En Route   Forty kilometers (twenty-five miles) southeast of Kungsbacka (on E6 and Route 153) is the shopping mecca of Ullared, once a single discount store, now a whole town of huge outlet stores and malls visited by 3 million Swedes each year. It's overwhelming, but even the most resolute nonshoppers may find it difficult to resist the selection and the prices.

Varberg

40 km (25 mi) south of Kungsbacka, 65 km (40 mi) south of Göteborg.

Varberg is a busy port with connections to Grenå in Denmark. Although the town has some good beaches, it's best known for a suit of medieval clothing preserved in the museum inside the 13th-century **Varbergs Fästning** (Varberg Fortress). The suit belonged to a man who was murdered and thrown into a peat bog. The peat preserved his body, and his clothes are the only known suit of ordinary medieval clothing. The museum also contains a silver bullet said to be the one that killed Karl XII. ☎ *0340/18520.* ⌦ *SKr 30.* ⊗ *Weekdays 10–4, weekends noon–4. Hourly guided tours mid-June–mid-Aug., daily 10–7; May–mid-June and mid-Aug.–Sept., Sun. 10–7.*

Dining and Lodging

$$ ✕ **Societen.** Housed in the cream-and-green carved-wood confection that is the 19th-century society house, this restaurant offers dining on a grand scale. Two huge, high-windowed dining rooms offer French-influenced dishes such as mussels with eggplant and garlic. There's foxtrot dancing on Friday and live bands and disco on Saturday. Two separate lively bar areas are on hand if you need to increase your intake of courage before taking to the dance floor. ⊠ *Societets Park,* ☎ *0340/676500. Reservations essential. AE, DC, MC, V.*

$$ ▦ **Kust Hotellet.** A former sanatorium on the beachfront, the Kust offers grandeur, as well as overly curly pieces of art nouveau furniture stuffed into every room. Bedrooms are a little small but comfortable. There is a large and well-equipped spa and sauna area. ⊠ *Nils Kreugers Vägen, 432 24,* ☎ *0340/629800,* ℻ *0340/629850. 106 rooms, 55 with bath, 38 suites. Restaurant, bar, indoor pool, sauna, spa. AE, DC, MC, V. BP.*

Falkenberg

❼④   *29 km (18 mi) south of Varberg, 94 km (58 mi) south of Göteborg.*

With its fine beaches and the plentiful salmon that swim in the Ätran River, Falkenberg is one of Sweden's most attractive resorts. Its Gamla Stan (Old Town) is full of narrow, cobblestone streets and quaint old wooden houses.

In the middle of Gamla Stan stands the 12th-century **St. Laurentii Kyrka** (Church of St. Laurentii). After the construction of a new church at the end of the 19th century, St. Laurentii was deconsecrated and used as a shooting range, a cinema, and a gymnasium, among other things. It was reconsecrated in the 1920s and is now fully restored with its 16th-century font and silver, as well as some awe-inspiring 17th- and 18th-century wall paintings.

Although it does have the usual archaeological and historical artifacts depicting its town's growth and development, the **Falkenberg Museum** also has an unusual and refreshing obsession with the 1950s. The curator here thinks that is the most interesting period of history, and you can make up your own mind once you've learned about the local dance-band scene, visited the interior of a shoe repair shop, and seen a collection of old jukeboxes. ⊠ *Skepparesträtet 2,* ☎ *034686125.* ⊡ *SKr 20.* ☉ *June–mid-Sept., Tues.–Fri. 10–4, weekends noon–4; mid-Sept.–May, Tues.–Fri. and Sun. noon–4.*

Falkenberg's first movie theater is now home to **Fotomuseum Olympia,** a fascinating display of cameras, camera equipment, and photographs dating back to the 1840s. ⊠ *Sandg. 13,* ☎ *0346/87928.* ⊡ *SKr 30.* ☉ *June–Aug., Tues.–Thurs. 1–7; Sept.–May, Tues.–Thurs. 5–7 and Sun. 2–6.*

When the weather gets hot, what better way to quench that raging thirst than a stroll around a cool brewery, followed by a glass of ice cold beer? At the **Falcon Bryggerier** you can do just that. Beer has been brewed on the premises since 1869, and a tour of the facility takes in both old brewing traditions and modern beer-making technology. The tour ends with a refreshing glass of the house brew. ⊠ *Åstadv.,* ☎ *0346/57000.* ⊡ *SKr 20.* ☉ *July–Aug., Mon.–Thurs. 10–1.*

Doktorspromenaden, on the south side of the river in the town center, is a beautiful walk set against a backdrop of heathland and shading trees. The walk was set up in 1861 by a local doctor, in an effort to encourage the townsfolk to get more fresh air. ⊠ *Doktorspromenaden.*

Dining and Lodging

$–$$ ✗ **Restaurant Hertigen.** This beautiful white villa is in wooded grounds on an island just outside the center of town. There is a large veranda and garden for outdoor eating in the summer. The classical French food served here is well done and is prepared with a nod in the direction of local cooking styles. ⊠ *Hertings Gård,* ☎ *0346/711880. Reservations essential. AE, DC, MC, V.*

$$ ⊞ **Grand Hotel Falkenberg.** Not as imposing as the name suggests, this pretty, yellow, 19th-century hotel is comfortable and friendly, with very large rooms. The interior is a jumble of furnishings from the last 30 years with the odd antique thrown in for good measure. Cherrywood and dark, rich fabrics are used throughout. ⊠ *Hotellg. 1, 311 23,* ☎ *0346/14450,* ℻ *0346/14459,* 🖳 *www.grandhotelfalkenberg.se. 70 rooms, 50 with bath, 3 suites. 2 restaurants, 2 bars, lounge, sauna, spa. AE, DC, MC, V. BP.*

$ ⊞ **Elite Hotel Strandbaden.** Built in 1992, this is a sprawling white wood and glass building right on the beach at the south end of town. The rooms here are quite small, but well equipped with cable TV; modem connections; minibars; and modern, comfortable furnishings. Most have a view of the sea. There is a state-of-the-art spa and health club in the hotel, and a very good restaurant decked out in startling blue and orange. ⊠ *Havsbadsallen, 311 42,* ☎ *0346/714900,* ℻ *0346/16111. 135* *rooms, 87 with bath, 5 suites. Restaurant, bar, brasserie, in-room data ports, minibars, sauna, spa, health club. AE, DC, MC, V. BP.*

Outdoor Activities and Sports

BEACHES

A 15-minute walk south from the town center is **Skrea Strand,** a 2-mi stretch of sandy beach. At the northern end of the beach is **Klitterbadhuset** (✉ Klitterv., ☎ 0346/86330, 🖃 SKr 30, ◷ Tues.–Sun. 9–7), a huge swimming complex with pools (including one just for children), water slides, a sauna, a whirlpool, and steam rooms. Farther south the beach opens out onto some secluded coves and grasslands.

FISHING

In the 1800s, Falkenberg had some of the best fly fishing in Europe. This prompted a frenzy of fishermen, including many English aristocrats, to plunder its waters. But despite the overfishing, the Ätran is one of few remaining rivers in Europe inhabited by wild salmon. Fishing permits and rod rentals can be arranged through the local **tourist office** (☎ 0346/14710).

Shopping

Törngren's (✉ Krukmakareg. 4, ☎ 0346/16920; 0346/10354, ◷ weekdays 9–5) is probably the oldest pottery shop operating in Scandinavia. The seventh generation of the founding family still owns and runs it. It's open during normal business hours, but you might have to call ahead to view the wares.

Halmstad

🌀 *40 km (25 mi) south of Falkenberg, 143 km (89 mi) south of Göteborg.*

With a population of 50,000, Halmstad is the largest seaside resort on the west coast. The Norreport town gate, all that remains of the town's original fortifications, dates from 1605. The modern Town Hall has interior decorations by the so-called Halmstad Group of painters, which formed here in 1929.

Most of Halmstad's architectural highlights are in and around **Storatorg,** the large town square. In the middle is the fountain *Europa and the Bull,* by the sculptor Carl Milles. Around the square are many buildings and merchants' houses dating from Halmstad's more prosperous days in the middle to late 19th century.

At the top of Storatorg is the grand **St. Nikolai Kyrka,** a huge church from the 14th century containing fragments of medieval murals and a 17th-century pulpit.

The Tropic Centre, just a few minutes' walk from the center of Halmstad, holds flora and fauna that come from outside Sweden. Tropical plants, birds, snakes, monkeys, spiders, and crocodiles are all safely tucked away behind glass, ready to both amuse and perhaps horrify you. ✉ *Tullhuset, Strandg.,* ☎ *035/123333.* 🖃 *SKr 60.* ◷ *Daily 10–4.*

No Swedish town would be complete without its local museum, and **Halmstad Länsmuseet** prevents Halmstad from being an exception. This one is more accomplished than most, however. Everything from archaeological finds to musical instruments to dollhouses are on display. There's also a haunting display of large figureheads taken from ships that sank off the local coastline. ✉ *Tollsg.,* ☎ *035/162300.* 🖃 *SKr 20.* ◷ *June–mid-Aug., Thurs.–Tues. 10–7, Wed. 10–9; late Aug.–May, Thurs.–Tues. 10–4, Wed. 10–9.*

★ The bizarre **Martin Luther Kyrka** is unique among churches. Built entirely out of steel in the 1970s, its exterior resembles that of a shiny tin can. The interior is just as striking, as the gleaming outside gives way to rust-orange steel and art deco furnishings that contrast with the outside. To some, Martin Luther Church may seem more like a temple to design than to anything else. ✉ *Långg.*, ☎ *035/15961*. ⊘ *Weekdays 9–3 and during services (Sun. 10)*.

In the 1930s the Halmstad Group, made up of six local artists, caused some consternation with their surrealist and cubist painting styles, influenced strongly by artists such as Magritte and Dalí. The **Mjällby Konstgård** (Mjällby Arts Centre) contains some of the most important works created over the group's 50-year alliance. ✉ *Mjällby (1 km/½ mi from Halmstad)*, ☎ *035/31619*. 🎫 *SKr 40*. ⊘ *Mar.–Oct., Tues.–Sun. 1–5*.

Dining and Lodging

$$ ✕ **Pio & Co.** Half informal bar and half bistro, this restaurant offers something for all. It's a bright and airy place with good service and excellent Swedish classics on the menu—the steak and mashed potatoes are wonderful. Their list of drinks is extensive. ✉ *Storg. 27*, ☎ *035/210669. AE, DC, MC, V.*

$$ 🏨 **Hotel Continental.** Built in 1904 in the National Romantic style, the interior of this hotel has been nicely preserved. The sophisticated design includes exposed-brick walls, subtle spotlighting, and light wood fittings. The rooms are bright, modern, and spacious. ✉ *Kungsg. 5, 302 45*, ☎ *035/176300*, 📠 *035/128604. 46 rooms, 8 with bath, 3 suites. Restaurant, bar. AE, DC, MC, V. BP.*

$$ 🏨 **Scandic Hotel Grand.** A shiny white tile floor, white ceiling tiles, and a circular podlike lobby create a strange first impression. But don't be alarmed. Rooms here come with all the space, comfort, modernity, and up-to-date technology you would expect from a Scandinavian hotel. ✉ *Rådhusg. 4, 302 43*, ☎ *035/2958600*, 📠 *035/2958611. 130 rooms without bath, 1 suite. Restaurant, bar, in-room data ports, sauna, spa, convention center. AE, DC, MC, V. BP.*

Nightlife and the Arts

The nightlife in Halmstad centers around the bars in Storgatan, the main street that runs into Storatorg. **Harry's** (☎ 035/105595) is worth a visit, if only to see its bizzare English phone box with a life-size model of Charlie Chaplin inside. The lovely **Kavaljeren** (☎ 035/124880) is housed in the basement of the town's 17th-century courts of law and has a fine vaulted ceiling.

Outdoor Activities and Sports

There are many good beaches around Halmstad. **Tjuvahålan**, extending west of Halmsted, has an interesting old smugglers' cove that provides pleasant walking. For details, contact the **tourist office** (☎ 035/109345).

Båstad

76 *35 km (22 mi) south of Halmstad, 178 km (111 mi) south of Göteborg.*

In the southernmost province of Skåne, Båstad is regarded by locals as Sweden's most fashionable resort, where ambassadors and local captains of industry have their summerhouses. Aside from this, it is best known for its tennis. In addition to the **Båstad Open**, a Grand Prix tournament in late summer, there is the annual **Donald Duck Cup** in July, for children ages 11 to 15; it was the very first trophy won by Björn Borg, who later took the Wimbledon men's singles title an unprecedented five times in a row. Spurred on by Borg and other Swedish champions, such as Stefan Edberg and Mats Wilander, thousands of youngsters take part in the Donald Duck Cup each year. For details, contact the **Svenska Tennisförbundet** (Swedish Tennis Association; ⊠ Lidingövägen 75, Stockholm, ☎ 08/6679770).

The low-rise, shuttered buildings in the center of Båstad give it an almost French provincial feel. In the main square is **St. Maria Kyrka** (St. Maria Church), which looks much more solidly Swedish. Dating from the 15th century the plain exterior hides a haven of tranquility within the cool, thick walls. The main point of interest in the church is the unusual altar painting depicting Christ on the cross, with human skulls and bones strewn beneath him.

Norrviken Gardens, 3 km (2 mi) northwest of Båstad, are beautifully laid out in different styles, including a symmetrical Japanese garden and a lovely walkway lined with rhododendrons. The creator of the gardens, Rudolf Abelin, is buried on the grounds. A restaurant, shop, and pottery studio are also on the premises. ⊠ *Båstad.* ☎ *0431/ 369040,* WEB *www.norrvikenstradgardar.se.* ☞ *SKr 35.* ☉ *Early June– mid-Aug., daily 10–6; late Aug.–May, daily 10:30–5.*

Dining and Lodging

$$ ✕ **Swenson's Krog.** Well worth the 3-km (2-mi) journey out of Bås- tad, this harborfront restaurant was originally a fisherman's hut. Swen- son's has been converted into a magnificent dining room with cornflower-blue walls, wooden floors, and a glass roof. The menu is full of Swedish classics such as fresh boiled red beets with salted but- ter and the most delicious homemade meatballs. The service is friendly, with the family atmosphere really shining through. ⊠ *Pål Romaresg. 2, Torekov,* ☎ *0431/364590. Reservations essential. AE, DC, MC, V.*

$ ✕ **The Wooden Hut.** Actually, this restaurant has no name: it's just a wooden hut on the harbor side. It has no tables either. It has no wine list, no waiters, no interior design, no telephone, and it doesn't accept credit cards. What this restaurant does have is a way to take you away from all the pomp and wealth that can sometimes bog down Båstad: by serving the most delicious smoked mackerel with potato salad. Walk past all the hotels and restaurants, smell the fresh sea air, and get ready for a great meal. ⊠ *Strandpromenaden,* ☎ *no phone. Reser- vations not accepted. No credit cards.*

$$ ✕▥ **Hotel Skansen.** Set in a century-old bathhouse, Skansen's interi- ors reflect the best of modern design. Wonderfully simple earth, cream, and moss-green tones create a sense of comfort, simplicity, and relax- ation. The rooms are bright, many with glass roof or wall features, and comfortable. Restaurant Sand ($–$$), with a sea view, serves stylish and well-prepared Swedish fare, with fish as a specialty. For those try- ing to avoid their rooms there is a well-stocked bar. The nightclub, how- ever, is nothing special. ⊠ *Kyrkog. 2, 269 21,* ☎ *0431/72050,* FAX *0431/ 70085,* WEB *www.hotelskansen.se. 112 rooms, 87 with bath, 1 suite. Restaurant, bar, sauna, nightclub. AE, DC, MC, V. BP.*

$ ▥ **Hotel Buena Vista.** Given its name, it's not surprising that this stone villa was built at the beginning of the 20th century by a Cuban émi- gré. The interior is a little dark and stuffy, since not much has changed since it first became a hotel in the '40s. All the same, it has pleasing touches of grandeur, such as the dark wood sweeping staircase. Rooms are large and well equipped, and the views from the front rooms, over the bay, are stunning. ⊠ *Tarravågen 5, 269 35,* ☎ *0431/7600,* FAX *0431/ 79100,* WEB *www.buena.se. 24 rooms without bath, 4 suites. 2 restau- rants, bar, no-smoking rooms, sauna, spa, chapel. AE, DC, MC, V. BP.*

Swedish Riviera A to Z

> *To research prices, get advice from other travelers, and book travel arrangements, visit www.fodors.com.*

BUS TRAVEL

Buses to Kungsbacka, Falkenberg, Halmstad, and Båstad leave from behind Göteborg's central train station. For details contact **Väst Trafik** (☎ 0771/414300).

CAR TRAVEL

Simply follow the E6/E20 highway south from Göteborg. It runs parallel to the coast.

TRAIN TRAVEL

Regular train services connect Göteborg's central station with Kungsbacka, Falkenberg, Halmstad, and Båstad. Contact SJ for information.
➤ TRAIN INFORMATION: **SJ** (⊠ Göteborg, ☎ 031/103000 or 020/757575).

VISITOR INFORMATION

➤ TOURIST INFORMATION: **Båstad** (⊠ Stortorget 1, ☎ 0431/75045). **Falkenberg** (⊠ Stortorget, ☎ 0346/17410). **Halmstad** (⊠ Lilla Torg, ☎ 035/109345). **Kungsbacka** (⊠ Storg. 41, ☎ 0300/34595). **Laholm** (⊠ Rådhuset, ☎ 0430/15216 or 0430/15450). **Varberg** (⊠ Brunnsparken, ☎ 0340/88770).

GÖTA CANAL

Stretching 614 km (382 mi) between Stockholm and Göteborg, the Göta Canal is actually a series of interconnected canals, rivers, lakes, and even a stretch of sea. Bishop Hans Brask of Linköping in the 16th century was the first to suggest linking the bodies of water; in 1718, King Karl XII ordered the canal to be built, but work was abandoned when he was killed in battle the same year. Not until 1810 was the idea again taken up in earnest. The driving force was a Swedish nobleman, Count Baltzar Bogislaus von Platen (1766–1829), and his motive was commercial. Von Platen saw the canal as a way of beating Danish tolls on shipping that passed through the Öresund. He also sought to enhance Göteborg's standing by linking the port with Stockholm on the east coast. At a time when Swedish fortunes were at a low ebb, the canal was also viewed as a way to reestablish faith in the future and boost national morale.

The building of the canal took 22 years and involved 58,000 men. Linking the various stretches of water required 87 km (54 mi) of man-made cuts through soil and rock, and building 58 locks, 47 bridges, 27 culverts, and 3 dry docks. Unfortunately, the canal never achieved the financial success that von Platen sought. By 1857 the Danes had removed shipping tolls, and in the following decade the linking of Göteborg with Stockholm by rail effectively ended the canal's commercial potential. The canal has nevertheless come into its own as a modern-day tourist attraction.

You may have trouble conceiving of the canal's industrial origins as your boat drifts lazily down this lovely series of waterways; across the enormous lakes, Vänern and Vättern; and through a microcosm of all that is best about Sweden: abundant fresh air; clear, clean water; pristine nature; well-tended farmland. A bicycle path runs parallel to the canal, offering another means of touring the country.

En Route   The trip from Göteborg takes you first along the Göta Älv, a wide waterway that 10,000 years ago, when the ice cap melted, was a great fjord. Some 30 minutes into the voyage the boat passes below a rocky escarpment, topped by the remains of **Bohus Fästning** (Bohus Castle), distinguished by two round towers known as Father's Hat and Mother's Bonnet. It dates from the 14th century and was once the mightiest fortress in western Scandinavia, commanding the confluence of the Göta and Nordre rivers. It was strengthened and enlarged in the 16th century and successfully survived 14 sieges. From 1678 onward, the castle began to lose its strategic and military importance; it fell into decay until 1838, when King Karl XIV passed by on a river journey, admired the old fortress, and ordered its preservation.

Just north of Kungälv along the Göta Canal is the quiet village of **Lödöse,** once a major trading settlement and a predecessor of Göteborg. From here, the countryside becomes wilder, with pines and oaks clustered thickly on either bank between cliffs of lichen-covered granite.

Trollhättan

🐂 *70 km (43 mi) north of Göteborg.*

In this pleasant industrial town of about 50,000 inhabitants, a spectacular waterfall was rechanneled in 1906 to become Sweden's first hydroelectric plant. In most years, on specific days the waters are allowed to follow their natural course, a fall of 106 ft in six torrents. The other main point of interest lies between what were once the falls and the series of locks that allowed the canal to bypass them. Here are disused locks from 1800 and 1844 and a strange Ice Age grotto where members of the Swedish royal family have carved their names since the 18th century. Trollhättan also has a fine, wide marketplace and pleasant waterside parks.

The best way to see the towns's spectacular waterfalls and locks is on the walking trail that winds its way through the massive system. The walk takes in the hydroelectric power station, the Elvius lock (the lowest in the system and never used, since its design was regarded as faulty), the great steps of the Lower Lock, and the canal museum. Part of the walk is a very pleasant stroll through the wooded cliffs that overlook the spectacular cascades of water. Details and directions can be found at **Trollhättans Turistbyrå** (tourist office; ☎ 0520/488472).

The canal and the locks gave Trollhättan its life, and a visit to the **Kanalmuseet** (Canal Museum) tells as full a history of this as you can find. Housed in a redbrick 1893 waterside building, the museum covers the history of the canal and the locks and displays model ships, old tools and fishing gear. ⊠ *Slussedsv. 2–8,* ☎ *0520/472206.* 🖃 *SKr 5.* 🕙 *Mid-June–mid-Aug., daily 10–6. Mid-Aug.–mid-June, weekends noon–5.*

The **Energihuset Insikten** (Insikten Energy Center) is considerably more interesting than you might at first imagine. Geared toward the non-scientific mind, it explains the workings of the nearby hydroelectric power station, an impressive 1910 castlelike building containing 13 massive generators. There is also an exhibit on the salmon and eel ladders, ingenious netlike contraptions used to lift the migrating animals over the powerful waterfalls so that they can continue on their journey to spawn in the inland lakes. For an extra SKr 40 you can take a four-minute cable car ride 30 m (98 ft) above the impressive falls and across the valley below. ⊠ *Österlang. 66,* ☎ *0520/88882.* 🖃 *SKr 10.* 🕙 *Daily noon–4.*

The **Saab Bilmuseum** (Saab Car Museum) surveys Saab's automotive output from 1946 to the present. Since the exhibition consists primarily of row upon row of cars, fenced off by rope, there's little here for any but true car enthusiasts. ☒ *Åkerssjövägan 10,* ☏ *0520/84344.* ☞ *SKr 10.* ☉ *June–Aug., daily 10–6; Sept.–May, Tues.–Fri. 1–4.*

Culture abounds at **Folketshus** (People's House), in the pedestrianized downtown area. Part of the building is given over to dramatic, ever-changing displays of contemporary art and art installations. ☒ *Kungsg. 12,* ☏ *0520/428607.* ☞ *Free.* ☉ *Tues.–Fri. noon–4, Sat. 10–2.*

En Route   Soon after leaving Trollhättan, the Göta Canal takes you past Halleberg and Hunneberg, two flat-top hills that are each more than 500 ft high; the woods surrounding them are extraordinarily rich in elk, legend, and Viking burial mounds. The canal then proceeds through **Karls Grav,** the oldest part of the canal, begun early in the 18th century. It was built to bypass the Ronnum Falls on the Göta River, which have been harnessed to power a hydroelectric project.

Dining and Lodging

$$ ✕ **Warf 36.** Here, you can choose between eating in a large, elegant dining room, decorated in traditional Swedish style, or, in summer at least, at an outdoor terrace, against a backdrop of humming waterfalls. Fish and seafood dishes are particularly good here. ☒ *Storg. 36,* ☏ *0520/10222. AC, MC, V.*

$ ✕ **Strandgatan.** This popular, relaxed café is in an 1867 building that once housed canal workers. There's always a good crowd, especially in summer, when outside seating is available. Locals come to while away the hours over coffee, bagels, home-cooked international cuisine, and beer and wine. ☒ *Strandg. 34,* ☏ *0520/83717. AE, DC, MC, V.*

$$ ☖ **Hotel Scandic Swania.** Stunning views over the waterfalls and locks on up to the hills above town are what distinguish this comfortable hotel near Trollhättan's center. Ask for a top-floor room at the front of the hotel and enjoy the sights. If you're up for a party, one of Trollhättan's few nightclubs is in the basement. ☒ *Storg. 49, 461 23,* ☏ *0520/89000,* ☎ *0520/89001. 309 rooms, 102 with bath, 3 suites. Restaurant, bar, lounge, no-smoking rooms. AE, DC, MC, V. BP.*

Outdoor Activities

Daily boat trips from the center of town take you right into the heart of the lock system and waterfalls. **MS Strömkarlen** (☏ *0520/32100,* ☞ SKr 100) leaves three times daily June–August.

Nightlife

Trollhättan's nightlife mostly revolves around the excellent **KK's Bar & Nightclub** (☒ Torgg. 3, ☏ 0520/481049), which is always crowded, mostly with those under 25. The bar is comfortable and fun and has a good cocktail selection. On Thursday those who are slightly older hit the dance floor.

Vänersborg

❼❽   *15 km (9 mi) north of Trollhättan, 85 km (53 mi) north of Göteborg.*

Eventually, the canal enters **Vänern,** Sweden's largest and Europe's third-largest lake: 3,424 square km (1,322 square mi) of water, 145 km (90 mi) long and 81 km (50 mi) wide at one point.

At the southern tip of the lake is Vänersborg, a town of about 30,000 inhabitants that was founded in the mid-17th century. The church and the governor's residence date from the 18th century, but the rest of the town was destroyed by fire in 1834. Vänersborg is distinguished by its fine lakeside park, the trees of which act as a windbreak for the gusts that sweep in from Vänern.

Fans of the esoteric may find the **Vänersborgs Museum** worth a visit. The oldest museum in Sweden, it has remained essentially untouched since it opened its doors in 1891: this applies as much to the dust that has gathered on the exhibits as it does to the exhibits themselves. Resolutely noninteractive, the dark rooms are filled mostly with stuffed African birds. It all makes for a sort of unintentional museum of museums. A gloomy apartment in which the museum's janitor once lived is now part of an exhibit instead—one that preserves the space in all its 1950s glory. ⊠ *Östra Plantaget,* ☎ *0521/264100.* 🎫 *SKr 20.* ☉ *June–Aug., Tues. noon–7, Wed.–Thurs. and weekends noon–4; Sept.– May, Tues. and weekends noon–4.*

A few minutes' walk from the center of town, **Skracklan Park** is a good place to relax. Take a break in the 1930s coffeehouse after walking along the park's promenade. A lake, parkland, and trees are set around the park's centerpiece, a statue of Frida, the muse of a famous local poet named Sjoberg. Frida always has fresh flowers stuffed into her bronze hand.

OFF THE
BEATEN PATH

HALLEBERG AND HUNNEBERG – Five kilometers (three miles) east of Vänersborg are the twin plateaus of Halleberg and Hunneberg. Thought to be 500 million years old, these geological wonders are the site of early Viking forts, and the resting place of early humans. But they are best known for their stunning natural beauty and the fauna they support: the county's biggest herd of elk. As tradition dictates, the king of Sweden still comes here every October for the Royal Hunt. To see the animals yourself, head for the walking trail that winds around Halleberg. At dawn or dusk the leggy, long-faced giant elk, inquisitive by nature, will be more than comfortable eating apples from your hand. Whether or not you'll be so comfortable, once you see the size of them, is another matter.

Dining and Lodging

$ ✕ **Pizzeria Roma.** Directly across the road from the hotel Ronnums Herrgård, this small restaurant is perfect for informal meals. The somewhat stark and brightly lit interior is offset by the very good and very cheap pizza and pasta served here. ⊠ *Nordkroksvågan 1,* ☎ *0521/ 221070. No credit cards.*

$ 🏨 **Hotell Strand.** Lodging choices are limited in Vänersborg, but the Hotell Strand's welcoming staff make it the best in town. ⊠ *Hamng. 7, 462 33,* ☎ *0521/13850,* FAX *0521/15900. 120 rooms. No-smoking rooms. AE, DC, MC, V. BP.*

$ 🏨 **Ronnums Herrgård.** A mile outside town, this old manor house has been converted into a hotel of some local repute. Some of the rooms are a little shabby, so try to get one in the main building. What you do get here is peace, natural beauty, and a very good hotel restaurant. The breakfast offered with the room is worthy of a king. ⊠ *Värgon, 468 30,* ☎ *0521/26000,* FAX *0521/260009. 60 rooms without bath. Restaurant, bar, no-smoking rooms. AE, DC, MC, V. BP.*

Nightlife

Nightlife is limited here, but at **Club Roccad** (⊠ Kungsg. 23, ☎ 0521/ 61200) there's always good modern dance music, and the cool, dark interior attracts a young, good-looking crowd that's serious about dancing.

Lidköping

55 km (34 mi) east of Vänersborg, 140 km (87 mi) northeast of Göteborg.

On an inlet at the southernmost point of Vänern's eastern arm lies the town of Lidköping, which received its charter in 1446 and is said to have the largest town square in Sweden. Nya Stadens Torg (New Town Square) is dominated by the old courthouse building, a replica of the original that burned down in 1960. Lidkoping had been razed by fire several times before that, leaving a lot of the old town gone. However, the 17th-century houses around Limtorget survived, and are still worth seeing today.

A pleasant enough town, Lidköping's villagelike layout comes from old rule forbidding buildings from being taller than the street it stands on is wider. The only exception seems to be the unfortunately ugly industrial park on the northern edge of town, which obscures an otherwise perfect view of Lake Vänern.

The **Rörstrands Porslins Museum** has on display a wealth of pieces that trace the history of china. Rörstrands, Europe's second-oldest porcelain company, also offers tours through its adjoining factory. If you have space in your luggage, the factory shop carries a large range of beautiful china at very reasonable prices. ⊠ *Fabriksg.,* ☎ *0510/82348.* 🖭 *Free; guided factory tour SKr 15.* ☉ *Weekdays 10–6, Sun. noon–4. Factory tours June and Aug.*

Väner Museet is dedicated to Lake Vänern's history, the life it supports, and the ways in which it has helped the surrounding area develop. What could be a slightly dull subject is vividly brought to life in this well-planned, modern museum, which has exhibits of meteorites and fossils as well as model ships and maritime photographs.⊠ *Framnäsvägen 2,* ☎ *0510/770065.* 🖭 *SKr 20.* ☉ *Tues.–Fri. 10–5, weekends noon–5.*

OFF THE BEATEN PATH

HUSABY HYRKA – This church, 15 km (9 mi) east of Lidköping, is a site of great religious and historical significance. The church itself, dating from the 12th century, houses some fine 13th-century furniture, 15th-century murals, and carved floor stones. But the biggest draw is outside the church, at St. Sigfrid's Well. Here, in 1008, King Olof Skötkonung converted to Christianity—the first Swedish king to do so—and was baptized by the English missionary Sigfrid. Since that time many Swedish kings have come to carve their names in the rock. Most signatures can still be clearly read today.

LÄCKÖ SLOTT – One of Sweden's finest 17th-century Renaissance palaces is 24 km (15 mi) to the north of Lidköping. It's on an island off the place where the eastern arm of Vänern divides from the western. Läckö Castle's 250 rooms were once the home of Magnus Gabriel de la Gardie, a great favorite of Queen Christina. Only the Royal Palace in Stockholm is larger. In 1681 Karl XI confiscated it to curtail the power of the nobility, and in 1830 all its furnishings were auctioned off. Many have since been restored to the palace. 🖭 *SKr 70.* ☉ *Daily 10–5. Closed June 9.*

Dining and Lodging

$$ ✕ **Gotes Festvaning.** Anything with pike (*gädda*) is particularly worth trying at this typical Swedish dining room serving good regional specialties. ⊠ *Östra Hamnen,* ☎ *0510/21700. AE, DC, MC, V.*

$$ 🏨 **Stadtshotel.** Like most town-hotels in Sweden, the Stadtshotel offers a faded grandeur with a lot of character. Rooms are a little on the

small side, but comfortable, with the best ones overlooking the river and the main town square. ✉ *Gamla Stadens Torg 1, 531 02,* ☎ *0510/22085,* FAX *0510/21532,* WEB *www.stadtlidkoping.se. 67 rooms, 2 suites. Restaurant, bar, no-smoking rooms. AE, DC, MC, V. BP.*

$ ☏ **Hotell Rådhuset.** This basic hotel is somewhat oddly located inside a former office building. The rooms are large and have cable TV. There are several computers at which you can check the Internet. ✉ *Nya Stadens Torg 8, 531 31,* ☎ *0510/22236,* FAX *0510/22214. 15 rooms. Breakfast room. AE, DC, MC, V. BP.*

En Route   On a peninsula 20 km (12½ mi) to the east of Lidköping, the landscape is dominated by the great hill of **Kinnekulle,** towering 900 ft above Lake Vänern. The hill is rich in colorful vegetation and wildlife and was a favorite hike for the botanist Linnaeus.

Mariestad

79   *40 km (25 mi) northeast of Lidköping.*

This town on the eastern shore of Lake Vänern is an architectural gem and an excellent base for some aquatic exploring. The town's center has a fine medieval quarter, a pretty harbor, and houses built in styles ranging from Gustavian (a baroque style named after King Gustav Vasa of the 1500s) to art nouveau. Others resemble Swiss chalets.

Domkyrkan, the late-Gothic cathedral on the edge of the old part of town, stands as a monument to one man's spite. Commissioned at the end of the 16th century by Duke Karl—who named the town after his wife, Maria— it was built to resemble and rival Klara Kyrka in Stockholm, the church of his brother King Johan III, of whom he was insanely jealous. Karl made sure that the church was endowed with some wonderfully excessive features, which can still be seen today. The stained-glass windows have real insects (bees, dragonflies, etc.) sandwiched within them, and the silver and gold cherubs are especially roly-poly and cute.

Vadsbo Museum is a museum of the local area's industry, which centers not surprisingly around the lake. The museum is on a small island just off the old town in the River Tidan, which flows off Vänern. Named after the old jurisdiction of Vadsbo, the museum—housed in the medieval judge's residence—has displays on the region from the prehistoric age to the 20th century. ✉ *Residensö, Marieholmn,* ☎ *0501/ 63214.* ✉ *SKr 20.* ☉ *Tues.–Sun. 1–4.*

OFF THE   **GULLSPÅNG** – Forty kilometers (twenty-five miles) north of Mariestad, this
BEATEN PATH town is the starting place for 20 km (12 mi) of railway track, originally
             built to improve Sweden's rail links in the 1960s but now used for
             leisure purposes. The tracks run through some beautiful countryside and
             along the Gullspångälv (Gullspång River), which has great swimming.
             You get to travel the tracks in handcars, which aren't often seen outside
             of cartoons and cowboy movies. The small cars are operated by having
             two people push a lever up and down. If you've got the energy, it's a
             great trip.

Dining and Lodging

$ ✕ **Old Ox.** Located on a boat permanently moored near the town, this bar-restaurant serves good steaks, burgers, and chicken at a very reasonable price. In the summer months you can sit out on deck and soak up the fresh Swedish air. ✉ *Hamng.,* ☎ *0501/13050. MC, V. Closed Sun.*

$$ ⊞ **Stadtshotellet.** The most luxurious choice in a town full of below-average hotels. The building is unobtrusive, but the rooms are comfortable, if a little bland in their furnishings. ⊠ *Nya Torget, 542 30, Mariestad,* ☎ *0501/77111,* ℻ *0501/77640. 110 rooms, 1 suite. Bar, no-smoking rooms. AC, DC, MC, V. BP.*

Nightlife and the Arts

Evenings can be fairly quiet and relaxing in Mariestad, but **Aquavit Blå Bar** (⊠ Kungsg. 5, ☎ 0501/71100) can be a lively spot for the young adults in town.

Outdoor Activities and Sports

The nearby island of **Torsö** is perfect for fishing and lying out on the beach. It's reachable only by boat. Boat trips can be taken farther out into Lake Vänern and up to the Göta Canal proper. For more information, including information on hiring equipment for fishing, contact the **tourist office** (⊠ Hamnplan, ☎ 0501/12140).

Sjötorp

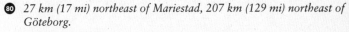 27 km (17 mi) northeast of Mariestad, 207 km (129 mi) northeast of Göteborg.

At the lakeside port of Sjötorp, the Göta Canal proper begins. A series of locks raises steamers to the village of Lanthöjden; at 304 ft above sea level it's the highest point on the canal. The boats next enter the narrow, twisting lakes of Viken and Bottensjön and continue to Forsvik through the canal's oldest lock, built in 1813. Boats then sail out into **Vättern,** Sweden's second-largest lake, nearly 129 km (80 mi) from north to south and 31 km (19 mi) across at its widest point. Its waters are so clear that in some parts the bottom is visible at a depth of 50 ft. The lake is subject to sudden storms that can whip its normally placid waters into choppy waves.

Vadstena

249 km (155 mi) northeast of Göteborg (via Jönköping).

This little-known gem of a town grew up around the monastery founded by St. Birgitta, or Bridget (1303–1373), who wrote in her *Revelations* that she had a vision of Christ in which he revealed the rules of the religious order she went on to establish. These rules seem to have been a precursor for the Swedish ideal of sexual equality, with both nuns and monks sharing a common church. Her order spread rapidly after her death, and at one time there were 80 Bridgetine monasteries in Europe. Little remains of the Vadstena monastery; in 1545 King Gustav Vasa ordered its demolition, and its stones were used to build **Vadstena Slott** (Vadstena Castle), a huge fortress created to defend against Danish attack. It was later refurbished and used as a home for Gustav's mentally ill son. Many of the original decorations were lost in a fire in the early 1600s. Unable to afford replacement decorations, the royal family had decorations and fittings painted directly onto the walls. Many of the "curtains" that can be seen today come from this period. Swedish royalty held court at Vadstena Slott until 1715. It then fell into decay and was used as a granary. Recent efforts have returned the castle to something approaching its former glory. Today it houses part of the National Archives and is also the site of an annual summer opera festival. ☎ *0143/15123.* ◺ *SKr 40.* ☉ *Mid-May–June and late Aug., daily noon–4; July–mid-Aug., daily 11–4. Guided tours mid-May–mid-Aug. at 12:30 and 1:30, late Aug. also at 2:30.*

The triptych altarpiece on the south wall of the **Vadstena Kyrka** (Vadstena Church) shows St. Birgitta presenting her book of revelations to a group of kneeling cardinals. Gustav Vasa's son's remains are stored here in a tomb covered with cherubs. St. Birgitta's bones are here as well. They're rather less grandly stored in a red velvet box inside a glass case.

Housed in what was once Sweden's oldest mental hospital, the **Hospital Museet** is a fascinating, moving reminder of centuries of misguided treatments and "cures" for the mentally ill. Devices on display include a chair into which patients were strapped and spun until they were sick and a bath in which unruly patients were scalded. Perhaps the most moving display includes photographs of inmates from the 19th century and the drawings they made of the tortures inflicted upon them. ⊠ *Lastköpingsg.*, ☎ *no phone.* ⊡ *SKr 25.* ⊙ *June–Aug., daily 1–3.*

The **Gottfrid Larsson-Gården** is a museum dedicated to the work of the leading sculptor Gottfrid Larsson (1875–1947), known for his studies of naked male manual workers. The museum also houses some temporary exhibits of other contemporary sculpture. ⊠ *Skäunningeg. 9,* ☎ *no phone.* ⊡ *SKr 10.* ⊙ *Tues.–Fri. 1–5, Sat. 1–3.*

OFF THE   **VÄVERSUNDA –** This scenic hamlet, 15 km (9 mi) southeast of Vadstena,
BEATEN PATH contains a pretty 12th-century limestone church. Inside there are some
             fine, restored wall paintings from the 13th century. Next to the church is
             a very popular bird-watching tower that overlooks a bird sanctuary.

Lodging

$$ 🏨 **Vadstena Klosterhotel.** Sweden's oldest secular building, parts of which date from the 13th century, is now a hotel. Rooms are modern and well appointed, and there are three comfortable lounges. You can choose a view of either Lake Vättern or the hotel's courtyard. The former is infinitely more preferable and only SKr 100 extra. ⊠ *Klosterområdet, off Lasarettsg., 592 30 Vadstena,* ☎ *0143/3150,* FAX *0143/13648. 29 rooms, 3 with bath. Restaurant, no-smoking rooms, meeting room. AE, DC, MC, V. BP.*

$ 🏨 **Kungs-Starby Wärdshus.** This functional guest house, reached via Route 50, is next to a renovated manor house and restaurant. The rooms use light wood throughout and have earth-tone carpets and green, blue, and brown color schemes. The complex is surrounded by a park on the outskirts of town. ⊠ *Ödeshögsv., 592 01 Vadstena,* ☎ *0143/75100,* FAX *0143/75170. 61 rooms. Restaurant, no-smoking rooms, indoor pool, sauna, meeting room. AE, DC, MC, V. CP.*

Motala

⑧¹   *13 km (8 mi) north of Vadstena, 262 km (163 mi) northeast of Göteborg.*

Before reaching Stockholm, the canal passes through Motala, where Baltzar von Platen is buried. He had hoped that four new towns would be established along the waterway, but only Motala rose according to plan. He designed the town himself, and his statue is in the main square. Motala itself is not an essential sight. Instead, it's the activities along the canal and lake, along with a few very good museums, that make Motala worth a stop.

★   Stop at the **Motala Motormuseum** even if you are not in the slightest bit interested in cars. All the cars and motorcycles on display—from 1920s Rolls Royces, through 1950s Cadillacs and modern racing cars—are presented in their appropriate context, with music of the day playing on contemporary radios; mannequins dressed in fashions of the time; and newspapers, magazines, televisions, and everyday household objects all helping to set the stage. More a museum of 20th-century technology and life than one of just cars, it makes for a fascinating look back at the last century. ⊠ *Hamnen*, ☎ *0141/58888*, WEB *www. motala-motormuseum.se.* ⊟ *SKr 40.* ☉ *June–Aug., daily 10–8; May and Sept., daily 10–6; Oct.–Apr., daily 10–3.*

The **Kanal och Sjöfartsmuseet** traces the story of the building of the Göta Canal, using original equipment and modern sound and light shows. Here, too, you can learn all about operating canal locks, and read about the close links with British engineers during the canal's construction. The Canal and Navigation Museum is located right on the harbor. ⊠ *Hamnen,* ☎ *0141/53510.* ⊟ *SKr 20.* ☉ *May–June and Aug., weekdays 9–5; July, daily 9–6.*

Europe's most powerful radio transmitter was built in Motala in 1927. In later years, radio became an important industry for this little town. The **Rundradiomuseet** uses interactive displays to present the history of radio's birth as well as a glimpse into its future. ⊠ *Radiovägan,* ☎ *0141/ 52202.* ⊟ *SKr 25.* ☉ *May, daily noon–4; June–Aug., daily 10–6.*

Dining and Lodging

$ ✕ **Hallen.** The best place to eat in town, Hallen is set in a 1920s food market that still has its original glazed-brick interior and a serving area and bar that resemble market stalls. The food is basic but well prepared. Fish from Lake Vättern are a specialty. If you're a beer lover, the 50 varieties of English and German beer should keep you happy all night. ⊠ *Storatorget,* ☎ *0141/219100. AE, DC, MC, V.*

$ ▦ **Göta Hotell.** Five kilometers (three miles) outside of town on Route 36A stands this small and welcoming hotel, built in 1912. It's a traditional, red wood building that's right on the water's edge. Most of the ground floor is taken up by a restaurant and bar and a veranda overlooking the canal. A large, central staircase takes you to bright, open landings. The spacious rooms have billowing linen drapes and are painted in shades of sunshine and citrus. The rooms with a view of the canal are the best, especially since they're available at no extra charge. ⊠ *Vid Kanalen, 591 31, Borensberg,* ☎ *0141/40060,* FAX *0141/ 40061. 9 rooms, 2 suites. Restaurant, bar, no-smoking rooms. AE, DC, MC, V. BP.*

En Route At Borenshult a series of locks takes the boat down to **Boren,** a lake in the province of Östergötland. On the southern shore of the next lake, Roxen, lies the city of **Linköping,** capital of the province and home of Saab, the aircraft and automotive company. Once out of the lake, you follow a new stretch of canal past the sleepy town of **Söderköping.** A few miles east, at the hamlet of Mem, the canal's last lock lowers the boat into Slätbaken, a Baltic fjord presided over by the **Stegeborg Slottsruin,** the ancient ruins of the Stegeborg Fortress. The boat then steams north along the coastline until it enters **Mälaren** through the Södertälje Canal and finally anchors in the capital at Riddarholmen.

Göta Canal A to Z

To research prices, get advice from other travelers, and book travel arrangements, visit www.fodors.com.

CAR TRAVEL
From Stockholm, follow E18 west; from Göteborg, take Route 45 north to E18.

CRUISE TRAVEL

For details about cruises along the Göta Canal, *see* Göteborg A to Z.

TRAIN TRAVEL

Call SJ Göteborg for information about service.
➤ TRAIN INFORMATION: **SJ** (✉ Göteborg, ☎ 031/103000).

VISITOR INFORMATION

➤ TOURIST INFORMATION: **Karlsborg** (✉ N. Kanalg. 2, ☎ 0505/17350). **Mariestad** (✉ Hamnplan, ☎ 0501/10001). **Motala** (✉ Repslagareg. 1, ☎ 0141/225254). **Skövde** (Västergötlands Turistråd; ✉ Kyrkog. 11, ☎ 0500/418050). **Uddevalla** (Bohusturist; ✉ Skansg. 3, ☎ 0522/ 14055). **Vadstena** (✉ Rådhustorget, ☎ 0143/15125).

VÄRMLAND

Close to the Norwegian border on the north shores of Vänern, the province of Värmland is rich in folklore. It was also the home of Alfred Nobel and the birthplace of other famous Swedes, among them the Nobel Prize–winning novelist Selma Lagerlöf, the poet Gustaf Fröding, former prime minister Tage Erlander, and present-day opera star Håkan Hagegård. Värmland's forested, lake-dotted landscape attracts artists seeking refuge and Swedes on holiday.

Karlstad

❷ *255 km (158 mi) northeast of Göteborg.*

Värmland's principal city (population 80,000) is situated on Klarälven (the Klara River) at the point where it empties into Vänern. Founded in 1684, when it was known as Tingvalla, the city was totally rebuilt after a fire in 1865. Its name was later changed to honor King Karl IX—Karlstad, meaning Karl's Town. In **Stortorget,** the main square, there is a statue of Karl IX by the local sculptor Christian Eriksson. East of the square is **Östra Bron** (East Bridge). Completed in 1811, it is Sweden's longest arched stone bridge, its 12 arches spanning 510 ft across the water. Anders Jacobsson, the bridge's builder, threw himself off it and drowned himself, for fear, it is claimed, that his great achievement would collapse. His name is carved on a stone in the bridge's center.

Consecrated in 1730, and all but destroyed by fire in 1865, **Karlstads Katedral** (Karlstad's Cathedral; ✉ Kungsg.), was subsequently rebuilt to its former glory. Particular features worth looking for are the altar, made of limestone with a crystal cross, and the font, also made of crystal.

One of only seven buildings that survived the great fire of 1865, the **Biskopsgården** (Bishop's Residence) is a beautiful two-story yellow wooden building that was built in 1781. The row of huge elm trees that surrounds the building acted as a natural firebreak and saved it from the flames. Guided tours can be arranged by the **tourist office** (☎ 054/222140).

The **Värmlands Museum** has rooms dedicated to both the sculptor Eriksson and the poet Gustaf Fröding. ✉ *Sandgrun, Box 335, Karlstad,* ☎ *054/143100.* ▣ *SKr 30.* ☉ *Thurs.–Tues. noon–4, Wed. noon–8.*

The **Marieberg Skogspark** (Marieberg Forest Park) is worth visiting. A delight for the whole family, the park has nature trails, walking tracks, restaurants, and an outdoor theater. ☉ *Early June–late Aug.,*

Thurs.–Tues. 11–5, Wed. 11–8; late Aug.–early June, Tues. and Thurs.–Sun. noon–4, Wed. noon–8.

Karlstad is the site of the **Emigrant Registret** (Emigrant Registry), which maintains detailed records of the Swedes' emigration to America. Those of Swedish extraction can trace their ancestors at the center's research facility. ⊠ *Norra Strandg. 4, Box 331, Karlstad,* ☎ *054/107727.* 🎟 *Free.* ☉ *May–Sept., daily 8–4; Oct.–Apr., Tues.–Sun. 8–4:30, Mon. 8–7.*

OFF THE
BEATEN PATH

SUNNEMO – Ten kilometers (six miles) north of Munkfors lies the little village of Sunnemo, with its beautiful wooden church.

KLARÄLVENÄLV – The Klarälven River runs for 500 km (312 mi) through Scandinavia, and offers great opportunities for rafting trips. Until 1991 the river was used for floating logs downstream to sawmills. Two companies, Sverigeflottan (☎ 0564/40227) and Vildmark i Värmland (☎ 0560/14040), operate trips along the river on two-person rafts. The water flows slowly, so on the way you can swim, fish, and contemplate the beautiful scenery and wildlife (elk, beavers, wolverines, and bears). At night you camp in tents on the water's edge.

Dining and Lodging

$$ ✕ **Inn Alstern.** Overlooking Lake Alstern, this elegant restaurant offers Swedish and Continental cuisine, with fish dishes as the specialty. ⊠ *Morgonv. 4,* ☎ *054/834900. AE, MC, V.*

$$ ✕ **Restaurang Munken.** Walking down the steps into this cellar restaurant is like stepping into a Three Musketeers movie. Low, arched stone ceilings, long wooden benches, and dim candlelight make this a cozy, informal spot. The food is warming, filling Swedish fare with a heavy Continental hand. Anything with veal is worth trying here. ⊠ *Västra Torgg. 17,* ☎ *054/185150. AE, DC, MC, V. Closed Sun.*

$–$$ ✕ **Ristorante Alfie.** The three dining rooms are dimly lit and the dark wood tables are close together, making Alfie a very sociable dining experience. The menu includes pizzas and pasta and a huge and varied steak menu. The entrecôte steaks, served extremely rare with béarnaise sauce, are some of the best around. ⊠ *Västra Torgg. 19,* ☎ *054/216262. AE, DC, MC, V.*

$$ 🛏 **Comfort Hotel Bilan.** Security will be the least of your worries staying here, since the hotel is in a converted old county jail. Not surprisingly, the outside is a little imposing and uninviting, but once inside, public areas and rooms all have bright furnishings and fabrics. In the basement there is a museum where you can look at the original cells and see letters and some of the objects—including a hacksaw—once sent to prisoners. ⊠ *Karlbergsg. 3, 652 24,* ☎ *054/100300,* 🅵🅰🆇 *054/219214. 86 rooms without bath. Restaurant, sauna. AE, DC, MC, V. BP.*

$$ 🛏 **First Hotel Plaza.** The very large rooms here are in soothing neutral tones and come with excellent amenities. There is a sauna and relaxation area on the top floor, which offers great views across the city. ⊠ *Västra Torgg. 2, E-655 25,* ☎ *054/100200,* 🅵🅰🆇 *054/100224. 131 rooms, 80 with bath, 5 suites. Restaurant, bar, lounge, in-room data ports, minibars. AE, DC, MC, V. BP.*

$$ 🛏 **Gösta Berling.** In town center, this small hotel, named for the hero of the Selma Lagerlöf novel, offers nondescript common areas but inviting, plushly carpeted rooms. ⊠ *Drottningg. 1, 652 24,* ☎ *054/150190,* 🅵🅰🆇 *054/154826. 49 rooms with bath. Breakfast room, no-smoking rooms, sauna, meeting room. AE, DC, MC, V. BP.*

$$ 🛏 **Stadshotellet.** On the banks of the Klarälven (Klara River), this hotel from 1870 is steeped in tradition. All of the rooms are decorated dif-

ferently, some in modern Swedish style, others in ways that evoke their original look. You can dine at the fancy Matsalon or in the more casual atmosphere of the Bishop's Arms, an English pub offering 50 types of beer. ⊠ *Kungsg. 22, S651 08,* ☎ *054/293000,* ℻ *054/188211. 143 rooms, 53 with bath. Restaurant, lounge, pub, no-smoking rooms, sauna, meeting room. AE, DC, MC, V. BP.*

Nightlife and the Arts

The choice of bars and pubs in Karlstad is good for a town of this size. **Harry's** (⊠ Kungsg. 16, ☎ 054/102020) is an American-style bar with a large wooden interior and good beer on tap. The English-style pub, the **Woolpack Inn** (⊠ Järnsvägsg. 1, ☎ 054/158016) is a perennial favorite with the locals.

For late-night dancing, try **N.Y. Nightclub** (⊠ Västra Torgg. 2, ☎ 054/100200), in the basement of the First Plaza Hotel. This is the place to be seen in Karlstad. Those in their mid-20s and beyond dance the night away to the latest club tunes, fueled by lavishly over-the-top cocktails and lots of beer.

Shopping

Stores selling clothes, jewelry, furniture, antiques, and crafts are all concentrated on the streets of Drotninggatan and Östra Torggatan. All the main national retail brands are here, as well as individual boutiques.

En Route   Värmland is, above all, a rural experience. Drive along the **Klaräalven,** through the beautiful Fryken Valley, to Ransater, where author Erik Gustaf Geijer was born in 1783 and where Erlander, the former prime minister, also grew up. The rural idyll ends in **Munkfors,** where some of the best-quality steel in Europe is manufactured.

Sunne

63 km (39 mi) north of Karlstad, 318 km (198 mi) northeast of Göteborg.

A small village more than a town, Sunne is mainly known for two things. First, the famed Swedish author Selma Lagerlöf has many connections here. Sunne is also known for the prominent spa that dominates the entrance road to the village. It's a haven for stressed executives from all over Sweden.

In the middle of town, **Sundsbergs Gård** is a beautiful building said to have inspired one of the settings in Selma Lagerlöf's novel *Gösta Berling.* Sundsberg's Manor House (built in 1780) is now a museum charting the last three centuries of Swedish domestic history. ⊠ *Ekebyv,* ☎ *0565/16400.* 🎫 *SKr 20.* ☉ *Tues.–Sun. noon–4.*

A small collection of old buildings make up **Sunne Hembygdsgården,** a museum showing life lived in the 1800s. The well-preserved buildings include a manor house, school, general store, and courthouse. ⊠ *Hembygdsvåden 7,* ☎ *0565/10120.* 🎫 *Free.* ☉ *By appointment.*

OFF THE
BEATEN PATH

MÅRBACKA – The estate on which Nobel Prize winner Selma Lagerlöf was born in 1858 can be found in this town, a stone's throw southeast of Sunne. Lagerlöf is considered the best Swedish author of her generation, and is known and avidly read by Swedes young and old. The house can be seen by guided tour. Her furnishings, including her study desk and beautiful, wood-panel library, have been kept much as she left them at the time of her death in 1940. ⊠ *Östra Ämtervik, 686 26,* ☎ *0565/31027.* 🎫 *SKr 40.* ☉ *Mid-May–June and Aug.–early Sept., daily 10–5, tours every hr; July, daily 9:30–5, tours every half hr.*

ROTTNEROS HERRGARDS PARK – On the western shore of Fryken Lake, 5 km (3 mi) south of Sunne, is Rottneros Manor, the inspiration for Ekeby, the fictional estate in Lagerlöf's *Gösta Berlings Saga* (*The Tale of Gösta Berling*). The house is privately owned, but you can go to the park, with its fine collection of Scandinavian sculpture. Here there are works by Carl Milles, Norwegian artist Gustav Vigeland, and Wäinö Aaltonen of Finland. The entrance fee covers both the sculpture park and the Nils Holgerssons Adventure Park, an elaborate playground for children. ⊠ *Rottneros,* ☎ *0565/60295.* ☑ *SKr 50.* ☉ *Mid-May–early June and late Aug., weekdays 10–4, weekends 10–6; late June, weekdays 10–5, weekends 10–6; July–Aug., daily 10–6.*

Dining and Lodging

$ ✕ **Köpmangården.** If you blink, you may miss this tiny bar and restaurant that's on a road of private residences. Looking like a derelict old house from the outside, the faded carpet, chipped and frayed furniture, and dingy rest rooms on the inside aren't much better. But the food is some of the best around. Everything is homemade. The tomato soup with crème fraîche, huge prawn sandwiches, and inch-thick steaks are all delicious. The warm welcome from the little old lady who runs the place is as good as the food. ⊠ *Ekebyv. 40,* ☎ *0565/10121. MC, V.*

$$ ✕🖭 **Quality Hotel and Spa Selma Lagerlöf.** This huge modern complex of a hotel is split onto two sides of the road leading into Sunne. Each side has large rooms furnished in a simple Scandinavian design, huge public rooms and lobbies, a bar, restaurant, and nightclub. The main hotel has a very well-equipped spa and fitness center with workout classes, gym, pool, fun pool, spa, saunas, solariums, massage, and treatment rooms. Guests can use most of the facilities for free, with a nominal charge for treatments. The restaurants ($$–$$$) in each hotel serve good Swedish classics, and French–influenced food, in a set dinner menu. Be sure to try the reindeer if it's available. The grounds of the hotel are extensive, and contain many wooded walking and jogging tracks. Be sure to ask for a room at the front of the hotel, as these have stunning views over the lake. ⊠ *Box 500, 686 28 Sunne,* ☎ *0565/688810,* ℻ *0565/16631,* ⅦℰⒷ *www.selmaspa.se. 340 rooms, 210 with bath, 18 suites. 2 restaurants, 2 bars, lounge, 2 pools, sauna, spa, health club, convention center. AE, DC, MC, V. BP.*

Shopping

If you're passing through Sunne and feeling a little ravaged by life, you can pick up some pick-me-ups at the local spa resort. **Quality Hotel and Spa Selma Lagerlöf** (☎ 0565/688810), offers all manner of wonderful herb, spice, mud, and clay concoctions to put in your bath, rub on your skin, or simply wallow in.

Outdoor Activities

If you're the nature-spotting type, you may be interested in taking an **elk safari** (☎ 0565/40016). Departures are every Wednesday and Friday in July and for SKr 150 you're almost guaranteed to see an elk.

Filipstad

⑧ *63 km (39 mi) northeast of Karlstad via Route 63.*

Filipstad is in the heart of Värmland's mining district. For hundreds of years, the town was the center for the area's mineral mining and metalworking. You can still see many of the ancient mining and stone-cutting methods and lifestyles in various working museums and villages such as **Nykroppa, Låban, and Persberg,** where Värmland's only surviving underground mine still produces limestone. Details of tours and prices can be obtained from **Filipstad Turistbyra** (tourist office; ☎ 0590/71560).

Filipstad's other mainstay is **Wasa** (☎ 0590/18100), Scandinavia's largest producer of crispbread. The factory runs guided tours, showing the history of the company and how the crispbread is produced. Call to arrange a tour.

Dining and Lodging

$$ ✕🍴 **Hennickehammars Gård.** The rooms are large and airy at this old Swedish manor house. They come with big windows, original wooden floors, and antique furniture. The restaurant ($$) serves traditional Swedish food in a fresh white-and-blue antique dining room with open fire. After your fill from dinner, a stroll around the peaceful grounds is a delight. ⊠ *Box 52, 682 22,* ☎ *0590/12565,* ⨳ *0590/608505,* 🌐 *www.hennickehammar.se. 54 rooms with bath, 3 suites. Restaurant, bar. AE, DC, MC, V. BP.*

Värmland A to Z

To research prices, get advice from other travelers, and book travel arrangements, visit www.fodors.com.

CAR TRAVEL
From Stockholm, follow E18 west; from Göteborg, take Route 45 north to E18.

TRAIN TRAVEL
There is regular service to Karlstad from Stockholm and Göteborg on SJ.

➤ TRAIN INFORMATION: **SJ** (⊠ Göteborg, ☎ 031/103000 or 020/757575).

VISITOR INFORMATION
➤ TOURIST INFORMATION: **Karlstad (Karlstad Conference Center)** (☎ 054/222140). **Filipstad** (⊠ Stora Torget 3, ☎ 0590/71560). **Sunne** (Turistbyrå; ⊠ Mejerig. 2, ☎ 0565/16400). **Värmlands Turistbyrå** (⊠ Tage Erlanderg. 10, Karlstad, ☎ 054/222550).

7 THE SOUTH AND THE KINGDOM OF GLASS

S OUTHERN SWEDEN IS CONSIDERED even by many Swedes to be a world of its own, clearly distinguished from the rest of the country by its geography, culture, and history. Skåne (pronounced *skoh-neh*), the southernmost province, is known as the granary of Sweden. It is a comparatively small province of fertile plains, sand beaches, farms, bustling, historic towns and villages, medieval churches, and summer resorts. These gently rolling hills, extensive forests, and fields are broken every few miles by lovely castles, chronologically and architecturally diverse, that have given this part of Sweden the name Château Country; often they are surrounded by beautiful grounds and moats. A significant number of the estates have remained in the hands of the original families, and many are still inhabited.

The two other southern provinces, Blekinge and Halland, are also fertile and rolling and edged by seashores. Historically, these three provinces are distinct from the rest of Sweden: they were the last to be incorporated into the country, having been ruled by Denmark until 1658. They retain the influences of the Continental culture in their architecture, language, and cuisine, viewing the rest of Sweden—especially Stockholm—with some disdain. Skåne even has its own independence movement, and the dialect is so akin to Danish that many Swedes from other regions have trouble understanding it.

Småland, to the north, is larger than the other provinces, with a harsh countryside of stone and woods, the so-called Kingdom of Glass. It is an area of small glassblowing firms, such as Kosta Boda and Orrefors, that are world-renowned for the quality of their products. In addition to visiting these works (and perhaps finding some bargains), you may also gain some insight into the poorer, bleaker way of life that led thousands of peasants to emigrate from Småland to the United States. Those who stayed behind developed a reputation for their inventiveness in setting up small industries to circumvent the region's traditional poverty and are also notorious for being extremely careful—if not downright mean—with money.

Perhaps the most significant recent event for the South has been the bridge that opened over the Öresund, linking Malmö to Copenhagen in Denmark. At 3 mi (5 km), the bridge is the longest combined railroad and tunnel in the world. It opened on July 1, 2000, amid hopes that it would bring a windfall to the South. As a tourist, your travel alternatives have improved.

Your itinerary should follow a route that sweeps from the western coastal town of Mölle around the southern loop and along the eastern shore, taking a side trip to the Baltic island province of Öland before heading inland to finish at Växjö. The entire route can be done by train, with the exception of Mölle and Helsingborg, Öland, and most of the glassworks in Småland—the Orrefors factory is the only one on the railway line. Continue your journey in any direction from Växjö.

Mölle

★ **84** *35 km (21 mi) northwest of Helsingborg, 220 km (132 mi) south of Göteborg, 235 km (141 mi) southwest of Växjö, 95 km (57 mi) northwest of Malmö.*

Mölle, in the far northwest of Skåne, is a small town set in spectacular isolation on the dramatic headland of the Kulla peninsula. It is an old fishing village with a beautiful harbor that sweeps up to the Kullaberg range. You will find beech forests, stupefying views, and rugged shores and beaches, surrounded on three sides by sea.

For those who love nature or want a break from cities and touring, Mölle is perfect. Not only is it a good base from which to explore, but the town itself has a charm that has never been tarnished by an over-abundance of tourists or a relentless drive to modernize at all costs.

But Mölle's past isn't all quaintness and tradition. In the late 19th century, the town was notorious throughout the country and the rest of Europe as a hotbed of liberal hedonism. This reputation was based on the penchant of locals to enjoy mixed-sex bathing, a scandalous practice at the time. Berliners loved it, and until the World War I there was a weekly train that went all the way to Mölle. But as soon as war broke out, the Germans disappeared.

Today it is a relatively wealthy place, as the elaborate residences and the upmarket cars crowding the narrow streets show. Much of this wealth supposedly arrived when the more fortunate men of the sea returned to build mansions. Many of the mansions have local, although perhaps distorted, legends about them.

The **Villa Italienborg** was completed in 1910 by a scrap dealer inspired by a trip to the Italian Riviera. The exterior is covered in striking red and white tiles that form a checked pattern, which was quite stylish at the time. ⊠ *Harastolsv. 6.*

The verandas, balconies, and sliding windows all make the **Villa Africa,** a beautiful two-story, stand out. It was built in a South African colonial style by a local captain to please his South African wife. Legend also has it that while wooing her he would claim that Mölle's climate was the equal of that of her homeland! ⊠ *N. Brunnsv.*

The **Kullaberg** nature reserve is just outside Mölle and covers more than 35 square km (13½ square mi). You can walk, bike, or drive in. This natural playground includes excellent trails through beech forests and along coastal routes. There's a lighthouse here set in stark land that resembles that of the Scottish Highlands—it even has longhaired Highland cattle. The park contains cafés, a restaurant, safe swimming beaches, and a golf course that's one of Sweden's most spectacular. Rock climbers consider the rock structure here to be similar to that of the Himalayas—many climbers planning to travel to that range first train here. ▤ *SKr 25 per car.*

Krapperup castle was built in 1570 over the ruins of a medieval stronghold dating back to the 13th century. The present building was extensively renovated in the late 18th century, although remnants of the stronghold still exist. The garden is among Sweden's best-preserved parks. There's an art gallery and museum inside, and concerts and performance theater are held here in the summer. It is 4 km (2½ mi) from Mölle on the main road to Helsingborg. ☎ *042/344190.* ▤ *SKr 60.* ☉ *Gallery Museum May–Sept.*

Just a few kilometers from town, the **Mölle Kapell** is a quaint white church that stands in fields under the Kullaberg. Despite its ancient appearance, the church was built in 1937. Much of the interior—the pulpit, the altar painting and pews—done by local artist Gunnar Wallentin.

The haunting **Nimis** and **Arx** artworks are built of scrap wood and stone and stand on a rugged beach that can be reached only on foot. The artist Lars Vilks has been working on the weird, highly controversial structures since the 1970s. They are the most visited sight in Kullaberg. Vilks has been under constant legal threat because he didn't apply for permission from the local government, which owns the land. *Head 2 km (1¼ mi) east out of Mölle to a road sign directing you to Himmelstorps Hembygdsgård. Following this sign you will reach a car park and an old farmhouse. From here it is a 1 km (½ mi) walk marked by small blue N symbols.* WEB *www.aim.se/art/Nimis Arx.*

OFF THE BEATEN PATH

ARILD – This fishing village has been important since the Middle Ages. It is 6 km (4 mi) east of Mölle. Today the town is a mix of bright fisherman's and sailor's cottages against a backdrop of a beautiful fishing harbor. The nicest place to stay is **Hotel Rusthållargården** (⊠ Utsikten 1, ☎ 042/347084), which costs SKr 695 per person. It has an excellent restaurant. If you're looking for a break, continue east from Arild for 2 km (1 mi) to reach the village of Skäret. Head for the copper sign shaped like a coffeepot, which marks **Flickorna Lundgren** (☎ 042/346044, ☉ May–Sept. 9), one of Sweden's most famous cafés. The outstanding gardens look out onto the sea, and the café's regular visitors have included King Gustav IV as well as V.

Dining and Lodging

Most of the cafés and restaurants in town are in hotels.

$$ ✕📖 **Turisthotell.** The rooms at this hotel are well appointed, and some have a view of the harbor. The breakfast, included in room rates, is generous and could see you through to dinner. The restaurant ($–$$) serves good food with a European flavor, focusing on meat entrées with Swedish side dishes such as lingonberries. The lamb, cooked medium rare with mint sauce, is outstanding. ⊠ *Kullabergsv. 32,* ☎ 042/347084, FAX 042/347484, WEB *www.molleturisthotell.se. 12 rooms with bath. Bar, dining room. AE, MC, V. Closed Jan.–Feb. BP.*

$–$$ ✕📖 **Grand Hôtel.** Although there are several accommodation options
★   in town, the spectacular Grand Hôtel—a turreted building set high up on a hill, has an unrivaled setting, great views, and a helpful staff. The best rooms are those with a sea view but they are all pleasant. For dining you have a choice of two restaurants, the hotel and the attached Captain's Room. The more expensive and adventurous meals are from the hotel dining room. ⊠ *Bökebolsvägen 11,* ☎ 042/362230, FAX 042/362231, WEB *www.grand-molle.se. 53 rooms with bath. 2 restaurants, bar, sauna, library, meeting rooms. AE, D, MC, V. BP.*

$$–$$$ 📖 **Hotel Kullaberg.** At this luxurious place, all the rooms are plush and decorated in themes. One room suggests *Out of Africa*, and another has a large biplane hanging from the ceiling. You may or may not love it, depending on your feelings about kitsch. But the Kullaberg is lush, with views of the sea and the harbor, ornate reading rooms, and a very good dining room. ⊠ *Gyllenstiernas Allé 16,* ☎ 042/347420, FAX 042/247431, WEB *www.hotelkullaberg.se. 18 rooms with bath. Dining room, library. AE, D, MC, V. Closed Feb. and Dec. 25–Jan. 1. BP.*

Shopping

In the otherwise unremarkable town of Höganäs, 35 km (22 mi) south of Mölle, is a good factory outlet store for ceramics and glassware. **Höganäs Keramik** (⊠ Vid Väg 111, Höganäs, ☎ 042/361131; ☉ Sept.–Apr., weekdays 10–6, Sat. 10–4, Sun. 11–4; May–June and Aug., weekdays 9–6, weekends 10–5; July, weekdays 9–7, weekends 10–5) sells brands such as BodaNova at discounts of up to 40%.

Outdoor Activities and Sports

The Skola Mölle Hamn (Special Sports School) caters to most outdoor activities. It organizes trips and provides gear and training for mountaineers, divers, and kayakers of all skill levels. ⊠ *Södra Strandvägen 6B,* ☎ 042/347705, 010/2924748, 070/7132791.

Kullens Höstskjutjar and Turridning organizes horseback riding. ☒ *Himmelstorp 765,* ☎ *042/346358.*

Mölle Golfklubb, one of the most spectacular 18-hole courses in Sweden, will slake the most fanatic golfers' thirst for their sport. ☒ *Kullagården,* ☎ *042/347520.* ☜ *Greens fee June–Aug. SKr 260, Sept.– May SKr 220.*

Side Trips from Mölle

Viken and **Lerberget** are two small villages on the way from Mölle to Helsingborg. Viken is a preserved fishing village with narrow, stone-walled streets; traditional cottages; and a well-kept example of the old windmills once used in Skåne. If you are here between late spring and fall, you may wish to stay the night, combining dinner at the Gula Boden seafood restaurant in Viken with a stay at the quaint Pensionat Solgården guest house in nearby Lerberget (a drive of two minutes).

$–$$ ✕ **Gula Boden.** With a local reputation for excellent fish meals and great views of the boat harbor and sunsets, Gula Boden is quite popular. Reservations are essential in July. ☒ *Vikens Hamn,* ☎ *042/238300. AE, DC, MC, V. Oct.–Apr.*

$ ⌂ **Pensionat Solgården.** Run by an artistic woman who spends six months of each year at the Tonga B&B, this pension hosts poetry readings outside in the summer. ☒ *Byav. 102, Lerberget,* ☎ *042/330430. Closed mid-Sept.–mid-Apr. BP.*

Helsingborg

85 *221 km (137 mi) south of Göteborg, 186 km (116 mi) southwest of Växjö, 64 km (40 mi) north of Malmö.*

Helsingborg (still sometimes spelled the old way, Hälsingborg), with a population of 120,000, may seem to the first-time visitor little more than a small town with a modern ferry terminal (it has connections to Denmark, Norway, and Germany). The town sees itself differently, claiming titles as Sweden's gateway to the Continent, and the pearl of the Øresund region. Helsingborg was first mentioned in a letter written by Canute, the King of Denmark, in 1085; later it was the site of many battles between the Danes and the Swedes. Together with its twin town, Helsingør (Elsinore in William Shakespeare's *Hamlet*), across the Öresund, it controlled shipping traffic in and out of the Baltic for centuries. Helsingborg was officially incorporated into Sweden in 1658 and totally destroyed in a battle with the Danes in 1710. It was then rebuilt, and Jean-Baptiste Bernadotte, founder of the present Swedish royal dynasty, landed here in 1810.

Built in 1897, Helsingborg's **Stadshuset** (Town Hall) has a small museum of exhibits on the city and the region. The stained-glass windows here depict scenes from the town's history, and the artist Isenstein's relief sculptures represent a stream of refugees—a gift from Danes who found safe haven here during World War II. A monument also recognizes Swedish help given to Norway and Denmark during the Nazi insurgency. ☒ *Södra Storg. 31,* ☎ *042/105963.* ☜ *SKr 30.* ☼ *May–Aug., Tues.–Sun. noon–5; Sept.–Apr., Tues.–Sun. noon–4.*

All that remains of Helsingborg's castle is **Kärnan** (The Keep), which was built in the late 14th century. It has walls 15 ft thick. This surviving center tower, built to provide living quarters and defend the medieval castle, is one of the most remarkable relics of its kind in the north. It fell into disuse after the Swedish defeated the Danes in 1658 but was restored in 1893–94. The interior is divided into several floors, which contain a chapel, an exhibition of kitchen implements, old castle fittings, and some weaponry. ☒ *Slottshagen,* ☎ *042/105991.* ☜ *SKr 30.*

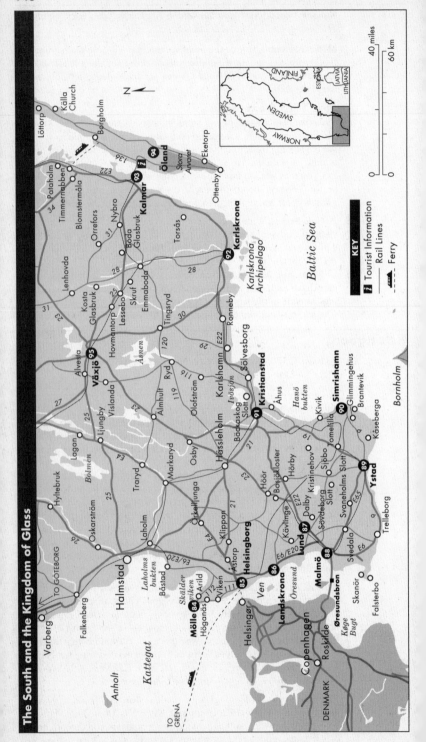

The South and the Kingdom of Glass

🕐 *June–Aug., daily 10–7; Apr.–May and Sept., Tues.–Fri. 9–4, weekends 11–4; Oct.–Mar., Tues.–Sun. 11–3.*

★ In 1864 **Sofiero Slott** (Sofiero Castle) was built in the Dutch Renaissance style by Prince Oscar and his wife, Sofia, as a summer home. Half a century later Oscar II gave the castle to his grandson, Gustav Adolf, and his wife, Margareta, as a wedding gift. Since the estate is now owned by the city of Helsingborg, you can gain access to Sofiero's park, a haven for more than 300 kinds of rhododendron, various statues donated by international artists, and a large English garden; nearby greenhouses have a number of plant exhibits. A café and fine restaurant are on the grounds. ⊠ *Sofierov. (on the road to Laröd),* ☎ *042/137400 or 042/140440.* 🎫 *SKr 40.* 🕐 *Mid-May–mid-Sept., daily 10–6; guided tours only. Park open year-round. Restaurant and café open Mar.–Dec.*

Maria Kyrkan, constructed beginning in the 14th century and finished 100 years later, is a fine example of Danish Gothic architecture. St. Mary's has several parts that are well worth checking out: the 15th-century reredos, the silver treasure in the sacristy, and a memorial plaque to Dietrich Buxtehude (1637–1707), a prominent composer as well as the church's organist. ⊠ *Maritorget, Södra Storg.,* ☎ *042/372830.* 🕐 *Aug.–June, daily 8–4, July, daily 8–6.*

The **Dunkers Kulturhus** is an ambitious arts and cultural project set to open in the spring of 2002. It will include a theater, a city museum, a music school, a concert hall, an art museum, a cultural center for children and youth, a multimedia center, and a restaurant. It was designed by Kim Utzon, the son of the controversial architect Jørn Utzon, the Dane who designed the Sydney Opera House. Prices and hours have yet to be finalized. ⊠ *Sundstorget,* 🌐 *www.dunkerskultuhus.com.*

Helsingborg's refurbished harborside area is called **Norra Hamnen.** The Northern Harbor has a pleasant marina with a string of architecturally impressive cafés and restaurants. The modern eateries and apartments in this once nondescript space were designed and built for a 1999 exhibition.

Dining and Lodging

$$$ ✕ **Gastro.** A long leather booth divides this dining room into two halves: one is packed with small tables for groups of two or three, the other with tables for five or six. Larger parties sit in the more formal back of the restaurant, but everyone orders from the same menu of Swedish-based international fare. Fish and seafood are the stars. ⊠ *Södra Storg. 11–13,* ☎ *042/243470. AE, DC, MC, V. Closed Sun.*

$$ ✕ **Oscar's Trapp.** Oscar's Trapp is housed in two towers that were built
★ in 1904 to resemble Kärnan, which sits at the top of the hill overlooking the town. In one tower is the dining area; in the other are a bar and lounge. The brick arches, antique furnishings, and the portraits and torches on the wall create an authentic, rustic setting: you have entered the knight's keep. The food is finely crafted and includes many meat dishes, such as the rack of lamb with rosemary and the perfectly cooked duck terrine. The accompaniments (new potatoes, lingonberry sauce) are Swedish classics. ⊠ *Stortorget,* ☎ *042/146044. AE, DC, MC, V. Closed Sun. and parts of July.*

$$ ✕ **Pälsjö Krog.** On the water, beside the pier that leads out to the Päl-
★ sjö Bath House, this restaurant offers a beautiful view of the Öresund. The owners have been restoring the restaurant to its original 1930s style—note the antique sofa in the lounge and the art on the walls. Seafood is the specialty in summer months; game in winter. ⊠ *Drottningg. 151,* ☎ *042/149730. Reservations essential in summer. AE, DC, MC, V.*

$$ ✕ **SS Swea** is a restaurant ship designed after cruise liners of old. Those with a nautical bent or nostalgia for past traveling days will be well served. The restaurant specializes in fresh seafood and international menus. Enjoy the wide-ranging menu but don't forget to disembark—there are no cabin bunks here. ⊠ *Kungstorget,* ☎ *042/131516. AE, MC, V.*

$–$$ ✕ **Restaurang La Petite.** If you are yearning for the delicacy of French cuisine and the genuine look and feel of a French restaurant, then look no further. La Petite has been here since 1975, suggesting success, and can also indulge the diner in Spanish and international meals. ⊠ *Bruksg. 19,* ☎ *042/219727. AE, MC, V. Closed Sun.*

$ ⌂ **Grand Hotel.** One of Sweden's oldest hotels has been completely ren-
★ ovated, maintaining its long-standing reputation for excellence. Antiques and fresh flowers fill the hotel, and the well-equipped guest rooms have cable TV, a hair dryer, minibar, and trouser press. The hotel is close to the railway station and ferry terminals. ⊠ *Stortorget 812, S251 11,* ☎ *042/380400,* FAX *042/118833. 117 rooms with bath. Restaurant, bar, no-smoking rooms, sauna, meeting rooms. AE, DC, MC, V.*

$ ⌂ **Hotel Högvakten.** This hotel on the main square has bright, fresh rooms with a mix of modern and antique furniture. Rooms can be a bit small, but the hotel is close to the main shopping street and the central station. ⊠ *Stortorget 14, 251 10,* ☎ *042/120390,* FAX *042/120095. 42 rooms with bath. Breakfast room, sauna, meeting rooms. AE, DC, MC, V. BP.*

$ ⌂ **Hotel Mollberg.** In the center of town, only a short walk from the central station, the Mollberg has spacious rooms with hardwood floors and large windows. Corner rooms have balconies that overlook a cobblestone square. The restaurant offers dining at reasonable prices. ⊠ *Stortorget 18, 251 14,* ☎ *042/373700,* FAX *042/373737. 97 rooms with bath. Restaurant, minibars, sauna. AE, DC, MC, V. BP.*

$ ⌂ **Marina Plaza.** This modern hotel, with its enormous central glass atrium, is right next to the Knutpunkten ferry, rail, and bus terminal. Relaxing and stylish, the Marina Plaza has spacious, elegantly decorated rooms. ⊠ *Kungstorget 6, S251 11,* ☎ *042/192100,* FAX *042/149616. 190 rooms with bath. Restaurant, bar, minibars, no-smoking rooms, sauna, meeting rooms. AE, DC, MC, V. BP.*

$ ⌂ **Villa Thalassa.** This youth hostel has fine views over Öresund. One large building contains 140 bunks in two-, four-, and six-bunk rooms. There are also 12 cottages near the water, each with two bedrooms (with double bed and bunk bed), bathroom with shower, and kitchen. The SKr 40 breakfast is not included. ⊠ *Dag Hammarskjölds väg, 254 33,* ☎ *042/210384,* FAX *042/128792. 140 beds with bath, 4- to 6-bed rooms (in winter 2-bed rooms also available). Breakfast room, meeting rooms. No credit cards. BP.*

Nightlife and the Arts

A plush culture and art center, Dunker's Kulturhus, is scheduled to open in spring of 2002.

The Tivoli is a place where you can cut loose. It concentrates on live rock bands, attracting major Swedish and international acts. The moderate-size dance floor has good lighting. If you're looking for a nightclub feel but want to be out of the razzmatazz, check out the vinyl bar. It has a restaurant, too. ⊠ *Hamntorget,* ☎ *042/187171,* WEB *www.thetivoli.nu.* ⊡ *SKr 60.* ☉ *Fri. and Sat. 10 PM–4 AM.*

Jazzklubben is an easy place to take in a variety of different live bands. If you strike the right night you may well find yourself in jazz heaven, since Jazz Club attracts musicians from all over. The atmosphere is intimate, even cozy. You can dine here, too. ⊠ *Nedre Långvinkelsg 22,* ☎ *042/184900.* ⊡ *Up to SKr 60.*

If pubs are your thing, try the **Charles Dickens,** which is the oldest in town. It has a real pub feel and you can easily settle onto your stool in this old-world place and take in a few beers or some wine. ⊠ *Söderg 43,* ☎ *042/135100.* ☉ *Mon.–Tues. and Sun.*

Outdoor Activities and Sports

Consider taking a relaxing dip in the sound at the late 19th-century **Pälsjö Baden** (Pälsjö Bath House) just north of town. The Helsingborg tradition of sweating in a sauna and then jumping into the cool waters of the channel—even in the winter months—might also appeal to you. After an evening sauna, nearby Pälsjö Krog is a good dinner option. ⊠ *Drottningg. 151,* ☎ *042/149707.* ▦ *Single visit SKr 25.*

Ramlösa Brunnspark (☎ 042/105888) is the source of the famous Ramlösa mineral water, which is served in restaurants and cafés throughout the world. Since it opened in 1707, the park has attracted summertime croquet players and those eager to taste the water (an outdoor café also serves beer and wine). Nearby is the **Ramlösa Wärdshus** (☎ 042/296257), which has been serving authentic Swedish cuisine since 1830. To reach the park by bus, take Bus 5 going south from central station.

If your bones are weary, visit **Öresundsmassage.** The professionally trained staff offers various massage services and can deal with problems such as cramping or help you improve your blood circulation. ⊠ *Roskildeg. 4,* ☎ *042/127042.* ▦ *30 min SKr 200, 40 min SKr 350.* ☉ *Mon., Wed., Fri. noon–9; Tues. and Thurs. 10–9.*

Skåne is a golfers' delight. There was a boom in golfing around 1990, when half the region's 58 golf courses were built; within an hour of Helsingborg you can find more than 20. Contact Skånes Tourist Information for more (☎ 042/104350).

Shopping

Helsingborg has convenient shopping, and it's a good place to do those errands you've been putting off. The best place to head is **Kullagatan,** which was the first pedestrianized street in Sweden. It is often described as being dominated by fashion but in fact it's a convenient collection of most of the sorts of shops you might need (e.g., there's a pharmacy, a photo shop, and a stationery store here). If it's cheaper, medium quality skins, furs, or leathers you want, try the **Skin and Fur Centre** at Kullagatan 7.

Landskrona

86 *26 km (16 mi) south of Helsingborg (via E6/E20), 41 km (25 mi) north of Malmö, 204 km (127 mi) southwest of Växjö.*

The 17th-century Dutch-style fortifications of Landskrona are among the best preserved in Europe. Though it appears to be a modern town, Landskrona dates from 1413, when it received its charter.

The eclectic **Landskrona Museum** has temporary exhibits as well as permanent coverage of Landskrona history and the Swedish contributions to art, medicine, aviation, and architecture. ⊠ *Slottsg.,* ☎ *0418/473120,* ▦ *www.landskrona.se/kultur.* ▦ *Free.* ☉ *Mon.–Sun. noon–5.*

Landskrona's **Citadellet** (castle) was built under orders of the Danish King Christian III in 1549 and is all that remains of the original town, which was razed in 1747 by decree of the Swedish Parliament to make way for extended fortifications. The new town was built on land reclaimed from the sea. ⊠ *Slottsg.,* ☎ *0418/473000.* ▦ *SKr 30.* ☉ *Early June–late Aug., daily 11–4.*

VEN – From Landskrona Harbor there are regular 25-minute boat trips to the island of Ven (🚢 SKr 60 round-trip; boats depart every 90 minutes 6 AM–9 PM). It's an ideal place for **camping**; check with Landskrona's tourist office (☎ 0418/473000). There are special paths across Ven for bicycling; rentals are available from Bäckviken, the small harbor.

The Danish astronomer Tycho Brahe conducted his pioneering research here from 1576 to 1597. The foundations of his Renaissance castle, Uranienborg, can be visited, as can Stjärneborg, his reconstructed observatory. The small **Tycho Brahe Museet** is dedicated to Brahe and his work. ⊠ *Landsv., Ven,* ☎ *0418/72530.* 🎫 *SKr 20.* ⊙ *May–Sept., daily 10–4:30.*

Outdoor Activities and Sports

Three kilometers (two miles) north of Landskrona lies the **Borstahusen** (⊠ 261 61 Landskrona, ☎ 0418/10837) recreation area, with long stretches of beach, a marina, and a group of 74 small cabinlike chalets.

Lund

87 *34 km (21 mi) southeast of Landskrona via E6/E20 and Route 16, 25 km (15 mi) northeast of Malmö, 183 km (113 mi) southwest of Växjö.*

One of the oldest towns in Europe, Lund was founded in 990. In 1103 Lund became the religious capital of Scandinavia and at one time had 27 churches and eight monasteries—until King Christian III of Denmark ordered most of them razed to use their stones for the construction of Malmöhus Castle. Lund lost its importance until 1666, when its university was established—the second-oldest university in Sweden after Uppsala.

★ Lund's **Domkyrkan,** a monumental gray stone Romanesque cathedral, is the oldest in Scandinavia, started around 1100 and consecrated in 1145. Since the Reformation, it has been Lutheran. Its crypt has 23 finely carved pillars, but its main attraction is an astrological clock, Horologum Mirabile Lundense, dating from 1380 and restored in 1923. The "Miraculous Clock of Lund" depicts an amazing pageant of knights jousting on horseback, trumpets blowing a medieval fanfare, and the Magi walking in procession past the Virgin and Child as the organ plays *In Dulci Jubilo.* The clock plays at noon and at 3 PM on Monday–Saturday and at 1 PM on Sunday. The oldest parts of the cathedral are considered to be the finest Romanesque constructions in Sweden. English and Swedish tours are available and there is an organ concert at 10 AM Sunday.

The Cathedral Museum and the Museum of History can be found in the building behind and a short distance north in Kraftstorg Square. The Cathedral Museum has exhibitions and a slide show about the Domkyrkan's history. The Museum of History has Sweden's second-largest collection of treasures from the Stone, Bronze, and Iron ages. It also houses one of the oldest human skeletal finds, dated to 5000 BC. ⊠ *Kraftstorg Square,* ☎ *046/2227944,* 🌐 *www.luhm.lu.se.* 🎫 *SKr 30.* ⊙ *Tues.–Fri. 11–4.*

One block east of the cathedral is the **Botaniska Trädgården** (Botanical Gardens), which contains more than 7,000 specimens of plants from all over the world, including such exotics as the Paper Mulberry Tree from the islands of the South Pacific. ⊠ *Östra Vallg. 20,* ☎ *046/2227320.* 🎫 *Free.* ⊙ *Gardens daily 6 AM–8 PM, greenhouses noon–3.*

On the other side of the Lundagård park from the Domkyrkan is where the oldest parts of **Lund University** stand. The main building is crisp white and easily spotted. The university was founded in 1666 and today has 30,000 students. Its **history museum** (☎ 046/350400) exhibits old texts, university regalia, and other items used in the university long ago. Just across Kyrkogatan from the university is a Lund institution—**Conditori Lund** (✉ Kyrkog. 17), a bakery and coffeehouse. It is easy to imagine the rooms once again filled with the smoke and loud opinions of the past's intellectuals. Refreshed, wander in behind the university among the ancient cobbled streets and traditional cottages. ✉ *Kyrkog.*

Just a short walk from the cathedral is the **Skissernas Museum.** Founded in 1934 in connection with Lund University, the Sketches Museum houses more than 20,000 sketches in addition to models and first drafts by major artists. The international collection contains the early ideas of artists such as Matisse, Picasso, Fernand Léger, and many others. ✉ *Finng. 2,* ☎ *046/2227283.* ✍ *SKr 30.* ☉ *Tues. and Thurs.–Sat. noon–4, Wed. 6:30–8:30, Sun. 1–5.*

Esaias Tegnér, the Swedish poet, lived from 1813 to 1826 in a little house immediately behind the cathedral. The house has since been turned into the **Tegnér Museet,** providing insight into his life and works. ✉ *Gråbrödersg.,* ☎ *046/291319.* ✍ *SKr 5.* ☉ *July–Aug., Sat. noon–3; Sept.–June, first Sat. each month noon–3.*

On the southern side of the main square is **Drottens Kyrkoruin** (the Church Ruins of Drotten), an underground museum showing life as it was in Lund during the Middle Ages. The foundations of three Catholic churches are here: the first and oldest was built of wood in approximately AD 1000. It was torn down to make room for one of stone around 1100; this was replaced by a second stone church built around 1300. ✉ *Kattensund 6,* ☎ *046/141329.* ✍ *SKr 10.* ☉ *Tues.–Fri. and Sun. noon–4, Sat. 10–2.*

☾ **Kulturen** (the Museum of Cultural History) is both an outdoor and an indoor museum, including 20 old cottages, farms, and manor houses from southern Sweden plus an excellent collection of ceramics, textiles, weapons, and furniture. ✉ *Karolinsplats,* ☎ *046/350400.* ✍ *SKr 30.* ☉ *May–Sept., Fri.–Wed. 11–5, Thurs. 11–9; Oct.–Apr., Tues.–Sun. noon–4.*

On the corner of Måtenstorget is **Lund Konsthallen** (Lund Art Gallery). The all-brick building may have a rather foreboding iron entrance and few windows, but skylights allow ample sunlight into the large exhibit room inside. The gallery has hosted some major works. ✉ *Måtenstorget 3,* ☎ *046/355000.* ✍ *Free.* ☉ *Mon.–Wed. and Fri. noon–5, Thurs. noon–8, Sat. 10–5, Sun. noon–6.*

★ The **Heligkorskyrkan i Dalby** (Holy Cross Church of Dalby) was founded in 1060, making it the oldest stone church in Sweden. It was for a short time the archbishop's seat until this was moved to Lund. Among the hidden treasures is a renowned baptismal font, brought here in 1150. The exposed brick within the church is original and many figures and icons date from medieval times, including a wooden relief at the front of the church called *Veronica's Napkin,* which shows the face of Jesus. The church is on a hill and less than 10 km (8 mi) from Lund. ✉ *Head east on Rte. 16, Lund's main road, and then follow signs,* ☎ *046/200065.* ✍ *Free.* ☉ *May–Aug., daily 9–6; Sept.–Apr., daily 9–4.*

OFF THE BEATEN PATH

BOSJÖKLOSTER – About 30 km (19 mi) northeast of Lund via E22 and Route 23, Bosjökloster is an 11th-century, white Gothic castle with lovely grounds on Ringsjön, the second-largest lake in southern Skåne. The castle's original owner donated the estate to the church, which turned it over to the Benedictine order of nuns. They founded a convent school (no longer in operation) for the daughters of Scandinavian nobility and built the convent church with its tower made of sandstone. The 300-acre castle grounds, with a 1,000-year-old oak tree, a network of pathways, a children's park, a rose garden, and an indoor-outdoor restaurant, are ideal for an afternoon outdoors. ⊠ Höör, ☎ 0413/25048. ✍ SKr 45. ⊙ Castle grounds May–Oct., daily 8–8, restaurant and exhibition halls May–Sept., Tues.–Sun. 10–6.

Dining and Lodging

$$ ✕ **Barntorget 9.** The restaurant-bar inside this 18th-century building
★ seems stuck in time: note the restored woodwork and paintings on the ceilings, the antique flowerpots and candleholders, and the classical statues in the corners of the room. The menu offers traditional Swedish dishes plus some more intriguing entrées such as smoked duck breast with a mushroom and endive salad and an orange vinaigrette. Barntorget 9 is a short walk from Lund's central train station. ⊠ Barntorget 9, ☎ 046/320200. AE, DC, MC, V. Closed Sun.

$$ ✕ **Godset.** Inside an old railroad warehouse right on the tracks near central station, Godset's modern tables and chairs stand on rustic wooden floors between brick walls. On one wall hangs a large 1950s clock taken from Mariakyrkan (Maria Church) in nearby Ystad. The menu offers seafood and meat dishes. Try the roasted venison poached in a cream sauce with raspberry vinaigrette. ⊠ Bang. 3, ☎ 046/121610. AE, DC, MC, V. Closed Sun.

$-$$ ✕ **Dalby Gästgifveri.** This is one of Skåne's oldest inns, and a gastronomic delight. The many red-meat dishes on the menu follow a tradition of history and quality, but innovative Swedish fare is served, too. Entrées such as the rich, somewhat gamey reindeer casserole are not for the faint of heart. Be sure to make reservations in the summer. ⊠ Tengsg. 6, ☎ 046/200006. AE, MC, V.

$-$$ ✕ **Restaurang Café Finn.** Connected to the Lund Konsthallen, Café Finn is an excellent option for lunch or dinner. The asparagus soup with mussels is perfect if you're not overly hungry, but for a more substantial meal go for the fried breast of pheasant with goose-liver pâté and port-wine gravy. The walls have an extensive collection of museum exhibit posters from the '60s, '70s, and '80s. Just outside is the Krognoshuset; built in the 1300s, it is Lund's best-kept medieval residence. ⊠ Mårtenstorget 3, ☎ 046/157646. AE, DC, MC, V.

$ ✕ **Ebbas Brödbar.** Just across the central station, Ebbas Bread Bar serves a number of excellent sandwiches on bagels, baguettes, or ciabattas (a flat Italian bread). ⊠ Bang. 8, ☎ 046/127127. AE, DC, MC, V.

$$ ▥ **Djingis Khan.** This English colonial–style Best Western hotel caters to business travelers but is also a great place for families or couples seeking a quiet location. The hotel's unusual name comes from a comedy show that has been performed at Lund University since 1954. With squash, tennis, and badminton courts nearby, along with a large swimming pool, it's ideal if you're looking to keep in shape. ⊠ Margarethev. 7, 222 40, ☎ 046/140060, FAX 046/143626. 55 rooms with bath. No-smoking rooms, hot tub, sauna, gym, bicycles, meeting room. AE, DC, MC, V. Closed July.

$ ▥ **Concordia.** This city-center Sweden Hotel property is in an elegant former home built in 1890. Rooms have a modern, clean look, but are somewhat colorless. ⊠ Stålbrog. 1, 222 24, ☎ 046/135050, FAX 046/137422. 65 rooms with bath. No-smoking rooms, sauna, meeting room. AE, DC, MC, V.

$ ▥ **Grand.** This elegant red-stone hotel is in the heart of the city, on a pleasant square close to the railway station. Renovated rooms have vintage turn-of-the-20th-century decor and charm. The fine restaurant of fers an alternative vegetarian menu. ⊠ *Bantorget 1, 221 04,* ☎ *046/ 2806100,* 📠 *046/2806150. 84 rooms with bath. Restaurant, no-smoking rooms, hot tub, meeting room. AE, DC, MC, V.*

$ 🖬 **Hotel Lundia.** Only a few hundred feet from the train station, Hotel Lundia is ideal for those who want to be near the city center. Built in 1968, the modern, four-story square building has transparent glass walls on the ground floor. Rooms are decorated with Scandinavian fabrics and lithographs. ⊠ *Knut den Stores torg 2, Box 1136, 221 04,* ☎ *046/ 2806500,* 📠 *046/2806510. 97 rooms with bath. Restaurant, lounge, no-smoking rooms, meeting room. AE, DC, MC, V.*

$ 🖬 **Oskar.** This centrally located hotel makes a pleasant resting place. ⊠ *Dygrareg. 3, S222 21,* ☎ *046/188085,* 📠 *046/373030. 6 rooms with bath. MC, V. BP.*

$ 🖬 **STF Vandrarhem Tåget.** So named because of its proximity to the train station (*tåget* means "train"), this youth hostel faces a park in central Lund. ⊠ *Bjerredsparken, Vävareg. 22, S222 37,* ☎ *046/ 142820. 108 beds without bath. No credit cards.*

Nightlife and the Arts

The **Lundia** (⊠ Knut den Stores Torg 2, ☎ 046/2806500) nightclub is in the Hotel Lundia, near the Burger King. It attracts groovers in their 20s and 30s. Women must be 23 or older, men over 25. It puts on a dance scene with electronic sounds that costs SKr 50 to get in.

★ At **Palladium** (⊠ St. Söderg. 13, ☎ 046/2116660), the dance scene is very popular, and the air is filled with mystical, symphonic sounds. The smallish dance floor creates intimacy. The venue also hosts live bands. On Friday and Saturday, the big nights, things don't get going until 11 and rage on until 3. Palladium draws young hipsters and will cost at least SKr 50 to get in, depending on the night.

The promotional manager at Palladium rates **Stortorget** (⊠ Stortorget 1, ☎ 046/139290) as the current hot spot in town. It has live music as well as a dance night and is popular with students. You won't get in here unless you are over 22.

Shopping

About 15,000 secondhand books are stacked in crazy piles in the **Åkards Antikvariat** (⊠ Klosterg., ☎ 046/2112499), making it full of the smells of aged literature. The oldest book dates to about 1500, around the time the printing press was developed. Any sort of book can be found, even an airport thriller.

The oldest coins date to 500 and 600 BC; **Lunds Mynthandel** (⊠ Klosterg. 5, ☎ 046/14436) often has specimens going back that far. It also carries books on numismatics.

Saluhalen (⊠ Corner of Mårtenstorget and Botulfsg.), "Foodhall," is an adventure in itself, an excellent example of the traditional Swedish food store but one that also stocks delicacies from Italy, Japan, and beyond. Cheese, meats, fresh and pickled fish, and pastries are all in great supply. It is the perfect place to get some food for a picnic in one of Lund's many squares and parks. The cheese selection at **Bengsons Ost** (⊠ Klosterg. 9) is hard to surpass. The people are friendly and it's a great spot to fill your picnic hamper. Bring your own wine and have a tasting session.

Since **Skånae–kraft** (⊠ Stora Gråbrödersg 4, ☎ 046/144777) carries a wide range of ceramics, crafts, and designer goods that changes frequently, finding something worthwhile depends on visiting when the stock happens to match your own taste. **Teahuset Java** (⊠ Vaster Mårtensg.), a well-known tea and coffee shop, sells leaves and beans

SWEET TOOTH

The Swedes, like every people of the earth, have developed an intricate web of storytelling and fairy tale. These are the realms of trolls and elves, of witches and spirits. The myths interweave the good and the bad, and reinterpret the experience of life as lived by people with few other ways to explain the apparently inexplicable.

With these thoughts in mind I was on my way to the the town of Gränna, on the mystical island Visingsö, which is said to have been created by a giant called Vist. Gränna is home to a great Swedish confectionery tradition: the making of the peppermint stick, which in Swedish is called Polkagris, and is exported around the world.

I walked into the factory of the oldest stick maker in the land, as the public is welcome to do, to watch the production process. Here the widow Amalia Erikson made the first red-and-white sweets in 1859. As a woman, she had to seek government permission to do so. Behind the glass window the craftsmen plied their trade: brewing, coloring, twisting, and turning something that looked like dough into fluorescent candy sticks. Some 2,000 a day are made in this factory alone. So much tooth-rotting sugar—about 75 percent of the product—it made sense of the elfin image: those wicked, toothless grins. Was evil afoot?

Oh yes. Like the bright-eyed child drawn to Grandma's candy drawer, I marveled at the colors as I watched the candy sticks roll out. It was inevitable that I would take the sugar hit that would take me to Mars. The first bite was pure pleasure, a crunching and splintering of the stick, and then the rush. But it was as if this event was written in the stars, foretold by a wise old troll. There was more crunch than I would have liked and, as if by magic, my tooth bounced onto the floor. The shopkeeper didn't know where to look. This adventure had extracted its price.

I beat an embarrassed retreat, beset with my own toothless grin. It was as if I had known not the facts of the future, but the sense of it. I took the ferry to Visingsö, with its timeless villages, eccentric art history, its rugged coast and people with their own enchanted look. In moments of mindless drift, I cast a weather eye toward the woods, the trees, and the toadstools. Would I see one of these underworld creatures? Did they have something to teach?

But the island, as magical as it seemed, proved to be a temporal place. The locals told me the elves mostly come out at night. I, however, saw Visingsö and its origins through the eyes of legend. The giant Vist, returning from a feast with his wife, discovered that, full of food, she could not take Lake Vättern in a step. With great might he lifted a piece of turf and placed it in the lake for her to step on. This is Visingsö's creation story.

As for me? Well, the lesson I had to learn, as I could best understand it, was one of the seven deadly sins, according to the Bible: that of avarice, or greed. From then on, Sweden could be seen only in a cautious, supernatural light. I never found a troll, but I believe they exist. My dental work is irrefutable and permanent proof.

from all over the world. You can also get all the paraphernalia that goes with brewing.

Malmö

88 *25 km (15 mi) southwest of Lund (via E22), 198 km (123 mi) south-west of Växjö.*

Capital of the province of Skåne, with a population of about 250,000, Malmö is Sweden's third-largest city. It was founded at the end of the 13th century. The remarkable 8 km (5 mi) bridge and tunnel from Malmö to Copenhagen that opened on July 1, 2000, began a new era of commercial shipping and leisure travel. Eight years in the making, the $3 billion Öresund Bridge provides drivers with an alternative to ferry travel between Sweden and Denmark; it also allows trains to travel between the two towns.

The city's castle, **Malmöhus,** completed in 1542, was for many years used as a prison (James Bothwell, husband of Mary, Queen of Scots, was one of its notable inmates). Today Malmöhus houses a variety of **museums,** including the City Museum, the Museum of Natural History, and the Art Museum, which has a collection of Nordic art. Across the street is the Science and Technology Museum, the Maritime Museum, and a toy museum. ⊠ *Malmöhusvägen,* ☎ *040/341000.* ▣ *SKr 40.* ☉ *June–Aug., daily 10–4; Sept.–May, Tues.–Sun. noon–4.*

℃ On the far side of the castle grounds from Malmöhus, the **Aq-va-kul** water park offers a variety of bathing experiences, from water slides to bubble baths. ⊠ *Regementsg. 24,* ☎ *040/300540.* ▣ *SKr 60.* ☉ *Weekdays 9–9, weekends 9–6; Mon. and Wed. adult sessions 7 PM–9:30 PM.*

In the same park as Malmöhus is the **Malmö Stadsbibliotek** (Malmö City Library), designed by the famous Danish architect Henning Larsen. Take a walk through the colossal main room—there's a four-story wall of glass that brings seasonal changes of colors inside. ⊠ *Regementsg. 3,* ☎ *040/6608500.*

A clutch of tiny red-painted shacks called the **Fiskehodderna** (Fish Shacks) is next to a dock where the fishing boats come in every morning to unload their catch. The piers, dock, and huts were restored in 1991 and are now a government-protected district. You can buy fresh fish directly from the fishermen Tuesday through Saturday mornings.

In Gamla Staden, the Old Town, look for the **St. Petri Church** on Kalendegatan; dating from the 14th century, it is an impressive example of the Baltic Gothic style, with distinctive stepped gables. Inside there is a fine Renaissance altar.

★ You can learn about Scandinavian art and design at the **Form/Design Centre,** just off Lilla Torg. The center is run by SvenskForm, a nonprofit association that promotes top-quality design in Sweden; Swedish and other Scandinavian artworks are on display throughout the center. ⊠ *9 Lilla Torg,* ☎ *040/664510.* ☉ *Aug.–June, Tues.–Wed. and Fri. 11–5, Thurs. 11–6, Sat. 11–4, Sun. noon–4; July, Tues.–Fri. 11–5, Sat. 10–4.*

The **Rådhuset** (Town Hall), dating from 1546, dominates Stortorget, a huge, cobbled market square in Gamla Staden, and makes an impressive spectacle when illuminated at night. In the center of the square stands an equestrian statue of Karl X, the king who united this part of the country with Sweden in 1658. Off the southeast corner of Stortorget is Lilla Torg, an attractive, small cobblestone square surrounded by restored buildings from the 17th and 18th centuries.

The **Idrottsmuseum** (Museum of Sport) occupies **Baltiska Hallen** (the Baltic Building), next to Malmö Stadium. It traces the history of sports, including soccer and wrestling, from antiquity to the present. ☎ 040/ 342688. ✉ Free. ☼ Weekdays 8–4.

One of Sweden's most outstanding art museums, **Rooseum,** is in a turn-of-the-20th-century brick building that was once a power plant. It has exhibitions of contemporary art and a quality selection of Nordic art. ✉ Gasverksg. 22, ☎ 040/121716. ✉ SKr 30. ☼ Tues.–Sun. 11–5. Guided tours in Swedish and English weekends at 2.

Look at contemporary art for free at the **Malmö Konsthall.** Founded in 1975, the Malmö Art Gallery is one of the largest in Europe, with a huge single room that's more than 20,000 square ft. It arranges about 10 exhibitions a year, from the classics of modern art to present-day experiments. Other activities include theater performances, film presentations, and poetry readings. ✉ St. Johannesg. 7, ☎ 040/341286. ☼ Thurs.–Tues. 11–5, Wed. 11–10.

Lilla Torg is a cobblestone square with some of the oldest buildings in the city. It is clustered with cafés, restaurants, and bars and in daytime is a great place to wander or watch the world go by. Walk into the side streets and see the traditional buildings, which were originally used mainly to store grain and produce. The building now housing the Form/Design Centre is a good example. By night, this is a bustling area. Check out the food hall, which contains one of Sweden's best coffee purveyors.

★ The **Øresundsbron** is an engineering miracle. Its train tracks and four car lanes stretch 8 km (5 mi) from the southern coastal suburbs of Malmö to Copenhagen. Designed under the auspices of Öresund Konsortiet, which was set up in 1992, the bridge is a minimalist beauty. ✉ Look-out at Øresund Ulställningen at the end of Utställningen Rd. Approach on E 20 highway, ᗯᴱᴮ www.oeresundsbron.com. ✉ SKr 275 each way for car.

The **European Housing Expo** was held around the Ribersborgsstranden waterfront in 2001. The houses and business buildings designed and erected for the show showcased the latest in architectural design. Wander around the development in order to see the exteriors of more than 500 homes, which include 58 different types of housing. They were sold after the expo was over. ✉ Ribersborgsstranden waterfront, ☎ 040/6680900 or 040/341200, ᗯᴱᴮ www.bo01.com.

OFF THE
BEATEN PATH

FALSTERBO AND SKANÖR – The idyllic towns of Falsterbo and Skanör are two popular summer resorts on a tiny peninsula, 32 km (20 mi) south-west of Malmö. Falsterbo is popular among ornithologists, who flock there every fall to watch the spectacular migration of hundreds of birds, especially swallows, geese, hawks, and eagles.

TORUP SLOTT – Built around 1550 near a beautiful beech forest, Torup Castle is a great example of the classic, square fortified stronghold. From Malmö, drive 10 km (6 mi) southeast on E65, then head north for another 6 km (4 mi) to Torup. ✉ Torup. ✉ SKr 30. ☼ May–June, week-ends 1–4:30. Group tours available at other times through Malmö Turist-byrå, ☎ 040/341853.

Dining and Lodging

$$–$$$ ✕ **Årstiderna i Kockska Huset.** Formed by merging two discrete restau-
★   rants that were in different locations, the combination is housed in a 16th-

century building with beautiful interiors. Several of the dining areas are in an underground cellar. Starting with traditional Swedish dishes that are often centered on beef, game, and seafood, the chef then gives them a contemporary twist. The restaurant's poached halibut, for example, is served with a citrus sauce with black pepper. Like the food, the wine list is excellent. ⊠ *Stortorget,* ☎ *040/230910. AE, DC, MC, V.*

$$ ✕ **Anno 1900.** This charming little restaurant sits in a former working-class area of Malmö. It is a popular local luncheon place with a cheerful outdoor garden terrace. Head here for such light dishes as salads and fishes as well as for traditional Swedish lunches built around the potato. The bread is outstanding. ⊠ *Norra Bulltoftav. 7,* ☎ *040184747. Reservations essential. AE, MC, V.*

$$ ✕ **B & B.** It stands for *Butik och Bar* (Shop and Bar) and is named as such because of its location in the market hall in central Malmö. There's always good home cooking, with dishes like venison and beef fillet with potatoes. Sometimes there's even entertainment at the piano. ⊠ *Saluhallen, Lilla Torg,* ☎ *040/127120. AE, DC, MC, V.*

$$ ✕ **Glorias.** This friendly little restaurant offers good value. The special menu, *Kvartersmenyn,* is an excellent bet, with a three-course prix fixe for SKr 175. The food is traditional, but dinner has a few American-inspired appetizers thrown in. Try the smoked salmon with new potatoes in season and herbed sour cream if it's being offered. ⊠ *Foreningsg. 37,* ☎ *040/70200. AE, DC, MC, V.*

$$ ✕ **Hipp.** This bar-restaurant first opened in 1899; today you can still marvel at the ornate columns that support a high ceiling painted with decorative flower patterns. If you sip your drink at the dark wood bar in the center of the restaurant, check out the heavy chandeliers hanging over you. Hipp's hearty fare is the perfect cap to a night at the city theater next door. The finely sliced raw salmon with black roe is a standout, as is the vegetable stir fry. Dry martinis are a specialty from the bar. ⊠ *Kalendeg. 12,* ☎ *040/974030. AE, DC, MC, V. Closed Sun. and Mon.*

$$ ✕ **Johan P.** This extremely popular restaurant specializes in seafood and shellfish prepared in Swedish and Continental styles. White walls and crisp white tablecloths give it an elegant air, which contrasts with the generally casual dress of the customers. An outdoor section is open in the summer. ⊠ *Saluhallen, Lilla Torg,* ☎ *040/971818. AE, DC, MC, V. Closed Sun.*

$–$$ ✕ **Nyströms Gastronomi.** Modern international cuisine with Mediter-
★ ranean hints; an elegant presentation; a polite, casual staff; and a warm atmosphere have earned this restaurant a sparkling reputation. The wine list is extensive and a cigar lounge is available. ⊠ *St. Pauli Kyrkog. 11,* ☎ *040/305303. AE, DC, MC, V. Closed Sun.*

$ ✕ **Spot.** A lively group of regulars flocks to this popular Italian restaurant for reasonable prices and unpretentious food. Lunchtime can get busy, but at night Spot is cozy. ⊠ *Corner of Stora Nyg./Kalendeg.,* ☎ *040/120203. AE, DC, MC, V. Closed Sun.*

$$$ 🏨 **Radisson SAS Hotel.** Only a five-minute walk from the train station, this modern luxury hotel has rooms decorated in several styles: Scandinavian, Asian, and Italian. There are even special rooms for guests with pets. Service is impeccable. The restaurant serves Scandinavian and Continental cuisine, and there's a cafeteria. ⊠ *Österg. 10, 211 25,* ☎ *040/6984000,* 𝖥𝖠𝖷 *040/6984001. 221 rooms. Restaurant, no-smoking room, sauna, gym, meeting room. AE, DC, MC, V.*

$$ 🏨 **Mäster Johan Hotel.** The unpretentious exterior of this Best West-
★ ern hotel disguises a plush and meticulously crafted interior. Created through a 1990 top-to-bottom redesign of a 19th-century building, with the focal point an Italianate atrium breakfast room, the Mäster Johan is unusually personal for a chain hotel. The rooms are impressive, with

exposed plaster-and-stone walls, recessed lighting, oak floors, Oriental carpets, and French cherrywood furnishings. ⊠ *Mäster Johansg. 13, 211 22,* ☎ *040/6646400,* FAX *040/6646401. 68 rooms with bath. Breakfast room, no-smoking rooms, room service, sauna, meeting room. AE, DC, MC, V.*

$ ★ 🛏 **Baltzar.** This turn-of-the-20th-century house in central Malmö converted in 1920 into a small, comfortable hotel. Rooms are modern, with thick carpets. ⊠ *Söderg. 20, 211 34,* ☎ *040/6655700,* FAX *040/ 236375. 41 rooms with bath. No-smoking rooms. AE, DC, MC, V.*

$ 🛏 **Prize Hotel.** In a rejuvenated part of Malmö Harbor, this low-overhead, minimal-service hotel has small but comfortable rooms equipped with satellite TV, telephone, and radio. The large front entrance and lobby atrium are inventively created out of a narrow strip of empty space between two buildings. Though the hotel doesn't add a surcharge to the telephone bill, breakfast does cost extra (SKr 65). ⊠ *Carlsg. 10C, 211 20,* ☎ *040/6112511,* FAX *040/6112310. 109 rooms with bath. Breakfast room. AE, DC, MC, V.*

$ 🛏 **Scandic Hotel Triangeln.** Ultramodern, in steel and glass, the Scandic is the city's only skyscraper—at a modest 20 floors. It provides excellent views all the way to Copenhagen on a clear day. Rooms are plain but comfortable. ⊠ *Triangeln 2, S200 10,* ☎ *040/6934700,* FAX *040/ 6934711. 214 rooms with bath. Restaurant, bar, in-room data ports, no-smoking room, sauna, gym, meeting room. AE, DC, MC, V.*

Nightlife and the Arts

The Bishop's Arms is a classic and busy English pub. It is in the former grill room of the Savoy Hotel and can hardly fail to impress the pub connoisseur. There's an excellent assortment of old whiskeys. ⊠ *Savoy Hotel, Nora Vallg. 62,* ☎ *040/70230.*

Étage is a centrally located nightclub for hipsters, with two dance floors. It also has a piano bar for relaxing, as well as a restaurant. The disco begins late under psychedelic light Thursday, Friday, and Saturday. Karaoke, roulette, and blackjack tables are available. ⊠ *Stortorget 6,* ☎ *040/232060.* 🎟 *SKr 50 or more.* ☉ *Mon., Thurs.–Fri., and Sat. 11 PM–5 AM.*

An old patrician apartment is the setting for the five rooms at **Klubb Plysch.** It's available for champagne, cigars, and lounging early in the evening, and dancing begins about 11. Take a seat in the superb velvet chairs. ⊠ *Lilla Torg 1.* ☎ *040/127670.* 🎟 *SKr 50.* ☉ *Weekend. 10 PM–3 AM.*

At **Wallmans Salonger,** the artistic, bohemian staff is part of the entertainment. They may burst into song, and they may start juggling. A dance show with terrific lighting begins at 7, and the nightclub proper begins at 11. There's also a casino and a restaurant here. ⊠ *Generalsg. 1,* ☎ *040/74945,* WEB *www.wallmans.com.* 🎟 *SKr 50–Skr 220.*

The Malmö Symphoni Orkester is a symphony orchestra that has a reputation across Europe as a class act. Each concert is a finely tuned event. Performances are held at many venues, including outdoors; some are at the impressive Malmö Konserthus. Phone for details about venues and costs. ☎ *040/343500.*

Shopping

Malmö has many quality housewares and design stores. **Duka** (Hansacompagniet Centre, Malmborgsg. 6, ☎ 040/121141) is a high-quality housewares shop specializing in glass, crockery, and glass art. Special tables are set up with Swedish products on display, and hand-carved and hand-painted wood Dala horses are for sale. **Cervera** (⊠ Södra Långg. 25, ☎ 040/971230) carries big-name glassware brands such as Kosta and Orrefors. There's an excellent selection of glass art as well as porcelain and china—and almost everything you might need as far as housewares.

The **Form/Design Centre** (⊠ Lilla Torg 9, ☎ 040/6645150) sells products related to its changing exhibitions on everything from ceramics to books. Also look here for the very latest in Scandinavian interior design. **Formagruppen** (⊠ Engelbrektsg. 8, ☎ 040/4078060) is an arts and crafts cooperative owned and operated by its 22 members. It sells high-quality woodwork, including cabinets. Quality ceramics, textiles, metalwork, and jewelry are also for sale. An arts and crafts shop with a Nordic twist, **Älgamark** (⊠ Östra Rönneholmsvågen 4, ☎ 040/974960) sells many antiques dating from Viking and medieval times and on through the 1600s. The shop also sells gold, silver, and bronze jewelry, much of which is also quite old.

Duxiana (⊠ Södra Promenaden 63, ☎ 040/305977) sells the world-famous Dux beds, which have elaborate spring systems and are built into wooden frames. Shipping can be arranged. Beds range in price from SKr 25,000 to SKr 57,000. **Outside** (⊠ Kyrkog. 3, Stortorget, ☎ 040/300910) specializes in high-quality outdoor gear. Everything from sleeping bags, boots, and tents to gas canisters and waterproofing products is stocked here. In addition to such brands as North Face and Patagonia, Outside is the only Scandinavian store to carry products from Mac Pac of New Zealand. At the summer market called **Möllevångstorget,** on the square of the same name, there is usually a wonderful array of flowers, fruit, and vegetables. It is an old working-class area and a nice place to stroll, even if you are not buying. The market is closed on Sunday.

Outdoor Activities and Sports

From Ribersborg Beach you can walk on a pier to the **Kallbadhuset Ribersborgsstranden,** which are old baths (the name translates as "cold bathhouses Ribersborg Beach"). Built in 1898, they are a popular place to swim, since a man-made harbor of boulders offers protection from the sea's turbulence. It also hosts cultural events such as poetry readings, and has a bar and café. To get to the beach, follow Citadellsvägen to the west from the central railway station. Walk alongside Öresunds Parken and turn right at the sign for Ribersborg. ⊠ Ribersborg Beach, ☎ 040/260366. ☞ SKr 35.

Paddle Boating on the canals is a great way to see the city. Each boat takes up to four people. Going south on Torg Bron from Gustav Adolf-storg, the boat stall is to your right on the walking path along the canal. ⊠ Turn off Torgg Bron. ☞ SKr 90 per hr. ☉ Mid-June–early Sept., daily 11–7.

En Route One of Skåne's outstanding Renaissance strongholds, **Svaneholms Slott** lies 30 km (19 mi) east of Malmö, on E65. First built in 1530 and rebuilt in 1694, the castle today features a museum occupying four floors with sections depicting the nobility and peasants. On the grounds are **Gästgiveri** (☎ 0411/40540), a notable restaurant; walking paths; and a lake for fishing and rowing. ⊠ Skurup, ☎ 0411/40012. ☞ SKr 25. ☉ May–Aug., Tues.–Sun. 11–5; Sept.–mid-Oct., Wed.–Sun. 11–4.

Ystad

⑧⑨ 64 km (40 mi) southeast of Malmö (via E65), 205 km (127 mi) southwest of Växjö.

A smuggling center during the Napoleonic Wars, Ystad has preserved its medieval character with winding, narrow streets and hundreds of half-timber houses dating from four or five different centuries. A good place to begin exploring is the main square, Stortorget.

The principal ancient monument, **St. Maria Kyrka,** was built shortly after 1220 as a basilica in the Romanesque style, though there have been later additions. The watchman's copper horn sounds from the church tower beginning at 9:15 and repeating every 15 minutes. It's to proclaim that all is well. The church lies behind Stortorget on Lilla Norregatan. The 16th-century Latinskolan (Latin School) is adjacent to the church—it's said to be the oldest schoolhouse in Scandinavia.

Charlotte Berlin's Museum is a well-preserved burgher's home from the 19th century. Charlotte Berlin left the home and the contents to the city upon her death in 1916. It has a variety of displays, including one that shows many antique clocks and watches. ⊠ *Dammg. 23,* ☎ *0411/18866.* 🎟 *SKr 10.* 🕑 *June–Aug., weekdays noon–5; weekends noon–4.*

The Franciscan monastery **Gråbrödraklostret** adjoins St. Peter's church. The oldest parts date back to 1267. Together, the church and monastery are considered the most important historical site in Ystad. Gråbrö-draklostret is one of the best-preserved cloisters in Sweden. ⊠ *Klosterg., off Stortorget,* 🎟 *SKr 20.* 🕑 *Weekdays noon–5; weekends noon–4.*

Sweden's best-preserved theater from the late 1800s, **Ystads Teater,** is a beautiful, ornate building. The dramatic interior adds a great deal to any performance seen here. Outside is a battery of cannons first used in 1712 to defend the harbor from its many marauders, especially the Danes. ⊠ *Sjömansg. 13,* ☎ *0411/577199.*

Ystads Konstmuseum houses a collection of important Swedish and Danish 20th-century art, as well as a photographic collection that includes a daguerreotype from 1845. ⊠ *St. Knuts Torg,* ☎ *0411/577285.* 🎟 *SKr 20.* 🕑 *Tues.–Fri. noon–5.*

OFF THE BEATEN PATH	**SÖVDEBORG SLOTT –** Twenty-one kilometers (thirteen miles) north of Ystad on Route 13 is Sövdeborg Slott. Built in the 16th century and restored in the mid-1840s, the castle, now a private home, consists of three two-story brick buildings and a four-story-high crenellated corner tower. The main attraction is the Stensal (Stone Hall), with its impressive stuccowork ceiling. It's open for tours if booked in advance for groups of at least 10. ⊠ Sjöbo, ☎ 0416/16012. 🎟 SKr 60.
★	**ALES STENAR –** Eighteen kilometers (eleven miles) east of Ystad, on the coastal road off Route 9, is the charming fishing village of Kåseberga. On the hill behind it stands the impressive Ales Stones, an intriguing 230-ft-long arrangement of 58 Viking stones in the shape of a ship. Believed to be between 1,000 and 1,500 years old, the stones and their purpose still puzzle anthropologists.
	GLIMMINGEHUS – About 10 km (6 mi) east of Ales Stones and 10 km (6 mi) southwest of Simrishamn just off Route 9 lies Glimminge House, Scandinavia's best-preserved medieval stronghold. Built between 1499 and 1505 to defend the region against invaders, the late-Gothic castle was lived in only briefly. The walls are 8 ft thick at the base, tapering to 6½ ft at the top of the 85-ft-high building. On the grounds are a small museum and a theater. There are concerts and lectures in summer and a medieval festival at the end of August. ⊠ Hammenhög, ☎ 0414/18620. 🎟 SKr 50. 🕑 Apr. and Sept., daily 10–4; May–Aug., daily 9–6; Oct., weekends 11–4.

Dining and Lodging

$–$$ ✕ **Bryggeriet.** A lovely cross-timbered inn, this restaurant brews its own beer—there are two large copper boilers near the bar. It has a pleasant garden, and the dimly lit interior is made out of bricks in the curved shape of an underground cavern. Hearty traditional fare, including reindeer and other game, is Bryggeriet's specialty. Try the duck, which is prepared in an elegant port sauce with an herb garnishing. ⊠ *Långg. 20,* ☎ *0411/69999.*

$–$$ ✕ **Lottas.** Beautifully set inside an architecturally interesting and fully renovated two-story building, Lottas is in the heart of town on the main square. The food includes several lighter fish dishes, including scallops in season. As is typically the case in Sweden, there are many red-meat options. The steaks are cooked and presented with care. ⊠ *Stortorget,* ☎ *0411/78800.*

$–$$ ✕🏠 **Hotel Continental.** The Continental opened in 1829 and is a truly
★ stunning building, both inside and out. Take a good look at the lobby with its marble stairs, crystal chandelier, stained-glass windows, and marble pillars. No two rooms are alike. The restaurant prepares food well, giving each dish its own individual flair. The meat dishes are served with a selection of root vegetables, including new potatoes, carrots, and what the British call swedes (rutabagas), when they're in season. ⊠ *Hamng. 13,* ☎ *04111/13700,* ℻ *0411/12570,* WEB *www.hotelcontinental-ystad.se. 52 rooms with bath. AE, MC, V. BP.*

$–$$ ✕🏠 **Stora Herrestad Gästgifvaregård.** This classic example of the state-sponsored roadside inns that were once common in Sweden dates from the 17th century. The inns were organized in such a way that none was more than 20 km (12½ mi) from the next. Travelers would each pay according to their means and be able to eat their fill, have a bed, and get water and hay for their horses. The rooms are simple but pleasant, and the excellent restaurant ($–$$), which serves traditional fare, is for guests and visitors alike. Originally, the inn was a courthouse—part of a complex of buildings that included a 12th-century church, a jail, and a mansion. ⊠ *Landsv. 32, about 5 km (3 mi) north of Ystad on Hwy. 19,* ☎ *0411/552036,* ℻ *0411/552039. 23 beds with bath, 10 rooms. Bar, dining room. AE, MC, V. BP.*

$ 🏠 **Bäckagården.** This homey, small hotel is centrally located. It dates from the 17th century, has a secluded garden, and serves breakfast. ⊠ *Dammg. 36,* ☎ *0411/19848,* ℻ *0411/65715. 7 rooms with bath. AE, MC, V. BP.*

Shopping

Amigo (⊠ Industig. 11, ☎ 0411/19488; ⊙ weekdays noon–6, Sat. 10–1) is a great shop for ceramics, glassware, and terra-cotta pots. Gifts, souvenirs, clothes, and various household items are sold at **Tidlöst** (⊠ Bökareg. 12, ☎ 0411/73029). The items are a mix of old and new. Head to **Sjögrens–Butikerna** (⊠ Stora Österg. 6, The Mall, ☎ 0411/17200) for an excellent selection of well-priced designware, including crystal, jewelry, glassware, china, and pottery.

Simrishamn

⑨⓪ *41 km (25 mi) northeast of Ystad via Route 9, 105 km (65 mi) east of Malmö, 190 km (118 mi) southwest of Växjö.*

This fishing village of 25,000 swells to many times that number during the summer. Built in the mid-1100s, the town has cobblestone streets lined with tiny brick houses covered with white stucco. The medieval **St. Nicolia Kyrka** (St. Nicolai's Church), which dominates the town's skyline, was once a landmark for local sailors. Inside are models of sailing ships. For most, Simrishamn doesn't warrant an overnight stay.

The **Frasses Musik Museum** contains an eclectic collection of music odd-ities, such as self-playing barrel organs, antique accordions, children's gramophones, and what may be the world's most complete collection of Edison phonographs. ⊠ *Peder Mörksvägen 5,* ☎ *0414/14520.* ⊠ *SKr 10.* ☉ *Early June–late Aug., Sun. 2–6; July, Sun.–Wed. 2–6.*

St. Nicolai Kyrka dates from the Middle Ages, though building began around 1161. The sculptures and reliefs inside the church are by the famous Swedish sculptor Carl Milles. In July there is a lunchtime con-cert starting at noon. ⊠ *Stortorget,* ☎ *0414/412480.* ☉ *Mar.–June 10 and mid-Sept.–Dec., weekdays noon–3, Sat. 10–1; June 11–mid-Sept., weekdays 10:30–6:30, Sat. 9:30–4, Sun. 11–4.*

OFF THE BEATEN PATH | **BRANTEVIK –** Less than 10 km (6 mi) south of Simrishamn on the coastal road is this classic but tiny southern fishing village. It has a marvelous harbor and the homes are small, brightly colored fishermen's cottages. Just 100 years ago only 1,100 people lived here, and it hasn't changed much since then. A good place for lunch is **Bronterögen**, a café that serves excellent meals and is right beside the harbor. It will cost between SKr 45 and SKr 125 for an entrée. For something a little more formal or even a night's stay, try the old inn **Brantevik's Bykrog and Hotel** (⊠ Mästergränd 2, ☎ 0414/22069). There are seven rooms here, along with a restaurant.

En Route   About 20 km (12 mi) north of Simrishamn is the tiny village of **Kivik.** You are now firmly in the heart of Sweden's apple country, a spectac-ular place to be when the trees are blooming in the spring. From Kivik, follow the signs to the **Äpplets Hus** (also called the Kiviks Musteri; ☎ 0414/71900), a museum that tells the history of apple orcharding in the area. Alongside is the cider brewery and a gift shop full of apple paraphernalia. On the way back from the Äpplet Hus is a small café— and a huge pile of boulders. This is the **Kivik grave,** one of the most remarkable Bronze Age monuments in Sweden. Dating from before 3000 BC, the tomb consists of a cairn nearly 250 ft across. Walk into the tomb and find the cist with eight tombstones engraved with symbols.

If you're in the area between July 1 and August 10, you might want to stop off at **Kristinehov,** about 8 km (5 mi) west of Brösarp and 35 km (22 mi) north of Simrishamn, via Route 9. A summer wine festi-val is presented at the castle by a local Swedish wine producer, **Åkersson & Sons** (☎ 0417/19700). Known as the pink castle, Kristinehov was built in 1740 by Countess Christina Piper. Although closed to the pub-lic since 1989, the castle is occasionally used for rock concerts and other summer programs.

Kristianstad

❾❶ *73 km (45 mi) north of Simrishamn via Routes 9/19 and E22, 95 km (59 mi) northeast of Malmö (via E22), 126 km (78 mi) southwest of Växjö.*

Kristianstad was founded in 1614 by Danish King Christian IV as a fortified town to keep the Swedes at bay. Its former ramparts and moats are today wide, tree-lined boulevards. For most, there isn't much of great interest in the town itself.

About 17 km (11 mi) east of Kristianstad and just north of the E22 highway is **Bäckaskog Slott.** Standing on a strip of land between two lakes, Bäckaskog Castle was originally founded as a monastery by a French religious order in the 13th century. Danish noblemen turned it into a fortified castle during the 16th century. It was later appropriated by the Swedish government and used as a residence for the cavalry. The castle was a favorite of the Swedish royalty until 1900. The museum inside has relics of those days. ✉ *Fjälkinge,* ☎ *044/53250.* ⛁ *SKr 30.* ⊙ *Mid-May–mid-Aug., daily 10–6; open off-season to groups by appointment only.*

En Route Six kilometers (four miles) east of Kristianstad on E22, take a left turn to Fjälkinge and follow brown signs marked with a white flower. The route, Humlesingan, is a scenic drive of 48 km (30 mi) around Skäne's largest lake, Lake Ivösjö. The geology dates from millions of years ago and is rich in minerals. It was a famed hops region until 1959. The old hop houses can still be seen—one is a café. The big mountainous island is Ivö, 440 ft high.

Karlskrona

❽❷ *111 km (69 mi) east of Kristianstad via E22, 201 km (125 mi) northeast of Malmö, 107 km (66 mi) southeast of Växjö.*

A small city built on the mainland and on five nearby islands, Karlskrona achieved great notoriety in 1981, when a Soviet submarine ran aground a short distance from its naval base. The town dates from 1679, when it was laid out in baroque style on the orders of Karl XI. Two churches around the main square, **Tre Faldighets kyrkan** and **Frederiks,** date from this period and were both designed by the architect Nicodemus Tessin the Younger.

Although the archipelago is not as large or as full of dramatic scenery as Stockholm's islands, Karlskrona is still worth the boat trip. One can be arranged through the **tourist office** (☎ 0455/303439). Because of the excellent state of preservation of the naval museum and other buildings in town, UNESCO designated Karlskrona a World Heritage Site in 1998.

The **Admiralitetskyrkan** (Admiralty Church) is Sweden's oldest wooden church, built in 1685. It is an unusual variant of the Swedish style of churches, which are generally made of stone. Although it was supposed to be temporary, the stone replacement was never built. The wooden statue of constable Matts Rosenborn, who froze to death here one New Year's Eve in the 18th century, stands outside tipping his hat to those who give alms. The church is on Bastionsgatan on the naval island. Walk east a few minutes from Stortorget, the main square.

★ The **Marinmuseum** (Naval Museum), dating from 1752, is one of the oldest museums in Sweden and has a superb collection perfect for those with a nautical bent. The shed for making rope is ancient (1692) and huge—nearly 1,000 ft long. In the museum are old maps and charts, old navigating equipment, ship designs, and relics from actual ships, as well as weaponry. The museum can also provide you with brochures of the port area, perfect for a pleasant walk.✉ *Admiralitetsslatten,* ☎ *0455/53902.* ⛁ *SKr 50.* ⊙ *June and Aug., daily 10–4; July, daily 10–6; Sept.–May, daily noon–4.*

Kungsholm Fort, on the island of Kungsholmen, is accessible only by a boat booked through the tourist agency (✉ Stortorget, ☎ 0455/303439) on the main island of Trossö. This stunning fortress was built in 1680 to defend the town's important naval port. The fortress was on full alert when the Russians blockaded Karlskrona in the 1780s and when the English were cruising the Baltic in 1801. Perhaps the most impressive aspect of the fort is the round harbor, built into the fort itself with only a narrow exit to the sea.

The Archipelago is made up of dozens of islands scattered off the coast of Karlskrona's mainland. They are stunning, low-lying islands that make excellent places to walk and picnic. Although some are accessible by road, the best way to take it all in is to go by ferry. The cruise takes half a day. Contact **Affärs Verken Båttrafik** (⌧ Fisktorget, ☎ 0455/78330, ☎ SKr 40–SKr 65), the ferry operators, with offices at the ferry terminal.

Dining and Lodging

$$ ✕ **Lisas Sjökrog.** Floating on the sea, Lisas Sjökrog is a great place to see a sunset and look out over the archipelago. In keeping with its location, the emphasis here is on seafood, including herring, halibut, and shellfish in season. You can also try well-prepared meat dishes and the popular summer salads. ⌧ *Fisktorget,* ☎ *0455/23465. AE, MC, V.*

$–$$ ✕ **Gourmet Grön.** This classy restaurant specializes in gourmet dishes and vegetarian food. Undoubtedly this is one of the finest eateries in Karlskrona. Fresh ingredients are a part of the ethos here, so the menu changes with the seasons. Antipasto dishes are superb, and almost everything tastes fresh. The vegetarian salads emphasize such delicacies as artichoke. Reservations recommended in the summer. ⌧ *Ronnebyg. 30,* ☎ *0455/333240. AE, MC, V.*

$ ✕ **Eat—The Home Company.** If you like to mix your dining with design, then Eat (placed within a home-design store) is a good choice. The menu is vaguely nouvelle, with beautiful presentations of small portions. The soups are terrific, ranging from mushroom to pumpkin. Try the lamb, cooked medium rare and served with mint. Trains were once repaired inside the 18th-century building. ⌧ *Bleklingeg 3, Lokstallarna,* ☎ *0455/300003. D, MC, V.*

$–$$ ▦ **First Hotel Statt.** The rooms are well appointed, the decor classic, and the style Swedish traditional at this property. Built around 1900, this immaculate hotel is in the heart of the city and is fully refurbished. Notice the ornate stairwell and the candelabras in the lobby. ⌧ *Varvsg. 1,* ☎ *0455/19250. 107 rooms with bath. Dining room, hot tub, sauna. AE, D, MC, V.*

$ ▦ **Carlscrona.** From this seaside hotel, the beach is a 10-minute walk away. The town center and the naval museum are even closer. Though the rooms are nothing special, many have good views. ⌧ *Skeppsbrokajen,* ☎ *0455/19630,* 🗏 *0455/25990. 80 rooms with bath. Dining room, in-room data ports, sauna, parking. AE, MC, V. BP.*

$ ▦ **Hotel Conrad.** For simple but functional accommodation at a reasonable price, the Hotel Conrad is good. It is a short walk from a good selection of shopping, restaurants, and entertainment. ⌧ *V. Köpmansg. 12,* ☎ *0455/82335. 58 rooms with bath. Sauna. AE, MC, V. BP.*

Nightlife and the Arts

Karlskrona is not overwhelmed by notable nightclubs, but **Bio Bar och Matsalar** (⌧ Borgmästareg. 17, ☎ 0455/311100, ☎ SKr 30, ◷ weekends until 3 AM) is one you might want to try if your tastes run toward the dramatic. It is a renovated old theater, very ornate with crystal chandeliers. The scene varies greatly but you're more likely to find Top-40 hits than the latest dance music. Making a modern attempt to play on the town's seafaring heritage, **Piraten Nattklubb** (⌧ Ronnebyg. 50, ☎ 0455/81853) serves up good cocktails among a decor that suggests the Middle Ages, despite the fact that its name means "Pirate Nightclub."

Outdoor Activities and Sports

Karlskrona has a reputation for both saltwater and freshwater fishing. **Senoren's Sportfishing Tours** (☎ 0455/44010) will take you to the outermost archipelago to fish by boat or from cliffs. **Hasslö Island Tourist**

and Fishing Service offers fishing in the ocean and in freshwater streams and lakes. Contact Kurta Ola Oftedal (☎ 0455/332492 or 070/332492).

Kalmar

⑨³ *91 km (57 mi) northeast of Karlskrona via E22, 292 km (181 mi) northeast of Malmö, 109 km (68 mi) southeast of Växjö.*

The attractive coastal town of Kalmar, opposite the Baltic island of Öland, is dominated by the imposing **Kalmar Slott,** Sweden's best-preserved ★ Renaissance castle. Part of it dates from the 12th century. The living rooms, chapel, and dungeon can be visited. ⊠ *Slottsvågen,* ☎ *0480/451490.* ⊠ *SKr 70.* ☉ *Mid-June–mid-Aug., Mon.–Sat. 10–6, Sun. noon–6; Apr.–mid-June and mid-Aug.–Oct., weekdays 10–4, weekends noon–4; Nov.–Mar., Sun. 1–3.*

The **Kalmar Läns Museum** (Kalmar District Museum), with good archaeological and ethnographic collections, contains the remains of the royal ship *Kronan,* which sank in 1676. Cannons, wood sculptures, and old coins were all raised from the seabed in 1980. Another exhibit focuses on Jenny Nystrom, a painter famous for popularizing the *tomte,* a rustic Christmas elf. ⊠ *Skeppsbrog. 51,* ☎ *0480/15350.* ⊠ *SKr 50.* ☉ *Mid-June–mid-Aug., Mon.–Sat. 10–6, Sun. noon–6; mid-Aug.–mid-June, Mon.–Tues. and Thurs.–Fri. 10–4, Wed. 10–8, weekends noon–4.*

Kalmar Domkyrkan is a highly impressive building designed by Nicodemus Tessin the Elder in 1660 in the Italian baroque style. Inside, the massive open spaces create stunning light effects. Strangely, the cathedral is the only one in Sweden without a bishop. Music is played at noon during the week. ⊠ *Stortorget,* ☎ *0480/12300.* ⊠ *Free.* ☉ *Daily 10–4.*

OFF THE **PATAHOLM AND TIMMERNABBEN –** On the mainland coast opposite BEATEN PATH Öland, along E22, numerous seaside towns dot the coastline, such as **Pataholm,** with its cobblestone main square, and **Timmernabben,** which is famous for its caramel factory. Miles of clean, attractive, and easily accessible—if windy—beaches line this coastal strip.

Dining and Lodging

$$ ✕ **Byttan.** Since the restaurant is surrounded by a large outdoor eating area and beautiful gardens, you can dine at a leisurely pace among the bushes and flowers when the weather is fine. Served with a vast range of freshly baked breads, the summer salads, especially the chicken salad served with limes, are terrific. You can also make the heartier choice of traditional herring with mashed potatoes. ⊠ *Slottsallé,* ☎ *0480/16360. MC, V. Closed Oct.–Apr.*

$$ ✕ **Källaren Kronan.** An eclectic, international approach to food is what is available here. Given the quality of the food, the meals are surprisingly cheap. Try the pheasant breast with Calvados sauce or the fillet of venison with black currant sauce. The building dates back to the 1660s and has been preserved as a cultural heritage site. ⊠ *Ölandsg. 7,* ☎ *0480/411400. MC, V.*

$–$$ ✕ **Ernesto Salonger.** This outdoor Italian restaurant serves everything from pizza to pasta. On Friday and Saturday nights a nightclub and casino are in action. ⊠ *Larmtorget,* ☎ *0480/20050.*

$–$$ ⊞ **Frimurare.** Set inside a spacious park inside an attractive building, the Frimurare radiates calm and peacefulness. Both the rooms and the hotel itself have old-timey touches. It's a short walk from here to the castle. ✉ *Lamtorget 2,* ☎ *0480/15230,* ℻ *0480/85887,* 🕸 *www. frimurarehotellet.gs2.com. 34 rooms, 31 with bath. D, MC, V.*

$ ☷ **Slottshotellet.** Occupying a gracious old house on a quiet street, Slottshotellet faces a waterfront park that's a few minutes' walk from both the train station and Kalmar Castle. Guest rooms are charmingly individual, with carved-wood bedsteads, old-fashioned chandeliers, pretty wallpaper, wooden floors, and antique furniture. The bathrooms are spotlessly clean. Only breakfast is served year-round, but full restaurant service is available in the summer. ✉ *Slottsv. 7, 392 33,* ☎ *0480/ 88260,* ℻ *0480/88266. 36 rooms with bath. Restaurant, no-smoking room, sauna, meeting room. AE, DC, V. BP.*

$ ☷ **Stadshotellet.** In city center, Best Western's Stadshotellet is a fairly large hotel with traditional English decor. The main building dates from 1907. Guest rooms are freshly decorated and have hair dryers and radios, among other amenities. There's also a fine restaurant. ✉ *Stortorget 14, 392 32,* ☎ *0480/15180,* ℻ *0480/15847. 140 rooms with bath. Restaurant, bar, no-smoking room, hot tub, sauna, meeting room. AE, DC, MC, V.*

Öland

★ ❾❹ *8 km (5 mi) east of Kalmar via the Ölandsbron bridge.*

The island of Öland is a magical and ancient place—and the smallest province in Sweden. The area was first settled some 4,000 years ago, and is fringed with fine sandy beaches and dotted with old windmills, churches, and archaeological remains. There's also spectacular bird life—swallows, cranes, geese, and birds of prey. Many migrate to Öland from Siberia. In 2000, UNESCO named the southern part of the island, known as Stora Arvaret, a World Heritage Site due partly to its striking, bleak beauty and unique flora and fauna.

To get to Öland, take the 6-km (4-mi) bridge from Kalmar. Be sure to pick up a tourist information map (follow the signs as soon as you get on the island). Most sights have no address, and are just scattered about. Close to the bridge is the popular **Historium,** where slide shows, wax figures, and constructed dioramas all show what Öland was like 10,000 years ago.

Head clockwise around the island. **Borgholms Slott,** the largest castle ruin in northern Europe, is just outside of the island's principal town, Borgholm (25 km/16 mi north of the bridge). Nearby is the royal family's summer home at **Solliden.**

NEED A
BREAK?
Borgholm has a pleasant square. Try Pappa Blå, a café that serves a variety of food from pizzas to sandwiches to steaks, SKr 60–SKr 150.

From Borgholm, follow the signs north to **Knisa Mosse,** a marshland area that's home to many bird species.

Heading farther north brings you to Löttorp. From here drive west to **Horns kungsgård,** a nature preserve on a lake that has a bird-watching tower and walking trails. Here is one of the few royal estates on the island. The government maintains it to look as it did in 1900.

Some 5 km (3 mi) north along the coast from Horns kungsgård is **Byrum,** a nature preserve with striking, wind-carved limestone cliffs. The botanist Linnaeus (Carl von Linné) discussed this area in his writings. Just a few more kilometers on is **Skäftekärr,** which has a culture museum, café, an Iron Age farm with an arboretum, and walking trails. At the northernmost tip is the Långe Erik lighthouse.

Turning back you will find one of the island's three nature centers, **Trollskogen.** On its trails are some majestic old oaks, prehistoric barrow graves, and pines. A little to the south is northern Europe's longest beach, a great swimming spot with sparkling white sand.

Pass back through **Löttorp,** heading south. Keep an eye out for the signs leading east off the main road for the intriguing **Källa** church ruins, some of the best on the island. Return to the main road and head south to **Kappelludden,** one of the island's best year-round bird sites. Medieval chapel ruins and a lighthouse make this coastal spot very scenic.

Gärdslösa, to the southwest of Kappelludden, has an excellently preserved medieval church. Look for the Viking inscriptions on its wall.

Continuing south, turn right at Långlöt for the **Himmelsberga Museum** (☎ 0485/561022, ⊙ May–Aug., 10–6, ⊠ SKr 50), a farm museum dating from the end of the 18th century. The buildings and furnishings include horse buggies and horse sleds. The old stables were home to the small, swift Öland horses, which were extinct by the beginning of the 19th century. Old documents claim that they could dance to horns and drums and jump through hoops.

Gråborg, a 6th-century fortress, with massive stone walls 625 ft in diameter, is a must-see. To get here, turn right at Norra Möckleby.

Return and head south. About 2 kms north of Seby are some strings of **rune stones**: engraved gravestones dating from 500 BC to AD 1050, stone circles, and cists and cairns. Head farther south down the road to come to the southeastern edge of Stora Alvaret. This bleak and eerie area has been farmed for 1,000 years.

Just before you reach the 5th-century fortified village of **Eketorp,** you'll reach a turnoff for the **Gräsgård,** an important fishing village. Eketorp's castle is partially renovated; the area includes small tenants' fields from the Iron and Middle ages. Admission to the castle and its grounds is SKr 45.

Continue on to **Ottenby** and the southernmost tip of Öland. This was a place for hunting as much as 5,000 years ago. It's now a popular site for bird-watching, and also has the largest Iron Age burial fields. The entrance fee to the burial fields is SKr 50 per car and SKr 20 per person.

Now drive north up the west coastal road. Shortly after **Södra Möckleby,** you'll come across the impressive burial grounds of **Gettlinge.** More than 200 graves lie across 2 km (1 mi). The site was in use from the time of Christ into the Viking era, which lasted until 1050. Beginning in late spring, the land north of here produces many different wild orchids. You may want to go have a look.

Farther on is **Mysinge Tunukus,** a Bronze Age site. A group of rune stones here are placed in a shape resembling a ship: it's beautiful at sunset. From here continue on back to the bridge and mainland Sweden.

Lodging

$ 🏨 **Eksgården Wärdshus.** The red cottages at this hotel resemble farmhouses. The pleasant dining room often hosts cultural performances. There's even a museum with farm and domestic implements and footwear, and an arts and crafts shop. ⊠ *386 93 Gårdby,* ☎ *0485/ 33450. 13 rooms with bath. Dining room, shop. Sept.–Jan.*

$ 🏨 **Grankullaviks Vandrarhem.** The beautiful setting for this hotel is right beside a beach on the northern coastline. The fishing is good and boats are for hire. ⊠ *380 75 Granullavik,* ☎ *0485/24040. 20 rooms without bath. Sept.–mid-June.*

$ 🏨 **Guntorps Herrgåd.** Spacious parkland surrounds this manor house, which is 800 m (2,500 ft) from the center of Borgholm. Outside, there's a heated pool. The dining room offers pleasant eating. ✉ *387 36 Borgholm,* ☎ *0485/13000,* 𝖥𝖠𝖷 *0485/13319. 6 rooms in main house and 14 small apartments, all with bath. Restaurant, pool. AE, MC, V.*

$ 🏨 **Halltorps Gästgiveri.** This 17th-century manor house has modernized duplex rooms decorated in Swedish landscape tones and an excellent restaurant. Driving north from Ölandsbron, it's on the left side of the road. ✉ *387 36 Borgholm,* ☎ *0485/85000,* 𝖥𝖠𝖷 *0485/85001. 35 rooms with bath. Restaurant, no-smoking rooms, 2 saunas, meeting room. AE, DC, MC, V.*

$ 🏨 **Värdshuset Briggen Tre Liljor.** Large trees stand alongside this lovely old stone-clad hotel, which is 25 km (16 mi) north of Borgholm. The rooms are very clean, spacious, and in an older style that may make you feel as if you've stepped back into the past. The restaurant serves good traditional food. ✉ *Lofta, 387 91 Borgholm,* ☎ *0485/26400,* 𝖥𝖠𝖷 *0485/26420. 17 rooms with bath. Dining room. AE, MC, V.*

$ 🏨 **Kastlö Stiftsgård.** Some of the rooms in this hotel once belonged to the nearby church and still have a religious feel. Other options include small huts. ✉ *Kostlüsa,* ☎ *0485/42775. 20 rooms without baths, 10 huts. Pool.*

The Kingdom of Glass

Stretching roughly 109 km (68 mi) between Kalmar and Växjö.

Småland is home to the world-famous Swedish glass industry. Scattered among the rocky woodlands of Småland province are isolated villages whose names are synonymous with high-quality crystal glassware. This spectacular creative art was at its height in the late 19th century. The conditions were perfect: large quantities of wood to fuel the furnaces and plenty of water from the streams and rivers. At the time demand was such that the furnaces burned 24 hours a day.

The region is still home to 16 major glassworks, many of them created through the merging of the smaller firms. You can still see glass being blown and crystal being etched by craftspeople. You may also be interested in attending a *Hyttsil* evening, a revival of an old tradition in which Baltic herring (*sil*) is cooked in the glass furnaces of the *hytt* (literally "hut," but meaning the works). Most glassworks also have shops selling quality firsts and not-so-perfect seconds at a discount.

Though the glass factories generally prospered before and during the 1900s, this wealth didn't filter down to many of their workers or to Småland's other inhabitants. Poverty became so widespread that the area lost vast numbers of people to the United States from the late 19th through the 20th century. If you're an American with Swedish roots, chances are your ancestors are from this area. The Utvandrarnas Hus (Emigrants' House) tells the story of this exodus.

The Kingdom of Glass's oldest works is **Kosta Glasbruk.** Dating from 1742, it was named for the two former generals who founded it, Anders Koskull and Georg Bogislaus Stael von Holstein. Faced with a dearth of local talent, they initially imported glassblowers from Bohemia. The Kosta works pioneered the production of crystal (to qualify for that label, glass must contain at least 24% lead oxide). You can see glassblowing off-season (mid-August–early June) between 9 and 3. To get to the village of Kosta from Kalmar, drive 49 km (30 mi) west on Route 25, then 14 km (9 mi) north on Route 28. ✉ *Kosta,* ☎ *0478/34500.* ⊙ *Late June–early Aug., weekdays 9–6, Sat. 9–4, Sun. 11–4; early Aug.– late June, weekdays 9–6, Sat. 10–4, Sun. noon–4.*

Orrefors is one of the best-known glass companies. Orrefors arrived on the scene late—in 1898—but set particularly high artistic standards. The skilled workers in Orrefors dance a slow, delicate minuet as they carry the pieces of red-hot glass back and forth, passing them on rods from hand to hand, blowing and shaping them. The basic procedures and tools are ancient, and the finished product is the result of unusual teamwork, from designer to craftsman to finisher. One of Orrefors's special attractions is a magnificent display of pieces made during the 19th century; you can appease bored children in the cafeteria and playground. From early June–mid-August, you can watch glassblowing from 9 to 10 and 11 to 3. ⊠ *On Rte. 31, about 18 km (11 mi) east of Kosta Glasbruk.* ☎ *0481/34000,* WEB *www.orrefors.se.* ◷ *Aug.–May, weekdays 10–6; June–July, weekdays 9–4, Sat. 10–4, Sun. 11–4.*

Mystical animal reliefs and female figures play a big role in the work at **Målerås,** which was founded in 1890. The glass workers are great to watch, using classic techniques with names such as "the grail." Overlooking the factory is a pleasant restaurant with panoramic views. ⊠ *12 km (7 mi) north of Orrefors.* ☎ *0481/31402.* ◷ *June–Aug., weekdays 9–6, Sat. 10–6, Sun. 11–5; Sept.–May, weekdays 10–6, Sat. 10–4, Sun. 11–4.*

Boda Glasbruk, part of the Kosta Boda Company, is the second-oldest glassworks, founded in 1864. The work here has an ethereal theme, with the designers drawing on cosmic bodies such as the sun and the moon. Much of the work has veils of violet and blue suspended in the crystal. ⊠ *Just off Rte. 25, 42 km (26 mi) west of Kalmar.* ☎ *0481/ 42400.* ◷ *Daily 9–4.*

Continue west from Boda Glasbruk for 20 km (12 mi) to the town of Lessebo. From mid-June to mid-August, you can visit the 300-year-old **Lessebo Handpappersbruk,** which is the only handmade-paper factory in Sweden. Since the 18th century the craftsmen have been using much the same techniques to produce fine paper, which is available from the shop. Guided tours take place on weekdays at 9:30, 10:30, 2:00, and 2:15. ⊠ *Lessebo,* ☎ *0478/47691.* ◷ *Jan.–Dec., weekdays 7–5, Sat. 10–4.*

Skruf Glasbruk began in 1896. Today it's a purveyor to the king of Sweden. The royal family, the ministry of foreign affairs, and the parliament have all commissioned work from Skruf. Local farmers encouraged the development of the glassworks because they wanted a market for their wood. The museum takes you through the historic eras of fine glasscraft in Småland. The factory specializes in lead-free crystal, which has a unique iridescence and form. ⊠ *10 km (6 mi) south of Lessebo. Turn left at Akerby.* ☎ *0478/20133.* ◷ *June and Aug., weekdays 9–6; July, weekdays 9–6:30; Aug.–June, weekdays 9–5, weekends 10–4.*

Founded in 1889, **Bergadala Glasbruk** is one of the most traditional glassworks. Alongside the main road are the former workers' homes, now used mainly as long-term rentals. Note the impressive circular furnace that stands in the middle of the wooden floor. Bergadala is often called the blue glassworks, since many of its pieces have a rich cobalt hue. A stone's throw from the smelter is a children's playground and a glass-painting workshop that will keep them quiet for hours. From here you are 10 km (6 mi) from Växjö. ⊠ *About 15 km (9 mi) northwest of Lessebo, toward Växjö.* ☎ *0478/31650.* ◷ *June, daily 9–5; July, daily 9–6:30; Aug., daily 9–6; Sept.–May, weekdays 9–5, weekends 10–4.*

Lodging

$ 🏨 **Hotell Björkäng.** Set in a park that will give you plenty of opportunity to take evening strolls, the Björkäng has well-kept rooms. They have some rustic decorations, such as traditional ornaments, wood carved by nature, and glass pieces. You also have the opportunity to spend an evening in the glassblowing room. The dining room offers a range of good traditional Swedish food. ⊠ *Stora Vägen 2, Kosta,* ☎ *0478/ 50000. 24 double and two single rooms, all with bath. Dining room, sauna, billiards. MC, V. BP.*

$ 🏨 **Orrefors.** The rooms are cozy, and the hotel is set in the authentic center of the Kingdom of Glass. The restaurant and bar offer good dining and a pleasant atmosphere. ⊠ *Kantav. 29, Orrefors,* ☎ *0481/30035,* FAX *0481/30056. 10 rooms with bath. Bar, dining room. MC, V. BP.*

$ 🏨 **Wärdhusset Flustret.** With a big garden, trees, and a forest surrounding you, this countryside inn can't help but be comforting. It's a great place from which to head out for a walk. ⊠ *Storg. 83, Lessebo,* ☎ *0478/ 10100,* FAX *0478/10103. 13 rooms, 5 with bath. MC, V.*

Växjö

● *109 km (68 mi) northwest of Kalmar via Route 25, 198 km (123 mi) northeast of Malmö, 228 km (142 mi) southeast of Göteborg, 446 km (277 mi) southwest of Stockholm.*

Some 10,000 Americans visit this town every year, for it was from this area that their Swedish ancestors departed in the 19th century. A large proportion of those emigrants went to Minnesota, attracted by the affordable farmland and a geography reminiscent of parts of Sweden. On the second Sunday every August, Växjö celebrates Minnesota Day: Swedes and Swedish-Americans come together to commemorate their common heritage with American-style square dancing and other festivities. Beyond this, the city is really just a base from which to travel onward.

The **Utvandrarnas Hus** (Emigrants' House) in the town center tells the story of the migration, when more than a million Swedes—one quarter of the population—departed for the promised land. The museum exhibits provide a vivid sense of the rigorous journey, and an archive room and research center allow Americans with Swedish blood to trace their ancestry. ⊠ *Museum Park, Box 201,* ☎ *0470/20120,* WEB *www.svenskaemigrantinstitutet.g.se.* ☒ *SKr 40.* ☉ *June–Aug., weekdays 9–5, Sat. 11–3, Sun. 1–5; Sept.–May, weekdays 9–4.*

The **Småland Museum** has the largest glass collection in northern Europe. The museum is famous for its presentation of the development of glass. It has an excellent display putting the area's unique industry into perspective and explaining the different styles of the various glass companies. ⊠ *Södra Jarnvägsg. 2,* ☎ *0470/45145.* ☒ *SKr 40.* ☉ *Weekdays 10–5, weekends 11–5.*

OFF THE
BEATEN PATH   **KRONOBERGS SLOTT** – About 5 km (3 mi) north of Växjö, this 14th-century castle ruin lies on the edge of the Helgasjön (Holy Lake). The Småland freedom fighter Nils Dacke used the castle as a base for his attacks against the Danish occupiers during the mid-1500s; now it's an idyllic destination. In summer, you can eat waffles from the café under the shade of birch trees or take a lunch or sightseeing cruise around the lake on the small, toylike *Thor,* Sweden's oldest steamboat. ☎ *0470/ 45145 castle; 0470/63000 boat tours.* ☉ *Tours offered late June–late Aug.* ☒ *Lunch cruise SKr 280, 2½-hr canal trip to Årby SKr 120, 1-hr around-the-lake trip SKr 85.*

Lodging

$ ⊞ **Esplanad.** In town center, the Esplanad is a small, family hotel offering basic amenities. ⊠ *Norra Esplanaden 21A, 352 31,* ☎ *0470/22580,* ℻ *0470/26226. 27 rooms with bath. No-smoking rooms. MC, V. BP.*

$ ⊞ **Hotel Statt.** Now a Best Western hotel, this conveniently located, traditional property is popular with tour groups. The building dates from 1853, but the rooms themselves are modern. The hotel has a cozy pub, nightclub, bistro, and café. ⊠ *Kungsg. 6, 351 04,* ☎ *0470/13400,* ℻ *0470/44837. 124 rooms with bath. Restaurant, café, pub, no-smoking rooms, sauna, gym, nightclub, meeting room. AE, DC, MC, V.*

The South and the Kingdom of Glass A to Z

To research prices, get advice from other travelers, and book travel arrangements, visit www.fodors.com.

AIR TRAVEL

CARRIERS

KLM, Malmö Aviation, and SAS serve the Malmö airport.
➤ AIRLINES AND CONTACTS: **KLM** (☎ 040/500530). **Malmö Aviation** (☎ 040/502900). **SAS** (☎ 040/357200 or 020/727000).

CUTTING COSTS

SAS offers discounts on trips to Malmö year-round; ask for the "Jackpot" discount package.

AIRPORTS

Malmö's airport, Sturup, is approximately 30 km (19 mi) from Malmö and 25 km (15 mi) from Lund.

Buses for Malmö and Lund meet all flights at Sturup Airport. The price of the trip is SKr 60 to either destination. For more information on bus schedules, routes, and fares, call the number below or the airport. A taxi from the airport to Malmö or Lund costs about SKr 250.
➤ AIRPORT INFORMATION: **Bus Information** (☎ 020/616161). **SAS Limousine Service** (☎ 040/500600). **Sturup** (☎ 040/6131100).

BOAT AND FERRY TRAVEL

Several regular boat services run from Copenhagen to Malmö, including hovercraft that make the trip in less than an hour. There is also a bus-ferry service from Copenhagen Station that goes to Lund. In addition, there are regular ferry connections between Denmark, Germany, and Poland from such Swedish ports as Malmö, Helsingborg, Landskrona, Trelleborg, and Ystad. Stena Line is one of the major Swedish carriers.

Day-trippers can pick up tickets at Malmö Harbor and catch one of the hourly Copenhagen-bound hovercraft operated by the following ferry lines: Flygbåtarna, Pilen, and Shopping Linje. SFL Skandlines runs the only car-ferry service between Dragör, Denmark, and Limhamn, Sweden, a town that adjoins Malmö's southern edge.
➤ BOAT AND FERRY INFORMATION: **Flygbåtarna** (☎ 040/103930). **Pilen** (☎ 040/234411). **SFL Skandlines** (☎ 040/362000). **Shopping Linje** (☎ 040/110099). **Stena Line** (⊠ Kungsg. 12–14, Stockholm, ☎ 08/141475; ⊠ Danmarksterminalen, Göteborg, ☎ 031/858000).

CUTTING COSTS

The *Malmökortet* (Malmö Card) entitles the holder to, among other benefits, free travel on the city buses, free parking, discounts on tours, and free admission or discounts to most museums, concert halls, nightclubs, theaters, the Royal Cab company, and many shops and restaurants. A one-day card costs SKr 150, a two-day card SKr 275, and a three-day card SKr 400. Cards are available from the tourist office in Malmö.

CAR RENTAL

If you are coming from Denmark and want to rent a car as soon as you arrive, several rental companies have locations at Malmö Harbor, including Avis, Hertz, and Europcar. Hertz car rentals are available for less than SKr 600 a day on weekends (less during the summer) if you book an SAS flight.

➤ MAJOR AGENCIES: **Avis** (☎ 040/77830). **Europcar** (☎ 040/71640). **Hertz** (☎ 040/74955).

CAR TRAVEL

You can now get between Copenhagen and Malmö by car across the new bridge. It costs SKR 275 to take a car across in one direction.

Malmö is 620 km (386 mi) from Stockholm. Take the E4 freeway to Helsingborg, then the E6/E20 to Malmö and Lund. From Göteborg, take the E6/E20.

Roads are well marked and well maintained. Traveling around the coast counterclockwise from Helsingborg, you take the E6/E20 to Landskrona, Malmö, and Lund, then the E6/E22 to Trelleborg; Route 9 goes along the south coast from there all the way to Simrishamn and then heads north until just before Kristianstad. It's there that you can pick up E22 all the way through Karlshamn, Ronneby, Karlskrona, and on across the east coast to Kalmar. From Kalmar, Route 25 goes almost directly west through Växjö to Halmstad, on the west coast between Helsingborg and Göteborg.

EMERGENCIES

As elsewhere in Sweden, call 112 for emergencies.

TRAIN TRAVEL

The major towns of the south are all connected by rail.

There is regular service from Stockholm to Helsingborg, Lund, and Malmö. Each trip takes about 6½ hours, and about 4½ hours by high-speed (X2000) train. All three railway stations are centrally located in their respective towns.

TRANSPORTATION AROUND THE SOUTH AND THE KINGDOM OF GLASS

A special 48-hour *Öresund Runt* (Around Öresund) pass is available from the Malmö Tourist Office: at SKr 149, the ticket covers a train from Malmö to Helsingborg, a ferry to Helsingør, a train to Copenhagen, and a ferry back to Malmö.

VISITOR INFORMATION

Jönköping and Skånes Turistråd (Skåne Tourist Council) have information covering the entire region. Other local tourist offices are listed below.

➤ TOURIST INFORMATION: **Helsingborg** (✉ Knutpunkten terminal, ☎ 042/120310). **Jönköping** (✉ Västra Storg. 18A, ☎ 036/199570). **Kalmar** (✉ Larmg. 6, ☎ 0480/15350). **Karlskrona** (✉ Borgnästoreg. 68, ☎ 0455/303490). **Kristianstad** (✉ Stora Torg, ☎ 044/121988). **Landskrona** (✉ Rådhusg. 3, ☎ 0418/473000; ✉ Landsv. 2, ☎ 0418/72420). **Lund** (✉ Kyrkog. 11, ☎ 046/355040). **Malmö** (✉ Skeppsbron at the Central Station, ☎ 040/300150). **Ronneby** (✉ Kallingev. 3, ☎ 0457/18090). **Skånes Turistråd** (✉ Skifferv. 38, Lund, ☎ 046/124350). **Växjö** (✉ Kronobergsg. 8, ☎ 0470/41410). **Ystad** (✉ St. Knuts Torg, ☎ 0411/77681).

8 DALARNA: THE FOLKLORE DISTRICT

DALARNA IS CONSIDERED the most traditional of all the country's 24 provinces, a place of forests, mountains, and red-painted wooden farmhouses and cottages by the shores of pristine, sun-dappled lakes. It is the favorite sight for celebrations on Midsummer Day, when Swedes don folk costumes and dance to fiddle and accordion music around maypoles covered with wildflower garlands.

Dalarna played a key role in the history of the nation. It was from here that Gustav Vasa recruited the army that freed the country from Danish domination during the 16th century. The region is also important artistically, both for its tradition of naive religious decoration and for producing two of the nation's best-loved painters, Anders Zorn (1860–1920) and Carl Larsson (1853–1915), and one of its favorite poets, the melancholy, mystical Dan Andersson (1888–1920). He sought inspiration in the remote forest camps of the old charcoal burners, who spent their days slowly burning wood to make the charcoal factory furnaces.

As for dining and lodging, do not expect too much in Dalarna. Traditionally, visitors to the area—many from elsewhere in Scandinavia or from Germany—make use either of the region's many well-equipped campsites or of *stugbyar* (small villages of log cabins, with cooking facilities), usually set near lakesides or in forest clearings.

Our itinerary circles Siljan, the largest of the 6,000 lakes in the province and the center of Dalarna's folklore. The main points can all be reached by train, except for the southern side of Lake Siljan.

En Route   Roughly 160 km (100 mi) from Stockholm on the way to Dalarna, just south of Avesta on Route 70, stands the world's biggest *Dalahäst,* or Dala horse, which is 43 ft tall. This version of the traditional symbol of Dalarna is painted bright orange-red and marks a modern roadside rest stop that has a spacious cafeteria and a helpful tourist information center.

Falun

96   *224 km (139 mi) northwest of Stockholm via E18 and Route 70.*

Falun is the traditional capital of Dalarna, though in recent years the nondescript railway town of Borlänge has grown in importance. Falun's history has always been very much bound to its copper mine, worked since 1230 by Stora Kopparbergs Bergslags AB (today just Stora), which claims to be the oldest limited company in the world. During its greatest period of prosperity, the 17th century, it financed Sweden's "Age of Greatness," and the country became the dominant Baltic power. In 1650, Stora produced a record 3,067 tons of copper; probably as a result of such rapid extraction, 37 years later its mine shafts caved in. Fortunately, the accident was on Midsummer Day, when most of the miners were off duty, and as a result no one was killed.

Today the major part of the mine is an enormous hole in the ground that, in combination with adjoining **Storamuseum,** has become Falun's principal tourist attraction. A look around the mine, which involves a mandatory one-hour guided tour, is well worth the time. The tour begins with a hair-raising ride in an old elevator 150 ft down into the mine, where you can walk through a network of old shafts and tunnels. Wear old shoes and warm clothing, since the copper-tinged mud can stain footwear and it's cold down there. The Stora Museum puts into perspective the lives of the men who worked the mines and has

Dalarna

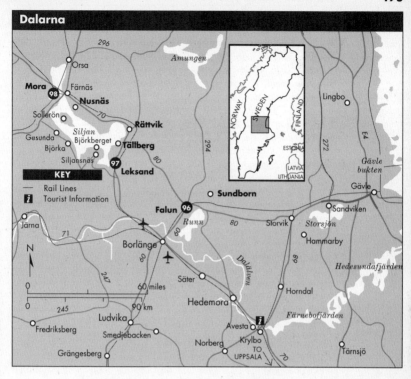

eye-opening displays on just how bad working conditions were be-lowground. ☎ 023/711475. 🎫 *Mine SKr 60, museum free with mine tour.* ⊙ *Mine May–Aug., daily 10–4:30; Sept.–mid-Nov. and Mar.–Apr., weekends 12:30–4:30; museum May–Aug., daily 10–4:30; Sept.–Apr., daily 12:30–4:30.*

The folk art, folklore, clothing, and music of the area are all well cov-ered at **Dalarnasmuseet** (the Dalarnas Museum). There is also a grand reconstruction of the study in which Selma Lagerlöf, the celebrated Swedish author, worked after she moved to Falun in 1897. ✉ *Stigareg. 2,* ☎ *023/765500.* 🎫 *SKr 20.* ⊙ *May–Aug., Mon.–Thurs. 10–5, Fri.– Sun. noon–5; Sept.–May, Mon.–Tues. and Thurs. 10–5, Wed. 10–9, Fri.– Sun. noon–5.*

Dining and Lodging

\$\$ ✕ **MS Slussbrunden.** This restaurant on a boat offers "prawn cruises." For a set price, diners feast on as many prawns as they can shell dur-ing the three-hour cruise. Live music acts serenade them all the while. Limitless bread and butter, cheese, fruits, and coffee are included. Wine and drinks are extra, and the choice is a little limited but good nonetheless. Combined with the beautiful scenery, the dinner cruise is a great hit. ✉ *Strandv.,* ☎ *023/63850. Reservations essential. AE, DC, MC, V. Closed Nov.–Apr.*

\$ ✕ **Blå Apelsinen.** The Blue Orange serves up what's known as *hus-manskost* (homey) Swedish food. Simple, hearty pork, beef, and fish dishes are all offered here in straightforward surroundings at reason-able prices. ✉ *Bergskolegränd 8A,* ☎ *023/29111. AE, MC, V.*

\$\$\$ 🏨 **Grand.** Part of the First Hotel chain, this conventional, modern hotel is close to town center. The bright rooms are decorated with Chippendale-style furniture. ✉ *Trotzg. 911, 791 71,* ☎ *023/18700,* ℻ *023/14143. 183 rooms. Restaurant, bar, minibars, no-smoking rooms, indoor pool, sauna, gym, convention center, free parking. AE, DC, MC, V.*

$$ 🏨 **Hotel Falun.** Rolf Carlsson runs this small, friendly, but bland-looking hotel just 1,300 ft from the railway station. The 12 rooms that share baths are offered at a lower rate. The front desk closes at 9 PM. ⊠ *Centrumhuset, Trotzg. 16, 791 71,* ☎ *023/29180,* FAX *023/13006. 27 rooms, 15 with bath. No-smoking rooms, meeting room. AE, DC, MC, V.*

$$ 🏨 **Hotel Winn.** This small, cozy hotel in town center is built in tradi-
★ tional Dalarna style and filled with antique furnishings. There is a pleas-
ant relaxation area where the hot tub and sauna will let you unwind
from the day's stresses. ⊠ *Bergskolegränd 7, 791 26,* ☎ *023/63600,*
FAX *023/22524. 88 rooms, 65 with bath. Restaurant, no-smoking
rooms, hot tub, sauna, meeting room. AE, DC, MC, V.*

$$ 🏨 **Scandic.** Resembling a Lego structure, the ultramodern Scandic is
in the expanded Lungnet sports and recreation center outside Falun,
where the 1993 World Skiing Championships took place. The com-
fortable rooms have good views of the giant ski jump that's used for
competitions. ⊠ *Svärdsjög. 51, 791 31 Falun,* ☎ *023/22160,* FAX *023/
12845. 135 rooms. Restaurant, pub, no-smoking rooms, indoor pool,
sauna, meeting room. AE, DC, MC, V.*

$ 🏨 **Birgittagården.** The Stiftelsen Dalarnas Birgitta Systrar (the Dalarna
Sisters of Birgitta) religious order runs this small hotel, 8 km (5 mi)
outside town. It's smoke- and alcohol-free, and set in a fine park.
There are no telephones or televisions in the rooms. ⊠ *Uddnäsv., 791
46,* ☎ *023/32147,* FAX *023/32471. 25 rooms without bath. No-smok-
ing rooms, meeting room. No credit cards.*

Outdoor Activities and Sports

A 25-minute walk from the center of Falun, east on Svärdsjögatan, takes
you to **Lungnet** (☎ 023/83561), Falun's sports complex and national
ski stadium. Horseback riding, swimming, bowling, an indoor sports
center, and running tracks are all available. The ski stadium is home
to the 260-ft ski jump (used only in competitions). In the winter you
can watch the daredevil jumpers fly through the air, and in the sum-
mer, when the snow has gone, you can go to the top yourself and ad-
mire the view across Falun and beyond.

SKIING

At the **Bjursås Ski Center** (☎ 0250/46200), 25 km (15 mi) northwest
of Falun on Route 80, snow lovers can make use of the resort's 7 lift
systems and 16 varied pistes. It's open between December and April
and has numerous hotels, restaurants, and cafés.

Sundborn

10 km (6 mi) northeast of Falun off Route 80.

★ In this small village you can visit **Carl Larsson Gården,** the lakeside home
of the Swedish artist (1833–1915). Larsson was an excellent textile de-
signer and draftsman who painted scenes from his family's busy, do-
mestic life. The house itself was creatively painted and decorated by
Larsson's wife, Karin, also trained as an artist. Their home's turn-of-
the-20th-century fittings and furnishings have been carefully preserved;
their great-grandchildren still use the house on occasion. Waits for guided
tours in summer can take two hours. ☎ *023/60053 May–Sept.; 023/
60069 Oct.–Apr.* ☞ *Guided tours only, SKr 65.* ☉ *May–Sept., daily
10–5; Oct.–Apr., visits by advance reservation.*

Rättvik

48 km (30 mi) northwest of Falun via Route 80.

Surrounded by wooded slopes, Rättvik is a pleasant town of timbered
houses on the eastern tip of Lake Siljan. A center for local folklore,

A SWEDISH BATH

It is autumn on the Stockholm archipelago island of Finnhamn today, but you could be forgiven for thinking it is winter. The ice has barely melted and an arctic wind scythes bitterly across the landscape. To the north, clouds that are surely laden with snow creep south and the people shiver. You need heat, and lots of it.

There is a solution, one forged in defense against the cold for eons of time by the people who have populated these frozen lands. And it is as traditionally Swedish as Absolut Vodka and just as warming. The *bastu* (sauna) has been the answer to frozen Nordic bones since long before medieval times, although no certain dates of origin have been determined.

The bastu takes many different shapes and forms, but the classic model is little more than a small wooden shed, parked beside a freezing lake or the sea—set in an eternal nature. The one on Finnhamn looks like something from the fairy-tale writings of Hans Christian Anderson (admittedly Danish). It is painted traditional rust red and is no more than 16 ft long. It sits on a creaky wooden pier under bleak, leafless trees, plumb against the sea.

This evening, it is a welcome sight and there is no alternative but to take the plunge, into a dry heat that will soar to 80 or 90 degrees Celsius. The snow clouds have arrived and snowflakes the size of golf balls are swirling and drifting. The sea is churning and the wind is coaxing the trees into an eerie dance. Through a small glass window, you can see the storm.

Taking a sauna has reached a fine art in Sweden. It is often a social event. Some men do business here (a last bas-tion of gender exclusion) and there is a definite ritual. The practice is about heat and cleansing. In fact the bastu has historically been the primary cleaning place, in times when running water was scarce. Nordic people came here for their once weekly (or less often) bathing routine. It was also used as the place for medical attention, due to its hygiene. Babies were born here. Corpses were brought to lie here. They were once a sacred place.

To begin, the initiate should first shower off the wrath of the day. You must then be completely dry, allowing the heat to properly open the pores for a clean, free sweat. Take a seat, buck naked, on a towel—a must for hygienic protocol.

Now the work begins. And it is work although it may not feel like it at first. It will take a while, but the sweat will trickle, then flood. Put some water on the coals to wet the air. When you reach near-fission, the next and most daring step awaits: the big freeze. On Finnhamn, I stepped unadorned into the snow, down the frozen steel ladder. Sha-la-la! By the powers, it was cold, head-splitting cold.

Back on terra firma within microseconds, the skin begins to tingle and the head spins in dizziness and shock. Absolute elation. Make haste to the bastu. The next rule is to dry off in the warming room. This is one full cycle. Keep going until you can take no more. At the end an ocean of warmth and exhaustion will engulf you.

The Swedish believe in the practice as an elixir and proclaim it aids good health, vigor, and life. But do beware: those with a heart condition or other matters of ill health have come to grief in the bastu. Everything in moderation, as the saying goes. Proceed with caution.

the town has several shops that sell handmade articles and produce from the surrounding region.

Every year in June, hundreds of people wearing traditional costumes arrive in longboats to attend midsummer services at the town's 14th-century church, **Rättvik Kyrka,** which stands on a promontory stretching into the lake. Its interior contains some fine examples of local religious art.

The open-air museum **Rättvik Gammalgård,** a 20-minute walk along the banks of the lake north of Rätvik, reconstructs peasant lifestyles of bygone days. More than 3,500 pieces of art, clothing, ceramics, tools, and furniture are on display in the old buildings, including many typical of the region. Tours in English can be arranged through the Rättvik **tourist office.** ✉ *Free; guided tour SKr 20.* ☉ *Mid-June–mid-Aug., daily 11–6; tours at 1 and 2:30.*

Just to the west of Rättvik, heading up into the forest, is **Vidablick.** The top of this tall wooden tower, more than 100 years old, will give you some of the most stunning views across Lake Siljan that you can find. It's quite a climb to get there—about an hour long.

Once a lucrative open chalk mine, the huge multitier quarry left at **Dalhalla** (7 km/4½ mi north of Rättvik) has become one of the world's most beautiful outdoor stages. One side is banked with seats, and the stage, surrounded with water and supported on pillars, appears to float on the cobalt-blue lake at the quarry's bottom. Opera, rock concerts, and amazing light shows are all presented here, where the sound is enhanced by the quarry's incredible acoustics. There is also a museum covering the meteor crash that formed Siljan 460 million years ago, the chalk mining that still takes place, and everything in between. Guided tours of the more remote parts of the quarry can be booked year-round, or you can just sit at the top and gaze down in wonder at its construction. ✉ *Knihsg. 13, Rättvik,* ☎ *0248/797950.* ✉ *SKr 40 for the museum and tour.* ☉ *Museum June–Sept., daily 10–5.*

Dining and Lodging

$ ✕ **Strandrestaurangen.** A family-style restaurant with a huge outdoor seating area right on the lake, Strandrestaurangen serves such standard Swedish fare as meatballs, sausages, and pork chops. It's all well cooked and filling. For the children, there's a beach, minigolf, an ice cream bar, and a swimming pool. For the adults, there's a pub attached, which has live music in the evening. ✉ *Rättvik,* ☎ *0248/13400. AE, MC, V.*

$ ▥ **Hotell Gärdebygården.** Set on its own grounds, with a pleasant view of the lake from the veranda, this small hotel makes a welcome, relaxing stop. Rooms are modern and cleanly furnished, and there's a small private beach where you can take to the water, if it's warm enough. ✉ *Hantverksbyn, 795 36,* ☎ *0248/30250,* ☏ *0248/30660. 50 rooms without bath. Bar, beach. AE, DC, MC, V. BP.*

Tällberg

9 km (5 mi) south of Rättvik via Route 70, 57 km (35 mi) northwest of Falun via Route 80.

Tällberg is considered by many to be the real Dalarna. Once a sleepy town that few knew about, an 1850 visit from Hans Christian Andersen put an end to all that. He extolled its virtues—tiny flower-strewn cottages, sweet-smelling grass meadows, stunning lake views—to such an extent that Tällberg quickly became a major tourist stop. This tiny village, one of the smallest in the region with only about 200 permanent residents, still becomes packed with crowds in summer.

The farm buildings that make up the **Klockargården** have become a living museum of handicrafts and local industry. Artists and craftsmen work in the old buildings, performing such skills as blacksmithing, baking flat bread, making lace, and weaving textiles. ⊠ *Tällberg,* ☎ *0247/ 50260.* ⊞ *Free.* ◷ *June–Aug., Thurs.–Tues. 10–8, Wed. 10–6.*

Dining and Lodging

Because Tällberg is such a tourist attraction, there are many more restaurants and hotels here than you might expect for a town of its size.

$$ ✕⊞ **Åkerblads.** A sprawling, low-built hotel, with parts dating from
★ the 1400s, Åkerblads is known primarily for its gourmet achievements. The restaurant ($$–$$$) serves an interesting blend of Swedish and French cuisine, including such dishes as pork roasted with eggplants and blueberries, and salmon with asparagus, truffle, and Burgundy wine sauce. The hotel rooms are comfortable and most have very good views of the lake. ⊠ *Sjögattu 2, 793 70,* ☎ *0247/50800,* FAX *0247/50652,* WEB *www.arkeblads-tallberg.se. 67 rooms, 8 with bath, 25 suites. Restaurant, bar, pool, sauna, spa. AE, DC, MC, V. BP.*

$$ ✕⊞ **Hotel Dalecarlia.** There's a homey feel to this first-class hotel, which has exacting standards and good lake views. The lobby has comfy sofas and darkened corners for the weary traveler to sink into. Rooms are large and softly furnished, and there is a good spa and fitness center with pool, sauna, and beauty treatments. The restaurant ($–$$) is candlelit and reminiscent of a farmhouse. It has oak beams, crisp white linen, and a large open fireplace perfect for warming your after-dinner brandy. The food is well presented and emphasizes local and regional specialties. The game is especially good. ⊠ *Tällberg, 793 70,* ☎ *0247/89100,* FAX *0247/50240,* WEB *www.dalecarlia.se. 80 rooms, 2 with bath, 5 suites. Restaurant, bar, pool, sauna, gym, convention center. AE, DC, MC, V. BP.*

$ ⊞ **Tällbergsgården.** A classic Dalarna red-wood building, this one claiming to be the oldest in the village, is home to a small, comfortable hotel with fresh rooms and good lake views. The bedrooms are light and airy, with neutral shades and wooden floors. ⊠ *Holgattu 1, 793 70,* ☎ *0247/50850,* FAX *0247/50200,* WEB *www.tallbergsgarden.se. 37 rooms without bath, 2 suites. Restaurant, bar, sauna, spa, meeting rooms. AE, DC, MC, V. BP.*

Shopping

In the middle of the village is **Silversmide** (⊠ Jungvasgården, ☎ 0247/ 50443), a small metalworking shop in which beautiful, one-of-a-kind pieces of jewelry in silver, gold, and iron are made and sold. If you're searching for a special gift, this place may be your solution.

Leksand

97 *9 km (5½ mi) south of Tällberg via Route 70, 66 km (41 mi) northwest of Falun via Rättvik.*

Thousands of tourists converge on Leksand every June for the Midsummer celebrations; they also come in July for *Himlaspelet* (*The Way that Leads to Heaven*), a traditional musical with a local cast that's staged outdoors near the town's church. It is easy to get seats; ask the local tourist office for details.

Leksand is also an excellent vantage point from which to watch the "church-boat" races on Siljan. These vessels are supposedly the successors to the Viking longboats. They were used in the 13th and 14th centuries to take peasants from outlying regions to church on Sunday. On Midsummer Eve, the longboats, crewed by people in folk costumes, skim the lake once more.

In the hills around Leksand and elsewhere near Siljan are many *fäbodar*, small settlements in the forest where cattle were taken to graze during the summer. Less idyllic memories of bygone days are conjured up by **Käringberget**, a 720-ft-high mountain north of town where alleged witches were burned to death during the 17th century.

★   The oldest parts of **Leksands Kyrka** date from the 13th century, and the current exterior dates from 1715. The Leksands Church's interior contains some interesting touches: a German font from the 1500s, a crucifix from 1400, and Dalarna's oldest organ. But what makes this church really shine is its location, perhaps one of the prettiest in the country. The peaceful, tree-lined churchyard and the view across the entire lake are both breathtaking. ⊠ *Kyrkudden,* ☎ *0247/80700.*

At the **Hembygdsgårdar,** the site of the oldest farm buildings in Dalarna, you can find out more about the famous red structures that dot the region's landscape. Other displays look at building techniques that arose in the Middle Ages as well as the history of country living in Dalarna. ⊠ *Kyrkallen,* ☎ *0704/095044.* 🗐 *SKr 10.* 🕙 *June–Aug., daily noon–4.*

Famous local doctor and author Axel Munthe built **Munthes Hildasholm** as a present for his English wife in 1910. The house and gardens, filled with exquisite antiques, paintings, and furniture from across Europe, can now be visited and seen exactly as they were left. Since there's a café here, you can take coffee and cake in the beautifully manicured gardens and lawns. ⊠ *Kykrudden,* ☎ *0247/10062.* 🗐 *SKr 60.* 🕙 *June–Sept., daily 11–6.*

En Route   From Leksands, drive along the small road toward Mora by the southern shores of Siljan, passing through the small communities of Siljansnäs and Björka before stopping at **Gesunda,** a pleasant little village at the foot of a mountain. A chairlift will take you from there to the top for unbeatable views over the lake.

☺   **Tomteland** (Santaland), near Gesunda, claims to be the home of Santa Claus, or Father Christmas. Toys are for sale at Santa's workshop and at kiosks. There are rides in horse-drawn carriages in summer and sleighs in winter. ⊠ *Gesundaberget, Sollerön,* ☎ *0250/29000.* 🗐 *SKr 95.* 🕙 *Mid-June–late Aug., daily 10–5; July, daily 10–6; late Nov.–early Jan., call ahead for daily schedule.*

The large island of **Sollerön** is connected to the mainland by a bridge at Gesunda, from which there are fine views of the mountains surrounding Siljan. Several excellent bathing places and an interesting Viking gravesite are also here. The church dates from 1775.

Dining and Lodging

$ ✗ **Bosporen Restaurang.** The large terrace outside this restaurant is a great place to dine in summer. The menu here is long and interesting, with some great Swedish classics. But for the best eating, have a look at Bosporen's very accomplished pizza menu, which makes use of such ingredients as rocket salad, pine nuts, Gorgonzola, and pears. Wine by the glass is of good quality, and the beers are wide-ranging and cheap. ⊠ *Stortorget 1,* ☎ *0247/13280. AE, DC, MC, V.*

$ 🏨 **Hotell Korstäppan.** The beautiful rooms, many with traditional tile fireplaces and all with wooden floors, are the main attraction at this large, yellow wooden hotel. All the rooms are spacious and simply furnished with stylish antiques and beautiful old rugs. ⊠ *Hjortnäsv. 33,*

793 31, ☎ 0247/12310, ⅻ 0247/14178. *30 rooms without bath. Breakfast room, convention center. AE, DC, MC, V. BP.*

$ ⅻ **Leksands Gästhem.** Simplicity bordering on minimalism is the theme at this converted old school near a farmyard just outside Leksand. The bedrooms have plain, scrubbed wooden floors, large windows, and only pale-blue chairs. All rooms share a bathroom with one or two others. In the hallway—where you can still see the low coat hooks for the schoolchildren—is a sweeping wood staircase that leads to a TV and lounge area. Wonderful breakfasts are included in the rate; everything is homemade. ✉ *Krökbacken 5, 793 90,* ☎ *0247/13700,* ⅻ *0247/ 13737,* ⅱ *www.leksandsguesth.nu. 13 rooms without bath. Breakfast room, lounge. AE, DC, MC, V. BP.*

Outdoor Activities and Sports

Leksand is the perfect base for a bike ride around Lake Siljan. There are many paths and tracks to choose from, and maps and rental bikes are available from the **tourist office** (☎ 0247/796130).

Mora

● *50 km (31 mi) northwest of Leksand, 83 km (52 mi) northwest of Falun via Route 70.*

To get to this pleasant and relaxed lakeside town of 20,000, you can take Route 70 40 km (25 mi) directly from Rättvik along the northern shore of Lake Silja, or follow the lake's southern shore through Leksand and Gesunda to get a good sense of Dalarna.

Mora is best known as the finishing point for the world's longest cross-country ski race, the Vasalopp, which begins 90 km (56 mi) away at Sälen, a ski resort close to the Norwegian border. The race commemorates a fundamental piece of Swedish history: the successful attempt by Gustav Vasa in 1521 to rally local peasants to the cause of ridding Sweden of Danish occupation. Vasa, only 21 years old, had fled the capital and described to the Mora locals in graphic detail a massacre of Swedish noblemen ordered by Danish King Christian in Stockholm's Stortorget. Unfortunately, no one believed him and the dispirited Vasa was forced to abandon his attempts at insurrection and take off on either skis or snowshoes for Norway, where he hoped to evade King Christian and go into exile.

Just after he left, confirmation reached Mora of the Stockholm bloodbath, and the peasants, already discontented with Danish rule, relented, sending two skiers after Vasa to tell him they would join his cause. The two men caught up with the young nobleman at Sälen. They returned with him to Mora, where an army was recruited. Vasa marched south, defeated the Danes, and became king and the founder of modern Sweden.

The commemorative race, held on the first Sunday in March, attracts thousands of competitors from all over the world, including the Swedish king. There is a spectacular mass start at Sälen before the field thins out. The finish is eagerly awaited in Mora, though in recent years the number of spectators has fallen thanks to the fact that the race is now usually televised live.

You can get a comfortable glimpse of the Vasalopp's history in the **Vasaloppsmuseet,** which contains a collection of the ski gear and photos of competitors, news clippings, and a short film detailing some of the race's finer moments. ✉ *Vasag.,* ☎ *0250/39225.* ⅻ *SKr 30.* ◷ *Mid-May–Aug., daily 10–6; Sept.–mid-May, daily 11–5.*

Mora is also known as the home of Anders Zorn (1860–1920), Sweden's leading impressionist painter, who lived in Stockholm and Paris before returning to his roots here and painting the local scenes for which he is now known. His former private residence—**Zorngården**—a large, sumptuous house designed with great originality and taste by the painter himself, has retained the same exquisite furnishings, paintings, and decor it had when he lived there with his wife. The garden, also a Zorn creation, is open to the public. Next door, the **Zorn Museet** (Zorn Museum), built 19 years after the painter's death, contains many of his best works. ✉ *Vasag. 36,* ☎ *0250/16560.* ✉ *Museum SKr 30, home SKr 30.* ☉ *Museum mid-May–mid-Sept., Mon.–Sat. 9–5, Sun. 11–5; mid-Sept.–mid-May, Mon.–Sat. 10–5, Sun. 1–5; home (guided tours only) mid-May–mid-Sept., Mon.–Sat. 10–4, Sun. 11–4; mid-Sept.–mid-May, Mon.–Sat. 12:30–4, Sun. 1–4.*

On the south side of town is **Zorns Gammalgård,** a fine collection of old wooden houses from local farms, brought here and donated to Mora by Anders Zorn. One of them was converted in 1995 into the **Textil Kammare** (Textile Chamber), the first exhibit of Zorn's collection of textiles and period clothing. ✉ *Yvradsv.,* ☎ *0250/16560 (June–Aug. only).* ✉ *SKr 20.* ☉ *June–Aug., daily 11–5.*

OFF THE
BEATEN PATH

SILJANSFORS SKOGSMUSEUM – Partly because there's always been a lot of wood available for firing furnaces, the area around Mora is well known for its metalworking. This outdoor museum shows the smithies' many connections to local forestry, in particular with the art of charcoal burning. A track through the forest will take you to smithies, ironworks, woodcutting sheds, and charcoal-burning towers. The walks are all linked together at the information center near the entrance. ✉ *12 mi southwest of Mora on Rte. 45,* ☎ *0250/20331.*

Dining and Lodging

$$ ✕ **Jernet Bar & Matsal.** Situated in one of Mora's oldest industrial buildings (1879), Jernet serves high-quality Swedish and international dishes, which may include roast elk with mustard potatoes and lingonberries and breast of chicken stuffed with Brie and apricots. The tables are bare, antique oak; the wooden chairs are of a traditional Leksand style; and the crisp linen napkins are woven locally. In the bar area, furnished in birch and stainless steel, the large windows allow for great views over the lake. ✉ *Strandg. 6,* ☎ *0250/15020. AE, DC, MC, V.*

$$ ⊡ **Kung Gästa.** This modern, reasonably sized hotel is 2 km (1 mi) from town center and only 330 ft from the Mora train station. The small rooms are brightly furnished, with wood floors and large windows. ✉ *Kristeneberg, 792 32,* ☎ *0250/15070,* FAX *0250/17078. 47 rooms, 22 with bath. Restaurant, no-smoking rooms, indoor pool, sauna, gym, meeting room. AE, DC, MC, V. BP.*

$$ ⊡ **Mora.** This pleasant little Best Western hotel is in town center 5 km (3 mi) from the airport. Its comfortable rooms are brightly decorated and have minibars and radios. ✉ *Strandg. 12, 792 01,* ☎ *0250/71750,* FAX *0250/18981. 138 rooms, 2 with bath. Restaurant, bar, minibars, no-smoking rooms, indoor pool, sauna, meeting room. AE, DC, MC, V. BP.*

$$ ⊡ **Siljan.** Part of the Sweden Hotel group, this small, modern hotel has views over the lake. Rooms are standard, with radio, television, and wall-to-wall carpeting; most are single rooms with sofa beds. ✉ *Morag. 6, 792 01,* ☎ *0250/13000,* FAX *0250/13098. 45 rooms, 1 with bath. Restaurant, bar, no-smoking floor, sauna, gym, dance club, meeting room. AE, DC, MC, V. BP.*

$ ⚑ **Mora Parken.** This modern, brightly furnished hotel sits in a park by the banks of the Dala River, not far from town center. Rooms are small and simply furnished with pastel fabrics and plain wood furniture and floors. ✉ *Parkgarten 1, 792 25,* ☎ *250/27600,* FAX *250/ 27615. 75 rooms with bath. Restaurant, no-smoking rooms, sauna, convention center. AE, DC, MC, V. BP.*

Outdoor Activities and Sports

SKIING

Dalarna's principal ski resort is **Sälen,** starting point for the Vasalopp, about 80 km (50 mi) west of Mora. Snow here is pretty much guaranteed from November to May, and there are more than 100 pistes to choose from, from simple slopes for the beginner to challenging black runs that weave through tightly forested slopes. For more information, contact any of the tourist offices in Dalarna.

WALKING

For the energetic traveler, it's possible to walk the 90 km (56 mi) **track from Sälen to Mora** that's used for the Vasalopp ski race in March. Along the way you may very well see some elk wandering through the forest. Day shelters, basic night shelters, fireplaces, tables, signposts, and rest rooms are set up along the trail. Facilities are free, but a donation of SKr 25 is suggested for the night shelters. Maps and other details can be obtained from the **Mora tourist office** (☎ 0250/567600).

OFF THE BEATEN PATH

ORSA – Fifteen kilometers (nine miles) north of Mora on Route 45 is a small, sleepy town that becomes a big chaotic symphony every Wednesday in July. It's then that the Orsa Spelmän, groups of traditional folklore music players, take part in what's called the Orsayran (Orsa rush). The musicians take over the streets of the town, wandering and playing their instruments. This soon becomes a free-for-all in which all the people in town, whether accomplished or not, bring out their instruments and play. It's great fun.

ORSA GRÖNKLITTS BJÖRNPARK – Just outside Orsa is this wildlife reserve inhabited by Sweden's native brown bears and other animals, including wolves. There's a limited chance of spotting one of these shy creatures among the bear park's forests, mountains, and lakes, but if you do it is an unforgettable sight. (Be sure to follow common sense safety rules, not approaching the bears too closely. It's important to not make them feel threatened; that's when bears tend to attack).

Nusnäs

6 km (4 mi) southeast of Mora via Route 70, 28 km (17 mi) northwest of Falun.

The lakeside village of Nusnäs is where the small, brightly red-painted wooden Dala horses are made. These were originally carved by the peasants of Dalarna as toys for their children, but their popularity rapidly spread with the advent of tourism in the 20th century. Mass production of the little horses started at Nusnäs in 1928. In 1939 they achieved international popularity after being shown at the New York World's Fair, and since then they have become a Swedish symbol—today some of the smaller versions available in Stockholm's tourist shops are, however, made in East Asia. At Nusnäs you can watch the genuine article being made, now with the aid of modern machinery but still painted by hand.

Shopping

You may want to buy some painted horses to take home; the place to visit is **Nils Olsson** (✉ Edåkervåen 17, ☎ 0250/37200). Shops in the area are generally open every day except Sunday.

Dalarna A to Z

To research prices, get advice from other travelers, and book travel arrangements, visit www.fodors.com.

AIR TRAVEL

CARRIERS

Mora Airport is served by Holmström Air.

➤ AIRLINES AND CONTACTS: **Holmström Air** (☎ 0250/30175).

AIRPORTS

There are 11 flights daily from Stockholm to Dala Airport, which is 8 km (5 mi) from Borlänge. There are half-hourly bus connections on weekdays between Dala Airport and Falun, 26 km (16 mi) away. Bus 601 runs every half hour from Dala Airport to Borlänge; the trip costs SKr 15. Mora Airport has five flights daily from Stockholm on weekdays, fewer on the weekends. The airport is 6 km (4 mi) from Mora; there are no buses from it.

A taxi from Dala Airport to Borlänge costs around SKr 100, to Falun approximately SKr 215. A taxi into Mora from Mora Airport costs SKr 90. Order taxis in advance through your travel agent or when you make an airline reservation. Book a cab by calling the DalaFalun taxi service.

➤ AIRPORT INFORMATION: **Dala Airport** (☎ 0243/64510). **DalaFalun Taxi** (☎ 0243/229290). **Mora Airport** (☎ 0250/30067).

BUS TRAVEL

Swebus runs tour buses to the area from Stockholm on weekends. The trip takes about four hours.

➤ BUS INFORMATION: **Swebus** (☎ 020/640640).

CAR RENTAL

Avis has offices in Borlänge and Mora. Europcar has its office in Borlänge. Hertz has offices in Falun and Mora.

➤ MAJOR AGENCIES: **Avis** (✉ Borlänge, ☎ 0243/87080; ✉ Mora, ☎ 0250/16711). **Europcar** (✉ Borlänge, ☎ 0243/19050). **Hertz** (✉ Falun, ☎ 023/58872; ✉ Mora, ☎ 0250/28800).

CAR TRAVEL

From Stockholm, take E18 to Enköping and follow Route 70 northwest. From Göteborg, take E20 to Örebro and Route 60 north from there.

EMERGENCIES

For emergencies dial 112. There are no late-night pharmacies in the area, but doctors called to emergencies can supply medication. Vasen Pharmacy in Falun is open until 7 PM weekdays.

➤ CONTACTS: **Falun Hospital** (☎ 023/82000). **Mora Hospital** (☎ 0250/25000). **24-hour medical advisory service** (☎ 023/82900). **Vasen Pharmacy** (✉ Åsg., ☎ 023/20000).

TOURS

Call the Falun tourist office for English-speaking guides to Falun and the region around Lake Siljan; guides cost about SKr 900.

BOAT TOURS

Just next to the train station, on the quay in the center of town, is the MS *Gustaf Wasa,* a beautiful old steamship that's used for sightseeing tours of Lake Silja. Trips can take from two to five hours and range in price from SKr 50 to SKr 300. They are a good way to see the stunning countryside from another perspective. ☎ *010/2523292.*

TRAIN TRAVEL

There is regular daily train service from Stockholm to both Mora and Falun.

VISITOR INFORMATION

➤ TOURIST INFORMATION: **Falun** (✉ Stora Torget, ☎ 023/83050). **Leksand** (✉ Norsg., ☎ 0247/80300). **Ludvika** (✉ Sporthallen, ☎ 0240/86050). **Mora** (✉ Ångbåtskajen, ☎ 0250/567600). **Rättvik** (✉ Railway Station House, ☎ 0248/70200). **Sälen** (✉ Sälen Centrum, ☎ 0280/20250).

9 NORRLAND AND NORRBOTTEN

THE NORTH OF SWEDEN, Norrland, is a place of wide-open spaces where the silence is almost audible. Golden eagles soar above snow-capped crags; huge salmon fight their way up wild, tumbling rivers; rare orchids bloom in Arctic heathland; and wild rhododendrons splash the land with color.

In the summer the sun shines at midnight above the Arctic Circle. In the winter it hardly shines at all. The weather can change with bewildering speed: a June day can dawn sunny and bright; then the skies may darken and the temperature drop to around zero as a snow squall blows in. Just as suddenly, the sun comes out again and the temperature starts to rise.

Here live the once-nomadic Lapps, or Sámi, as they prefer to be known. They carefully guard what remains of their identity while doing their best to inform the public of their culture. Many of the 17,000 Sámi who live in Sweden still earn their living herding reindeer, but as open space shrinks, the younger generation is turning in greater numbers toward the allure of the cities. As the modern world makes its incursions, the Sámi often exhibit a sad resignation to the gradual disappearance of their way of life. A Sámi folk poem says it best: "Our memory, the memory of us vanishes/We forget and we are forgotten."

Yet there is a growing struggle, especially among younger Sámi, to maintain their identity, and, thanks to their traditional closeness to nature, they are now finding allies in Sweden's Green movement. They refer to the north of Scandinavia as *Sapmi,* their spiritual and physical home, making no allowance for the different countries that now rule it.

Nearly all Swedish Sámi now live in ordinary houses, having abandoned the *kåta* (Lapp wigwam), and some even herd their reindeer with helicopters. Efforts are now being made to protect and preserve their language, which is totally unlike Swedish and bears far greater resemblance to Finnish. The language reflects their closeness to nature. The word *goadnil,* for example, means "a quiet part of the river, free of current, near the bank or beside a rock."

Nowadays many Sámi depend on the tourist industry for their living, selling their artifacts, such as expertly carved bone-handle knives, wooden cups and bowls, bark bags, silver jewelry, and leather straps embroidered with pewter thread.

The land that the Sámi inhabit is vast. Norrland stretches 1,000 km (625 mi) from south to north, making up more than half of Sweden; it's roughly the same size as Great Britain. On the west there are mountain ranges, to the east a wild and rocky coastline, and in between boundless forests and moorland. Its towns are often little more than a group of houses along a street, built around a local industry such as mining, forestry, or hydropower utilities. Thanks to Sweden's excellent transportation infrastructure, however, Norrland and the northernmost region of Norrbotten are no longer inaccessible. Even travelers with limited time can get at least a taste of the area. Its wild spaces are ideal for open-air vacations. Hiking, climbing, canoeing, river rafting, and fishing are all popular in summer; skiing, ice-skating, and dogsledding are winter activities.

A word of warning: in summer mosquitoes are a constant nuisance, even worse than in other parts of Sweden, so be sure to bring plenty of repellent (you won't find anything effective in Sweden). Fall is perhaps the best season to visit Norrland. Roads are well maintained, but be careful of *gupp* (holes) following thaws. Highways are generally traffic free, but keep an eye out for the occasional reindeer.

Dining and lodging are on the primitive side in this region. Standards of cuisine and service are not nearly as high as prices—but hotels are usually exceptionally clean and staff scrupulously honest. Accommodations are limited, but the various local tourist offices can supply details of bed-and-breakfasts and holiday villages equipped with housekeeping cabins. The area is also rich in campsites—but with the highly unpredictable climate, this may appeal only to the very hardy.

Norrbotten is best discovered from a base in Kiruna, in the center of the alpine region that has been described as Europe's last wilderness. You can tour south and west to the mountains and national parks, east and south to Sámi villages, and farther south still to Baltic coastal settlements.

Kiruna

99 *1,239 km (710 mi) north of Stockholm.*

About 145 km (90 mi) north of the Arctic Circle, and 1,670 ft above sea level, Kiruna is the most northerly city in Sweden. Although its inhabitants number only around 26,000, Kiruna is one of Sweden's largest cities—it spreads over the equivalent of half the area of Switzerland. Until an Australian community took the claim, Kiruna was often called "the world's biggest city." With 20,000 square km (7,722 square mi) within the municipal limits, Kiruna boasts that it could accommodate the entire world population with 150 square ft of space per person.

Kiruna lies at the eastern end of Lake Luossajärvi, spread over a wide area between two mountains, Luossavaara and Kirunavaara, that are largely composed of iron ore—Kiruna's raison d'être. Here is the world's largest underground iron mine, with reserves estimated at 500 million tons. Automated mining technology has largely replaced the traditional miner in the Kirunavaara underground mines, which are some 500 km (280 mi) long. Of the city's inhabitants, an estimated fifth are Finnish immigrants who came to work in the mine.

The city was established in 1890 as a mining town, but true prosperity came only with the building of the railway to the Baltic port of Luleå and the northern Norwegian port of Narvik in 1902.

Like most of Norrland, Kiruna is full of remarkable contrasts, from the seemingly pitch-black, months-long winter to the summer, when the sun never sets and it is actually possible to play golf round-the-clock for 50 days at a stretch. Here, too, the ancient Sámi culture exists side by side with the high-tech culture of cutting-edge satellite research. In recent years the city has diversified its economy and now supports the Esrange Space Range, about 40 km (24 mi) east, which sends rockets and balloons to probe the upper reaches of the Earth's atmosphere, and the Swedish Institute of Space Physics, which has pioneered the investigation of the phenomenon of the northern lights. The city received a boost in 1984 with the opening of Nordkalottvägen, a 170-km-long (106-mi-long) road to Narvik.

One of Kiruna's few buildings of interest is **Kiruna Kyrka** (Kiruna Church), on Gruvvägen, near the center of the city. It was built in 1921, its inspiration a blending of a Sámi kåta with a Swedish stave church. The altarpiece is by Prince Eugen (1863–1947), Sweden's painter prince.

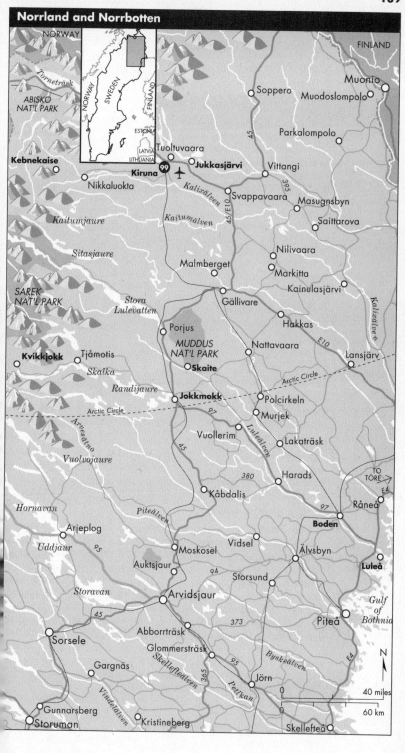

Norrland and Norrbotten

NORWAY

FINLAND

Torneträsk

ABISKO
NAT'L PARK

NORWAY SWEDEN FINLAND

ESTONIA

LATVIA
LITHUANIA

Muonio

Soppero Muodoslompolo

Parkalompolo

45

Kebnekaise

Tuoltuvaara

Kiruna 99 ✈ **Jukkasjärvi** Vittangi

Nikkaluokta

Kalixälven Svappavaara Masugnsbyn

395

45/E10

Saittarova

Kaitumjaure *Kaitumälven*

Sitasjaure Nilivaara

Malmberget Markitta

Kainulasjärvi

**SAREK
NAT'L PARK** *Stora
Lulevatten* Gällivare

Kalixälven

Porjus Hakkas

Kvikkjokk Tjåmotis **MUDDUS
NAT'L PARK** Nattavaara

E10 Lansjärv

Skalka **Skaite**

Arctic Circle

Randijaure **Jokkmokk** Polcirkeln

Arctic Circle 97 Murjek

Arvesjätno Vuollerim Lakaträsk

Vuolvojaure *Luleälven*

45

380 Harads

TO
TÖRE

Hornavan Kåbdalis 97 Råneå

E4

Piteälven **Boden**

Arjeplog

Uddjaur 95 Moskosel Vidsel Älvsbyn

Auktsjaur **Luleå**

Storavan 94 Storsund

Arvidsjaur *Gulf
of
Bothnia*

45 373 Piteå

Sorsele Abborrträsk E4

Glommersträsk 95 *Byskeälven*

Gargnäs *Skellefteälven* 365 Jörn

Vindelälven *Pettkan*

N

Gunnarsberg Kristineberg 40 miles

Storuman 60 km

Skellefteå

Lodging

$$ 🏨 **Ferrum.** Part of the RESO Hotels chain, this late-1960s-vintage hotel is near the railway station. Rooms have wall-to-wall carpeting and modern, standard furniture. ⊠ *Lars Janssonsg. 15, Box 22, 981 31,* ☎ *0980/398600,* FAX *0980/398611. 171 rooms. 3 restaurants, 2 bars, no-smoking rooms, sauna, gym, dance club, meeting room. AE, DC, MC, V.*

$ 🏨 **Jarnvagshotellet.** Dating from 1903, this small hotel has the advantage of being close to the railway station. ⊠ *Bangårdsv. 9, 981 34,* ☎ *0980/ 84444,* WEB *www.jarnvagshotellet.com. 18 rooms. Restaurant, breakfast room, no-smoking rooms. DC, MC, V. BP.*

$ 🏨 **Kebne och Kaisa.** These twin modern hotels—named after the local mountain, Kebnekaise—are close to the railway station and the airport bus stop. Rooms are bland but modern and comfortable. The restaurant is one of the best in Kiruna; it's open for breakfast and dinner. ⊠ *Konduktörsg. 3 and 7, 981 34,* ☎ *0980/12380,* FAX *0980/68181. 54 rooms with bath. Restaurant, no-smoking rooms, 2 saunas. AE, DC, MC, V.*

En Route   Driving south from Kiruna toward Muddus National Park, you'll pass several small former mining villages before coming into the **Kalixälv** (Kalix River) valley, where the countryside becomes more settled, with small farms and fertile meadows replacing the wilder northern landscape.

Jukkasjärvi

16 km (10 mi) east of Kiruna.

The history of Jukkasjärvi, a Sámi village by the shores of the fast-flowing Torneälven (Torne River), dates from 1543, when a market was already here. There is a wooden church from the 17th century and a small open-air museum that evokes a sense of Sámi life in times gone by.

If you are gastronomically adventuresome, you may want to sample one of the most unusual of all Sámi delicacies: *kaffeost,* a cup of thick black coffee with small lumps of goat cheese. After the cheese sits in the coffee for a bit, you fish it out with a spoon and eat it, then drink the coffee.

Dining and Lodging

$ ✕🏨 **Jukkasjärvi Wärdshus och Hembygdsgård.** The restaurant spe-
★ cializes in Norrland cuisine—characterized by reindeer, wild berries, mushrooms, dried and smoked meats, salted fish, fermented herring, rich sauces using thick creams—and is the lifework of its manager, Yngve Bergqvist. The manor has one large honeymoon suite with wood floors and antique furniture; there are 45 cabins around it, 30 with bathroom, kitchen, and two bedrooms with bunk beds. Fifteen "camping cabins" are simple shelters that share the use of a common house with toilets, showers, sauna, kitchen, and washing machine. Breakfast is not included. River-rafting and canoeing trips can be arranged. ⊠ *Jukkasjärvi, Marknadsv. 63, 981 91,* ☎ *0980/66800; 0980/66842 restaurant,* FAX *0980/ 66890. 1 suite, 45 cabins, 30 with bath. Restaurant, sauna, meeting room. AE, DC, MC, V.*

$$$ 🏨 **Ice Hotel.** At the peak of winter, tourists are drawn by the annual
★ construction of the world's largest igloo, which opens for business as a hotel from mid-December through April, after which it melts away until being revised and built again nine months later. Made of snow, ice, and sheet metal, the Ice Hotel offers rooms for 40 guests who spend the night in specially insulated sleeping bags on top of layers of reindeer skins and spruce boughs. At the Absolut Icebar, colored electri-

lights liven up the solid ice walls. Breakfast is served in the sauna, with a view of the (nonelectric) northern lights. The entire hotel is designated nonsmoking, as it takes only a few puffs to tarnish the snow-white interiors. ✉ *Marknadsv. 63, 981 91 Jukkasjärvi,* ☎ *0980/66800,* FAX *0980/66890,* WEB *www.icehotel.com. 120 beds without bath, 18 suites. Restaurant, bar, sauna, cross-country skiing, snowmobiling, chapel, meeting room. AE, DC, MC, V. Closed May–Nov.*

Outdoor Activities and Sports

A challenging local activity is riding the rapids of the Torne River in an inflatable boat. In winter Jukkasjärvi also offers dogsled rides and snow-mobile safaris. For more information, call the Gällivare tourist office.

Kebnekaise

85 km (53 mi) west of Kiruna.

At 7,000 ft above sea level, Kebnekaise is Sweden's highest mountain, but you'll need to be in good physical shape just to get to it. From Kiruna you travel about 66 km (41 mi) west to the Sámi village of Nikkaluokta. (There are two buses a day from Kiruna in the summer.) From Nikkaluokta it is a hike of 19 km (12 mi) to the Fjällstationen (mountain station) at the foot of Kebnekaise, though you can take a boat 5 km (3 mi) across Lake Ladtjojaure. Kebnekaise itself is easy to climb provided there's good weather and you're in shape; mountaineering equipment is not necessary. If you feel up to more walking, the track continues past the Kebnekaise Fjällstationen to become part of what is known as Kungsleden (the King's Path), a 500-km (280-mi) trail through the mountains and Abisko National Park to Riksgränsen on the Norwegian border.

Lodging

$ ⊞ **Kebnekaise Fjällstation.** This rustic, wooden mountain station consists of six separate buildings. Choose between the main building, with its heavy wood beams, wood floors, and wood bunk beds—five per room—and the newer annexes, where more modern rooms each contain two or four beds. All guests share the use of a service house, with toilets, men's and women's showers, and sauna. Though the main lodge is closed in fall and winter, one annex stays open year-round. The facility is 19 km (12 mi) from Nikkaluokta and can be reached by footpath, a combination of boat and hiking, or helicopter. Guided mountain tours are available. ✉ *981 29 Kiruna,* ☎ *0980/55000,* FAX *0980/55048; off-season, contact Abisko tourist office. 196 beds without bath. Restaurant, bar, sauna. AE, V. Closed mid-Aug.–mid-Mar.*

Outdoor Activities and Sports

All the regional tourist offices can supply details of skiing holidays, but never forget the extreme temperatures and weather conditions. For the really adventuresome, the Kebnekaise mountain station offers combined skiing and climbing weeks at around SKr 3,800. It also offers week-long combined dogsledding, skiing, and climbing holidays on the mountains, which vary in price from SKr 4,200 to SKr 5,400. Because of the extreme cold and the danger involved, be sure to have proper equipment. Consult the **mountain station** (☎ 0980/55000) well in advance for advice.

Kvikkjokk and Sarek National Park

310 km (193 mi) southwest of Kiruna via Route 45.

Sarek is Sweden's largest high-mountain area and was molded by the last ice age. The mountains have been sculpted by glaciers, of which there are about 100 in the park. The mountain area totals 487,000 acres, a small portion of which is forest, bogs, and waterways. The remainder is bare mountain. The park has 90 peaks some 6,000 ft above sea level.

The Rapaätno River, which drains the park, runs through the lovely, desolate Rapadalen (Rapa Valley). The area is marked by a surprising variety of landscapes—luxuriant green meadows contrast with the snowy peaks of the mountains. Elk, bears, wolverines, lynx, ermines, hare, arctic foxes, red foxes, and mountain lemmings inhabit the terrain. Bird life includes ptarmigan, willow grouse, teal, wigeon, tufted ducks, bluethroat, and warblers. Golden eagles, rough-legged buzzards, and merlins have also been spotted here.

Visiting Sarek demands a good knowledge of mountains and a familiarity with the outdoors. The park can be dangerous in winter because of avalanches and snowstorms. In summer, however, despite its unpredictable, often inhospitable climate, it attracts large numbers of experienced hikers. At Kvikkjokk, hikers can choose between a trail through the Tarradalen (Tarra Valley), which divides the Sarek from the Padjelanta National Park to the west, or part of the Kungsleden trail, which crosses about 15 km (9 mi) of Sarek's southeastern corner.

Skaite and Muddus National Park

192 km (119 mi) south of Kiruna via E10 and Route 45.

Established in 1942, Muddus National Park is less mountainous and spectacular than Sarek. Its 121,770 acres are mainly taken up by virgin coniferous forest, some of whose trees may be up to 600 years old. The park's 3,680 acres of water are composed primarily of two huge lakes at the center of the park and the Muddusjåkkå River, which tumbles spectacularly through a gorge with 330-ft-high sheer rock walls and includes a waterfall crashing 140 ft down. The highest point of Muddus is Sör-Stubba mountain, 2,158 ft above sea level. From Skaite, where you enter the park, a series of well-marked trails begins. There are four well-equipped overnight communal rest huts, and two tourist cabins. The park shelters bears, elk, lynx, wolverines, moose, ermines, weasels, otters, and many bird species. A popular pastime is picking cloudberries (a kind of raspberry) in autumn.

Jokkmokk

205 km (127 mi) south of Kiruna via E10 and Route 45.

Jokkmokk is an important center of Sámi culture. Each February it is the scene of the region's largest market, nowadays featuring everything from stalls selling frozen reindeer meat to Sámi handcrafted wooden utensils. If you're an outdoor enthusiast, Jokkmokk may be the best base in Norrland for you. The village has three campsites and is surrounded by wilderness. The local tourist office sells fishing permits, which cost SKr 50 for 24 hours, SKr 100 for three days, SKr 175 for one week, and SKr 350 for the entire year. The office can also supply lists of camping and housekeeping cabins.

Lodging

$$ 🏨 **Hotel Jokkmokk.** A modern hotel this luxurious seems incongru-
★   ous in this remote region but is welcome nevertheless. Rooms are car-
peted, and six of them are designated as "Ladies' Rooms," which
basically means they're done up with pastels and florals. The hotel i
in town center, but the staff can arrange dogsled rides and helicopte
trips to the Sarek and Muddus national parks; there is excellent fish

ing nearby. ⊠ *Solg. 45, 962 23,* ☎ *0971/77700,* FAX *0971/77790,* WEB
*www.hoteljokkmokk.se. 75 rooms with bath. Restaurant, no-smok-
ing rooms, sauna, meeting room. AE, DC, MC, V.*

$ 🏠 **Gästis.** This small hotel in central Jokkmokk opened in 1915.
Rooms are standard, with television, shower, and either carpeted or
vinyl floors. ⊠ *Herrev. 1, 962 31,* ☎ *0971/10012,* FAX *0971/10044.
30 rooms with bath. Restaurant, no-smoking rooms, sauna, meeting
room. AE, DC, MC, V.*

$ 🏠 **Jokkmokks Turistcenter.** This complex is in a pleasant forest area,
near Luleälven, 3 km (2 mi) from the railway station. Rooms have bunk
beds, a small table, and chairs; showers, toilets, and a common cooking area are in the hall. ⊠ *Box 75, 962 22,* ☎ *0971/12370,* FAX *0971/
12476. 26 rooms without bath, 84 cabins with bath. 4 pools, sauna,
meeting room. MC, V.*

Boden

*290 km (180 mi) southeast of Kiruna, 130 km (81 mi) southeast of
Jokkmokk on Route 97.*

Boden, the nation's largest garrison town, dates from 1809, when
Sweden lost Finland to Russia and feared an invasion of its own territory. The **Garrisonsmuseet** (Garrison Museum), contains exhibits
from Swedish military history, with an extensive collection of weapons
and uniforms. ⊠ *Garrisonsmuseet, Sveav. 10,* ☎ *0921/68399.* 🖼
Free. ☉ *Mid-June–late Aug., Mon.–Sat. 11–4, Sun. noon–4.*

Luleå

340 km (211 mi) southeast of Kiruna via E10 and E4.

The most northerly major town in Sweden, Luleå is an important port
at the top of the Gulf of Bothnia, at the mouth of the Luleälv (Lule
River). The town was some 10 km (6 mi) farther inland when it was
first granted its charter in 1621, but by 1649 trade had grown so much
that it was moved closer to the sea. The development of Kiruna and
the iron trade is linked, by means of a railway, with the fortunes of
Luleå, where a steelworks was set up in the 1940s. Like its fellow port
towns—Piteå, Skellefteå, Umeå, and Sundsvall—farther south, Luleå
is a very modern and nondescript city, but it has some reasonable hotels. A beautiful archipelago of hundreds of islands hugs the coastline.

The **Norrbottens Museet** (Norrbotten Museum) has one of the best collections of Sámi ethnography in the world. ⊠ *Hermelinsparken 2,* ☎
0920/243502. 🖼 *Free.* ☉ *Weekdays 10–4, weekends noon–4.*

Dining and Lodging

$$ ✕🏠 **Arctic.** Right in town center, the Arctic is known locally for its restau-
★ rant, which serves local specialties. The hotel is warm and cozy, with
tastefully decorated, rustic rooms. ⊠ *Sandviksg. 80, 972 34,* ☎ *0920/
10980,* FAX *0920/60787. 94 rooms with bath. Restaurant, no-smoking
rooms, hot tub, sauna, meeting room. AE, DC, MC, V.*

$$ 🏠 **Elite Stads Hotellet.** This large, central Best Western hotel has
nightly—sometimes boisterous—dancing. Rooms in the building dat-
ing back to 1901 are spacious and carpeted, with turn-of-the-20th-cen-
tury furnishings. ⊠ *Storg. 15, 972 32,* ☎ *0920/67000,* FAX *0920/
67092. 135 rooms with bath, 3 suites. Restaurant, café, lounge, minibars, no-smoking rooms, sauna, dance club, meeting room. AE, DC,
MC, V. BP.*

$$ 🏠 **Scandic.** This hotel on Lake Sjö has an extremely pleasant setting and
is 2 km (1 mi) from the railway station. ⊠ *Banv. 3, 973 46,* ☎ *0920/*

276400, FAX 0920/276411. *160 rooms with bath. Restaurant, no-smok-ing rooms, indoor pool, sauna, gym, meeting room. AE, DC, MC, V.*

$ ⊞ **Amber.** A particularly fine old building, listed on the historic reg-ister, houses this hotel close to the railway station. Rooms are mod-ern, with plush carpeting, minibars, and satellite television. ⊠ *Stationsg. 67, 972 34,* ☎ *0920/10200,* FAX *0920/87906. 16 rooms with bath. Mini-bars, no-smoking rooms. AE, DC, MC, V.*

$ ⊞ **Aveny.** Rooms are of varying sizes and colors, but all are spotless and fresh. It's close to the railway station. ⊠ *Hermelinsg. 10, 973 46,* ☎ *0920/221820,* FAX *0920/220122. 24 rooms with bath. No-smoking rooms. AE, DC, MC, V.*

Norrland and Norrbotten A to Z

To research prices, get advice from other travelers, and book travel ar-rangements, visit www.fodors.com.

AIR TRAVEL
CARRIERS
There are two nonstop SAS flights a day from Stockholm to Kiruna Airport, 5 km (3 mi) from Kiruna, and three additional flights via Luleå. Check SAS for specific times.
➤ AIRLINES AND CONTACTS: **SAS** (☎ 020/727727).

AIRPORTS
In summer, buses connect Kiruna Airport, which is 5 km (3 mi) from Kiruna, to the city center; the fare is about SKr 50. A taxi from the airport to the center of Kiruna costs about SKr 160; book through the airline or call the number below.
➤ AIRPORT INFORMATION: **Kiruna Airport** (☎ 0980/68001). **Taxi Kiruna** (☎ 0980/12020).

CAR RENTAL
➤ MAJOR AGENCIES: **Avis** (⊠ Kiruna Airport, Kiruna, ☎ 0980/13080). **Europcar** (⊠ Forv. 33, Kiruna, ☎ 0980/80759). **Hertz** (⊠ Industriv. 5, Kiruna, ☎ 0980/19000).

CAR TRAVEL
Since public transportation is nonexistent in this part of the country, having a car is essential. The few roads are well built and maintained, although spring thaws can present potholes. Keep in mind that habi-tations are few and far between in this wilderness region.

EMERGENCIES
For emergencies dial 112. A medical advisory service in Luleå is avail-able 24 hours a day.

There are no late-night pharmacies in Norrbotten, but doctors called to emergencies can dispense medicine. The pharmacy at the Gallerian shopping center in Kiruna is open weekdays 9:30–6 and Saturday 9:30–1.
➤ CONTACTS: **Gallerian Pharmacy** (⊠ Föreningsg. 6, ☎ 0980/18775). **Jokkmokk Health Center** (⊠ Lappstav. 9, ☎ 0971/44444). **Kiruna Health Center** (⊠ Thuleg. 29, ☎ 0980/73000). **Sunderbu Hospital Luleå** (☎ 0920/282000).

TOURS
Local tourist offices have information on guided tours. Same Lanüs Resor arranges tours to points of interest in Lappland. Call the Swedish Sámi Association for Sámi tours.

➤ FEES AND SCHEDULES: **Same Lanüs Resor** (✉ c/o Rental Line I Jokkmokk, Hermelinsg. 20, 962 33, Jokkmokk, ☎ 0971/10606). **Swedish Sámi Association** (✉ Brog. 5, 903 25, Umeå, ☎ 090/141180).

TRAIN TRAVEL

The best and cheapest way to get to Kiruna is to take the evening sleeper from Stockholm on Tuesday, Wednesday, or Saturday, when the fare is reduced to SKr 595 for a single. The regular one-way price is SKr 600 when sharing the cabin with six people and SKr 700 when sharing the cabin with three people, double for return. You'll arrive at around lunchtime the next day. To book a train, call Tag Kompaniet, the rail company that handles northern Sweden.

➤ FEES AND SCHEDULES: **Tag Kompaniet** (☎ 020/444111).

VISITOR INFORMATION

Norrbottens Turistråd is the regional tourist office. Local tourist offices are listed below by town.

➤ TOURIST INFORMATION: **Norrbottens Turistråd** (✉ Kronan H3, Luleå, ☎ 0920/434510). **Abisko** (✉ 980 24 Abisko, ☎ 0980/40200). **Gällivare** (✉ Storg. 16, ☎ 0970/16660). **Jokkmokk** (✉ Stortorget 4, ☎ 0971/12140 or 0971/17257). **Kiruna** (✉ Folkets Hus, ☎ 0980/18880). **Luleå** (✉ Kulturcentrum Ebeneser, ☎ 0920/293500).

10 PORTRAITS OF SWEDEN

SWEDEN AT A GLANCE: A CHRONOLOGY

ca. 12,000 BC The first migrations into Sweden.

ca. 2000 BC Tribes from southern Europe, mostly Germanic peoples, migrate toward Denmark.

ca. AD 770 The Viking Age begins. For the next 250 years, Scandinavians set sail on frequent expeditions stretching from the Baltic to the Irish seas, and even to the Mediterranean as far as Constantinople and to North America, employing superior ships and weapons and efficient military organization.

ca. 800– ca. 1000 Swedes control river trade routes between the Baltic and Black seas; establish Novgorod, Kiev, and other cities.

830 Frankish monk Ansgar makes one of the first attempts to Christianize Sweden and builds the first church in Slesvig, Denmark. Sweden is not successfully Christianized until the end of the 11th century, when the temple at Uppsala, a center for pagan resistance, is destroyed.

1000 King Olof Skötkonung becomes the first Swedish king to be baptized and becomes the country's first Christian king.

1100 Christianity is spread throughout Sweden as a result of German missionaries in the 800s and English in the 1000s.

1248 Erik Eriksson appoints Birger as jarl, in charge of military affairs and expeditions abroad. Birger improves women's rights, makes laws establishing peace in the home and church, and begins building Stockholm.

1250 Stockholm is officially founded.

1319 Sweden and Norway form a union that lasts until 1335.

1370 The Treaty of Stralsund gives the north German trading centers of the Hanseatic League free passage through Danish waters and full control of Danish herring fisheries for 15 years. German power increases throughout Scandinavia.

1397 The Kalmar Union is formed as a result of the dynastic ties between Sweden, Denmark, and Norway, the geographical position of the Scandinavian states, and the growing influence of Germans in the Baltic. Erik of Pomerania is crowned king of the Kalmar Union.

1477 University of Uppsala, Sweden's oldest university, is founded.

1520 Christian II, ruler of the Kalmar Union, executes 82 people who oppose the Scandinavian union, an event known as the "Stockholm bloodbath." Sweden secedes from the union three years later. Norway remains tied to Denmark and becomes a Danish province in 1536.

1527 A Swedish national church is created by parliamentary decree at the Swedish Riksdag in Västerås.

1523 Gustav Ericsson founds Swedish Vasa dynasty as King Gustav I Vasa.

1534 Count Christoffer of Oldenburg and his army demand the restoration of Christian II as king of Denmark, initiating civil war between supporters of Christian II and supporters of Prince Christian (later King Christian III).

1541 The Bible is published in Swedish.

1593 The Swedish national church becomes Lutheran.

1611–16 The Kalmar War: Denmark wages war against Sweden in hopes of restoring the Kalmar Union.

1611–60 Gustav II Adolphus, the great warrior king, begins this crucial era, dying in 1632. During this time, Sweden defeats Denmark in the Thirty Years' War and becomes the greatest power in Scandinavia as well as northern and central Europe.

1632–54 Queen Christina reigns. In 1654 she abdicates the throne, converts to Catholicism, leaves for Rome, and is accepted by the pope.

1660 Peace of Copenhagen establishes modern boundaries of Denmark, Sweden, and Norway.

1666 Lund University, Scandinavia's largest university, is founded in Lund, Sweden.

1668 Bank of Sweden, the world's oldest central bank, is founded.

1700–21 Sweden, led by Karl XII, first broadens then loses its position to Russia as northern Europe's greatest power in the Great Northern War.

1773 Gustavo III creates the Swedish Opera Institution, which is still functioning today.

1782 The Royal Opera House in Stockholm, designed by the architect C. F. Adelcrantz, is inaugurated.

1801–14 The Napoleonic Wars are catastrophic for Denmark economically and politically: the policy of armed neutrality fails, the English destroy the Danish fleet in 1801, Copenhagen is devastated during the bombardment of 1807, and Sweden, after Napoléon's defeat at the Battle of Leipzig, attacks Denmark and forces the Danish surrender of Norway. The Treaty of Kiel, in 1814, calls for a union between Norway and Sweden despite Norway's desire for independence. The Danish monarchy is left with three parts: the Kingdom of Denmark and the duchies of Schleswig and Holstein.

1807 During the Napoleonic Wars, Swedish King Gustav III joins the coalition against France and reluctantly accepts war with France and Russia.

1809 Sweden surrenders the Åland Islands and Finland to Russia, Finland becomes a grand duchy of the Russian Empire, and the Instrument of Government, Sweden's constitution, is adopted.

1818 Sweden takes a Frenchman as king: Karl XIV Johann establishes the Bernadotte dynasty.

ca. 1850 The building of railroads begins in Scandinavia.

1889 The Swedish Social Democratic Party is founded.

1896 The first moving picture film is shown in Sweden.

1901 Alfred Nobel, the Swedish millionaire chemist and industrialist, initiates the Nobel prizes.

1905 Norway's union with Sweden is dissolved.

1911–1960 Jussi Björling lives to become Sweden's most renowned tenor singer and is said to be the world's second best in history, after Caruso.

1914 At the outbreak of World War I, Sweden declares neutrality but is effectively blockaded.

1918 Swedish women gain the right to vote, with some restrictions.

1918 Birgit Nilsson, Sweden's best known and most acclaimed woman opera singer, is born. In 1958, she became the first non–Italian to open the famed season of Opera La Scala in Milan.

1920 Scandinavian countries join the League of Nations.

1921 Restrictions on women's suffrage are lifted.

1929–37 The first Social Democratic government takes office in Sweden.

1939 Sweden declares neutrality in World War II.

1946 Sweden joins the United Nations.

1949 Sweden declines membership in NATO.

1952 The Nordic Council, which promotes cooperation among the Nordic parliaments, is founded.

1957 A Swedish referendum votes yes to a compulsory state pension for people age 67 and over.

1972 Sweden, on the basis of its neutral foreign policy, declines membership in the European Union (EU).

1974 The pop group ABBA wins the European song contest in Brighton, England, with the song *Waterloo*.

1975 Sweden's Instrument of Government of 1809 is revised and replaced with a new Instrument of Government. This constitution reduces the voting age to 18 and removes many of the king's powers and responsibilities.

1980 Fifty-eight percent of Sweden's voters advocate minimizing the use of nuclear reactors at Sweden's four power plants.

1980 Björn Borg wins his fifth consecutive Wimbledon tennis title.

1981 Björn Borg wins the French Tennis Open for the sixth time.

1982 Swedish actress Ingrid Bergman, the winner of three Oscar awards, dies at the age of 67. Best known for the films *Casablanca* and *Spellbound*.

1986 Sweden's prime minister, Olof Palme, is assassinated for unknown reasons. Ingvar Carlsson succeeds him.

1986 Sweden is the first country to detect nuclear fallout from the Soviet power plant in Chernobyl, unknown of in the West at the time.

1987 The Swedish national ice hockey team, Tre Kronor, wins the world ice hockey championship in Vienna, the first time in 25 years.

1991 The Social Democrats are voted out of office and the new government launches a privatization policy.

1992 Sweden's Riksbank (National Bank) overnight raises interest rates to a world record of 500% in an effort to defend the Swedish krona against speculation.

1995 Finland and Sweden join the EU in January.

1998 Stockholm is the 1998 Cultural Capital of Europe, hosting arts, culture, and nature events throughout the year.

2000 The Öresund road and rail bridge linking Sweden with Denmark is opened, effectively connecting Sweden to continental Europe.

2001 Sweden holds the presidency of the EU for six months.

REFLECTIONS OF STOCKHOLM

A T A RECEPTION for visiting dignitaries, the mayor of Stockholm surprised his guests by serving them glasses of a clear liquid that turned out to be water. It came, he explained, from the water surrounding this island city, and the purpose of the tongue-in-cheek gesture was to demonstrate that modern cities can afford clean environments. In fact, Stockholm has won the European Sustainable City Award in competition with 90-odd other cities, and a large swathe of Stockholm, including the vast royal domains, has been declared a national park for the benefit and enjoyment of the populace.

There were sound, practical reasons for building Stockholm on the 14 islands that command access from the Baltic Sea to Lake Mälaren. Back in the 13th century, after the Vikings had retired from plunder and discovery, Estonian pirates had taken to pillaging the shores of the lake, which extends deep into the Swedish heartland. Birger Jarl, the ruler who founded Sweden's first dynasty, put a stop to all that by stockading the islands the pirates had to pass. His effigy lies in gilded splendor at the foot of the city hall tower.

Stockholm without water would be unthinkable. It's the water that gives it beauty, character, life. The north shore and the south are, to be truthful, rather Germanic in character, not too different from, say, Zürich or Berlin. But watch them from across a busy waterway, mirrored in the blue lake, and they become invested with a lively charm.

The pearl in the oyster, however, is the small island known as Gamla Stan, or Old Town, dominated by the tawny-colored, massive Royal Palace, designed by Nicodemus Tessin in the 17th century and completed in the 18th. In the Middle Ages, so many German merchants settled here that a law was passed to limit their number on the city council to less than half of the members. The winding streets are lined with old houses in yellow, ochre, and occasional oxblood red. Some of the city's most attractive small hotels, gourmet restaurants, and lively jazz clubs are here. To many peo-

ple, the greatest treasure is found inside Storkyrkan, the Stockholm cathedral, next door to the palace: a larger-than-life, polychrome wooden statue of St. George slaying the dragon from 1489.

Skeppsholmen, a smaller island east of Gamla Stan and once the nation's principal navy base, is an idyllic place for a stroll, and great for art lovers. The Museum of Modern Art by the Spanish architect Rafael Moneo opened in 1998 and is one of the great contemporary museums. It blends in well with other structures, such as the "old" modern museum, a former armory and a trendsetter since its opening in 1958; it is now becoming the Museum of Architecture. Also on Skeppsholmen is the exquisite East Asiatic Museum, another Tessin creation, which houses one of the world's finest collections of Chinese art.

After you cross the bridge from Skeppsholmen on your way back to the city center you'll walk past the National Museum. You'll do well to stop there—not just for its Rembrandts and Swedish masters of centuries past but also for its new atrium restaurant, one of the city's best, in the piazzalike inner courtyard.

The piers of Stockholm's islands are lined with so many vessels of every category, from cruise ships and seagoing roll-on/roll-off vessels to island-hopping steamboats and pocket-size ferries, that it would seem impossible to squeeze in another motorboat, sailboat, or sloop. There were more than 100,000 of them at last count, and still the number keeps growing. The waterborne traffic jam when they return on a Sunday night in summer after a weekend at sea is something to behold.

Most of the Stockholm sailors travel no farther than to one of the 25,000 islands and skerries that make up the Stockholm archipelago, extending 73 km (45 mi) east into the Baltic Sea. A red timbered cottage on one of these islands in the Baltic is most Swedes' idea of ultimate bliss, and there they seek to re-create the simple life as they imagine their forefathers to have lived it.

A fair approximation of archipelago life is just a 25-minute ferry ride away from the city center. This is Fjäderholmarna, or Feather Island, an islet that not long ago was a navy munitions dump. The rock is worn smooth by retreating Ice Age glaciers, there's a clump of yellow reeds at the water's edge, and on the rock the inevitable red cottage, windows and corners trimmed with white, against a backdrop of dark green foliage. There's a restaurant serving excellent Swedish specialties and a small colony of craftsmen making high-quality souvenirs.

Take a boat trip west from the city, and you're in a different world, verdant and tranquil. An hour away and you're at Drottningholm Palace, also designed by Nicodemus Tessin and now the residence of the royal family. The palace and its formal French garden are impressive and the little Chinese Pavilion enchanting, but the real gem is the 200-year-old and perfectly intact Drottningholm Court Theater, where period performances of operas by Mozart, Gluck, and other 18th-century composers are presented every summer. The orchestra wears wigs, the singers appear in original costumes, and the ingenious old stage machinery produces thunder and storms.

As you wander through the reception areas and dressing rooms you'll be struck by the sparse, cool elegance of the decor and furnishings, a style borrowed from Louis XV but stripped down to the bare essentials. It may strike you, too, that this is not very different from modern Swedish interiors and design. Then you will have discovered a well-hidden truth: the Swedes, who take such pride in being modern, rational, and efficient, are secretly in love with the 18th century.

— Eric Sjogren

Eric Sjogren, a Swedish travel writer based in Brussels, is a frequent contributor to the *New York Times* and other publications.

ASTRID LINDGREN

APPROPRIATELY, the career of Astrid Lindgren, Sweden's best-known children's writer, author of the *Pippi Longstocking* books and many others, had a fairy-tale beginning. Once upon a time, Karin, her seven-year-old daughter, ill in bed with pneumonia, begged her, "Tell me a story . . .tell me the story of Pippi Longstocking."

"Neither she nor I know where on earth she got that name from," said Lindgren. "That was the first time I ever heard it. I made up the character right there and then, told her a story, and only wrote it down much later."

Thus was born one of the most memorable characters in children's fiction, her adventures translated from Lindgren's native Swedish into more than 50 languages.

"A few years later, I was awarded a prize for the stories and offered to share it with Karin," recalled Lindgren, "but by then she decided that she was too old. She said she was bored with Pippi."

With younger children all over the world, however, Pippi continues to strike a responsive chord: a little girl of indeterminate age with a gap-toothed smile, freckled face, and a wild mop of ginger hair from which a braid juts lopsidedly out over each ear.

Phenomenally strong, irrepressibly cheeky, she lives independent of adults, with a horse and monkey in a tumbledown house, supporting herself from a hoard of gold coins. She has no table manners and doesn't go to school. She does just what she likes, when she feels like doing it.

"Bertrand Russell once said that children dream of power the way that adults dream of sex," said Lindgren. "I was impressed with that at the time, and I think I must have had it in mind when I created Pippi."

Despite vociferous protests from educationalists and child psychologists, Pippi won immediate favor with kids. Lindgren also created several other memorable characters, but Pippi remained the basis of her enormous popularity in her home country.

The independent spirit that created such an unconventional character as Pippi Longstocking was evident in the author throughout her life. Using her awesome popularity, Lindgren was partly responsible for the fall of one Swedish government and for forcing a second one in 1989 to draft radical new legislation protecting the rights of pets and farm animals, about which she cared deeply.

During her lifetime, she remained refreshingly unspoiled by all the adulation and attention she received.

"When I go out, people come up to me in the street and tell me how much they've enjoyed my books, and children will hug and kiss me," she used to say. "Of course, that's very nice, but you know, somehow I always feel it's not happening to *me*.

"It's as though someone else had all that celebrity and I am standing alongside her."

She would dismiss any suggestions that she wielded power. "Power? I have only the power of the word," she would say. "I wouldn't want power in the real sense. That's the worst thing I know. People always abuse it."

Yet it seemed that, Pippi-like, she reveled in the influence she, an ordinary (or perhaps one should say, extraordinary) citizen, could use to inject rebellious ideas into the heads of her youthful public and bend Sweden's rulers to her will.

One of her characters is *The World's Best Karlson*. Lovable figment of a little boy's imagination, Karlson is a jovial type who laughs at reality and flies around the house aided by a propeller set in the middle of his back. The Karlson books are particularly popular in Russia, where *Literaturnaja Gaseta*, a literary review, described the character as "the symbol of innocent, uncorrupted childhood, the childhood we as adults find so difficult to remember and accept."

The Satirical Theater in Moscow staged a play based on the character in the 1960s, and Lindgren used to say that whenever she visited Russia, taxi drivers would always talk to her about Karlson.

When former Swedish Prime Minister Ingvar Carlsson visited Moscow, she was delighted to hear that many Russians were disappointed because he wasn't the *real* Karlson.

ACCORDING TO LINDGREN, it was the stories of the Bullerby children that most closely approximated her own childhood. These feature the adventures of children from three families in a little village somewhere in Sweden and eulogize rural life set against a fondly painted picture of seasonal contrast. The Bullerby children are Lindgren's *nicest* characters: playful but, unlike Pippi, unwilling to overstep the line.

Bullerby is based on the little village of Sevedstorp, set amid the dense pine-and-spruce forests that cover the southern Swedish province of Småland, birthplace of her father, Samuel August Ericsson, who by the time Astrid was born, in 1907, had moved to the nearby town of Vimmerby.

Home was a simple clapboard house, painted red and with a glassed-in porch, surrounded by well-tended flower beds, daisy-strewn lawns, and apple trees. Her father had started life as a hired hand but wound up running his own farm. The family was reasonably well off, though there was rarely money left over for luxuries. Samuel Ericsson was an excellent storyteller, and many of the anecdotes he told his children surfaced later in Lindgren's books. Her mother, Hanna, wrote poetry in her youth and at one time dreamed of becoming a schoolteacher.

Lindgren was one of four children. She had an elder brother, Gunnar (born 1906), and two younger sisters, Stina (born 1911) and Ingegerd (born 1916). All displayed literary talents of some kind or another: Gunnar became a member of parliament renowned for his political satires, Stina a translator, and Ingegerd a journalist.

The innocent childhood fun and games described in the Bullerby books were, by and large, those of Astrid herself and her brother and sisters. She used to say: "We played the whole time from morning to night, just like the children in the Bullerby stories."

She enjoyed a warm relationship with Samuel August, a fact that is reflected

time and again in her books, peopled in the main with warm, understanding, though often gruff fathers. She described their mother, on the other hand, as a rather distant person, recalling that Hanna hugged her only once when she was a child. It was from her that she inherited her willpower, energy, and stubbornness, she said.

The creator of Pippi Longstocking rebelled against Hanna's authority just once as a child: "I was quite young—perhaps three or four—and one day I thought she was stupid so I decided to run away and hide in the outside toilet. I wasn't there for too long, and when I came back in my brother and sisters had been given sweets. I thought this was so unfair that I kicked out in Mother's direction. I was taken into the front room and beaten."

When she started at the local school at the age of seven, in 1914, she was overcome with shyness (a traditional Swedish handicap) when the teacher called out her name and, instead of answering "yes," burst into tears.

The priest in charge of registering the new arrivals told her she could go and sit down instead of standing with the other children. "I absolutely didn't want to go and sit down." The tears subsided, and she came to see the incident as the day she broke through her "wall of shyness."

She was a conscientious pupil, remembered by classmate Ann-Marie Fries, the model for Madicken, another of her characters, as "unbelievably nimble. I remember her in the gym; she could climb from floor to ceiling like a monkey."

Astrid also began to show evidence of literary talents. Her essays were frequently read to the rest of the class, and, when she was 13, one of them was even published in *Wimmerby Tidning*, Vimmerby's local newspaper. This was titled "Life in Our Backyard" and described two small girls and the games they played. "They joked and called me Vimmerby's answer to Selma Lagerlöf, and I decided that if there was one thing I would never be it was an author."

She recalled her teens as a melancholy episode. "Like most teenagers, I thought I was ugly," she said, "and I just *never* fell in love. Everyone else was in love."

She left school at 16 and was given a job on *Wimmerby Tidning*, reading proofs and even covering some local events such as weddings and funerals as a reporter.

In 1926 Astrid's blissful childhood came to a very definite end, when, at the age of 18, she had an affair with a man and became pregnant. In recent years Sweden has developed a reputation for liberality in such matters, but in those days, pregnant and unmarried, she created a huge scandal in Vimmerby, a small town steeped in traditional Lutheran values.

Astrid left home and traveled to the capital, Stockholm. "Of course, my parents weren't pleased, but I wasn't thrown out or anything like that," she explained. "Wild horses wouldn't have kept me there."

She knew nobody in Stockholm. "I was terribly alone at first," she said. "I had left behind all my friends. I was very unhappy. Childhood is one thing," she said philosophically. "Youth is something else."

She took solace in reading the works of Norwegian author Knut Hamsun. Hamsun's book *Hunger* made a deep impression on her and she named it as her principal literary influence. Lonely and poor herself, she identified strongly with Hamsun's graphic descriptions of the life of a starving young writer in Norway.

In an essay for the mass-circulation Stockholm evening newspaper *Expressen* in 1974, she recalled sitting under a bird-cherry tree outside a church, reading *Hunger*. "That was the greatest literary experience I've ever had," she said.

She gave birth to a son, Lars, whom she handed over to foster parents in Copenhagen, returning to Stockholm to study shorthand and typing and to land a job at a local firm working for the father of Viveca Lindfors, the Swedish actress.

"I soon started to make friends in Stockholm, and I went to Copenhagen as often as I could to see Lars. There was never any question of his being adopted. He was my son and I loved him deeply," she said.

On one occasion she left her job during working hours to take the train to Copenhagen, only to be spotted by her boss. She was sacked.

However, her luck seemed to have turned. Astrid found an editorial job with KAK, the Swedish automobile association. There

she met Sture Lindgren, whom she married in the spring of 1931. Her son came to live with them, and in 1934 she gave birth to her daughter, Karin.

T HE FAMILY LIVED IN the part of Stockholm known as Vasastan, at first in a small apartment close to the main railway line to the north of Sweden, later in a spacious, light apartment overlooking a park.

It was in the winter of 1941 that Karin asked her to tell the story of Pippi Longstocking. "Much later I was out walking in the park when I slipped and sprained my ankle," she recalled. "I was forced to lie in bed, so I began to write down the stories I had told to Karin."

She typed a manuscript and sent it to Bonniers, one of Sweden's leading publishing houses. It was refused. Undaunted, she wrote a girl's story, *Confidences of Britt Mari*, which she entered for a contest organized by another, much smaller, publishing house, Rabén and Sjögren. She won second prize, and in 1944 the story was published. Lindgren also began working for the company as an editor.

The following year Rabén and Sjögren published her follow-up, titled *Kerstin and I*. Then in 1945 the company announced a new contest for books aimed at children age 6–10.

Lindgren revised her Pippi Longstocking manuscript and entered it for the contest, along with a new effort, *All About the Bullerby Children*, in which she lovingly re-created her childhood in Vimmerby. *Pippi Longstocking* won first prize. *All about the Bullerby Children* failed to take an award but was bought for publication. The first Pippi Longstocking book was well received by both critics and public and soon sold out. However, a year later, the follow-up, *Pippi Goes Abroad*, caused a furor, with Lindgren accused of undermining the authority of parents and teachers.

Professor John Landquist, writing in the evening newspaper *Aftonbladet*, accused Lindgren of "crazed fantasy" and said Pippi's adventures were "something disagreeable that scratches at the soul."

Today there is a different perspective. Viví Edström, professor of literature at the

University of Stockholm, has described Pippi as "a child's projection of everything that is desirable" and claims her as a major influence on Swedish literature.

"In the still prim and moralizing children's literature of the 1940's, Astrid Lindren's breakthrough meant that children had a literature on their own terms," says Edström.

The third and last Pippi Longstocking book, *Pippi in the South Seas,* was published in 1948. In this, Pippi sails away to a Pacific island for a reunion with her father, returning to Sweden for Christmas, which she spends alone. It could be an allegory on the fate of nonconformists in Sweden, a country where the good of the collective has always been prized above that of the individual.

Physically, the model for Pippi was a red-haired, freckle-faced friend of daughter Karin, Sonja Melin, who today sells vegetables in Hötorgshallen, one of Stockholm's few surviving indoor markets. "She was just so lively as a child. As soon as I saw her, I thought, 'That's my Pippi!' " said Lindgren.

Lindgren has created many other well-loved and sometimes controversial characters in the 30 books she wrote since.

Mio My Son, written in 1954 (perhaps significantly, two years after the death of husband Sture) is one of Lindgren's most ambitious books: a highly advanced fairy story that explores difficult themes such as fear and death.

In 1985 a journalist asked Lindgren on Swedish Radio, "Isn't *Mio My Son* actually a pretty nasty book?"

She replied, "Of course; that's why children love it."

A**LTHOUGH SHE NEVER** attempted a "serious" adult novel ("I never really wanted to; I'm not sure I'd be any good at it"), she was not shy about exploring themes considered improper for children. In 1973 controversy raged once more, this time over *The Brothers Lionheart,* in which a dying child dreams of meeting, in another world, the brother he idealizes who has died heroically in a fire. The two boys ride off to fight the forces of evil.

Shortly after this, in 1976, Lindgren, a lifelong voter for the Social Democrats, caused a still greater fuss when she became embroiled in a row with Sweden's Socialist government.

It all started with a demand from the tax authorities, which would, she calculated, along with her social-insurance contributions, exceed her actual income. She wrote a fairy story for *Expressen,* the Stockholm newspaper. Its main character, Pomperipossa, has always loved her country and respected its rulers. Now she turns against them: "'O you, the pure and fiery social democracy of my youth, what have they done to you?' thought Pomperipossa, 'How long shall your name be abused to protect a dictatorial, bureaucratic, unjust, authoritarian society?' "

The barb went home, and in the Swedish parliament (*Riksdag*) then finance minister Gunnar Sträng (his surname translates into English as "Strict") reprimanded Lindgren. "The article is a combination of inspired fantasy and total ignorance of tax policy," he said. "Astrid Lindgren should stick to what she knows, namely making up stories."

Lindgren hit back: "He may not be good at arithmetic, but he's certainly good at telling fairy-tales. I think we should trade jobs, he and I."

In that year's general election the Social Democrats lost power, after more than 40 years in office. An analysis of the result by the influential Sifo public-opinion research institute named the controversy over Lindgren's story as a major contributory factor.

Ronia, the Robber's Daughter, published in 1981, returned to a "straight" fairy-tale format, the story of a boy and girl from two different, warring bands of robbers, who run away together. This was turned into an award-winning Swedish film by comedian/director Tage Danielsson. Eleven of her books have been filmed, and Lindgren herself took an active interest in each project.

She was positively deluged with prizes, including in 1989 the Albert Schweitzer Award, for her work on behalf of animal rights. At a time in life when most people would be content to wind down, she joined forces with veterinarian Kristina Forslund in a campaign to persuade Sweden to introduce more stringent rules on animal husbandry.

A string of articles and open letters soon brought the government to its knees. Prime Minister Carlsson announced new legislation that he dubbed "Lex Astrid" and called on Lindgren personally to tell her about it.

Despite the fact that the laws are considered the most advanced in the world, Lindgren was not satisfied. She described them as "toothless." "They are full of loopholes," she said. "Now we have to fight to get them tightened up."

"I really don't know what I would have been if I had not become an author," said Lindgren. "Maybe I could have been a lawyer. I might have been rather good at that."

Astrid Lindgren passed away on January 28, 2002, at the age of 94.

— Chris Mosey

STOCKHOLM'S ARCHITECTURAL PROCESSION

AS IN MANY OTHER SWEDISH CITIES, a single afternoon walk in Stockholm offers a jouney through centuries of architectual change and innovation. There are, of course, the classics. Take Kungliga Slottet (Royal Palace) on Gamla Stan. Designed by Nicodemus Tessin the Younger and built between 1690 and 1704, it's a rather austere palace—no domes, no great towers—and yet it commands a certain respect sitting so regally over the water. Nearby, on Riddarholmen, observe the gorgeous, medieval Riddarholmskyrkan (Riddarholm Church), with its lattice spire pointed toward the heavens. And let's not forget Drottningholm, a 17th-century château-esque structure—designed by Tessin the Elder and finished by his son—that has been the home of the royal family since 1981. Also at Drottningholm is the Court Theater (1766), which, remarkably, still contains its original decor and fully functional stage machinery.

Stadshuset (City Hall) is also a must-see on any architectural walking tour. Completed in 1923, the building contains more than 8 millon bricks and 19 million gilded mosaic tiles. Each year the Nobel Prize ceremony is held in the building's Blå Hallen (Blue Hall). Built a few years later is Stadsbiblioteket (City Library), designed by Eric Gunnar Asplund—one of Sweden's most renowned architects. The library's eye-pleasing yet simple design foreshadows the *Funkis* (Functionalist) movement that Gunnar helped spearhead in the 1920s and '30s.

Skattehuset (Tax House), also known as Skatteskrapan (a play on "skyscraper"), is hard to miss, looming mercilessly as it does over Södermalm. Completed in the early 1950s as part of an attempt to consolidate the nation's tax offices, the singularly dull gray 25-story building is often criticized for having ruined the southern skyline of Stockholm. Except for the annual siege of thousands of Stockholmers flooding it with last-minute tax declarations every May, the building sees few visitors.

Farther south, another architectural oddity plagues, or enhances, depending on whom you ask, the skyline. Globen (The Globe), the world's largest spherical building, looks something like a colossal golf ball, or a futuristic space-station still awaiting its launch into orbit. Unveiled in 1988, it's the main arena in Stockholm for indoor sporting events (especially hockey) and rock concerts. Despite debates concerning its aesthetic (or lack thereof), a look at the cables and beams inside reveals Globen's architecture marvel.

Another much debated architectural undertaking is Hötorgscity, across from the highly influential Kulturhuset at Sergels Torg. This post-war compound of five 18-story buildings was constructed in the mid-'50s and shares the oppressive style of its near-contemporary, the Skatteskrapan. Hötorgscity was built to house retail stores and offices, and thus bring more commerce to downtown Stockholm. The project failed. A significant chunk of historic Stockholm was lost. Vandalized by ne'er-do-wells and ignored by prospective tenants, the buildings were shut down in the '70s, although today there is a renewed interest in the top floors of the buildings, especially among young business owners.

What is most striking about the buildings that make up Stockholm's architectural portfolio is their collective diversity. You'll glean a particularly remarkable sense of them if you visit them all in one day. Centuries of history involving both failures and successes are reflected in the styles these structures represent. Every building in Stockholm, new or old, tells a story.

BOOKS AND VIDEOS

Books

A History of the Vikings (Oxford University Press, 1984) recounts the story of the aggressive warriors and explorers who during the Middle Ages influenced a large portion of the world, extending from Constantinople to America. Gwyn Jones's lively account makes learning the history enjoyable.

Captain Nemo's Library was written by Per Olov Enquist, born in 1934. He is a novelist and playwright. The book is a family drama set in the 1940s on the northern coast of Sweden. *Private Confessions* is by theater and film director Ingmar Bergman, born in 1918. In this book he reveals some of his own background and, maybe, gives us a clue as to why he is one of Woody Allen's role models.

Since his poetry was first published in 1954, the writer and poet Tomas Tranströmer's work has been much admired in Sweden. Unfortunately, only his more obscure titles have been translated into English, including the collection titled *For the Living and the Dead. Black Water* by Kerstin Ekman is a thriller set in the secluded landscape of the Swedish north.

Selma Lagerlöf wrote *The Wonderful Journey of Nils Holgersson* in 1906, on request, as a geography textbook for schoolchildren. As a reader you are taken on an adventure through the entire country, expanding your horizons with the main character, a little boy called Nils Holgersson. She won the Nobel Prize in literature in 1909. *Myth and Religion of the North,* by E. O. G. Turbille-Petre, was published in London in 1964. It investigates and explains the history and the evolution of the diverse mythological tales and pagan religions of Sweden.

One of the easiest and certainly most entertaining ways of learning about modern Swedish society is to read the Martin Beck detective series of thrillers by Maj Sjöwall and Per Wahlöö, all of which have been translated into English. One of these, *The Terrorists,* was even prophetic, containing a scene in which a Swedish prime minister was shot, a precursor to the assassination of Olof Palme in 1986.

Similarly, an entertaining insight into how life was in the bad old days when Sweden was one of the most backward agrarian countries in Europe can be obtained from Vilhelm Moberg's series of novels about poor Swedes who emigrated to America: *The Emigrants, Unto a Good Land,* and *The Last Letter Home.*

The plays of Swedish writer August Strindberg greatly influenced modern European and American drama. Perhaps the most enduringly fascinating of these, *Miss Julie,* mixes the explosive elements of sex and class to stunning effect.

One of the most exhaustive and comprehensive studies in English of the country published in recent years is *Sweden: The Nation's History,* by Franklin D. Scott (University of Minnesota Press). Chris Mosey's *Cruel Awakening: Sweden and the Killing of Olof Palme* (C. Hurst, London 1991) seeks to provide an overview of the country and its recent history seen through the life and assassination of its best-known politician of recent times and the farcical hunt for his killer.

Videos

Sweden was home to Ingmar Bergman, who is recognized as one of the greatest Swedish directors of all time. His works include such classics as *The Virgin Spring* (1959), *Wild Strawberries* (1957), and *Fanny and Alexander* (1982). He was also a poet.

The Seventh Seal was released in 1957 and directed by Ingmar Bergman. It is a religious drama set in a medieval context starring great Swedish actors, including Max Von Sydow, who also starred in the film *Snow Falling on Cedars.* Another of Bergman's masterpieces, *Fanny and Alexander* (1982) was filmed by internationally acclaimed Sven Nykvist. It was awarded four Oscars in 1984, including one for best foreign film. It is a story about an upper-middle-class family, set at the beginning of the 20th century.

My Life as a Dog (1985) was directed by Lasse Hallström. Although it failed to win an Oscar, it got the New York Film Critics Circle award for Best Foreign Language Film in 1987. Hallström's big break in the United States came with *What's Eating Gilbert Grape*, starring Johnny Depp and Leonardo DiCaprio. He lives outside New York with his wife, actress Lena Olin.

The Twins, an American film from 1942, showcases the famous Swedish actress Greta Garbo. She was born in 1905 and became known as "the Divine" for her reluctance to speak about herself, which lent her an air of integrity and mystery. She mostly played grand but tragic roles, with the one major exception being *Ninotchka*, where her continuous laughter almost seemed out of character.

SWEDISH VOCABULARY

	English	Swedish	Pronunciation
Basics			
	Yes/no	Ja/nej	yah/nay
	Please	Var snäll;	vahr snehll
		Var vänlig	vahr vehn-leeg
	Thank you very much.	Tack så **mee**-keh	tahk soh mycket.
	You're welcome.	Var så god.	vahr shoh **goo**
	Excuse me. (to get by someone)	Ursäkta.	oor-**shehk**-tah
	(to apologize)	Förlåt.	fur-**loht**
	Hello	God dag	goo **dahg**
	Goodbye	Adjö	ah-**yoo**
	Today	I dag	ee **dahg**
	Tomorrow	I morgon	ee **mor**-ron
	Yesterday	I går	ee **gohr**
	Morning	Morgon	**mohr**-on
	Afternoon	Eftermiddag	**ehf**-ter-meed-dahg
	Night	Natt	naht
Numbers			
	1	ett	eht
	2	två	tvoh
	3	tre	tree
	4	fyra	fee-rah
	5	fem	fem
	6	sex	sex
	7	sju	shoo
	8	åtta	oht-tah
	9	nio	nee
	10	tio	tee
Days of the Week			
	Monday	måndag	mohn-dahg
	Tuesday	tisdag	tees-dahg
	Wednesday	onsdag	ohns-dahg
	Thursday	torsdag	tohrs-dahg
	Friday	fredag	freh-dahg
	Saturday	lördag	luhr-dahg
	Sunday	söndag	sohn-dahg
Useful Phrases			
	Do you speak English?	Talar ni engelska?	tah-lahr nee ehng-ehl-skah
	I don't speak . . .	Jag talar inte svenska . . .	yah tah-lahr **een**-teh **sven**-skah
	I don't understand.	Jag förstår inte.	yah fuhr-**stohr een**-teh
	I don't know.	Jag vet inte.	yah **veht een**-teh

I am American/ British.	Jag är amerikan/ engelsman.	yah ay ah-mehr-ee-**kahn**/ **ehng**-ehls-mahn
I am sick.	Jag är sjuk.	yah ay **shyook**
Please call a doctor.	Jag vill skicka efter en läkare.	yah veel **shee**-kah **ehf**-tehr ehn **lay**-kah-reh
Do you have a vacant room?	Har Ni något rum ledigt?	hahr nee noh-goht **room leh**-deekt
How much does it cost?	Vad kostar det?/ Hur mycket kostar det?	vah **kohs**-tahr deh/hor **mee**-keh **kohs**-tahr deh
It's too expensive.	Den är för dyr.	dehn ay foor **deer**
Beautiful	Vacker	**vah**-kehr
Help!	Hjälp	yehlp
Stop!	Stopp, stanna	stop, **stahn**-nah
How do I get to . . .	Kan Ni visa mig vägen till . . .	kahn nee **vee**-sah may **vay**-gehn teel
the train station?	stationen	stah-**shoh**-nehn
the post office?	posten	**pohs**-tehn
the tourist office?	en resebyrå	ehn-**reh**-seh-**bee**-roh
the hospital?	sjukhuset	**shyook**-hoo-seht
Does this bus go to . . . ?	Går den här bussen till . . . ?	gohr dehn hehr **boo**-sehn teel
Where is the W.C.?	Var är toilett/ toaletten	vahr ay twah-**leht** twah-**leht**-en
On the left	Till vänster	teel **vehn**-stur
On the right	Till höger	teel **huh**-gur
Straight ahead	Rakt fram	rahkt **frahm**

Dining Out

Please bring me . . .	Var snäll och hämta åt mig	vahr snehl oh hehm-tah oht may
menu	matsedeln	maht-seh-dehln
fork	en gaffel	ehn gahf-fehl
knife	en kniv	ehn kneev
spoon	en sked	ehn shehd
napkin	en servett	ehn sehr-veht
bread	bröd	bruh(d)
butter	smör	smuhr
milk	mjölk	myoolk
pepper	peppar	pehp-pahr
salt	salt	sahlt
sugar	socker	soh-kehr
water	vatten	vaht-n
The check, please.	Får jag be om notan?	fohr yah beh ohm **noh**-tahn

212

INDEX

NOTES

NOTES

NOTES

NOTES

NOTES

NOTES